# AUTHORING **autism**

**thought in the act**   *a series edited by* ERIN MANNING AND BRIAN MASSUMI

Melanie Yergeau

# AUTHORING **autism**

*/ on rhetoric and neurological queerness*

Duke University Press   Durham and London   2018

All rights reserved
Printed in the United States of America on acid-free paper ∞
Text designed by Courtney Leigh Baker
Typeset in Whitman and Myriad Pro by Westchester
Publishing Services

Library of Congress Cataloging-in-Publication Data
Names: Yergeau, Melanie, [date] author.
Title: Authoring autism : on rhetoric and neurological
queerness / Melanie Yergeau.
Description: Durham : Duke University Press, 2017. |
Series: Thought in the act | Includes bibliographical
references and index.
Identifiers: LCCN 2017022894 (print)
LCCN 2017044088 (ebook)
ISBN 9780822372189 (ebook)
ISBN 9780822370116 (hardcover : alk. paper)
ISBN 9780822370208 (pbk. : alk. paper)
Subjects: LCSH: Autism. | Disability studies. | Autistic
people. Classification: LCC RC553.A88 (ebook) | LCC
RC553.A88 Y474 2017 (print) | DDC 616.85/882—dc23
LC record available at https://lccn.loc.gov/2017022894

Cover art: Dan Miller, Untitled (DM 294), 2017. Acrylic
and ink on paper. Courtesy of Creative Growth Art Center.

Duke University Press gratefully acknowledges the support
of the University of Michigan Office of Research, Institute
for the Humanities, and College of Literature, Science, and
Arts, all of which provided funds toward the publication of
this book.

/ *contents*

/ *acknowledgments*

I would like to begin my acknowledgments section by thanking the Electric Light Orchestra. They don't know who I am, but I know who they are, and without them, there would be no perseveration and hence no book.

Equally seriously, if not more so, I have many people to whom I am deeply grateful. I didn't consider myself a disability studies anything, much less a disability studies scholar, until I began graduate school. My many mentors at DePaul University—Carolyn Goffman, Liz Coughlin, Darsie Bowden, Anne Bartlett, Craig Sirles, Jan Hickey, and Pete Vandenberg—gave me the time, space, and guidance to think about my place in the world as a scholar-activist.

This is the book I've long wanted to write, and it represents well over a decade of thinking and labor. At Ohio State, my dissertation committee modeled for me generosity, incisiveness, patience, and the underresearched yet necessary role of candy in the writing process. Cindy Selfe and Brenda Brueggemann, my cochairs, offered invaluable commentary on my work, including this book (which is not my dissertation—Cindy and Brenda read a lot). Likewise, I want to thank so many people at Ohio State—in English, disability studies, disability services, and the Nisonger Center—for letting me return, every summer, to tinker and dwell among the many cool ideas and projects happening in Columbus. Scott DeWitt and Amy Spears generously hosted me at the annual Digital Media and Composition Institute (DMAC)—for seven years in a row—as I worked on this project and others, and they continue to help me think through the digitality of autistic worlds. My other mentors at Ohio State have continued to spark so many ideas, kindly dedicating their time at DMAC, at conferences, and via Skype: Louie Ulman, Susan Delagrange, Beverly Moss, Kay Halasek, Kathleen Griffin, Dickie Selfe, Scott Lissner, Enjie Hall, Jonathan Buehl, and Nan Johnson. Our dissertation reading/writing group breathed such energy and passion into all things rhetoric: Genevieve Critel, Paige Banaji, and Lauren Obermark. Elizabeth Brewer, Kate Comer, Katie DeLuca, Deb Kuzawa, and Erika Strandjord read portions of this book, provided instrumental feedback, and/or smiled and nodded whenever I entered rant mode (sometimes these things happened all at once). So many thanks to Jen Herman, Annie Mendenhall, Julia Voss, Jen Michaels, Krista Bryson, Nick Hetrick, Heather Thompson-Gillis, Silas Hansen, Mike Bierschenk, Vera Dukaj, Anne Langendorfer, Christina LaRose, Tiffany Anderson, and Tim Jensen—for attending protests, for helping me as I worked through different ideas, for encouraging me to eat doughnuts.

While at University of Michigan, I have received incredible support at all stages of the writing process, including a subvention in support of permissions and copyediting. This book was also in part supported by a fellowship through UM's Institute for the Humanities. I benefited immensely from a wonderfully interdisciplinary group of colleagues at the institute, who read and commented on many drafts of my work: Sid Smith, Doretha Coval, Patrick Tonks, Sara Ahbel-Rappe, Maria Cotera, David Green, Holly Hughes, Alison Joersz, Elizabeth Keslacy, Nancy Linthicum, Sarah Linwick, Pascal Massinon, Rostom Mesli, Rachel Neis, Asaf Peres, Christian Sandvig, Tobin Siebers, Bonnie Washick, and Wang Zheng.

I also could not have moved forward on this book were it not for the manuscript workshop hosted by my department, which was organized by Terri Tinkle and coordinated by a reading committee, Anne Curzan and David Gold. Alison Kafer and Cindy Lewiecki-Wilson provided vital feedback on the scope and direction of the project, and they graciously read subsequent material, postworkshop. The readers at the workshop turned an event I had nervously dreaded into an engrossing conversation that energized me for months—for this I am ever thankful to Aliyah Khan, Madhumita Lahiri, John Whittier-Ferguson, Alison Adlaf, and Kris Harrison.

My department has been incredibly supportive. The administrative staff—Jane Johnson, Karly Mitchell, Jane Sullivan, Amy Argersinger, Karena Huff, Senia Vasquez, Jennifer Catey, and Denise Looker—have routinely helped me figure out how things work. Lucy Hartley frequently offered advice, wisdom, and encouragement as I moved through a number of stressful moments. As well, numerous colleagues have taken time to ask provocative questions, engage my work, and offer welcome commiseration about the weather, stale doughnuts, and literal and metaphorical potholes that the universe seems to have purposefully organized: Anne Gere, June Howard, Tung-Hui Hu, Petra Kuppers, Scott Lyons, Victor Mendoza, Josh Miller, David Porter, Alisse Portnoy, Michael Schoenfeldt, Tobin Siebers, Megan Sweeney, Ruby Tapia, and

Gillian White. To my colleagues in Sweetland, disability studies, and digital studies—your tireless efforts have sustained my resolve: Lisa Nakamura, Jane Berliss-Vincent, Anna Schnitzer, Patricia Anderson, Lloyd Shelton, Anna Kirkland, Robert Adams, and Naomi Silver.

Lorelei Blackburn and Andrea Riley Mukavetz have helped me survive Ann Arbor, which, I have learned, is not Columbus, Ohio. So too have local disability studies people helped me feel more at home: D. L. Adams, Liat Ben-Moshe, Kim Nielsen, Jim Ferris, Beth Currans.

Throughout the life span of this book, I've been privileged to attend conferences and spend time with many, many remarkable colleagues. Thank you, Angela Haas and Janice Walker, for all that you do in service of the Graduate Research Network at Computers and Writing. To Gail Hawisher, Patrick Berry, Tim Lockridge, and my fellow editors at Computers and Composition Digital Press, your work continues to inspire me. I have had amazing and, at many junctures, mind-blowing conversations (mental image: if autism could hold a leaf blower) with Jonathan Alexander, Kristin Arola, Garrett Avila-Nichols, Cheryl Ball, Kris Blair, Casey Boyle, Hugh Burns, Matt Cox, Doug Eyman, Bill Hart-Davidson, Debra Journet, Claire Lauer, Tony O'Keefe, Liza Potts, Malea Powell, Jackie Rhodes, Donnie Sackey, Jentery Sayers, and Barbi Smyser-Fauble.

The Society for Disability Studies as well as the Disability Studies Standing Group at the Conference on College Composition and Communication have been amazingly supportive, and I've learned from many people, including Dev Bose, Sushil Oswal, Michael Salvo, Franny Howes, Maren Linett, Stephanie Wheeler, Casie Cobos, Catherine Prendergast, Jason Palmeri, Janine Butler, Allison Hitt, Craig Meyer, Patricia Dunn, Chad Iwertz, Ruth Osorio, Jordynn Jack, Shannon Walters, Aimi Hamraie, Bre Garrett, George Williams, Christina Cedillo, Corbett OToole, Carol Gill, Carrie Sandahl, Phil Smith, Sami Schalk, Emily Nusbaum, Nirmala Erevelles, Bernice Olivas, and Amanda Booher. Margaret Price has long served as my mentor, and I am most appreciative of the years of socks (years. of. socks.). (This is in no way sarcastic, for socks are serious business. But also: I am honored to have you in my life.) Stephanie Kerschbaum's accountability checks, encouragement, and academic valentines enabled me to get through, one page at a time. Jay Dolmage has read and reassured me through multiple panic attacks. Amy Vidali and Tara Wood provided critical feedback on talks I delivered, which later were absorbed into the book.

At Duke University Press, Elizabeth Ault and Ken Wissoker devoted incredible time and offered encouragement at every step of the process. Erin Manning and the anonymous readers provided so much in the way of commentary and energy, and this book is a better project for it. I would also like to thank Liz

Smith and Karen Fisher for managing and copyediting this project as it moved into its final stages, as well as Paula Durbin-Westby for indexing.

To my autistic blogging and activist communities: I am humbled by your kindness and your willingness to put yourselves out there, for your continued perseverance and your courage. I am grateful to Ibby Grace, Bridget Allen, Athena Lynn Michaels-Dillon, Nick Walker, N. I. Nicholson, Alyssa Hillary, Lydia Brown, Paula Durbin-Westby, Ari Ne'eman, Scott Robertson, Meg Evans, Julia Bascom, Katie Miller, Emily Titon, Kerima Çevik, Ariane Zurcher, Beth Ryan, Emma Zurcher-Long, Judy Endow, Elesia Ashkenazy, Alex Kimmel, Anne Carpenter, Amy Sequenzia, Finn Gardiner, Moreniké Onaiwu, Sam Harvey, Dani Ryskamp, Corina Becker, Savannah Logsdon-Breakstone, Rachel Cohen-Rottenberg, Sparrow R. Jones, Kassiane Sibley, Dora Raymaker, Lei Wiley-Mydske, Emily Baillou, Lauri Swann Hunt, Brenda Rothman, Michelle Sutton, Deanne Shoyer, C. J. Shiloh, Jonas Blauer, Jean Kearns Miller, Corbin Kramer, Justin Rooney, Stephanie Ballam, Jeffrey Strasser, Rachel Klippenstein, Elizabeth Beu, Benzion Chinn, and so many others that I am sure to be forgetting. Any and all omissions are my own error.

Thank you to Meredith K Ultra, whose artwork appears in chapter 2. Your work is amazing. Many thanks, as well, to Ai Binh Ho, Molly Parsons, Pam Saunders, and Bonnie Tucker, all of whom read, researched, and contributed so very much to this project.

Ralph Savarese, John Duffy, Paul Heilker, Chris Foss, Julia Miele Rodas, Bev Harp, Morton Gernsbacher, Pam Block, Michele Friedner, Bryce Huebner, and Shelley Tremain: you routinely encouraged me, often in moments when I was experiencing great personal distress.

Finally, thank you to my family, who promised not to make fun of my flowery language. I am holding you to this.

Parts of the introduction appeared in an earlier form in "Occupying Autism: Rhetoric, Involuntarity, and the Meaning of Autistic Lives," in *Occupying Disability: Critical Approaches to Community, Justice, and Decolonizing Disability* (Springer, 2015).

# INTRODUCTION. involution

My mother has a set of stories, narratives she wields depending on her mood. One such story involves an infant me, lying in my crib on Saturday mornings. In the first telling, I am a well-behaved child. "You never cried," she remarks, sipping her coffee. "You'd let me sleep until noon. You were such a quiet baby." Her words emit a sense of nostalgia as my younger brother tears through the room and bodychecks a friend on the living room floor.

Other days, the narrative starkly changes. "I'd come to your crib on Saturday mornings," she shudders, "and I'd find you with poop up to your neck." She pauses for dramatic effect. "*Up to your neck.*" Sometimes, she recounts how I'd grab my feces and lob them at the wall, or smear them on my face, or rub them against the bars of the crib. The story then diverges into toddlerhood, my first forays into kindergarten—how I'd wet myself at school, how I didn't have friends, how I spent hours in my room memorizing road maps from AAA. There is a solemnity about this story, an absent acknowledgment that there was something about me, something about me that they should have known back then. If only.

Years later, as a young adult, I was diagnosed with autism.

What autism provided was a discursive framework, a lens through which others could story my life. My hand and full-body movements became self-stimulatory behaviors; my years-long obsession with maps and the Electric Light Orchestra became perseverations; my repetition of lines from the movie *Airplane!* became echolalia. My very being became a story, a text in dire need of professional analysis. This, my body, this was autism—and suddenly, with the neuropsychologist's signature on my diagnostic papers, I was no longer my body's author.

As John Duffy and Rebecca Dorner relate, autism is a narrative condition. In particular, they note that "diagnoses of autism are essentially storytelling in character."[1] Here they emphasize the identities and languages that any claim to autism might afford, on the part of both autistic and nonautistic people. Through diagnosis, autistics are storied into autism, our bodyminds made determinable and knowable through the criteria of neurodevelopmental disability.[2] Through diagnosis, nonautistic stakeholders become authorized as autism somethings—as autism parents, as autism researchers, as autism therapists and specialists and mentors and advocates. Even when autism is depicted as a condition that resists the narratable (which, as I discuss later, is an unfortunately typical move), the narrating impulse remains entrenched in the act of diagnosing unto itself: Traits and check boxes tell a story. In turn, those who have been so storied likewise respond, albeit in sometimes unexpected ways. Autistic stories might culminate in angry blog posts, video narratives, comics, memoirs, or extended middle fingers. Autistic stories often bristle against the well-meaning intentions of what autistic blogger Kassiane Sibley terms "helper personalities" or nonautistic people whose so-called charity is self-serving.[3] Autistic stories might take shape as screaming in a supermarket, or as banging one's head against the hard edges of a radiator, or as jumping joyously in a mud puddle. Often, autistic stories aren't beheld as stories at all, but rather as symptoms as jaw-dropping as poop throwing. These stories, in all of their heterogeneity, promote radically different (non)meanings and affective responses. Here it is important to note the political difference that autism-as-modifier and autistic-as-modifier make. The former relates to broader discourse on autism that is typically authored by nonautistic people, whereas the latter imparts that which is autistically created.

Are you, dear reader, autistic or nonautistic? Can there ever really be any in-between?

Following the above, what's important for our purposes is Duffy and Dorner's claim that autism is typically characterized as that which contrasts—as that which contrasts with language, humanness, empathy, self-knowledge, understanding, and rhetoricity.[4] And, indeed, this particular claim about autism as contrast orders clinical literature on the condition. Contrariness, antithesis, enigma—these are not autism tropes, but arguably autism's essence. Or, put alternatively, autism has been essentialized and thereby made (un)known as a condition of opposing fields, as a condition that, in toto, defies. If we listen for these stories, we encounter them everywhere. *Assessment of Autism Spectrum Disorders*, a reference guide for physicians, represents autism as a "most perplexing condition" due to its "unusual combination of behavioral weaknesses and a lack of biological models."[5] Media accounts of autistic people communicate the sensationalism of savant-beings who are at once so extraordinary yet so epistemically distant and critically impaired. We are bombarded with anecdotes of children who refuse to hug their parents, of children whose worlds are supposedly so impoverished that they spend their days spinning in circles, or flapping their hands, or screaming or self-injuring or resisting—ardently and fixatedly resisting.

Were we to return to toddler me, we might have a case in point. Shit smearing, as one parent contends in Chloe Silverman's *Understanding Autism*, stands among the more lurid narratives that configure parental experiences of autism: "If you hang around [autism] parents enough, all we talk about is poop."[6] Poop talk exemplifies the pathos-driven genres upon which Duffy and Dorner primarily focus, and yet, as they note, these narratives are typically nonautistic, canonized by individuals who have (presumably) never smeared their own shit (or spent their days spinning in circles, or self-injuring, or ardently and fixatedly resisting). We can access autism poop talk across many rhetorical domains, including clinical literature on scatolia and pica (smearing and eating, respectively) as well as guidebooks for caregivers on autistic misbehavior, such as Autism Speaks's "Challenging Behaviors Tool Kit" or resource sites from developmental disability agencies.[7] Parental poop talk is perhaps the most affectively loaded of all poop talk, in large part because it relates smearing, eating, and rectal digging in graphically humanizing terms. Someone has to clean it up. Someone has to act, to intervene. The humanization in autism poop talk, of course, is rarely about the human whose poop has been thrust into the spotlight. And, especially in the case of parent blogs and other digitally born life writing, poop talk is often divulged without the full and informed consent of the autistic person being depicted. This isn't to deny the dangers or stresses associated with a loved one's ingestion of harmful bacteria, or the distress involved in attending to the spread of literal shit, or the community and support a parent might garner from sharing intimate stories online. My point, rather, is that these narratives are shittier than the shit they claim to represent. These are shitty narratives—rhetorical commonplaces that author autistic people as victim-captives of a faulty neurology, as rhetorically degraded and rhetorically suspect. In these constructions, our shit holds more rhetorical power than we do.

While this book is not about literal shit, it is about the figurative shit that contemporary autism discourse has flung upon autistic bodies. These shitty narratives persist, I argue, because their rhetorical power derives from the figure of the autistic as unknowable, as utterly abject and isolated and tragic, as a figure whose actions are construed less like actions and more like neuronally willed middle fingers.[8] At root, these shitty narratives are rhetorical projects: they apprehend neuroqueerness as interlocking series of socially complex impairments, impairments that impact the domains of relatedness, intent, feeling, sexuality, gender identity, and sensation—indeed, all of that which might be used to call oneself properly a person. Joelle Smith, blogger at *Evil Autie*, relates shitty stories as stories that work to "shock and outdo."[9] In particular, Smith observes that poop talk is emblematic of the "need to do anything, no matter what the risk, to cure us."[10] It is this need to do anything to stop autism—this critical exigence—that positions autism as a rhetorical problem and autistics as rhetorically problemed. Earlier, I related the example of the child who refuses to hug, which is a common exemplar of autism's queerly asocial and thereby heartrending symptoms. But the figure of the hug-avoidant autistic child is a remarkably acontextualized figure, a figure with whom a receiving audience is not supposed to identify. (The parent—or the person who isn't being hugged—is, without fail, represented as the empathetic character.) Framing a child's bodily comportment as refusal resorts to deficit-laden and negativistic terminology; it likewise, especially in the case of autistics whose languages aren't spoken or voiced, attributes (non)intentions in the face of scant rhetorical evidence. When nonautistic publics mourn and inquire about the why—why would a child refuse a hug?—the why recedes from the rhetorical and moves into the neurological (or, as Jordynn Jack terms it, the neurorhetorical). The hug-avoidant autistic child is reduced to terms of neuronal motion, of synaptic plasticity and mindblindness and sensory disintegration and gut flora. There is something contrary here, something neurologically askew.

If there is one takeaway from what I here write, it is this: what we do not know, and what we often purposively ignore, are autistic narrations of such rhetorical events, the interbodily potentials, desires, and moments that structure an autistic life, or any life. To whom do we listen? The autistic or the nonautistic? Can there ever really be an in-between? What of my shit? What of my unhuggable body? What of me? What of *autos*, the self that so consumes the presumably autistic? Where the fuck are we?

Despite autistic people's increased visibility and, indeed, increased participation in public policy and political advocacy, autistic stories are not the autism stories that circulate, dominate, or permeate. One could make the argument that this sentiment is becoming less true, that terms like *neurodiversity* are welcomed with broader social currency, that the proliferation of autism books signals some optimism, that autistic-run nonprofits are changing public discourse on autism research and support, that Temple Grandin has replaced Rain Man as the autist du jour and thus the world is a happier place for autistic people. I, however, do not approach *Authoring Autism* with that same kind of optimism, nor do I necessarily take the above items as cumulative wins for autistic people.

Three autistics on a federal committee who are routinely berated by their nonautistic cohort, as is the case with the U.S. IACC, is not sufficient evidence of policy inclusion.[11] Wonderful autism books continue to be written by wonderful nonautistic people, but this does not of necessity make the world more welcoming of autistics and autistic modes of communicating. The exclusion of autistic people of color from the broadest reaches of both nonautistic and autistic-led advocacy does not and should not translate to "the world is happier." And, as a white autistic who has attained considerable education—I am a professor who can, even if only infrequently, access reliable speech—I write this book with great trepidation, and resignation, that autism politics routinely reward those who are multiply privileged. The logics of ableism are intertwined with the logics of racism, classism, and heterosexism. And while autism unto itself reduces my ethos as an interlocutor, whiteness, class, and speech configure my claims to personhood very differently than those who occupy more marginal positions. Following the above, Temple Grandin's routine proclamations that autism teachers should emulate the social practices of the 1950s is not a socially just nor revolutionary approach to neuroqueer sociality, but a demonstrably racialized orientation toward the world. Such autism awareness is better termed perilous than it is positive or gainful.

As I discuss momentarily, I do believe in autistic futures, in autistic people's cunning expertise in rhetorical landscapes that would otherwise render us inhuman. I believe in the potentialities of autistic stories and gestures, of neuroqueering what we've come to understand as language and being. I believe that autistic rhetorics complicate what we traditionally hold dear across a plurality of fields. But whatever progress we might attribute to our present moment, it is impossible to deny that the arguments structuring public knowledges, understandings, and felt senses of autism are grossly ableist, powerfully violent, and unremarkably nonautistic.[12] And because these knowledge warrants, to channel Ibby Grace, saturate almost every discipline and discourse community, the rhetorical beings and doings of autistic people have been figured as anything but rhetorical.[13]

With no small irony, I write this book in equal parts as a rhetorician and autistic activist, roles that have inevitably shaped the ways in which I apprehend this thing we call autism. My dual positionality is no small irony because I have, at many junctures, been told that autism precludes me from being rhetorical, much less a rhetorician. I have been told these things by a range of persons, including colleagues and therapists. Those who come to this book from fields beyond rhetorical studies might genuinely wonder why this is a bad thing—to be nonrhetorical, to lack or have diminished capacity for rhetorical exchange. In everyday parlance, most people who discuss "other people's rhetoric" use rhetoric as a stand-in for "fucked-up language and trickery." And while fucked-up language and trickery are indeed part of rhetoric proper, I am invoking a deeper lineage here, a more contested set of meanings. I am invoking ethics, philosophy, cognition, and politics. I am invoking not only the ways in which autism has been figured as lacking in these domains, but also the ways in which autistic people seek to queer those domains, to fuck up that which is already fucked up.

It is not uncommon, for example, for rhetoricians to claim that rhetoric is what makes one human. This is a belief that persists in spite of rhetorical studies' various turns toward things, ecologies, affect, and complex vitalisms: if one is arhetorical, then one is not fully human.[14] Rhetoric's function as a precondition for humanness or personhood is typically and deeply connected to how we conceive sociality, or our modes of relating and relatedness with our (neurotypically human) surrounds. In this way, rhetoric is, as Craig Smith makes clear, "involved in the most important decisions of our lives, it is *ontological*; that is, it concerns the why we exist and how we exist. Rhetoric's making-known function is epistemological because it helps us obtain knowledge. Thus, rhetoric touches on the two most important branches of our lives: how we learn things and how we live."[15] To repeat: Rhetoric comprises how we learn things and how we live. Autism, by contrast, signals the dissolution of such learning. This dissolution is sometimes presented as all-encompassing and at other times is claimed as a matter of degree or severity. We, the autistic, are that which contrasts. If clinical discourse on autism is, as Duffy and Dorner declare, storied around rhetorics of "scientific sadness," then autistic rhetorics, in all of their contrastive resonances, queer the motifs, structures, modes, and commonplaces of what nonautistics have come to narrate and thereby know about autism. To author autistically is to author queerly and contrarily.

Voluntary Rhetorics

I very clearly remember the long process of being toilet trained. These memories starkly diverge from the ways in which other people typically narrate their own experiences with learning to use the bathroom—which is to say, other people typically don't. By contrast, I do not remember learning to read. Decoding symbols felt less effortful, even as a toddler, but decoding my body—decoding sensations, recognizing which tightness meant which function, rehearsing the order of bodily motions required to use a toilet—these things long eluded me, and even still do not always remain in the past tense. When I read parent narratives that bemoan their autistic kindergarteners wearing diapers, I am visited with a sense of surreality, as though my own privacy, my own unwilled body, has been breached. Am I hungry? How do I make my fingers grasp a utensil? At what stage in the process do I flush the toilet? Toward what or whom does my bodymind intend?

In our work together, Paul Heilker and I have made arguments about autism's rhetorical potentials—that autism is a profoundly rhetorical phenomenon, that autism is begging for rhetorical scrutiny.[16] It's important to highlight the radicalness of these statements—that autism embodies the narrativistic, that autism embodies the rhetorical, that autism is or has potential—because they represent a major departure from what scholarly literature, across cognitive studies disciplines, often suggests about autism. Many scholars have argued, for instance, that autism precludes the ability to both compose and enjoy stories. Over the past decade, numerous articles in the *Journal of Autism and Developmental Disorders*, one of the flagship autism journals, have characterized autistic autobiography as lacking narrative structure and coherence, as lacking rhetorical facility and audience awareness, and as lacking self-reflection.[17] Autistic language has been variously cataloged as a "rigid pre-symbolic mode of representation," as "egocentric," and as work that "should not be overrated."[18] In all things discursive, autism represents decided lack. These are the stories through which we know autism, even as these same stories claim that autism remains unknowable, unnarratable.

In many respects, this medicalized storying of lack is the crux of this book—or, rather, subverting this medicalized storying is the crux of this book. For autism is medically construed as a series of involuntarities—of thought, mode, action, and being. As this book narrates throughout, involuntarity dominates much of the discourse on autism, underlying clinical understandings of affect, intention, and socially appropriate response. And, as I'll discuss shortly, because involuntarity stretches across clinical and popular domains, it is often used in service of denying the narrative capabilities—and the narrative value—of autistic people.

We, the autistic, are merely the residues of rhetoricity.

When neurodivergence enters the fold, involuntarity can signal myriad concepts. In many instances, the discourse(s) of involuntarity governs autism as a condition. Most obviously, autism is not a voluntary condition—one doesn't choose autism, per se. Many parent narratives about autism echo this line of thought and speak of autism as something happening to them, as though their entire family had been struck by lightning. Particularly iconic, for instance, is the Autism Speaks Learn the Signs campaign, in which autism prevalence is compared to car crash fatalities, hypothermia, kidnapping, and pediatric cancer.[19] (All of these things, despite autism being a nonfatal disability.) Numerous stakeholders in the autism world, from parents to journalists to bioethicists to autistic people themselves, have posed the following question: Who would choose autism? (Or, more broadly, who would choose any disability?)

Because autism isn't a switch that can be turned off at will (trust me, I've tried), autism is frequently conceived as essentialized involuntarity. But beyond the illusion of choice, autism's essence, if you will, has been clinically identified as a disorder that prevents individuals from exercising free will and precludes them from accessing self-knowledge and knowledge of human others. Its subjects are not subjects in the agentive sense of the word, but are rather passively subject to the motions of brains and dermis gone awry. Deborah Barnbaum's *The Ethics of Autism* is one such account.[20] A philosophical treatise, the book promotes a portrait of autism that is the antithesis of both community and communicability, echoing the stereotypical sentiment that autistics are closed off from the larger world. "There is something intrinsically limiting in an autistic life," writes Barnbaum.[21] And, later, "Autism cuts people off from people."[22] What Barnbaum and others suggest is that autism is a world without people, that a world without people is a world without rhetoric, and that an arhetorical life is a life not worth living—a life beyond the realm of voluntary action and intentionality.

Of course, framing autism as neurological involuntarity is a false construct. After all, does anyone really choose their neurology?[23] And yet, even though neurotypicality is as much an involuntarity as is mental disability or neurodivergence, the construct of involuntarity is culturally inscribed into autism as a condition.[24] Autistics wrench and scream and rock their bodies, and they have no choice; they have no agency; they project little to no rhetorical or narrativistic purpose.

Within this passivity-centric framework, involuntarity might encompass shit smearing or body rocking; it likewise encompasses any act of communication, or what white-coat types might otherwise reduce to inappropriate behaviors; it encompasses embodiment; it encompasses how one dwells in the world. It signifies a lack of purpose, a lack of audience awareness, a lack of control over one's own person—and under the banner of *person*, I'm including how we conceptualize mind, body, being, and self-determination. My flapping fingers and facial tics signify an anti-discourse of sorts: Where is my control? Where is my communicability? Would anyone choose a life of ticcing? How can an involuntary movement, an involuntary neurology, a state of being that is predicated on asociality—how can these things be rhetorical?

In many ways, I am over-narrating this involuntary narrative, this story that autistic people are lacking in all things selfhood. We could call my storying hyperbole, or we could call it an autistic symptom. (My neurology supposedly primes me, after all, to be oversensitive, black-and-white, and hypertruthful about the world around me.) At many junctures in this book, I defer to the hyperbolic, and the narratives I create around medical stories relate keenly sense-felt experiences of dehumanization. To be clear, what I am here calling hyperbole is not my hyperbole, for hyperbole assumes a shared, and often neurotypical, referentiality. It is one of those rhetorical tropes that I suspect was created by a rhetorician whose blood possessed the mystical properties of benzodiazepines, or maybe Quaaludes. What disabled subjects might experience as the mundane and everyday, nondisabled subjects might experience as hyperbole, and vice versa. These are rhetorical negotiations as much as they are sensory or perceptual negotiations: In contending that popular autism narratives represent autistics as involuntary, I am drawing upon long-standing histories and motifs that have come to dictate the whatness of autism. Mass institutionalization. Refrigerator mothers. Anti-vaxxers. Puzzle pieces. All of these figures, and more, create their exigencies through stories about autism's tragedy and victims, through stories about lack of choice. These stories are also animated beyond the domain of academic research: What Simon Baron-Cohen says in a neuroimaging journal is read, interpreted, and ultimately applied by practitioners on the ground. These translations and clinical applications of theory are stories unto themselves, stories that wield the harshest of material effects. But, more than this, I am also relating the stories that autistic people tell about these stories—meta-stories, of sorts. Who, then, is to be believed? If autism has taken over our brains, are we to be trusted? Does the condition of being nonautistic provide more agency, or rhetoricity, or voluntariness, even if only incrementally so?

Of course, involuntarity, I am arguing, is not an inherent part of autism as a condition. It is a story that structures and mediates autistic people's experiences of the world, but it is not an essential property in the way that clinicians or fundraisers might relate it. Rather, involuntarity's stories are those of abuse, of disbelief, of suffering and non-agency and pain. Involuntarity is forcibly imposed onto autistic bodies, onto neurodivergent bodies writ large, often to violent effect. Involuntary logics are the logics that delivered me to the psychiatric ward of the local hospital; they are the logics that forcibly absented me from a high school education; they are the logics of overmedication, eugenic futures, institutionalization; they are the logics that narrate shit smearing as brain gone awry. Involuntarity wreaks violence, even when violence is wrought voluntarily.

Throughout this book, I am thinking through the logics of involuntarity across two domains. First is the domain of autism itself, or autism's supposed propensity to impede or reduce the intentionality, will, volition, and/or goal direction of those affected. This is the domain on which I've primarily lingered thus far. The second, and closely related, is the creed of compliance and coercion that attend autism intervention services, most especially those that are behaviorist in form. In these therapies, autism is not so much an ecology of neuroqueer experience but rather an ecology of joint and forcible prosthesis, an ecology in which the autistic is physically made to comply with the therapeutic and social demands of nonautistic publics. In other words, if involuntarity isn't ascribed to autistics on a genetic or neurological level, it is most certainly inscribed in the treatment enterprises that structure an autistic child's life. Following Luckett, Bundy, and Roberts, we might ask, "to what extent could [autistic people's] choices be said to be voluntary rather than conditioned responses?"[25] Is an autistic rhetoric a rhetoric of operant conditioning and reinforced response? And, if so, can we even call this a rhetoric?

A number of disability studies scholars have commented upon the ways in which neurodivergent interlocutors have been rendered effectually nonrhetorical.[26] Taken together, their central arguments revolve around residual characterizations of neurodivergence (in particular, mental illness) across clinical and popular texts. When I invoke the term *residual*, I mean to suggest that mental disability always leaves something behind. And, in leaving something behind, mental disability takes over. When one is schizophrenic, for example, her rhetorical actions are rendered less as symbolic actions and more as biological motions: schizophrenia causes the person to act. The schizophrenic person, in these constructions, has no volition—or whatever volition she has is tempered by the schizophrenia. In this regard, it's important to note that whatever the placeholder—whether schizophrenia, autism, depression, cerebral palsy, ADHD, bipolar—mental disability signals a kind of rhetorical involuntariness. Mental disability wields more agency than mentally disabled people.

Involuntarity is a project of dehumanization.

This, then, is how the neurodivergent are often storied into (non)rhetoricity. We are conditioned to believe that our selves are not really selves, for they are eternally mitigated by disability, in all of its fluctuations. Autism is, in many respects, an apt and kairotic case study in rhetoric's in/voluntary violences. Most any text or tract about autism comes adorned in numbers, alarming figures crafted to inspire exigency and fear. Six hundred percent increases in diagnosis. One in sixty-eight children. Three million dollars in lifetime care. But beyond the numbers, which remain situated in rhetorics of crisis and doom, autism is frequently storied as an epic of asociality, of nonintention. It represents the edges and boundaries of humanity, a queerly crip kind of isolationism. We, the autistic, are a peopleless people. We embody not a counter-rhetoric but an anti-rhetoric, a kind of being and moving that exists tragically at the folds of involuntary automation. Our bodyminds rotely go through the motions, cluelessly la dee da. As rhetorician Todd Oakley once described, "rhetorical practices must . . . pose some form of an intentional agent to be coherent, and there is no better evidence to that effect than studies of autistic people, beings who lack the human rhetorical potential."[27]

Nowhere is the syllogism clearer:

—One must be human in order to be rhetorical.
—Autistic people are not rhetorical.
—Autistic people are not human.

Ignore, for a moment, that an autistic person derived the above syllogism. The irony might cause a headache. Also ignore that an autistic person might know what irony is. Ignore too that rhetoricians have written about the ways in which nonhuman animals are rhetorical, or even the ways in which objects are rhetorical.[28] Furniture may bear rhetoricity, but autistic people lack the Socratic gusto of futons.

Although I question rhetoric's human-centeredness in subsequent chapters, the following remains my chief concern: the ways in which non-rhetoricity denies autistic people not only agency, but their very humanity.

Autism is, of course, looming in the public consciousness. At a time when we know more about autism than we've ever known, what we know is very little, and what we know is decidedly nonautistic. There have been numerous attempts at god theories, or theories that purport to explain the many reasons why autistic people are nonpeople. These god theories transpose facets of autistic personhood into sterile symptom clusters, pathologizing character traits such as "intense and fulfilling interests" with clinically ornate buzzwords such as "perseveration of autistic psychopathy." But among the most prominent of such god theories, I'd argue, are theories about theory of mind (ToM) and theories about autistic behavior (in particular, that of applied behavior analysis, ABA). Whereas ToM stories autism in terms of internal states and cognitive processes, behavior analysis stories the autistic through observation, bodily comportment, and external behavior. Taken together, ToM and ABA construe the autistic as involuntarily willed and involuntarily drafted—beholden not only to neuronal desires but to the desires of therapists and caregivers and social norms.

In examining these god theories, *Authoring Autism* questions and rejects their canonicity in clinical research and practice, as well as the indictments these theories make about rhetorical action. Like any god theory, these theories are nuanced and complex, arguably disciplines unto themselves. But what they share in common is a persistent disbelief in the capacities of autistic people to be volitional, to be social, and to be selves. Given autism's classification as a disorder of social communication, these (dis)beliefs about autism are themselves theories of rhetoric, theories that privilege restrictive notions of what it means to interact and interrelate.

In chapters 1 and 2, I deconstruct as I story these god theories, both of which have radically shaped how clinicians and families understand autistic people. But here I want to linger on one god theory in particular, ToM, because this god theory has been hugely influential in the trajectory and staying power of autism research, grant funding, and clinical approaches to treatment. Theory of mind is a cognitive mechanism that autistic people are claimed to lack, or in which they are grievously impaired. In short, ToM is the ability to understand that other people have their own unique mental states, feelings, beliefs, and desires. It is the ability not only to recognize intentional stances, but to apprehend that intentional stances exist to begin with. Yet contemporary theories about ToM also invoke and assert other cognitive phenomena—including, but not limited to, mentalizing, metacognition, self-awareness, imaginative play, and expressing empathy.[29] In other words, to lack a theory of mind is not simply to lack a theory of others' minds—it is also to lack an awareness of one's own mind.[30]

Simon Baron-Cohen is perhaps the scholar most readily associated with ToM research and is particularly well known for having coined the term *mindblindness*, the notion that autistic people are pathologically impaired in recognizing and attributing mental states. Mindblindness, then, functions as a rhetorical foil that renders the autistic non-rhetorical at worst, and residually rhetorical at best. As R. Peter Hobson quips of the mindblind, "their difficulty in shifting among person-centred perspectives undermines both their grasp of what it means to hold a perspective and, beyond this, what it means to claim that any given perspective is true of that which transcends individuals' perspectives, namely reality."[31]

Reality is beyond the autist's grasp. Autism is that which contrasts. In Hobson's commentary I am reminded of Kenneth Burke's work on god theories, in which he claims that "in any term we can posit a world."[32] What, then, is an autistic world, if such a world bears no credible claim to a credible reality?

Under such logics, I have written this book, presumably unaware of my reader and my (non)self. The involuntary actions, thoughts, writings, and behaviors of my autistic body negate my claims to writerhood, rhetorichood, and narrativehood. Instead, this book might be better understood as a cluster of symptoms.

*Achoo.*

You're welcome.

## Autistic Machines

Symptoms only take us so far—and the landing point is generally a sterile one. When I describe my bodily comportment in terms of symptoms, I reduce how I move through physical space to a mere check box on a patient intake form. My body is more than this reduction. I have stimmy hands, hands that wave, and flap, and tussle rubber bands—hands that create and transform space as much as they occupy it. My hands story and proclaim, denounce and congratulate. My hands say both *fuck you* and *thank you*. Sometimes I am the only person who knows what my hands are meaning. Sometimes even I don't know what my hands mean—but why must I always cherish or privilege meaning? Description cannot contain my hands. And yet, my former neuropsychologist described my movement as autistic stereotypy. My therapist described my movement as self-stimulatory gesticulation. In all of their describing, I find that little about me is described. Instead, my body is reduced. Erased. Medicated.

And so, symptoms only take us so far. My own capacious reimagining of symptomatology, of both autism and rhetoric, invokes what Victor Vitanza, in a nod to Deleuze, calls the "involution" of rhetorical spaces.[33] Involution calls into question ideas about rhetoric's supposed human-centeredness (what of a "hands-on" rhetoric?), as well as the ways in which traditional conceptions of intentionality dehumanize neurodivergent interlocutors. Vitanza positions *involuting* as mashup of *involuntary* and *revolution*, imagining rhetorical domains in which involuntarity reconfigures our felt sense of rhetoric's very project. Because what, after all, is this thing we call rhetoric?

Traditionally, rhetoric has been conceived as the art of persuasion. But the centrality of argument to rhetorical traditions has long been questioned, most especially by feminist rhetorical theorists. James Berlin has described rhetoric as the thing which mediates reality by means of discourse.[34] But if we return again to questions of belief, voluntariness, and hyperbole, it is hard to construct an autism rhetoric—or, indeed, an autistic rhetoric—when the mediators, realities, and discourses have been storied as so fantastically different. Bruno Bettelheim, one of autism's earliest and most notorious figures, famously called autistics prisoners of the fortress, comparing autism to concentration camps. Importantly, Bettelheim storied his own experiences as a survivor of Buchenwald and Dachau, employing his narrative to signify how autistic people have it far worse—because autism is a living death.[35] These stories position autism as a mechanistic entelechy, a life force that is ironically typified by death. So too does the trope of the alien order autism discourse, with even autistic-authored cultural texts and web forums bearing titles such as Wrong Planet or Resident Alien. We might turn again to Kenneth Burke and the argument that rhetoric's identifications are its divisions, that one can only identify with another if some kind of mediating difference organizes their encounter: for it is in this clashing, this coming together, that persuasion arises. But how to be a persuading body when one's body has been storied as unpersuasive, as inhuman and deadly? From where in the ether can an autistic rhetoric hail?

As I relate in chapter 1, rhetoric's modes and stories—and rhetoric's privileges—are incredibly wide-ranging and diffuse. But with autism, what at once seems so sprawling and profound a construct as rhetoric becomes incredibly narrow. The clinicalization of autism requires a clinicalization of rhetoric, because how else to measure that which the autistic lacks? Speech, as in words audibly escaping the contours of human mouths; writing, as in words that are arranged to be read and meaningfully understood by humans; intent, as in actions that not only bear a kind of purpose or deliberate meaning, but actions that likewise work to infer or deduce purposes and deliberations from human others, all presumably accomplished with neurotypical magical superpowers; emotion, and imagination, and socialization—I could keep going. Each of these items is a construct that rhetoric prizes and privileges. Each of these items is a construct that autistics are claimed to lack.

Take, for instance, my narrative approach thus far. It strikes me that I might be read as incredibly self-absorbed, if only because I have diagnostic papers that affirm this very sentiment. I am storying autism academically and rhetorically, yes, but I am also storying an autistic version of me—as though I am living out, on the page, the paradoxical autos of autism in all of its glory. I am simultaneously selfless and self-centered, and these things are mutually sustaining. If I had a fully developed sense of self, then I would have a more fully developed sense of others, and vice versa. What autism presents, then, is an opportunity for readers to diagnose the very form of this book, as though this book were an invitation for symptomatological scrutiny.[36]

I am autistic. I live and dwell and will forever remain among the lacking.

To be honest, it is only in recent years that I think about my shit so often, and so rhetorically. My shit never really stained any walls. My family was always moving, hopping from one location to the next, desperate as my parents searched for work, as my parents searched for a school system that didn't object to students who crapped themselves during math class. But I am not thinking about my shit as a symptom, as a sign of how I lack empathy or perspective for others' feelings (or others' desires to wash cribs and walls and hands). Rather, I am thinking about the narrativity of my shit. A weird thing, I realize—and perhaps that I am even sharing this with a public audience further signals how impaired my ToM really is. (I kid.)

The connection between shit smearing and ToM might appear tenuous at first glance. But in many respects, I'd posit, they occupy an interlocking, mutually constitutive narrative about autistic selfhood: Autistics are considered residually rhetorical because their symbolic actions, in the words of Burke, have been reduced, scientistically, to nonsymbolic motion.[37] That is, autistic motion is the domain of neurobiological behavior, which is the domain of the nonsymbolic and automatic, or the automatonic. We see this narrative all the time, most often in behaviorist writings that proclaim autistic speech acts and gestures as behaviors lacking in meaning, purpose, or social value.[38] Francesca Happé echoes this line of thought when she describes autism as a world bereft of inference and intent: "Without mentalizing ability, the transparency of intentions that allows humans to use language in a truly flexible way is not open to autistic communicators."[39] To be clear, this is a story that structures how nonautistic others come to know autism, and thereby autistics, in the present day. We can see this story alive and well in clinical scholarship, just as we can locate this story in the social skills curricula that dominate special education programs. Michelle Garcia Winner's Social Thinking and Carol Gray's Social Stories are but two exemplars of the ways in which the biomotion of ToM theories structures the logics of autism intervention and response.[40] Each intervention presumes something has gone awry in the neurosocial circuitry of autistic brains, and each intervention endeavors to teach autistics the utterly unteachable: to understand that humans exist in more than a fleshy, body-occupies-a-space kind of way. Humans exist perspectivally and intentionally, and without this knowledge, autistics are absented from the larger project of being human.

In the stories we tell and encounter about biological motion, autistics and humans unfortunately operate as a clinical binary. Autistics are *robots-en-organisme*, mindblindly spewing and spreading our shit because full communicability is beyond our reach. Autistics are not Burke's "symbol-using animals," at least not in a consistent or socially appropriate sense. What communicability autistics do possess is merely residual. Or, put alternatively, autism is an entity much like nonautism, or *allism*, is an entity.[41] Whereas autism is represented as compulsions toward the self (autos), allism is fashioned as a turning-toward the other (*allos*). These entities—the neuro-orientational impulse toward self or other—both reside and recede, reside and recede. And, importantly, in invoking allism throughout this book, my intent is not to reify the notion that nonautistics are empathetic social butterflies or that autistics are mindblind egocentrists. Rather, what allism signifies is the absurdities of these constructions, as well as the ways in which cultural understandings of what it means to be nonsocial are deeply entrenched in values of human worth.

Following the above, what might autistic shit signify? What is so symbolic and compelling and kairotic about my shit? Shit only signifies if the autist intends it to signify, and, as scholars have asserted repeatedly, if one is a true autist, then signification lies beyond one's grasp. When autistry recedes, intended signification may be a goal, may be a dim reality: For the purported high-functioning, perhaps shit on the wall does hold meaning. And yet, the rub: Autism always bears residue. One can never wholly escape its grasp. Even stories of so-called recovery, even the most optimistic high-falutin'-functioning narratives posited by behaviorist demigod Ole Ivar Lovaas himself, proclaim that autism always inheres.[42] Its ephemera trail, never fully dissociable from the being upon which it once latched. To be autistic is to live and to lie in a between space. The autistic symbolic is always a reduction, a motion rather than a rhetorical repertoire. It is mechanistic, rigid, routinized, reducible. Consequently, its significations are never more than quasi-significations. Autism's significations are the significations of impairment, of symptoms, of disorder, of crippling residual effects.

The answer, then, to my shit smearing is that I didn't (don't) know what shit is. Shit means nothing. It is neither figurative nor literal: It exists, but it doesn't project. Otherwise, why would an autistic person (read: machine) cake it on walls? In what reality can I dwell when I cannot reliably conjure or imagine the mental states of others, including poopy others?

In scholarly texts, autism's wills and misfires are variously framed. But as it is commonly represented, autism is not ingrained in, nor is it part of, human will. Autism is instead conceived as ancillary to—and parasitic of—an allistic will. Whatever intent an autistic possesses begins with her presumed prior or core self, the allistic self. When autism is diagnosed, it is thought to reside, to push out the normalcy and invade, body-snatcher style. As in, autism made toddler me throw and smear and lick my own shit. As in, autism is making me write this book, and you, dear reader, should be skeptical at all turns. This changeling narrative is potent, rearing its head in texts ranging from Jenny

FIGURE I.1. A smiling poop emoji is positioned above a caption that reads, "Ceci n'est pas un caca." The image is an (autistic) homage to René Magritte's *The Treachery of Images* and Foucault's *Ceci n'est pas une pipe*. Image created by Phantom Open Emoji, used via Wikimedia Commons, Creative Commons Attribution 3.0 Unported License.

*Ceci n'est pas un caca*

McCarthy's parenting memoirs to Google's genomic database of autism tissue samples. Autism—autism is what's moving and breathing.

And so, autism does have a will, but its will is one of nonsymbolic motion, not symbolic action. It follows, then, that in being nonactors, autistic people's wills are merely the wills of neurobiology, of distilled movements and motions and mechanisms whose remnants and residences occupy higher priority than rhetorical, symbolic intent.

Even autistic people themselves have narrated a similar kind of story. Autistic life writer Wenn Lawson, for example, famously titled one of his books *Autism: Taking Over*.[43] In *Songs of the Gorilla Nation*, Dawn Prince described autism as living behind glass, wherein all motions, commotions, and symbolic exchanges happen always at a remove, cognitively filtered and distorted.[44] But, in many respects, this story is an old autistic story. It is an early and emergent narrative script, a script that autistic people have since diverted, evolved, repeated, rebuked, and queered. I could claim that autism's wills were shitty wills—shitty in that autism took me hostage and shitty in that autism plays with actual shit. But I instead suggest that my autistic motions are better read as mediators and preconditions of autistic actions, actions that cloud the lines of sociality and asociality. Must shit smearing have an audience in order to be a rhetorical act? What if childhood shit smearing were read as autistic communication instead of autistic behavior? And might we think of shit—the actual, organic object—as a coagent unto itself? Manning and Massumi suggest that "from the autistic, we hear neither a rejection of the human, nor a turning away from relation."[45] What, then, are autistic objects, and in what ways do they rhetorically mediate? Rhetoric has long storied intent as a kind of distribution, one whose affects, effects, and motions obscure how we think of bodies, environments, machines, nonhuman animals, and things.[46] Why, then, does autism so pathologically diverge from these stories?

As I suggest throughout *Authoring Autism*, autistic stories are, at root, queer stories. Here I borrow my deployment of *queer* from José Esteban Muñoz to suggest queer as a kind of verbing, as an always-futurity. Muñoz begins *Cruising Utopia* with the pithy claim that "queerness is not yet here."[47] In this construction, Muñoz positions queerness as an ideal, as a rejection of arrival and a rhetoric of potentiality. Importantly, Muñoz's focus on hope and potentiality is a critical assessment of the antirelational turn within queer studies, which, he maintains, "moves to imagine an escape or denouncement of relationality as first and foremost a distancing of queerness from what some theorists seem to think of as the contamination of race, gender, or other particularities that taint the purity of sexuality as a singular trope of difference."[48] As I discuss in subsequent chapters, *arelationality* and *asociality* are terms of work that position the autistic as deadly or death-wishing, collapsing the autistic into all that is alarmingly inhuman. In fact, these terms of work are often used interchangeably with *autism* itself. And these terms of work, as Muñoz writes of antirelational queer theories, likewise result in the whitening and masculinizing of autistic people: if an autistic future is bleak, it is racistly and transmisogynistically represented as bleaker—"contaminated"—when its subjects are persons of color, women or genderqueer, poor, and/or nonspeaking. Drawing upon Muñoz, Jonathan Alexander describes queerness's "motion of futurity" as "a working through impossibility."[49] The queer motion toward the "not yet here" is what propels Alexander to assess the field of composition and rhetoric as an inherently straightening enterprise—and, I would add, a thereby inherently ableist enterprise.[50] He suggests that there can be no queer pedagogy, no queer composition, because pedagogy and composition are, at root, social(izing) and norming projects (and, in this vein, composition pedagogy unfurls as a white, straight, masculine project). To compose is to comply; to teach is to inculcate compliance. Conversely, queering, Alexander maintains, "confronts all of us with the incommensurabilities of desires and identities and socialities."[51]

The above reveals much that is relevant to autism. We might, for instance, consider autism as a kind of neurologically queer motioning. To be autistic is to be neuroqueer, and to be neuroqueer is to be idealizing, desiring, sidling. But rather than story such motioning as parasitically unwilled, or as a grope toward mindblindness, I'd instead suggest that autism is a neurologically queer motioning that is asocially perverse, a lurching toward a future that imagines "incommensurabilities of desires and identities and socialities," a ticcing toward rhetorical residues. This asociality, while often represented by clinicians as a nonsociality, is inherently relational in that it defies, reclaims, and embraces the expansiveness that countersocialities can potentially embody. Jay Dolmage has offered a similar vision of disability rhetorics, construing dis-rhetoricity as a way to move that is cunning, sideways, and creeping toward disabled futures.[52]

Autistic machinations, however, are rarely portrayed so idealistically. Autism research operates on the hope that there will be no autistic future. As Alison Kafer laments, the "presence of disability signals . . . a future that bears too many traces of the ills of the present to be desirable."[53] Such are the rhetorical shapings of neuroqueer subjects. Because autism resides, even futures that predict improvement or mitigation of symptoms still bear traces—traces of mindblind, involuntary motion. Theories about ToM often function as a metanarrative for this antifuturistic logic. Autism might be better termed an autpocalypse.

Theories about ToM arguably constitute their own interdisciplinary enterprise. We might even term this enterprise ToM studies. There are a variety of theories about how and in whom ToM operates, such as whether ToM is an innate capacity, a developmental milestone, or a processual ability that emerges through experience, simulation, and/or projecting one's concept of self onto another. My intent (oh, wait—my motion) is not to provide an overhaul of theories about ToM here. Nor is my intent to suggest which theory is best or most humane, because—and this is important—I believe all incarnations of ToM to be decidedly inhumane. Instead, I am interested in the ways in which ToM stories autistic people, as well as the effects it has on how we come to know and understand autistic people. These effects, I suggest, are lingering and often violent. Among the many terms of work employed by ToM studies is *modularity*. It is not uncommon for cognition to be represented as computeristic, regardless of whether autism is the focal point of conversation.[54] Although hotly debated, ToM is often posited as a cognitive module—or even a series of cognitive modules—mechanisms in which brains (dis)engage.[55] The general idea is that there is a mechanism(s) in the human brain that bears responsibility for ToM, and we know this to be true because autistic people seem not to have such a module. This logic is, of course, circuitous and questionable. The state of our knowledge is that a ToM module exists because one core group of people seems to lack it organically.

Modularity is, of course, its own kind of metaphorization of the brain. When modularity is invoked in ToM discourse, it is often in reference to the theory that ToM abilities occupy their own distinct, domain-specific cognitive module (or modules, plural, that work in tandem to coordinate all of ToM's many functions). But I would argue that ToM doesn't modularize the human brain so much as it modularizes autistic people. Theory of mind defines and dissects autistic people in and as discrete components. Remember that ToM begs at more than mere intention—it crafts an involuntary landscape that traverses self-knowledge, sociality, empathy, recognition of mental states, and even imagination. These are some of the many domains in which autism resides, in which we can sport and spot autistic traces.

Importantly, Muñoz maintains that queerness is constitutive of motion and ephemera, of traversals and traces. Autism, I am claiming, is always residual and is always fluctuating, ticcing, trembling. Its ephemera are marked and marketed in ToM scholarship, and if I were so inclined, I might pull out a copy of the *Diagnostic and Statistical Manual of Mental Disorders* (DSM) and locate autism's traces and motions, its histories and presences, across bullet points and checklists and clinical catalogs and modularistic models. I have so far, in this introduction, resisted this common DSM impulse—for isn't every statement on autism a statement about its diagnostic criteria?

But my autism resides far beyond diagnosis, much like my pansexuality resides far beyond coming out. Disclosure bears its own kind of residual effects. My neuroqueer disclosures inflect and infect—they suggest an interpretive lens through which others feel an impulse to story my life, to story my being. Is autism responsible for my paragraph structure? Did a neuroqueer neuron operationalize my word choice? To what extent do we need—or want—a rhetorical theory of modularity?

Vitanza's involution project figures the tic, the stim, the vocalization, and the unconscious gesture as the fabric upon which, in the words of Thomas Rickert, rhetoric has capacity to emerge.[56] In other words, without ticcing, without involuntary motion, there is no rhetorical action. My shit, as perverse as it may seem, is a precondition for rhetoricity. It is rhetoricity. And while I cannot speak to the in/voluntariness of my feces-smearing child self, I can speak to the ways in which my bodymind writes and is written into autism's non-rhetoricity. My facial tics and complex hand movements involute social fabrics. Chorus of tics, emerge.

## Autistext

While autism is certainly a disability, it is, as I have suggested, a constellation of stories—stories about embodiment and intention, stories about humanity and hierarchy, stories about diagnosis and detection and prevention. This constellation, as Phil Bratta and Malea Powell describe, is an assertion about normalcy as much as it is a question of what and why something comes to be configured as normal or dominant.[57]

But autism is also a story about communication more generally, about enriching our ideas of rhetoricity and eye contact and the beauty of shiny objects. It's a story about disability culture. It's a story about stories, and what or who is determined to be storyable. It's a story about empathy and expression and reclamation. In my adult years, as I've struggled to locate a sense of identity, the idea of storying brings both comfort and distress. Autism is core to my very being. It's how I sense, interact with others, and process information. Autism is my rhetoric. But what's at risk here is who tells my story and, more broadly, who tells the story of my people. What's of concern is who gets to author our individual and collective identities, who gets to determine whether we are, in fact, narrative creatures, whether we are living beings in rhetorical bodies, whether we are even allowed to call ourselves human.

Many autistics have told their stories—or nonstories, if you will. Arguably, the first published autie-biography was David Eastham's 1985 *Understand: Fifty Memowriter Poems*, a small chapbook that was scarcely circulated. Importantly, 1985 is the same year that Simon Baron-Cohen, Alan Leslie, and Uta Frith published "Does the Autistic Child Have a Theory of Mind?," the first such article to suggest lack of ToM as a causal explanation for autism.[58] In quick succession, and with broader public reach, came a number of published autie-biographies, most famously Temple Grandin's *Emergence: Labelled Autistic* (1986) and Donna Williams's *Nobody Nowhere* (1992). Other texts published at the turn of the 1990s included Sean and Judy Barron's *There's a Boy in Here* (1992), David Miedzianik's *My Autobiography* (1993), and Thomas McKean's *Soon Will Come the Light* (1994).

The stories of Grandin and Williams—and with them the barrage of autistic stories that soon followed—forced clinicians, parents, educators, and lay publics alike to reassess their archly held views of autism, to reconsider theories about the autistic's capacity for thought. But after the shock of autistic literacy began to wane, clinicians sought new and inventive theories—something, anything, to maintain order over disorder.[59] For example, Bernard Rimland, founder of the Autism Society of America, was quick to suggest that Grandin and Williams had both recovered from their autism—because how could an autistic have an inner life, much less narrate one?[60] In like manner, Francesca Happé suggested that autie-biographers were exceptional occurrences, so-called able-disabled people who, while still autistic, brought little of worth to discussions of autism. Asked Happé at the time, "What can we point to in their writing that deserves the label 'autistic'?"[61]

And so opened the floodgates. Following Grandin and Williams, cognitive studies researchers seeded autism journals with articles on autie-biography and autistic life writers, elaborating any conceivable problem, error, or rhetorical faux pas they could find. And find these things, they did. As I discuss in chapter 3, such accounts have often focused on what the autistic writer has left unsaid, importing the logics of ToM to purport that the writer lacks, in varying degrees, capacity for self-awareness and/or audience awareness. Happé's 1991 analysis of Grandin's work has become somewhat iconic in its rhetorical approach to autism: "These autistic writers," she notes, "may not be interested in, or capable of writing on those subjects which we [allistics] should most like to hear their views."[62] Some twenty years later, the sentiment remains. Studies tell us that autistic writers supposedly employ fewer mental state terms, or terms that signal an awareness of others' intentions, beliefs, feelings, desires, and even existence.[63] So too are autistics claimed to relate fewer personal experiences in spontaneous conversational narratives.[64] Autistic people are likewise claimed to have a "lesser propensity to adjust to alternative perspectives" and are theorized to possess not only ToM impairments but broader impairments in role-taking as well.[65] Helen Tager-Flusberg relates such narrative failures thusly: "These errors reflect difficulties in conceptualizing notions of self and other, as they are embedded in shifting discourse roles."[66] The refrain is clear: Autistics don't tell us what we want to hear, nor do they tell it to us in the manner in which we wish to hear it.

While studies on autistic narrative competence vary in their results and foci, taken together, these studies convey a scalar portrait of the autist as suspended in perpetual non-rhetoricity, no matter how far ze proceeds along the scale. Incrementally, autistics can make gains in rhetorical or narrative competence. But on the whole, one would not be designated with the label *autistic* if ze weren't a queerly (non)rhetorical creature. If we autistics use so-called internal states language in our writing or speaking, it's still possible that we might shift the topic of discourse too quickly or too routinely. If we are able to maintain a topical stance, we might reverse our pronouns or use only proper names. If we finally master normative pronominal conventions, we might still yet rely on the literality of language rather than discern the intentionality or figurative meanings of another interlocutor. If we grok metaphor, we still lack intention and sociality in other ways: We fail to share in the enjoyment of others; we might not speak, at all, ever; we flat out refuse to adjust our narratives in accordance with new or contextually relevant information. (Have I mentioned yet that my favorite band is the Electric Light Orchestra?)

In this way, our discursive partiality becomes metonymic for our human partiality. Autistic people do not tell allistics what they want to know; and because autistic people do not tell allistics what they want to know, autistics are presumed to hold variable impairments in those cognitive and neurological domains that control or mitigate social-intentional function. In other words: Unlike allistic rhetors, our narrative practices cannot be read outside neurology, for without neurology we cannot map or filter autism onto our narratives. Ours are neuroqueer brains whose synapses routinely fire blanks, and something as banal as our pronoun (mis)use supposedly evidences our distinctiveness from all other persons. Autism's rhetorical function—in genetics, neurology, psychology, philosophy, and more—is to contrast those who are otherwise presumed to be cognitively and thereby humanly whole.

Yet, in spite of the pessimism that slithers throughout this chapter and (spoiler) others, autistic people have continued to write, publish, agitate, advocate. We continue to tell allistics what they don't want to hear. Catalogs teem with autistic-authored books, many of which are oriented toward autistic audiences and together culminate to suggest the breadth and heterogeneity of autistic publics. Autistics.org, for instance, hosts a list of autistic-authored books that numbers well over a hundred, and Lindsay at the blog *Autist's Corner* maintains an extensive "autiebibliography." Autistic culture, as a movement, boasts at least three decades of activism, much of it digitally born. Self-published and transmedia collections such as the *NeuroQueer* group blog, *Loud Hands: Autistics, Speaking, All the Weight of Our Dreams: On Living Racialized Autism,* and *Typed Words, Loud Voices* emerged from digital communities of autistic and other neurodivergent people. While new media scholars bemoan the death of the blog, the autistic blogosphere thrives. Autism Acceptance Month (April), Autistic Pride Day (June 18), Autistics Speaking Day (November 1)—these campaigns, and more, are some of the many virtual gatherings in which autistic people multimodally narrate their lives, communities, cultures, and ways of being in the world. And while it is beyond the scope of this book to count pronouns or internal states language in these texts (although that would be a fun Sunday), my broader contention is that these items do not disqualify people from rhetoricity. Rather, autistic conventions can be more capaciously read as a neuroqueer mode of engaging, resisting, claiming, and contrasting the interstices of sociality.

Autistic narrative persists. It persists in the face of discourses that would render us arhetorical and tragically inhuman. It persists across genre and mode, much of it ephemeral and embodied in form. Autistic people persist and insist in the narrativity of their tics, their stims, their echoed words and phrases, their relations with objects and environs. We persist in involuting, in politicizing the supposedly involuntary. We can't help it, after all.

## Autie-ethnography/Autistethnography

Storying is my method throughout this book, a method I've engaged for myriad reasons, including and especially my inability not to be self-absorbed.[67] First, I believe that autistic stories, both my own and those of others, resist the cultural inscriptions that autism as a diagnosis suggests. As Irene Rose contends in her work on autistic life writing, such "narratives work at a connective emotional level to resist the pathologisation of difference."[68] Rose explores, in particular, the resonances of terming autistic life writing autie-ethnography rather than autie-biography. Among other items, Rose considers the power in testimony and witnessing, as well as the activist strands that often travel through autist texts, or what I might term *autistexts*. Ultimately, Rose contends that autistexts transcend the solitary construction of autos—in both autism and the autobiographical—and work intertextually to narrate and protest oppression. Rotating between *autie-ethnographic* and *testimonio* as terms of work, Rose writes, "the primary concern of *testimonio* is sincerity of intention, not the text's literariness, an intention that in autistic autobiography is supported by editorial decisions that have allowed distinctly non-rational ontological experience to be included—and therefore validated—in some autistics' texts."[69] Intention is but one domain, then, in which autistexts queer the contours of a diagnosis, as well as the rhetorical traditions that attend such diagnosis. Autistic stories are interrelational, even if that interrelationality does not extend toward allistics, or even humans more generally.

Second, I believe that autistic stories reconfigure what it means to be self-focused and without self, in all of the paradoxicality of that simultaneity. These stories are queerings in that they narrate a confluence of excess and lack; or, put another way, the rhetoricisms of autistic storying defy rhetoricism. As such, these stories are theoretical texts unto themselves, worthy of the page weight accorded to the prominent autism scholars I've cited in this book. Ibby Grace, an autistic educational philosopher, offers one such perspective in her own storying of coming to an autistic identity.[70] Grace expands Rose's focus on intertextuality and life writing to suggest that all autistic storying—regardless of genre, mode, or delivery—functions as a kind of autistethnography. In this way, the flap of a hand or the fluttering of a wrist becomes a rhetorical act that exceeds the mereness of needing to be studied. More importantly, Grace makes the concerted shift from the *autie* to the *autist* prefix, noting that the former has taken on an increasingly diminutive quality over the past decade. When allistics speak of auties and aspies, she warns, they not only appropriate community terms but frequently attempt a cutening and thereby a rhetorical lessening of autistic subjects. For Grace's part, her autistethnography makes little mention of autism, while simultaneously queering the genre of typical autism ethnographies and clinical case studies. She begins her essay by observing, for instance, "It is a surprise that in our society it is not more disabling to live your whole life unaware that folding the symbolic kissing cherry blossoms together just so creates a regular pentagonal dodecahedron. But I am glad people can live fulfilling lives that way, because does anybody wish ill to people who are without that inner visual ability to properly spin things?"[71] Were a ToM scholar to analyze Grace's work (or mine, for that matter), I can only imagine (pun) where they might begin in their analysis, in their attempts to locate rhetorical pathology. Grace's refrain throughout her autistethnography is "maybe the reader can make inferences," a none-too-subtle appeal to those capacities in which autistics are figured as lacking.[72] But more, this demicommand—"maybe the reader can make inferences"—makes no such assumption that readers can, or will be able to, understand or share in the beauty or absence of visualization abilities. Grace's autistethnography, rather complexly, defends her rhetoricity while concomitantly telling it to fuck off.

Storying, then, holds potentiality. These "cultures of one," as Dawn Prince famously described autistics, culminate to form a kind of counter-rhetoric in all of their anti-rhetoricity.[73] We might behold autistic storying—and the unearthing of nonautistic stories about autism—as methods for queering futures, for projecting autistic desires and autistic ideals. The story of my shit, the story of my stims, the story of my diagnosis and involuntary entrance into this communing, incommunicable community. In authoring autism throughout this book, I am relating my own autistic narrative while also drawing upon the narratives of other autistics, even to the point of excess. As I mentioned previously, I engage the narrativistic—as a theoretical rather than a literary or analytic function—because ours is a condition that summons disbelief. Sometimes this disbelief is leveled at the disability itself ("but you can't be autistic"), and sometimes this disbelief is leveled at the scholarship we produce ("you are too autistic to write unbiasedly about autism"). In many regards, I am playing with a complicated autistic topos, that of the overshare, and talking about shit and queerness and self-injury more generally as a means to unsettle, digress, and, ultimately, center those who have traditionally been decentered.

These, of course, are rhetorical risks. Narrative methodologies have long been held suspect within academe, often viewed as a kind of nonresearch and/or rhetorical self-absorption. Such is the challenge, then, of positing autistethnography as a method and a genre worthy of scholarly attention. Disability studies, much like other cultural studies fields, has not been immune from such critique. Disabled people's autobiographical musings are typically cast as "narcissistic," as pathological compositions produced by otherwise scholarly incapable bodyminds.[74] Yet, despite such characterizations, disability studies persists as a highly narrativistic field, one that seeks to foreground individual narratives within larger sociopolitical and often rights-based discourses.

In ticcing toward the autie-ethnographic, *Authoring Autism* provides a(n) (alternative) (neuroqueer) narrative of autism's history and rhetorical meaning(s). This project, at root, aims to deconstruct cognitive studies scholarship that reifies the inhumanity and neurological passivity of autistics, while also claiming that autistic people queer the lines of rhetoric, humanity, and agency. Importantly, the rhetorical narrative in this project is interconnected with queerness in competing ways—as action, analytic, identity, and movement. First, I argue that, in its past and present clinical formations, autism is contextually situated within societal responses to and of gay panic. We can locate queerness in nineteenth-century fears about the feeble-minded and sexual deviance; we can locate queerness in the mainstreaming of ABA, which is used to eliminate "feminine sex-typed behaviors" and "cross-gender identification" in gender-variant children and to make autistics "indistinguishable from their peers";[75] we can locate queerness in theories about ToM, which are premised on the idea that autistics, regardless of gender identity, have an extreme male brain;[76] and we can locate queerness in the self-identifications of autistic people, who, anecdotally, have a far higher preponderance of queer identifications than do nonautistic populations. Often, discourse on the queer takes shape with regard to autistic people's identifications, but it also takes form as a verbing of that which supposedly makes autistic people antisocial and non-rhetorical creatures.

The autistic subject, queer in motion and action and being, has been clinically crafted as a subject in need of disciplining and normalization. What autism provides is a backdoor pathologization of queerness, one in which clinicians and lay publics alike seek out deviant behaviors and affectations and attempt to straighten them, to recover whatever neurotypical residuals might lie within the brain, to surface the logics and rhetorics of normalcy by means of early intensive behavioral intervention (EIBI).[77] Queer bodies and autistic bodies betray rhetoricity in gesture, relationality, emotion, and intent. How better, then, to refute—or to exceptionalize—the life writing of autistic people, who are so often presumed to be both cognitively challenged and cognitively queer/ed?

But, more than the above examples, which call upon queerness as identity (often in the LGBTQA sense of identity), autism is figured as a kind of neurological queering: Autistics are not only actively antisocial, defying the bounds of multiple social fabrics, but we are the ultimate asocial beings, forwarding self over others, humanizing objects and objectifying humans, rigid in our gaze and our gait and our affect.[78] The neurologically queer, contends Micki McGee, "is a site of panicked—indeed, epidemic—contestation."[79] The ToM discourse that governs empirical study of autism premises itself on cultural panics about what might be termed prosocial behaviors. Autistic bodies, mindblind bodies—these are bodies that not only defy social order, but fail to acknowledge social order's very existence. Autism, then, poses a kind of neuroqueer threat to normalcy, to society's very essence.

The term *neuroqueer* is itself a relatively new and web-based invention, at least in its current iteration, having evolved through the collaborative work of autistic bloggers Ibby Grace, Athena Lynn Michaels-Dillon, Nick Walker, and myself. As Walker in particular relates, *neuroqueer* resists a definition, even in its uptake within identitarian discourses. Instead, he maintains, neuroqueer identities are those in which subjects perform the perversity of their neurotypes, noting rather circumlocutiously, "A neuroqueer individual is an individual whose identity has in some way been shaped by their engagement in practices of neuroqueering. Or, to put it more concisely (but perhaps more confusingly): you're neuroqueer if you neuroqueer."[80] In these constructions, neuroqueer subjects are verbed forms, more accurately and radically conceived as cunning movements, not neuronal states or prefigured genetic codes. Given autism's particular threats to social orders, autism's queerity is often storied by means of disorientation: Autistics are so rhetorically impaired that they remain unoriented toward all that is normative and proper, whether empathy or eros or gender (performance and concept unto itself).

Autism treatment enterprises, many of which share origin stories with gay conversion therapies, enact a rehabilitative response as a means of de-queering the autist. In the vein of crip-queer studies scholars Robert McRuer and Abby Wilkerson, Jay Dolmage has described such clinical impulses as a kind of "compulsory sociality."[81] Affirming the work of disability rights activists who model their work on queer liberation, Dolmage claims that "resistance to compulsory sociality can be recognized as a possible disability rhetoric, even in a world in which the individuating and isolating construction of disability can be used against people with disabilities."[82] In support of this claim, Dolmage draws upon Julia Miele Rodas—in particular, her argument that autistic resistance to sociality is a condition of autistic survival. Writes Rodas, "Resistance to the encroaching world, and to tyrannical expectations of compulsory sociality, is necessary to autistic survival and self-determination."[83] In other words, that which supposedly makes autistics non-rhetorical is what makes them queer/ed, and is also what enables them to survive, to tic into autistic futures.

Narrating Neuroqueer Histories

As a clinical marker, autism is relatively nascent. Its emergence in psychiatric literature dates to the 1920s, but the earliest sustained case studies didn't transpire until World War II and the immediate postwar years, with studies led by Leo Kanner, Hans Asperger, Bruno Bettelheim, and others. As important as these studies are to constructions of autistic neuroqueerness, eugenicist histories and their focus on eliminating disabled and racialized people predate autism by a number of decades.[84] Even though the constellation of symptoms and traits we now know as autism was not named autism until the 1930s, autism is haunted by broader narratives of so-called racial betterment, as well as narratives concerned with eradicating intellectual and psychiatric disability.

Importantly, physicians at the time contended that masturbation and sexual deviance were the direct cause of mental disability.[85] In our contemporary moment, one that swells abuzz with the activity of neuroscientific rigor and fMRI machines, the autism-queer connection suggests autism as a neurophysiological trigger for queerness (all postulated around hormonal imbalances, white matter discrepancies, and impaired ToM modules). Conversely, through the early twentieth century, a moralistic approach to sexuality claimed the reverse—that aberrant sexual activity was the root cause of cognitive difference. (And so, the age-old question for autistic queers: Which came first—the autism or the gay?) In the United States, Samuel Gridley Howe represented one such theorist; John Harvey Kellogg represented another (and, among other things, codeveloped Corn Flakes as a cure-all for masturbation in the asylum, and also mutilated the genitalia of his child patients).[86]

I here want to fast-forward several decades, to 1974. In the interim time period, autism was born and blamed on the coldness of so-called refrigerator mothers. But as studies on autistic-imbued queerness were just beginning to ramp up, studies on nonautistic, gender-nonconforming children were already well under way, under the heading of ABA.

What is in 2014 considered the "gold standard autism therapy" (see the Autism Speaks website) was the predominant therapy used to train out the queer in children perceived to be trans, effeminate, and/or homosexual in the 1960s and 1970s.[87] To put it briefly, ABA represents a suite of therapeutic modalities whose end goal involves behavioral shaping toward the normative, toward the prosocial, toward compliance. It is, in combination with aversion therapy, one of the primary methodological forerunners of what might now be termed reparative therapy. Paradoxically, it remains the contemporary autism therapy of choice, endorsed by numerous medical authorities, including the U.S. Surgeon General. With regard to queer histories of ABA, some readers may recall the 1974 study by George Rekers and Ole Ivar Lovaas, which featured a four-year-old boy named Kraig who cross-dressed and displayed "pronounced feminine mannerisms, gestures, and gait, as well as exaggerated feminine inflection and feminine content of speech."[88] Rekers, now a prominent gay conversion advocate, chronicled the process by which Kraig's effeminate behaviors were punished—variously by abuse from his father and silent treatment from his mother—and his masculine behaviors were rewarded (with praise and toys). In our present-day moment, we now know Kraig to be Kirk Murphy, who committed suicide at the age of thirty-eight.

In later years, Lovaas distanced himself from his sex-role deviance research while Rekers based his entire career on it. Notably, Rekers and Lovaas's project—known as the UCLA Feminine Boy Project—was not only a federally funded program, but the largest program in U.S. history designed to intervene in the lives of so-called "sissy boys" and prevent "transvestism, transsexualism, [and] some forms of homosexuality."[89] As Phyllis Burke notes of the Feminine Boy Project in *Gender Shock*, "$218,945 went to UCLA from the NIMH with Dr. Lovaas as Principal Investigator (PI) in this project. For the early 1970s, this was an extraordinary amount of money for such a research grant, and because he was the PI, Dr. Lovaas was also the kingpin, the one whose reputation secured the grant, and the one who determined how the money would be allocated."[90] And yet—when autism enters the mix, ABA as queer cure-all resumes, posed as a methodology that recoups normalcy for the abnormally brained. Most states, for instance, recommend an average of forty hours per week of intensive ABA for autistic children. In the autistic community there has emerged a distinctive ex-ABA movement, one led by traumatized autistics and parents alike. Survivors of ABA speak of hours-long sessions spent on inculcating compliance, assent, and normalized gender roles, hours spent on social stories that reinforce stereotypical and cis/heteronormative behaviors.

As I discuss in chapter 2, these moments that attend autism and behavioral shaping stand among many such horrific moments in neuroqueer histories. But these moments remain iconic, for they reify heterocentric conceptions of gender and sexuality, while concurrently assuming that autistics are fundamentally, deviantly, and neurologically queer. These moments are also historically pervasive, feeding both accepted medical practice and pseudo-scientific approaches toward recovery and cure. Today's common practices include forced medication, ranging from sterilization to heavy sedation. For instance, one of the antidepressants I took for years, mirtazapine, has been studied in autistic populations only for its potential to curb masturbation and fetishism.[91] Another drug, Lupron, a chemical castration agent, has been used to control the aggression and sexual expression of autistic teens.[92]

Of course, these rhetorical webs of autism and queerness are not just notable for their horrors. They invoke all of the tough, meaty questions that any kind of intersectionality demands. How do we account for where queerness begins and disability ends? It may well be that I am queer only because my neurological disability predisposes me to queerness. But does that matter? What are the consequences of saying that I'm queer because I'm autistic—or, conversely, that I'm autistic because I'm queer?

Or, to step back even further: How do we theorize the neurologically queer? Even though my focus here is on autism, in many respects, this isn't a book on autism at all. Madness and mental disability are inextricable from queer histories. In what ways are categories such as OCD or bipolar disorder shaped and controlled by the heterocentric residue of the psychiatric establishment? What ethical lapses surface when we take on the task of teasing out the multiply identified, when we assert causality, when we find new and inventive ways of remarginalizing the marginalized, all in the name of scholarly pursuit?

The often violent ephemera of neuroqueer histories leave indelible traces on our presents and futures. I write this book, in part, because I don't know what to do with this stuff anymore. What to do when a rhetorician describes ToM as a "perfect phrase"?[93] What to do when a philosopher in one breath claims ToM is a "fundamental aspect of human relationships" and then in the next claims that autistic people do not have a "fully functioning theory of mind"?[94] What to do when leading autism researchers claim that autistic writing is inherently unreliable and that "it might be a mistake to take what is said at face value"?[95] What to do when a rhetorician claims that autistic people are "masked by a cloud of social solitude"?[96] What to do when a journalist maintains that autistic writing is "transmitted on suspect equipment"?[97] What to do with scholarship that denies autistic rhetoricity, denies autistic voice, denies autistic personhood?

How does an autistic person argue against the above? Anything I claim here is held suspect on the basis of my very being—because I am autistic, I lack a theory of mind. And because I lack a theory of mind, I lack both a theory of my mind and a theory of the minds of others. And because I lack a theory of my mind and the minds of others, anything I say is inherently unreliable, idiosyncratic, and special. My rhetorical moves are not rhetorical moves, but are rather symptoms of a problemed and involuntary body. Reason, topoi, tropes, narrative arcs, diplomacy—these will only ever be attempts, or, as Happé calls them, "hacks" toward a normative embodiment, hacks toward a normative rhetoric.[98] Appearing to know myself or others is merely *appearing* to know myself or others. I can appear, but I can never know. I have symptoms, and they have rhetoric.

Under such a construction of symptomatology, the only arguably reliable story I've offered in this introduction comes from my presumably nonautistic mother, her competing narratives of my autistic selfhood. Her words about autistic identity and shit smearing carry far more weight than my own. In many respects, this is how I feel about the world of rhetoric—it is a steaming pile of competing, ableist theories about distant Others that extend up to my neck. How to lob rhetoric at the wall? How to smear it on my face? Where is my intentionality? Must one have intentions in order to be rhetorical? Theory of whose mind?

I ask these questions somewhat desperately. There is an exigency here. How can we—in the classroom, in the clinic, in the pages of our scholarly annals—how can we transform social spaces in ways that enable those distant Others to speak back? How might we reinvent discourse on rhetoricity and intentionality and in/voluntarity and abjection in ways that are critically savvy and conscious of disabled embodiment?

For my part, I want a rhetoric that tics, a rhetoric that stims, a rhetoric that faux pas, a rhetoric that averts eye contact, a rhetoric that lobs theories about ToM against the wall.

Overview of Chapters

If my want of a lobbing rhetoric brings to mind the image of movement, then I have succeeded in offering a metaphorical trajectory for this book. The chapters herein are circuitous and unfolding in their design, each one serving as a queering of the chapter preceding it. Chapter 1, "Intention," calls into question the centrality of intentionality and purpose within the rhetorical tradition. Not only do I call into question theories that deny autistic people's capacity for free will and intent, but I also argue that rhetoricity itself should not remain contingent on a rhetor's intent, or, more pointedly, on the perceptions of a rhetor's intent. Clinical rhetorics, regardless of their disciplinary home, craft the actually autistic as rhetorically residual subjects, as rhetors who are not quite rhetors, as demi-rhetors. The autistic person's supposed incapacities for intentionally acting are intricately bound in scholarly approaches to autistic (non)rhetoric.

Demi-rhetoricity, I posit, is a horrifically useful strategy for denying the agency, rhetorical being, and personhood of autistic people. As a construct, demi-rhetoricity enables clinicians to claim the best of both worlds when they respond to autistic disclosures: (1) they can argue that autistic people are not autistic enough to make claims about autism; and (2) they can likewise argue that autistic people are too autistic to make claims about autism. This chapter weaves scholarship from queer theory on ephemera and residuality as well as classical rhetorical exegeses on halving and motion (Zeno's paradoxes) to suggest that demi-rhetoricity is the major topos from which clinicians draw when they wish to refute the desires or claims to identity of those whom they study. But here I also suggest that autism's queer potentials—or entelechies—lie in their defiance and reclamation of the residually rhetorical.

Chapter 2, "Intervention," rhetorically examines—and rhetorically demolishes—what it means to intervene in the residual motions and actions of autistic people. In particular, I turn my attention to ABA, a suite of behavioral methodologies that is arguably the most popular, most funded, and most recommended of clinical interventions available in autism markets.

I contend that ABA maintains its distinction as a gold standard autism therapy because it pathologizes neuroqueer commonplaces (including, but not limited to, gesture, orientation, invention, and style).[99] In service of this argument, I examine ABA's clinical history as a therapy used to dequeer young children beginning in the 1960s at UCLA, therapeutic practices that remained in effect through the 1980s under the branding of ABA and continue in the present under the banner of reparative therapy. One of the main contributions of this chapter is the comparative analysis of ABA dequeering research against ABA scholarship on autism, particularly that undertaken by ABA forebear Ole Ivar Lovaas. In engaging these comparatives, I argue that ABA's queer(less) histories coterminously emerged as a therapy for autistic children because autism, since its clinical inception, has been implicated in discourses in/around queer panic and eugenics. Practitioners of ABA, I maintain, deny the rhetoricity of neuroqueer subjects while concurrently admitting that ABA overwrites its subjects' rhetoricity with compliance. In this construction, queerness and autism are at best liminal cases, and at worst are constituted outside the bounds of rhetoric. Practice is only practice when it is able, straightened, and compliant.

The third chapter, "Invitation," dissects and interrogates the ways in which personal disclosures about autism diagnosis culturally function as invitational, residual, and demi-rhetorical. Autism disclosure is often agonistic, expectant of allistic refutation. The ability to say, "I have autism," for example, is often viewed as evidence that one does not have autism—or, at least, not real or severe autism. In this vein, I contend that spectra might be termed, in the words of Burke, a master trope for disability. Spectra enable nondisabled others to position a disabled person's claim to disability as elliptic: it is never the whole story. Examining what I term elliptic rhetoric, I argue that nonautistic interlocutors interpret autistic utterances as inherently partial. Following this logic, a claim to autism is read as incomplete and in need of nonautistic correction, clarification, or rehabilitation. In this chapter, then, I examine autistethnographic texts, including blogs and memoirs, and the ways in which autistic rhetors incite and invite refutation in their personal disclosures. Autistic people have long theorized invitational rhetoric in autistic cultural spaces, often surfacing what Judy Endow and Brenda Smith Myles have termed the "hidden curriculum" to unearth ableist practices that frame autistic ethos as partial or nonexistent.[100]

Earlier, in chapters 1 and 2, I focus on the ways in which clinicians incrementally halve autistic rhetoricity. Chapter 4, "Invention," builds upon this line of inquiry by suggesting that halving is but one employ of demi-rhetoricity. Drawing upon queer theory's figures of demisexuality and demigenderness, I suggest that demi-rhetoricity holds potential as a reclamatory strategy for those who publicly disclose an autistic identity. Rather than conceptualize identity or rhetoricity as points along a linear spectrum, deminess might instead be queerly viewed and queerly practiced as a kind of neuroqueer orientation. It might be regarded as a way of thinking not about "how much rhetoric or how much autism can my brain hold," but rather about rhetorical attraction or rhetorical desire, and what it means to roll, crip-queerly, outside the bounds of rhetoric.

As well, chapter 4 argues that autistic rhetorics are not sites for intervention but rather sites of invention. Partiality, residuality, and deminess are inventional resources from which autistic people may draw—sometimes rhetorically, sometimes involuntarily, sometimes queerly. In support of these claims, I analyze blogs and vlogs created by activists who identify as autistic and/or queer (including blogs such as Julia Bascom's *Just Stimming*, Amy Sequenzia's *Non-Speaking Autistic Speaking*, Ido Kedar's *Ido in Autismland*, and Cynthia Kim's *Musings of an Aspie*).

If autism is a rhetoric unto itself, I argue, then researchers must confront the idea that being autistic confers ways of being, thinking, and making meaning that are not in and of themselves lesser—and may at times be advantageous. Not only is autism a world (a la Sue Rubin), but autism is a nondiscursive world. And, while at times these nondiscursive worlds may be idiosyncratic or mutually unintelligible, these worlds hold value and meaning, as much as they might bristle at value and meaning. They are inventional sites, which, much like sign languages have already done in the fields of linguistics and rhetoric, promise to (make us) question long-held notions about language itself. This chapter identifies numerous such inventional sites, including perseveration (rigidity, obsession, and routinization), echolalia (repetition of words and phrases), and self-stimulation.

Finally, in the epilogue of this book, I revisit questions of what it means to interrelate when one's bodymind has been deemed pathologically asocial, or residually rhetorical. Among an encyclopedic list of impairments, autistics are said to lack metarepresentational and empathic abilities, a lack that is supposedly evidenced by our misuse of pronouns—swapping first and third person, privileging proper nouns over pronouns, and engaging other such usage errors. What is sociality without a *you* or a *me*? As a means of closing, I posit a queering of autistic pronouns, a queering of relational indexes. An asocial present is often rendered by clinicians as a nonexistent future, an autpocalypse: More people are becoming autistic; therefore, more people are becoming nonpeople.

# ONE. intention

[Autistic children] are in continuous motion, never still.
—O. Ivar Lovaas, *The Autistic Child*

Where does rhetoric lie?

This question has many meanings, many potential interpretations. When I ask where rhetoric lies, I want to know both where it resides and where it deceives. Where does rhetoric live? What does rhetoric obscure? Whom does rhetoric fool? Where, what, and whom does rhetoric betray?

I am interested in looking at where rhetoric lies because such questions inform what we think of as symbolic or socially shared: In what ways is symbolism central to rhetorical action? Where does the symbolic map itself onto rhetorical terrains? Is symbolism ever true?

These are important questions for rhetoric, and they are likewise important questions for autism. Rhetoric has its own traditional quarters, but it redisposes itself when autistic bodies make themselves known. Autism's earliest meanings were psychodynamic in scope, referring to specific pathology as well as categorical self-absorption.[1] Autism, Žižek once claimed, is the "destruction of the symbolic universe."[2] (In Žižek's defense, it was the 1980s, and he modified the word autism with *radical*.) Frances Tustin, one of the predominant autism psychoanalysts of the twentieth century, figured autism as a traumatic refusal to differentiate self from other, in which the autistic child develops a "somatic allergy" for the "not-me."[3] As a means of self-soothing, autistics partialize and self-absorb the human, remaking others' organs—such as others' breasts or hands—into autistic objects.[4] Importantly, autism in these constructions is figured as a defusion of drives, as impulses that unfold rather than intend.

If autism results in the death of symbolism and the refusal to engage human others, then autism surely kills (at) parties. When I enter a social space, the electricity of the other, intervening bodies recedes in my presence. Dynamics have shifted, not to accommodate my presence, but to redirect the electricity elsewhere, toward the not-me. There is a certain awkwardness that inheres in rhetorical situations touched by the autistic. A clinical paradigm might locate that awkwardness in my autistic body, identifying the rigidity of my joints, my wayward gaze or monotonic speech, my lumbering body parts that paw their way through public spaces, as if my feet were unaware that objects existed beyond them. Under this framework, my body disrupts rhetorical situations because my body is rhetorically degraded.

Of course, I don't for a moment believe that autistic people are rhetorically degraded, nor do I believe us to be symbolically autpocalyptic. Rather, I believe that rhetoric's arrangements forcibly absent the autistic. That is, rhetoric builds spaces that occlude the autistic because the autistic supposedly represents the asocial edges of rhetoric. My modus operandi in this chapter is partial, partial in the sense that I break down rhetoric not into a definitional, or a matter of what rhetoric is, but rather what rhetoric *privileges* or *obscures* in its designs, what rhetoric refuses to traverse. Because rhetoric's topoi are many, my approach is associational at times, (de)constructing one cherished topos and bridging over to the next. Rhetoric's topographies shore up that which autistics are time and again claimed to lack: intentionality, symbolic capacity, sociality, and audience awareness, among other rhetorical means. In this way, claiming that autistics are arhetorical or pseudo-rhetorical seems a matter of principle or fact—on the level of a philosophical or natural law. If a given rhetorical tradition structures its theoretical body around intentionality, and if autistic people are said to lack intentionality, then autistic non-rhetoricity remains a logical condition of the syllogism. And, if autistic people have difficulty inferring or communicating an intention, does a nonautistic *we* really need to listen? Depending upon the rhetorical tradition from which we draw, we might replace *intentionality* with any number of darlings—pathos, reason, context, speech. For as many topoi as rhetoric proclaims to be central, there are as many deficits and symptoms that render the autistic as rhetorical antonym. In this way, the rhetorical degradation that attends autism is planar, multiple. Whatever the rhetoric of the week is, we are claimed not to have it.

Take, for instance, what we think we know about sociality. In many respects, sociality is the glue of this chapter, and, more broadly, this book. As Judy Holiday contends, rhetoric is firmly situated in the "realm of the social."[5] Rhetoric is social, and neuroqueer people are purported to be sociality's nemesis. In calling upon the social, I am invoking Holiday's claim that "rhetoric both *invents* and is *invented* by humans, individually and collectively."[6] Engagement, reciprocity, empathy—these things, and more, are configured as that which rhetoric requires in order to effect change. And, more importantly, each of these items is deeply connected to intentionality, which is itself multivariate. In linguistics, intention is typically configured around the social dimensions (or, pragmatics) of language, and is understood as invoking multiple cognitive phenomena. Intention, then, calls upon not only shared goal direction but also mobilizes complex relationships to time, place, and bodyminds (both one's own and others'). Bruno Bara and his coauthors assert that intentionality and sociality are implicated in one another.[7] In order to be considered "communicative," they claim, an intention needs to "communicate a meaning to someone else, plus the intention that the former intention should be recognized by the addressee."[8] In other words, intentionality only becomes rhetorical when it is social, when its effects are mutually recognizable. Intention requires a theory of one's own as well as other minds.

If we were to define intentionality rather simply, we might cast it as that toward which we turn as well as the action of turning-toward unto itself. Intentionality encompasses both the process of inference and the physical action of communicating or making that inference known. It is determined by both cause and effect, the latter of which is made recognizable on the body—through speech, through gesture, through gaze, through paralinguistic cues such as throat clearing, or feet shuffling, or kiss blowing. In this regard, intention can be strikingly normative. When intent is offered in conjunction with the neuroqueer, it becomes illegible: we only know what intent is when that intent is read via prosocial measures.

Autism, in its queerly contrastive ways, harbors different stories, stories of nonintention at worst and failed intention at best. Autism is less of a motive and more of a force. Mikhail Kissine notes that autistics behold their addressees less as humans and more "as a tool to attaining a certain goal."[9] Kissine's approach, while reminiscent of psychodynamic fixations on autistic objects, is distinctly concerned with theory of mind (ToM) and the pragmatics or social functions of language. Ours is a sociality of things; ours is an intentionality of motricity and instrumentality. A pointed finger isn't necessarily about goal direction or sharing attention with others; instead, a pointed finger might hold infinite autistic meanings or potential meanings or even nonmeanings. What of an autistic instrumentality of the arm, of the raised finger? What of the stim, the tic, the involuntary or even the misunderstood gesture? Following Kissine, autistic movements are not intentions or intentioned but are rather their own drives. Or, as I suggest momentarily, these autistic propensities might be better recognized as entelechies, as queerly asocial potentials that are realized through the beingness of being autistic.

Sociality, then, is but one means among many of rhetorically degrading the autistic. But this degradation is not always negativistic or self-defeating. While up until this point I have foregrounded the violence that attends rhetorical denials, it is worthwhile asking whether or not autistics should even desire rhetorical recognition. In positing that rhetoric degrades the autistic into non-rhetoricity, I draw upon José Estaban Muñoz's ephemeral hermeneutics. Muñoz figures ephemera as a queer kind of evidence, as that which is left behind by, or in the wake of, fact. In this telling, fact doesn't represent that which is Absolutely True so much as that which is visible, normative, and hegemonic. Writes Muñoz, "Ephemera are the remains that are often embedded in queer acts, in both stories we tell one another and communicative physical gestures such as the cool look of a street cruise, a lingering handshake between recent acquaintances, or the mannish strut of a particularly confident woman."[10] Importantly, ephemera comprise the temporary, the discardable, the gestural, the residual, and at times the imperceptible. There is a certain collecting impulse that attends the ephemeral, and it is from this impulse that I trace autism's residuality, autism's entelechies. Autism's ephemera might be called perseverative, or that which builds toward climax by means of repetition, obsession, stiltedness, and echo. For in determining the ways in which rhetoric denies the autistic, I am likewise motioning toward the whatness of an autistic rhetoricity. What is an autistic rhetoric? What is an autistic non-rhetoric? How to capture the many (non)rhetorical forces that might culminate to shape and be shaped by autistic lives, in all of their diversity?

In piecing together rhetoric's project, and its rampant exclusions of autistic people from that very project, I am likewise tracing what might be termed autistic cultural practices. These practices are at times codified and rhetorically positioned in the life writing of autistic people, and at times these practices are unnarratable, are so embodied and temporal and uncontainable that they remain extant from rhetoric's symbolic bounds. Autistic activist Lydia Brown impassionedly maintains that autistic people "are more than the discursive and rhetorical constructs of autism and ability and disability. . . . Our history is not taught or acknowledged. Our leaders, pioneers, and innovators exist on the margins of mainstream society, politics, and history. We are so commonly erased that many disabled people only learn that our communities are vibrant and widespread after they've already become adults."[11] As Brown observes, rhetoric has so dehumanized the autistic that even autistic people have difficulty in thinking of themselves as part of community, culture, or rhetorical practice—often not being exposed to such notions until adulthood. What's more, autistic people's most visible accounts of autistic being have typically taken shape as best-selling memoirs, notably by individuals who have been lauded for achieving financial or personal success, "despite" their disabilities.[12] Yet even in these widely circulated texts, autism resides—autistic life writers are still thought to be autistic, and thereby not wholly rhetorical or trustworthy.[13] While a number of autistic people have published memoiristic accounts with autism trade presses, autistic writing is often self-published, disseminated online or by means of vanity presses or zines.[14] There is, then, a certain ephemerality to many of these artifacts, an ineffability greater than that which discourse can contain. There have been some notable attempts to archive such texts, many of which, due to small distribution or lapses in online hosting, encounter difficulty in surviving. However, there are just as many contemporary archives that have proved longevity and sustainability. *All the Weight of Our Dreams: On Living Racialized Autism*, Autistics.org, the Ed Wiley Lending Library, and the Loud Hands Project are among such autistic-led archival efforts.

But, more importantly, many autistic activists do not write and/or speak, and it is here that their rhetoricity is further halved, further degraded, further absented from archives. Tics, screeching, body twirling, shit smearing, repeating the words and motions of nonautistic others, or repeating the words and motions of the gecko on a Geico commercial from 2005—these of-the-moment movements, in which persuadability inheres, in which motions and commotions send awkward electricity via spinal waves, felt across every interlocutor in a given room—often, these are unrecorded moments, rhetorical situations that are dismissed as arhetorical, as the involuntary blips of autistic brains sending autistic signals, all to the effect of allistic disgust, allistic pity, allistic fear. What is so remarkable about allism is its assumption that allos and autos are binaristic poles, blips on a continuum that speak toward the autistic's lack of sociality and thereby moral degradation. But what is an other-centeredness if that centeredness cannot center the autistic Other?

Autistics are multiply bound to non-rhetoricity. In many respects, the idea of an autistic culture is often rendered as the cute or pathological machinations of autistic people who lack insight into the horrors of their arhetorical circuitry. But, as Brown notes, "Autistic culture is more than a passing, perfunctory phrase wrapped in a convenient package."[15] Autistic culture—and its flirtatious bristling against rhetorical norms—is a queering of rhetoric's conditions. And, as Muñoz contends of the queer, the autistic rhetorical is in many ways a not-yet-here and a not-yet-known. Autism is, as Byron Hawk writes of entelechy, a striving unto itself that "generates multiple lines of divergence as a residual effect."[16] If autism defies ideas about symbolism, intention, and social meaning, then what are we tracing? What might be advantageous in claiming a residual rhetoricity, or tracing an asocial symbolic, for autistic people? What of my ticcing fingers, this skin and bones?

And so, I am interested in discerning how autistic rhetors are denied rhetoricity. But I am more interested in how this denial is rhetorically accomplished, as well as how autistic people expertly respond to such denials. As I argued in the introduction, I believe rhetorical denials are often effected by means of arguments regarding partiality or remnants. That is, neuroqueer subjects might have some residual capacity for rhetorical action and practice (especially when a clinician intervenes or rehabilitates what little might be there), but they are never fully there, fully whole, or fully capable. In other words, traces of rhetoric are not enough to amount to rhetoric, for even a minute presence of The Autism™ radically destroys symbolic universes, a la Žižek.

While this chapter primarily assays the ways in which autistics are degraded from rhetoricity, I likewise begin the project of building toward an autistic rhetoricity that queers what we've come to understand as rhetoric. Queer rhetorics are anti-rhetorics, are rhetorics cunning enough to claim and embody the arhetorical. Although I devote more attention to autistic queering in chapters 3 and 4, my immediate focus here is to claim the exigency and necessity of queering while concurrently examining those discourses that would render the neuroqueer residual, lesser, and inhuman. That is, I suggest we construct autistic rhetoricity by tracing autistic people's queer gesturing, toward that which both embraces and fucks with rhetoric—toward involution. Autistic people embody the both/and of symbolism and nonsymbolism.

In the pages that follow, I leverage discourse on rhetorical remnants against clinical constructions of gradation: spectra, functioning, and severity, which operate like a series of bell curves nested within bell curves, infinitely halving neuroqueer subjects' rhetorical capacities. These clinical logics work to deny neuroqueer rhetoricity, in part, by predetermining what rhetoric can mean, effect, or contain. But these rhetorical residues are also animated in how we frame the thereness of rhetoric: where and in whom it is presumed to live (brains, bodies, humans, nonhumans, objects, spaces, temporalities), whether rhetoricity is ever innate (often taking shape in debates about art versus science/skill), how and in whom the rhetorical is identified (aesthetically, pedagogically, clinically), and so on. I am repeatedly struck by Lennard Davis's description of disability culture, when he asks, "Is there a there?"[17] I am interested in asking the same of rhetoric.

The thereness of rhetoric also comes into play when we think about topoi—sets of inventional resources from which rhetors may draw. Rhetorical invention has long histories of being conceived topographically and ecologically. Location, Holiday insists, "underwrites all rhetorical situations, shaping and circumscribing knowledge, perception, and invention."[18] Heuresis is a spatiality unto itself. Rhetoricians such as Jay Dolmage or Shannon Walters, for example, have adopted the rhetorical concept of mētis as a disability rhetoric.[19] Conceived in Greek traditions as a kind of cunning, mētis is uniquely tied to the god of fire and metallurgy Hephaestus, whose feet twisted around sideways, indicating a crablike, side-to-side kind of movement. A disability rhetoric, in their estimation, involves cripping/creeping/sidling among all the available means—even if those means exist outside the bounds of persuasion.

More importantly, however, mētis is not (and should not be represented as) simply the rhetorical renderings of a Greco-Roman (and thereby colonial and Eurocentrist) rhetorical tradition. As Dolmage points out, metis, mestiza, and mestijaze instigate "'doubleness and divergence' from across quite different rhetorical traditions," unfolding constellated embodiments that traverse race, ethnicity, trauma, survivance, disability, and sexuality.[20] But so too do these terms invoke metaphors of mixing, not to mention colonial violences, that Gloria Anzaldúa describes throughout her oeuvre.[21] Anzaldúa's is a reclamatory project, one in which the mestiza is both clever and slippery in her rhetorical prowess: "Deconstruct, construct. She becomes a nahual, able to transform herself into a tree, a coyote, into another person. She learns to transform the small 'I' into the total self."[22] Here, and throughout Borderlands / La Frontera, Anzaldúa relates the cunning, askance motions of a rhetor who seeks to make a "conscious rupture with all oppressive traditions of all cultures and religions."[23]

Mētis, then, holds multiple locational resonances, signifying the unruly unfixity of those who are racialized, disabled, and queered. Whereas allistics (or, nonautistics) conceive autism as residential, as that which lies on top (of a brain, of a neuron, of a synapse), neuroqueer activists portray crip rhetorics that are crabbily and transformatively beside, or co-occurring, or pervading, or creeping.

This chapter, then, involves rooting out the many valences of thereness and lying as they pertain to autism—and how autistic people themselves figure and literalize their thereness, even in the midst of being clinically and rhetorically figured as absent. To do this, I consider autism's rhetorical potentials and the ways in which autism's slippery locatedness defies arrival. Autism's movements are sly and indirect, gestures that accrue their power through their not-always-intendedness. Intention, in many respects, serves as the connective tissue for all of the (non)potentials and imperfections that supposedly and rhetorically plague autistic people. I examine several sites in which these rhetorical remnants make their presence effable and known: rhetoric's privileging of linear or developmental trajectories, of a social symbolic, and of normatively brained means and motives. Each of these topoi circles back to intention, to complex ideas around the ways in which autistic movement lacks the requisite goal direction and voluntariness to effect social or symbolic action. In this regard, I contend that autistic locatedness is often distributed across rhetorical continua while paradoxically being framed entelechially as a failure to arrive. Here we might think of these distributions and fixities as their own kinds of lying about rhetoric and motion, simultaneously a residential lying as well as a symbolic or pretensive lying.

Consider, for instance, autism's very categorization as a developmental disability. What we know from clinical research is that autism's developmental impairments are tripartite and impermeable, affecting social, communicative, and motoric domains—indeed, all domains in which rhetoric is claimed to dwell.[24] The god terms that unite this triad of impairments overwhelmingly concern themselves with sociality and ToM. Lorna Wing, Judith Gould, and Christopher Gillberg echo this line of thought, insisting that "the fundamental problems underlying all autistic conditions and the Triad of Impairments, is absence or impairment of the social instinct present from birth in the great majority of cases."[25] Importantly, Wing, Gould, and Gillberg carry profound ethos in offering this sentiment, as each has been instrumental in the formation of autism as a modern diagnosis. Wing, for instance, is notable for having popularized Hans Asperger's work—indeed, the very idea of an Asperger's syndrome or so-called high-functioning autism—to English-speaking audiences. Gould's work, often in collaboration with Wing, cultivated the concept of autism as a spectrum, and Gillberg's diagnostic criteria for Asperger's syndrome influenced the ICD classifications of autism spectrum disorders.[26]

This claim, then—that autism is, at root, known for its asociality—is not one without power. But where, we might ask, do such claims lie? How do they locate autism, and in what ways do they suspend the rhetorical capacities of autistic people?

It is from these questions that this chapter draws its exigency. In the pages that follow, I traverse rhetoric's many fixities, including and especially those theories and figures central to what might be termed a Western and neurorhetorical canon: Aristotle and Kenneth Burke, as well as Francesca Happé, Simon Baron-Cohen, and other cognitive theorists. These canonical figures are thrown into relief when juxtaposed against the motions and narrations of neuroqueer subjects, or those whose very being is so typically construed as rhetorically twitchy. In consideration of where rhetoric resides and recedes, I begin by examining autism's paradoxical placements along a variety of clinical continua. From there, I move to trickier, more pejorative matters. How has sociality been storied? If I lie right now, am I intending to lie, or is autism intending for me? Or, still more: Am I conditioned to lie because of social skills curricula? And in what ways might this conditioning degrade my voluntary capacity for rhetorical action? With criss-crossed neurons and wonky hemispheres like these, what rhetorical potentials do I hold? Autism, I am suggesting, is a mode of becoming, is continuous motion that defies the clinical.

## Demi-rhetoricity and Paradoxes of Motion

When it comes to autism's stories, paradoxes abound. Autism is always residual because autism resides. It is clinically represented as an entity, as parasitic. Though potentially improvable, autism is unremovable. Once an autistic, always an autistic. Studies of optimal-outcome autistics (variously referred to in clinical literature as recovered or asymptomatic autistics) have long documented autism's residual effects. That is, even when the autistic child performs so allistically as to warrant the removal of her diagnosis, autism somehow still remains.[27] Its remnants linger. Its residuals lie (*lay* and *lie*) in pragmatics, semantics, symbolic in/capacities, gesture, bodily comportment. Much like the Dude, autism abides.[28]

Those familiar with Aristotle's *Physics* or Plato's *Parmenides* might recall Zeno of Elea, known for his paradoxes of meaning and motion. Zeno, a student of Parmenides, practiced argumentation to the point of absurdity, reducing complex phenomena to simplistic conclusions, conclusions that often worked to deny seeming realities—for example, there is no such thing as motion. Such reductio ad absurdum, I am suggesting, is what guides popular notions of autism. In *Parmenides*, for example, one such paradox concerned whether or not entities could have plural meanings. In particular, Zeno, using the foil of *like* and *unlike*, suggests that the idea of the many cannot exist. He reasons that if two unlike items share certain likenesses, then they would be one and not many; and if two like items or phenomena were in any way unlike one another, then they are not of the same phenomenon and thus cannot be claimed to be many, because they are separate, singular, unlike things. In defense of Zeno's denial of plurality, Parmenides at one point notes that "every part is part of a whole," suggesting that partiality isn't salient for its multiple parts but is rather defined in totality, by the cumulation of all parts.[29]

In another paradox, alluded to in *Parmenides* as well as *Physics*, Zeno contends that the concept of place is an infinite regress, akin to nesting dolls.[30] If

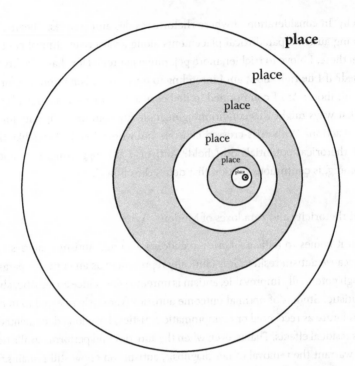

**FIGURE 1.1.** Zeno's paradox of place. In this image, a series of concentric circles, each labeled with the word *place*, are nested one within the other, ad infinitum. Place keeps multiplying and expanding to contain all other places.

place exists, he argues, then there must be other places within place, and more places still within those places, ad infinitum. In this way, place is always a singular, drawing back to Zeno's paradox of plurality: one place absorbs another, parasitically, such that place is never more than one and is always expanding to swallow yet more places into place. Place is so limitless that it remains solitary.

Yet still, it is in *Physics* that Aristotle discusses Zeno's paradoxes of motion, which are among his more well-known paradoxes. In the Achilles paradox, for example, Zeno suggests that a runner who halves his distance as he runs will never reach the finish line, for distance can be infinitely halved, forever. In another paradox, that of Achilles and the tortoise, Zeno presents a scenario in which the tortoise is given a head start in a race, and Achilles fails to catch up, because by the time he reaches the tortoise's starting point, the tortoise will already be ahead by some increment.[31] This incremental leading repeats ad infinitum: Achilles reaches the tortoise's last resting point, only for the tortoise to remain incrementally ahead. Finally, there is also Zeno's paradox of the arrow

FIGURE 1.2. Arrows at rest, one of Zeno's motion paradoxes. In this freeze-frame image, a sprung arrow remains at rest at many points, midair.

in flight, wherein Zeno claims that motion does not exist. Zeno presents the example of an arrow being sprung into the sky, suggesting that, were the trajectory of the arrow to be freeze-framed at any point in time, the arrow would appear to be at rest. Zeno thus maintains that upon being fired, the arrow occupies a state of rest, and is thereby motionless.[32]

The above paradoxes have, of course, been widely debated and debunked since their very inception. I relate all of these paradoxes here, however, because I believe the same paradoxes are at work in (non)rhetorical renderings of autism. As the Cultural Rhetorics Theory Lab suggests, "Linearity imposes ideas about causality or origins, both of which are generally also obscuring many of the other meaningful relationships between places, spaces, events, people, and communities. And it traps subjects who are literally held in place, skewered by multiple discourses."[33] In this vein, consider, for instance, the figure of the incrementum and its relation to Achilles and the tortoise. Jordynn Jack and Jeanne Fahnestock have argued that the incrementum functions as a master trope in the rhetoric of science. Fahnestock defines the incrementum as a gradation between two antithetical poles, and Jack clarifies that "an incrementum is simply a scale, but one that can be used for rhetorical purposes."[34] In the case of autism, we might consider allism to occupy one pole and autism to occupy the other, with the remainder of human neurology situated in the vast expanse in between. In such an expanse, were we to follow Zeno, sit infinite points among the autism–allism (or self–other) continuum.

Of course, in clinical discourse, because autism is typically storied as residual—never abating, no matter how far one progresses toward allism—allism (or normalcy) generally is not represented as the end pole. Rather, much like disability writ large, allism is a middle or average pole, with yet more disability occurring on the other edges of the expanse. Another word for this particular incrementum, though it is often visually represented as bulbous rather than straight-lined, is the bell curve. As Fahnestock notes, whereas some series are created for their ends, "other series are constructed for the sake of their middles."[35]

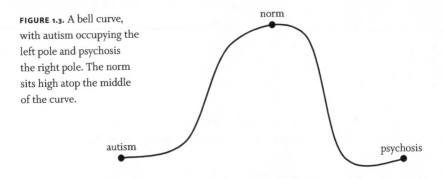

**FIGURE 1.3.** A bell curve, with autism occupying the left pole and psychosis the right pole. The norm sits high atop the middle of the curve.

norm

autism                                                                    psychosis

If we look to recent scholarship on autism and intention, we can see one such bifurcation occurring with schizophrenia or psychosis more generally. Ciaramidaro and her coauthors, for example, contend that autism is a condition typified by hypointentionality, whereas schizophrenia is typified by hyperintentionality: both modes of being are storied and, indeed, essentialized according to their respective positions in the domains of social cognition and communication.[36] Autistic people fail to attribute intentions to other minds, whereas people with schizophrenia overattribute intentions to other minds. Thus, in the case of bell curves, autism might represent the beginning pole; normalcy might represent the middle or norm; and psychosis might represent the ending pole.[37]

Residual models of bell curves frequently apply a Zeno-esque logic: if autism resides, then one's movement from the autism pole to the normal middle requires infinite traversals. In these constructions, motion is illusory. Paradoxically, autistics, who are so often claimed to be in continuous embodied motion, cannot escape their places on the bell curve. Again deferring to Zeno, autism's residences swallow other residences: autism's placeness overtakes the brain's placeness, which overtakes neurons' placeness, and on down the line of neurological locales, ad infinitum. There is only one place for autistics, and that place is autism.

Because autism is frequently conceived as rhetoric's antithesis, autistic people can never reach rhetoricity. They are forever suspended, occupying only spaces of rest, imprisoned in never-ending points of locomotion, always halved. Were we to mesh the Achilles paradox with the paradox of plurality, we could begin to see the ways in which half-rhetoricity, or what I call demi-rhetoricity, functions effectually as non-rhetoricity. That is, even when autistics' symbolic and intentional capacities are represented as matters of degree, their unlikeness in relation to the nondisabled supersedes any likeness. Karen Zelan, a psychotherapist who chronicled her work with forty-five autistic children in *Between Their World and Ours*, maintains that notions of unlikeness inhere in autism diagnoses, reinforcing Zeno's paradox of plurality: "If we force upon the diagnosis of autism the implicit or explicit notion that because autists are in important ways unlike us, they are in *all* ways unlike us."[38]

As a result, autistics are considered singularly as opposed to dwelling among a many—for there can be no autistic plurality or community, and certainly not in combination with those who are nonautistic.[39] These rhetorical constructions of rhetorical halving and effectual singularity frequently attend discourse on ToM. Theory of mind scholars ranging from Baron-Cohen to Frith and Happé to Williams dabble in matters of degree.[40] Frith and Happé, for instance, discuss autistic ranges between "impaired" and "intact abilities," and they likewise pair "handicapped" and "talented" autistics as another such opposing range.[41] In like manner, Williams tackles the genre of autie-biography to suggest that ToM represents a continuum of impairment among autistics, with some high-functioning people possessing a bit more ToM, though still never quite enough, than other autistics: "Firstly, the impairment in reading others' minds amongst individuals with autism is not taken by any researcher in the field as being an all-or-nothing deficit. Certainly, these autobiographers have some understanding of the minds of other people, even if this understanding is diminished relative to their typical peers, and/or if this understanding has been acquired through an atypical developmental process and is based on compensatory mechanisms."[42] Theory of mind, of course, is but one such cognitive module or capacity along which autistic people are charted, normed, and infinitely halved. And while ToM is a god theory with particular staying power in autism discourse, it is not the only body of work that seeks to explain and contain the autistic. Given autism's sheer bodily force—it is, after all, designated as a pervasive developmental disorder, conceivably impacting all things bodymind—a host of etiological theories structures clinical research. Autism's stories are radically transdisciplinary, and its causation theories ford genetics, neurology, cognition, psychology, and linguistics. It is autism's supposed pervasiveness that leads Victoria Brunsdon and Francesca Happé to posit autism as a fractioned and fractionable disorder, as a disorder whose symptomatological features arise from myriad causes.[43] Under these logics, so-called fractionable autism represents "a theory in which the social and nonsocial symptoms of ASD are suggested to have distinct causes at the genetic, neural, cognitive and behavioural levels."[44] In this regard, autism's coherence as a condition isn't putatively explainable under one genetic or neurological rubric, but rather comes into being through the confluence of multiple behavioral markers, each of which might surface with fluctuating degrees of severity and each of which possesses diverging causes (e.g., ToM dysfunction representing a cause for social impairment and weak central coherence representing a cause for embodied and locomotive divergence). In other words, fractionable autism becomes autism when multiple enminded phenomena collide.[45]

Fractionable autism theories, however, become god theories through their very resistance to god theories. In these stories of fractionation, autism's demi-rhetoricity intensifies, straddling multiple neuro-continua. Not only are autistic capacities charted under the cohesive banner of disorder, but they are charted under the diffusive banner of the syndromic: our rhetorical capacities, one by one, are meted out according to our cognitive impairments, our genetic deletions or duplications, our hormonal levels both pre- and postnatally, our color gradients on PET scans and fMRI readings, or our linguistic performances during narrative intakes. Rather than one of these measures symbolizing the demi-rhetoricity that is autism, each of these fractional gauges works in tandem to present the autist as rhetorically involuntary, subject to the juices or electric blips of our malfunctioning bodies. In this way, the stories that attend fractionation become all consuming, despite any emphasis on the partial or dispersed. A god term, Richard Weaver warns us, creates rhetorical exigencies in "which all other expressions are ranked as subordinate and serving dominations and powers. Its force imparts to the others their lesser degree of force, and fixes the scale by which degrees of comparison are understood."[46] Put alternatively, fractionated autism draws its rhetorical power through the partialization of other god theories. No longer is ToM the master of autistic dysfunction, but rather one of several potential causal factors of not only autism unto itself, but even autistic traits such as impaired social goal direction or failure to seek enjoyment. These, then, are the myriad ways in which autistics are authored into demi-rhetoricity. Ours is a continuous motion across not one but infinite diagnostic and symptomatological scales.

Indeed, the notion of an autism spectrum unto itself is a demi-rhetorical construct: individuals deemed low functioning are disqualified from rhetorical subjectivity because of their disabilities. But individuals deemed high-functioning are likewise disqualified from rhetorical subjectivity—because their autism resides, because they are too far from the autism pole but not close enough to the normalcy pole, because they never really progress to full-fledged allism, which requires an infinite number of steps. Whatever autistics intend—and how can we intend when our intentions are merely demi-intentions?—our arrival at rhetoricity can never be fully realized.

Numerous scholars in disability studies have engaged these paradoxes of meaning and motion, albeit often with different terminology. Jasbir Puar's move from discourses of disability to discourses of debility and capacity is one such example.[47] Puar examines the ways in which "neoliberal regimes

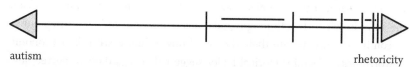

distance = *infinitely halved*

autism                                                                rhetoricity

**FIGURE 1.4.** A continuum that runs from autism to rhetoricity. The continuum is segmented, from the midpoint onward, into halved units, never quite reaching rhetoricity's resting place.

of biocapital produce the body as never healthy enough, and thus always in a debilitated state in relation to what one's bodily capacity is imagined to be."[48] In this construction, bodies are judged based along an incrementum of capacity and debility. Importantly for Puar, neoliberal discourses will always deem bodies in some way debilitated: for the traversal toward capacity is always halved, and one's body—due to aging, racialization, trauma, illness, or disability—will never be good enough, will never have momentum enough to arrive. Puar's broader point, both here and in *Terrorist Assemblages*, is that identitarian frameworks (whether queer or crip) are inextricably ensnared in the violences of empire, which work to demarcate queer-cripness as the respectable, homonormative politics of white queers.[49] And while queerness is frequently figured as a way of moving, neoliberal imperatives toward productive, high-functioning citizenry impose violent logics in which "bodies actually lose their capacity for movement, for flow, for (social) change."[50] Citing Puar, Kelly Fritsch likewise underscores how rhetorics of gradation police and commodify marginal subjects, especially those who are brown, black, queer, indigenous, and/or disabled. "Rather than clear distinctions being made between who is normal and who is abnormal," notes Fritsch, "emphasis instead is placed on 'variegation, modulation and tweaking.' "[51] In other words, these demi-rhetorical paradoxes are not new paradoxes, nor can they be read outside constellations of race, sexuality, nation, gender, trauma (historical and present), disability, or class. White supremacy compels stasis, as does ableism and transantagonism, among other rhetorical means: we can always make ourselves better, if by "made better" we mean "do violence to our selves and our cultures."

In this regard, then, we might think about the ways in which demi-rhetorical logics are not only resonant of, but constitutive of, neoliberal ideologies. When autism resides—always lingering, always attached—autistic bodyminds become forever-works-in-progress, sites in need of perpetual intervention.[52] We might, for example, look to the many lobbies and institutional sites that have come to dictate not only the whatness of autism, but autism's supposed remedies—all of which are long-term, therapeutic modalities that ford one's life span.[53] As well, we might consider the capitalistic logics of the term *functioning* unto itself, and the ways in which functioning's gradations (from high to low) entrap autists in continua that correlate their rhetorical unworthiness with their economic unworthiness.[54] Demi-rhetorical logics suggest that regardless of degree, low-functioning and high-functioning bodies are effectually nonfunctioning bodies, are bodies inhospitable for workplaces, are bodies in need of vocational, occupational, and behavioral interventions, all means and manner of treatment that works in service of crafting independent persons capable of producing and laboring. In this vein, no autistic person is ever high-functioning enough, much like no autistic person is ever low-functioning enough. The latter argument works to reject social assistance and support services for autistic people—because there will always be more steps in the way of being wholly, truly low functioning. The poles, being unreachable, forever suspend autistic people in places from which they cannot argue, cannot assert, cannot intend. Autism's residences are permanent, whereas rhetoric's residences are migratory.

As I hope I have made clear, clinical stories, regardless of their disciplinary home, craft neuroqueer subjects as rhetorically residual subjects, as rhetors who are not quite rhetors, as demi-rhetors. Our every action, emanating as it does from our impaired brains, is locatable on a clinically indebted rhetorical continuum. That is to say: neuroqueer people are thought to be arhetorical at worst, and partially rhetorical at best. That is to say: spectra are master tropes for neurodivergence. That is to say: not only are mental disabilities rhetorical disabilities—they are agonistic disabilities, disabilities whose very existence is unhinged, ever-shifting yet paradoxically stationary along a variety of clinical continua, subject to refutation and sensationalization.[55] Our rhetorical prowess is storied as relative rather than realized.[56]

If it weren't already clear, I believe that demi-rhetorical logics are horrifically useful strategies for subjugating the motions, rhetorical being, and personhood of autistic people. Demi-rhetoricity is, I believe, the major topos from which clinicians draw when they wish to refute the desires or claims to identity of those whom they study. As a construct, demi-rhetoricity enables clinicians to claim the best of both worlds when they respond to autistic rhetors:

1  They can argue that autistic people are not autistic enough to make claims about autism.
2  They can likewise argue that autistic people are too autistic to make claims about autism.

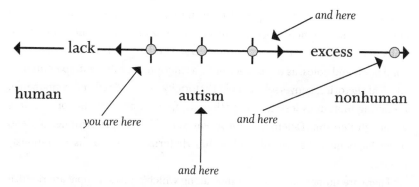

**FIGURE 1.5.** Crip teleportation? A continuum runs from human at one pole to nonhuman at the other. Autism sits in the middle. Along the continuum are various points of occupation, demarcated by arrows and the phrase "you are here" (and here, and here, and here).

Often, clinicians will make these arguments simultaneously and of the same autistic person. As noted earlier, we might, for instance, readily identify this logic within the context of functioning or severity labels. Ironically, champions of functioning labels often purport that eradicating such labels would collapse or singularize autistic difference; and yet, all the while, such continua are themselves a profound flattening of the diversity of humanity one might find under the label *autism*. Under demi-rhetorical constructions, all autistics are both too high-functioning and too low-functioning. Much like autistics can never reach allism's edges, autism likewise evades a real: an autistic person's fullness or realness is always subject to debate. As with all queer things, this convergence of excess and lack enables clinicians to refute autistic rhetors without having to overtly deny or dispute the autistic person's autism or rhetoricity. It's not that autistics are not autistic—it's more that autistics have too much autism and not enough autism, all at the same time, and this makes them inherently unreliable, inherently and rhetorically halved. While demi-rhetoricity often renders its subjects effectively non-rhetorical, its construction as a kind of rhetorical residue fosters the illusion that the demi-rhetorical are (or can aspire to be) participating bodies.

Spectra are reductionist and paradoxical tropes. In claiming that neurology is incremental, a host of reductionist moves transpires—not only in reducing neurology to a line with antithetical poles, but in reducing being, body, self-hood, rationality, intentionality, rhetoricity, and symbolism to the domain of spatialized brains. These residual logics are the inverse of that which Muñoz forwards in his "hermeneutics of residue."[57] Whereas Muñoz seeks to trace queerness, or that which is "rarely complemented by evidence," clinical rhetorics take evidence and fact and parcel them into discrete units, all in service of derhetoricizing the neurologically queer.[58] Muñoz describes ephemeral rhetoricity as continuous and gestural, as embodied and expired, as the expanse beyond point and poles, as the not-yet-here, as motions teeming with potentiality. Clinical rhetorics, conversely, behold rhetoricity as contained and containable, rendering motion as lesser, noncontinuous, freeze-framed points of rest. It is as though Bergson, Deleuze, Merleau-Ponty, and Massumi's critiques of Zeno never happened. We are *still* still within rhetoric. Continua discontinuously reduce.

There are numerous such continua along which autistic people are rhetorically distributed. As I will now relate, questions around the autistic's capacity for symbolic action are probably the most engrossing of these continua—for symbolicity cherishes certain ideas around intending, moving, lying, and being human.

## Tricky Rhetorics

Here I wish to return to an earlier question: Where does rhetoric lie?

This chapter began—and unfolded—in search of rhetoric's residences, or the ways in which symbolic orders work to exclude autistic people from rhetorical citizenship, from rhetorical end points. But topography is only one dimension of how rhetoric and autism have come to be residually figured. And, in many respects, this residential figuring—this lying—is its own kind of lie.

Autistic people are clinically described as many things, and one of the most potent is literality or brazen honesty. Autistic language is often conceived as presymbolic or nonsymbolic at worst, and residually symbolic at best. Ami Klin and his coauthors, for instance, hold that "[autistic] individuals often acquire a large number of symbols and symbolic computations that are devoid of shared meaning with others."[59] In like manner, Susan Dodd contends that autistic children have "an impaired ability to symbolise, both in communication and in play."[60] And, going further, Lucille Hess suggests that autistic children's lack of "pretence development" is integrally connected to autistic deficits in social reciprocity, imagination, and intentionality.[61] What such responses hold in common are their shared emphases on intentional, directed social meaning. Symbols must be shared; meanings must proliferate.

To be clear, in attending to the social-symbolic, I am here primarily focused on the ways in which intentionality, in its voluntaried valences, is storied onto or against autism. My frame of reference is limited and is particularly neuroqueer, evoking a simultaneous engagement with how clinicians pejoratively queer the autistic and how autistics cunningly queer the clinical. And while clinicians tell many stories about autism, these stories extend beyond the peer-reviewed publication. Indeed, stories of the unintentioned autist morph and evolve, newer (and often more stigmatic) permutations trickling down into educational, caregiving, and policy domains. In a given study, researchers may restrict their demi-rhetorical purview to the domain of, say, predictive intention: for example, to what extent can an autistic person exercise and communicate foreknowledge when observing or interacting with an allistic interlocutor? Meanwhile, a practicing behavioral therapist might read this as a story about the pedagogical imperative of physical force, of autistic children's inability to voluntarily do or intend anything, of the need for behaviorists to seclude autistic children from their peers and restrain them during the school day.

Clinicians wield many justifications for claiming autistics are nonsymbolic and thereby non-rhetorical. Autistic people struggle with metaphor; autistic people do not speak and/or have speech patterns that bear evidence of neurodivergence; autistic people lack empathy, an ultimate kind of social symbolism; autistic people's bodies move involuntarily, void of goal direction; autistic people fail to imitate prosocial others or make social inferences; and so on. Often, scholarly literature places the autistic nonsymbolic against theories of imagination, play, and pretense. Each of these items represents a freeze-frame position along a developmental continuum (e.g., at what age does your child pretend that objects are something other than what they are?), and thus poses opportunities for potential intervention. A number of therapies for autistic children, for instance, focus on childhood play. Some of these interventions, such as various floor time modalities, involve a nonautistic person imitating the autistic child's mannerisms, fostering interpersonal and interbodily contact by mirroring the beautiful rigidity and ritual of autistic-type play. Other approaches, however, edge more toward normalization in their focus, prompting those play behaviors that are deemed most prosocial. For instance, a therapist may discourage an autistic child from spinning the wheels of a toy car, instead redirecting the child to make his car go *vroom* (because vrooming is prosocial for cars?). Play in these contexts becomes a modality for working toward reciprocity, or imitation, or intentioned movements toward a social end. The ﹋autistic child, always in motion, must be sprung, as if ze were a tightened coil, into symbolic action. Intention, in this regard, becomes conditioned as well as predicated on effect: autistic children are presumed unable to voluntarily play because their disabilities preclude them from prosocial forms of pretense. Consequently, whatever inferences or social sharing transpire are assumed to have been achieved through clinical rote and medical compliance. What appears to be voluntary may be a mere social script. Such are the mappings and trappings of rhetoric.

Deception, pretense, and social connection—these are the domains in which the autistic is said to be impaired. But these are also the domains of rhetoric, even if not totally or exclusively so. Rhetoricians have long contested the idea that rhetoric is unconcerned with truth, or that rhetoric is solely conceived as bending wills toward a rhetor's ways. Rhetoric, Dolmage assures us, is more than pejorative sentiment.[62] The art of persuasion has deception at its disposal, but it likewise has, as Kinneavy makes clear, other, truthier means as well.[63] Rhetoric is not philosophy's polar opposite, but rather its fun uncle. As rhetoricians, we might instead attend to what Royster and Kirsch herald as rhetoric's plurality, wherein rhetoric is more accurately construed as rhetorics, as multiple means for attending to the truths (even the false truths) of a given situation.[64] Importantly, plural rhetorics, as James Berlin maintains, do not locate their differences in the "superficial emphasis of one or another feature of the rhetorical act. The difference has to do with epistemology—with assumptions about the very nature of the known, the knower, and the discourse community involved in considering the known."[65] Consider, however, autism's relationship with knowledge. Were I to consider metaphors that have come to represent autism in the broader culture (a capacity which I supposedly lack), I might summon any number of tropes that intimate autism's occlusion of epistemic belonging and capacity. For autism is often figured as absent presence, an embodied state impervious to knowing. There is Bruno Bettelheim's empty fortress.[66] There are Suzanne Wright's kidnap victims.[67] There are the mind-blind, care of Simon Baron-Cohen.[68] And Autism Speaks, in conjunction with Google, renders the autistic as the MSSNG, so epistemically absented as to be without any instance of I.[69]

And yet, the question of rhetoric and trickery, or what Wayne Booth has called rhetrickery, strikes me as profoundly generative.[70] If rhetoric is the stuff of tricks and lies, then the unimaginative autist must surely not be the stuff of rhetoric. Indeed, in Lorna Wing's original triad of impairments, impoverished imagination occupied its own specific domain, broadly encompassing pretense, play, and deception, as well as the ability to think about and predict the actions of others—all necessary preconditions for traditional conceptions of rhetorical manipulation.[71] And while describing rhetoric as trickery or mere rhetoric invokes classical rhetoric and sophistry, rhetrickery could likewise be interpreted as a statement about symbolism in general.[72] Metaphors might be true, but on another, truer level, they are never true. In this regard, Olga Bogdashina suggests that distinguishing symbolic from perceptual signification might generatively enlarge rhetorical worlds, autistic and non.[73] Perceptual signification is literal in its immediacy and sometimes harsh materiality, but signifies in that meanings come into view through repetition of the autistic experiential. A number of autistic people echo, in our grand tradition of echoing, this line of thought. Autie-biographer Donna Williams, for instance, describes perceiving as having a sensorial purpose rather than a functional or significant one.[74] Following Williams, we could say, for example, that rubber bands are sensorily stretchy and gruff. They have a texturality that welts and constricts, and they carry smells that range from plastic to dirt. Rubber bands ignite elastic pressure; they capture the attention of hands and mouths with their potential velocity. Sensorily, perceptually—rubber bands squish and spring. Functionally, they tie things together—hair, papers, bunches of carrots. Symbolically, rubber bands might signify something about physics, or meticulous office personalities, or weight loss, or childhood pranks. Symbolic or non, it is evident that rubber bands signify, sensorily reference.

Whereas rhetoric's art lies in its lying, autistic perception might be described as the not-yet-realized, as queerly beheld and queerly "becoming," as entelechies or forever-directions unto themselves.[75] Erin Manning outlines autistic perception as "the opening, in perception, to the uncategorized, to the unclassified. This opening, which is how many autistics describe their experience of the world, makes it initially difficult to parse the field of experience. Rather than seeing the parts abstracted from the whole, autistic perception is alive with tendings that create ecologies before they coalesce into form."[76] Here (and elsewhere), Manning attends to autistic people's narration of their perceptual experiences, of their being in the world. Asserting that "non-speaking voices are rarely included in what we understand as knowledge-formation," Manning draws upon the work of nonspeaking autistics such as Mel Baggs, Ido Kedar, Tito Mukhopadhyay, and D. J. Savarese.[77] Among the topoi of autistic perception is that of "nonvolition," or involuntarity.[78] Languaging becomes barrier when bodies do not purposively act in accordance with an autistic rhetor's desires. Apraxia, then, shapes rhetoricity, affects perceptual worlds: bodies in movement queer the openings from which our sensory experientials occur. Ours is not the perceptual domain of "holistic gestalt," but rather unfiltered detail.[79] When I am having a meltdown, for example, my rhetorical situation is a literal, nonsymbolic assault. In these moments, I have no thoughts—only biting, biting of sounds, of bodily thrashes, of colors, of biting biting bites. The pieces take precedence, and yet I do not in those moments know them to be pieces.

Like Manning, autistic writer Star Ford relates autistic perception as a negotiation between foreground and field, between expanse and parts, in which detail isn't experienced as detail but as direction of focus, as textural totality.[80] Ford's project—titled *A Field Guide to Earthlings*—is an ambitious, highly detailed rendering of autistic and allistic differences in sensing and meaning making. Ford devotes entire chapters to symbolic action, framing symbols as the dominant discursive form in which allistics trade. Describing symbolicity as a "deadening," she writes, "The NT [neurotypical] brain learns to categorize and direct incoming signals. NTS 'catch' what comes at them; this deadens the impact. The act of deadening or filtering stimuli is called 'symbolic filtering.' . . . Symbolic filtering converts real world stimuli into a [sic] internal symbolic representation of the real world."[81] For Ford, autistic perception is an enlivening, is a literality, is that which precedes interpretation and co-occurs with the immediacy of an event. In other words: the autistic is a sensorimotor rhetoric of the non- or demi-symbolic. Accordingly, Ford suggests that autism is a divergent way of perceiving, an interbodily, beyond-the-skin experiential of detail and overwhelm and intricacy. It is not the prosocial rhetoric of making toy cars go vroom, but is rather an engagement with the materiality of the toy car and the rubbery feeling of wheels against skin.

Whereas rhetoric battles against those who would reduce it to mereness, autistics encounter similar battles when it comes to the perception of their perception, which is so often figured as intentionally wanting. Perception's mereness, when bounded within rhetoric, conjures Burkean notions of immanent movement being the lesser, nonsymbolic units that might one day aspire to be symbolic action. In other words, autistics cannot traverse the distance between motion and action; ours is a demi-symbolicity, in part because perception is perceived (ha) as lesser than verbosity or social exchange. "Things move," wrote Burke; "persons act."[82] Recall the epigraph of this chapter, wherein the autistic is in continuous motion, never still. What to make of autistic motioning, beyond its thingness, beyond its failures to arrive?

Full-body rocking, among the cherished topoi of autistic rhetorics, is no doubt what leads Autism Speaks to chide that "mere words" are of little use to autistics.[83] (After all, words are doubly mere when one presumes one's listening audience will not understand them.) What nonautistic people symbolically surmise is that autistic people are merely imperceptible. Whereas intention might derive its meaning from the openness of experience in other, nonautistic contexts, the perceptual contours that attend neurodivergent embodiment are at best considered (by neurotypicals) as rhetorically residual, enminded, or fatally mentalistic.[84] These stories about intention and interrelation, as I relate in subsequent chapters, flow across numerous rhetorical and embodied domains. For example, following Merleau-Ponty, Gayle Salamon has claimed sexuality as that which defies bodily containment and that which is located in "one's intentionality toward the other and toward the world," a clear rejection of rhetoric's scalar models.[85] What Salamon writes bears direct import for autism and for the neuroqueer more generally, for the Other in this context is not of necessity a human or allistic Other, and neither is the intentionality she describes based on reciprocity or personal choice.[86] This storying of intentionality, of desire and being-becoming, bristles against what clinical pronouncements would have us believe about autism as well as allism. While cognitive theorists routinely point out that intentionality can be nonsocial (e.g., the bodily motions of intending to drink a cup of coffee), these are not the intentionalities that preclude the neuroqueer from rhetorical citizenship or symbolicity.[87] These, rather, are intentionalities that might be better termed bodily drives or automatonic responses, neuro-worlds and neuro-motions that clinicians behold as tragically simplistic rather than desirously queer.

And so, for all of my reading, for all of my interpersonal engagement with autism specialists and rhetoricians, I am left wanting an understanding of symbolism's significance, and why its absence or mere residual presence supposedly impoverishes my autistic life. I could invoke Peirce, or Burke, or Saussure, or Freud, or Baron-Cohen—but what I am left with is this:

1  Symbols hold arbitrary or somewhat removed relationships with referents.
2  Symbols hold shared social meaning.
3  Social meanings hold meaning because they are intended and inferred, predicted and fulfilled, and allistically determined and determinable.
4  I have diagnostic papers that discount my ability to participate fully in numbers 1–3.
5  I keep these papers in a filing cabinet, and I sometimes think about lighting them on fire in my backyard.

Whereas philosophers and linguists contemporarily position symbolization as a force that affectively binds and transcends participating bodies, that (poststructurally) demands disruption and fragmentation, discourse on autism tends to presuppose symbolism as a mere brain module, as a place within a place within a place (e.g., module within brain within autism). Autistic children's varying capacities for autobiographical narrative, for example, have been linked to white matter compromise and a reliance "less on typical pathways and more on alternative ventral pathways" in the brain.[88] Spoken language has been similarly mapped and developmentally plotted in autistic people, with observed correlations between cortical volume and verbal IQ.[89] In the case of so-called ToM modules, atypical neural activation has been implicated in brain regions that are associated with social cognition and language processing.[90] Similarly, Goch et al. report that their MRI study of autistic children revealed reduced network centrality of Wernicke's area, which has been linked to language comprehension more broadly.[91] I could keep going—for there are innumerable studies that map language and sociality onto the autistic brain, each in search of those spaces in which autism makes its presence nonsymbolically known. Certainly, there have been neuroscientific studies of all kinds of brains, with all kinds of conclusions about where, exactly, we might chart symbolic capacities. But my larger point here, and elsewhere, is that autism's asocial meanings and neural locations have been authored, consumed, and constrained in ways that allism has not.

Put alternatively, if symbolism concerns allistic people, it's complicated; if symbolism concerns autistics, it's brain damage. Such discursive reasoning, per Burke, might be deemed reductively scientistic, in that its reductions slash bodies into empirically determined and manipulated mechanisms. Scientism, unlike dramatism, breaks down human action into mechanical motion. In its more cognitivist strands, rhetoric likewise locates symbolicity within one's mere headspace—at least when considering cognitively disabled people, that is. Whereas cognitive modules were all the rage for rhetors in the 1980s, the braining of rhetoricity has resurfaced in the 2000s primarily in relation to pathology. Todd Oakley, Andrea Greenbaum, and Ann Jurecic, to name but a few exemplars, exercise this particular approach with regard to autism: autistic people's ToM modules are missing or defective, resulting in demi-rhetors who cannot "inhabit a world of intentional stances."[92] Surely if there are arhetorical brains, then there are rhetorical brains—but the topography of those able to call themselves rhetorical is a landscape in which autistic people are prevented from living or lying.

Involuntarity—the motion of limiting autistic intent to a rigid, cognitively purposive standard that even neurotypicals don't need to live up to—has come to rhetorically typify the life of the neuroqueer. If our neuroqueer brains don't sap our volition, then surely clinical care, with all of its demands, does. The neuroscientific impulse to queer the brain, as Dussauge and Kaiser warn, works in practice as attempts to localize queer and genderqueer practices in gray matter, as if brain imaging were a rendition of *Where's Waldo*.[93] In this way, fMRI studies and genetic sequencing are not all that dissimilar from the localizing compulsions that attend autism research. (And, as I'll suggest momentarily, the autistic and the queer are often impermeable.) Dussauge and Kaiser classify these neuroscientific impulses as reemergences of innatist, determinist, reductionist, and essentialist discourses, where "brain constitution serves to predict behavior."[94] This "braining of the human" is not only enabled by the heterosexual gaze, but by an able-bodied fascination with identifying and containing that which is neurologically queer, à la Zeno's paradoxes.[95]

Such brain-localized fascination attends autism because autism purportedly represents the edges of sociality. It is not uncommon, for instance, for clinicians to sensationalize their autistic clients' literalisms. They might offer the example of the autistic child who screams in terror upon hearing the phrase "heads will roll," or the autistic adult who stares quizzically into the rainy sky in search of cats and dogs. The expectation, of course, is that nonautistic people will be the readers or listening parties encountering these autism anecdotes, and will thus find the stories exotic or intriguing or just plain weird. Whereas rhetoric's domain is interstitial and social for normates, rhetoric for autistics is conceived as a cranial absence, or cranial remnants of an undevelopable capacity, with symbolic impairment often evidencing these figures of lack. Even when autistics lie or wield tropes, the action of lying or troping is attributed more to neuronal motion than it is intrinsically motivated will. Iconic in this regard is ToM discourse on hacking, or the idea that autistic people who display metaphoric capacities only do so through rote or compensatory strategies. Hacking is, in a word, passing or scripting. "The question of parroting," Francesca Happé once wrote, "cannot, of course, be ruled out."[96] Involuntarity is the reductionist state of our being. Autistics fake rather than make rhetoric.

Following the above, I mean to articulate a dual, at times meandering, strand in this book: my first impulse is to argue that of course autistic people are rhetorical and capable of symbolic action. I feel a certain urgency in making this claim, in defending our asocial and antisocial rhetorical leanings, of rejecting the idea that autistic motions are little more than parroting or cognitive impulses. But, more importantly, I contend that, even if the reverse were true (e.g., autistic people lack or have impaired capacity for symbolic exchange), autistic people are still, nonetheless, rhetorical. Other than occupying the oxymoronic, what would it mean if literality were considered an autistic trope? Similarly, a nonsymbolic rhetoric forces us to confront ideas about audience and sociality: what is rhetoric without audience, without humanity? What is rhetoric, or language, without some kind of remove, some kind of covering or obscuring, some kind of lying? And, finally, how might an autistic rhetoric move beyond neurotypical obsession with the brain? I believe there are many such rhetorical models that preserve that which makes neuroqueer subjects neurodivergent, while also configuring perceptual worlds and embodied modalities that extend beyond the mere bounds of rhetoricity.[97] In being queerly rhetorical, neuroqueer subjects fuck with rhetoric.

## Intention Is for Neurotypicals

Rhetoric promotes a compulsory sociality. This compulsory sociality appeals to a given character's ethos and authority, but it also privileges "stock roles and personae."[98] That is, rhetoric's sociality is one of characters and characteristics, a line with definitive edges. Moreover, rhetoric is practiced, constrained, and reified by social bodies as a means of containing and delineating who and what constitutes a social body to begin with. Think, for example, of the Athenian chorus, or Perelman and Olbrechts-Tyteca's theorizing of cognitive presence and universal audiences, or Ede and Lunsford's engagement with audience addressed and invoked.[99] Clearly, rhetoric cherishes its audiences. These audiences, typically, contrast the characteristics we associate with the neurologically queer. Autistic people are known for "disturbances in the ability to relate to others and understand their thoughts and intentions, with consequent problems with friendships, play, and initiating and responding to social overtures."[100] Autistic traits, taken together, represent everything that allistics devalue in an audience or social exchange.

Whatever context I might bring to bear on my asocial status, autism is typically storied as the domain of the un- and in-credible, or what Jenell Johnson calls *kakoethos*.[101] Literally meaning "bad character," *kakoethos* rhetorically functions as antiethos. According to Johnson, this antiethos operates not as an absence but as a marked and stigmatic presence, "permanently arrest[ing] one's rhetorical ethos at the moment of imprint."[102] In this way, those of kakoethical character cannot escape their demi-rhetorical suspension, even if their rhetorical impairments are mere matters of degree, or mildness. Kakoethos forever impedes rhetorical arrival.

While Johnson notes that her turn to kakoethos is one of theoretical rather than historical import, it might be worthwhile, for our purposes, to consider the ways in which the demi-rhetorical machinations of the kakoethical have been historically constituted in medicine. Galen, an ancient Greek physician, described kakoethos in terms of chronicity and malignancy. In his discussion of ulcers, he wrote, "the chronicity is one part of all the essential aspects. It is not actually this chronicity itself, or being called and being chronic, which indicates the appropriate treatment, but from this [chronicity] it is possible to infer the bad state of the ulcerated part."[103] Here, Galen is rather overtly alluding to the metonymy of disability. If one were to substitute the ulcerated with the autistic, a story emerges about autism's effectual singularity, or Zeno's paradox of the like and unlike. Autism is a bad state. And this bad state is inferable from the behaviors we chart and map along the human body or, indeed, the body of rhetoric: motor control and coordination, proprioception, stims and tics, speaking and mutism, eye contact, the body's directedness toward others, the body's directedness toward things and surroundings, and so on. Later, Galen builds upon his contention that kakoethos is metonymic, represented by "visible signs pertaining to the whole body."[104] Even but a handful of the aforementioned embodied movements can generate an autism diagnosis, and once that diagnosis descends from the heavens, it is totalizing and thereby kakoethical. Symptoms and test results might indeed represent only a portion of being human, but their rhetorical effects are essentializing.

In this (bad) spirit of essentialization, here I offer a story from my childhood. Like many an autistic story, this one might be framed as a narrative about my supposed incapacity to make and maintain lasting friendships, to address a listening audience, to participate in a larger social body. In support of my friendless narrative, I could invoke the DSM ("Failure to develop peer relationships appropriate to developmental level"), or I could recount my preteen visits to the school shrink, wherein I fielded questions about my self-isolating tendencies and penchant for acontextually reciting lines from *Airplane!* ("The others are alive, but unconscious. Just like Gerald Ford!"). This story's kakoethical figuring involves a teenage me. In this story, I obliviously engaged with peers who sought to trap me in rhetoricisms, as though their words were flypaper. Unable to discern intention, I strategically (mis)apprehended these kinds of conversations at face value. In one such exchange, a group of my classmates cornered me while I awaited my ride home. One boy from the group—it might have been two, but this is a pithy narrative, and character development is such a drag for a lowly asocial autist (sarcasm)—one boy gazed deeply into my eyes, and asked in seeming seriousness, out of nowhere, "Do you experience genital itchiness?"

Were I rhetorically endowed (more sarcasm), I might have processed the ill intent of the question with some immediacy. But I'm autistic—you know, merely breathing and stiltedly perceiving—and the dynamics of this exchange seemed rife with nuance, sensory data that required logicizing. Why was this boy asking about genitalia, and in front of a mass audience of our peers? My initial thought was to regard the question suspiciously. Here, a group of teens had approached me, the echolalic autistic, about something that sounded like diaper rash. Genital itchiness was potentially being proffered as a symbol of queer disability: to admit to it could be to admit to mental defect, to perversion.

But, despite my suspicions, my admission was vested in literality. "*Of course* I have experienced genital itchiness," I responded—which was met with riotous laughter. Even days later, I experienced continued harassment and exaggerated groans of disgust whenever I set foot in a room with my peers. The bullying struck me as repugnant not because bullying is repugnant, but because I was the only person to make a truthful admission. The whole gambit seemed to me a trick question. To say anything other than *yes* would be to lie. Lying was the graver moral error, far graver than a social faux pas. Asociality had ironically fomented within me a kind of moral imperative, a kind of moral outrage. How dare they not admit to genital itching. How dare they pretend they'd never crotch scratched. (Just like Gerald Ford.)

My forthrightness, under a rhetorical lens, might be read as kakoethical to an extreme. For I have brought to bear two selves in this particular story—preteen Melanie and present Melanie. Not only have I divulged experiences of genital itchiness, but in the introduction I identified myself as a childhood feces smearer, as a toddler who routinely mouthed her own shit. The abjection of these narratives, and what might be perceived as my compulsive willing-ness to share, accrue infinite assumptions about autism's in/voluntariness and ever-residual presence. To dwell in shit is to dwell in a bad state. In writing this book, what with all of the big words, I might be assessed as having some rhe-torical capacity. But in discussing my bowel movements or employing echolalic profanity (fuck—just like Gerald Ford), I might be assessed as having difficulty with self-control and rhetorical context (this is a fucking academic book), pre-dictive understanding of readers' mental states and desires (who picks up an academic book and expects to read about shit?), or any number of autism's many arhetorical symptoms. I make my autistic self known in the presence of social bodies by means of the awkward, asyncopated motions that arhetorically world and queer my environment. Even if I am intentioned, autism unintends for me—its visible signs pertain to my whole body, my demi-rhetorical body.

Despite the social risks in narrating my shit, I engage the autobiographical, the autistethnographic. If we consider Jay Dolmage's conception of rhetoric—the circulation of power through discourse—we can more readily apprehend the neuroqueer potentialities of narrating and claiming the abject, the antisocial, the asocial.[105] My (non)intent is for these abject tellings to skew the contours of rhetoric, to queer ideas of communing (let's dwell with shit), community (let's dwell with shit), and sociality (let's dwell with shit)—items that rhetoric holds dear. Symbolic filtering is not the autistic me. Symbolic filtering is a con-stipatory act, a bottling of perception and immediacy. Autistic rhetorics are *kakokairos*, or an immediate awkwardness—not *like*, but *are*. Under these logics, autism is not only a bad state, but bad timing. (To quote Amy Sequenzia: bad*ass* timing?)[106]

Of course, had I not imparted my inner dialogue in my tale of itchiness, instead relaying only the observable facets of the rhetorical situation—that is, male ringleader of a group of teens asks if I have genital itchiness; I respond "yes"; the teenagers laugh—the rhetorical assessment of the moment would be very different. The removal of my inner dialogue would create a story in which my response is suggestive of robot-like precision and Pentium speed, unencumbered by embodied processes of deducing or directing intentionality because I wield impaired intentional capacities. This reading, of course, brings me back to an earlier point regarding not only autistic perception, but perception of autistic perception. As I discuss in chapter 2, clinical approaches to the question of what and how autistics perceive have come to be dominated by behaviorist methods. Even theories about ToM, which attempt to account for autistic mental states by assuming their absence or disrepair, often reduce autistic perception to behavioral or mechanistic terms, to impassable points on a chart. This is, in many respects, not all that dissimilar from Galen's approach to ulcers. The ulcer's chronicity is legible through bodily behavior rather than the actual ulcer; in like kind, autism's demi-rhetoricity is legible through bodily behavior rather than an observable autism module or node or blip on the brain. The kakoethical is paradoxically diffuse yet freeze-framed in its locatedness. In this way, theories about ToM, or autism fractionation, or defusion of drives defer to the inferential. Some of these inferences may be in part supported by neurological and genetic data, certainly. Largely speaking, though, neurologists and geneticists use these data in concert with their corresponding observations about autistic behavior to make yet more inferences. Inference is behaviorally correlative and normatively dependent. If children in an fMRI study have been diagnosed with language impairments, then any contrastive data that arise between autistic subjects and allistic controls is read through the lens and locatedness of language impairment.

These are but some of the ways in which behavior moves, in which behavior orients the autistic toward so-called bad states. Behaviorist framings of neuroqueer intention are, following Kenneth Burke, framings of motion (nonsymbolic) rather than action (symbolic). In this, we might recall Burke's claim that things move and people act. With regard to autism, this story often takes shape around socially directed versus object-oriented intention. Clinicians frequently story the autistic as being more immersed in the world of things than the world of people. This isn't to say that autistics do not narrate stories about more-than-human ecologies, but rather that clinical exegeses are damningly ableist in their inferences and approach. A chaise lounge named John Horgan once famously quipped that "autistics often seem to make no fundamental distinction between humans and inanimate objects, such as tables and chairs."[107] In these narratives, autistic people are claimed to lack understanding of mental states, and are also claimed to have impairments in sociality, based on their outward behavior. The allistic inference, then, is that an autistic person's gravitation toward things signals an incapacity or inborn ambivalence toward the humanly social. As Burke complained of B. F. Skinner and other behaviorists of the mid-twentieth century, behavioral terms rely on that which is external, working inward from inference only: "In brief, 'behavior' isn't something that you need but observe; even something so 'objectively there' as behavior must be observed through one or another kind of terministic screen that directs the attention in keeping with its nature."[108]

For Burke, terministic screens worked to select, deflect, and reflect a given reality by means of language. In the reality of the behaviorist, then, the seemingly value-neutral rhetorics of empiricism, surveillance, and observation function as terms of work, as terministic screens. And while these screens enable behavioral scientists to anatomize observed behavior into potentially infinite and discrete motions, these screens also prevent behaviorists from apprehending the fullness and symbolicity of that which they routinely cataloged and observed. In particular, Burke took up the example of "psychogenic illness" as a cause of verbal behavior, or biologically informed utterances that were nonetheless symbolic and thereby irreducible to mere behavior. Noted Burke, "True, one can experimentally drive animals crazy. But not with 'ideas!' I must work on the assumption that there is a fundamental difference between a device that removes food from a hungry animal . . . and the plight of a symbol-using animal who, if he gets drunk, always says exactly what he knows he shouldn't say."[109] Whereas the symbolic—the realm of ideas, the realm of the verbal— might at times reduce rhetorical action, its reductions are of the figurative sort, the metaphorical sort, that is, the lies that rhetoric/ian/s love. Behaviorism's reductions, however, purport to be within the realm of the real and empirical, resulting in negativistic and arhetorical reduction, a reduction of motion rather than action. If we were to apply this logic to the question of, say, autistic rhetoricity, a symbolic screen would figure autistic body movements and verbalizations as holding meaning and being organically purposive in their direction. A symbolic screen would, following Massumi, remove autism from the mereness and freeze-frame fixity of positionality, and instead regard autistics as being in continuous, unimpeded motion, traversing and gesturing toward and queering the fuck out of rhetoric.[110]

What is less clear, however, is how Burke's motion/action dichotomy might account for the arhetorical and asocial breadth that autistic perception in/voluntarily directs and accommodates. As I explore in chapter 4, one of the chief topoi in autistic narratives is the in/voluntary disconnect between cognitive desire and bodily action. Autism's so-called movement differences and disturbances—to use Anne Donnellan's language—result in actors whose bodies have wills unto themselves, gesturing and speaking in ways the actors do not fully intend.[111] These embodied forms, which contain causes and means unto themselves, might be more properly deemed entelechies. Autism is defined by the processual, by the ever unfolding. Even though all bodyminds, to some degree, engage in moments of involuntary dis/connection (e.g., just because you want to draw a photographic likeness of Gerald Ford doesn't mean that you can), autistic bodyminds have come to be typified by the excessive and intensive durational aspects of competing embodied and interbodily wills. In clinical estimations, autistic people have, in the words of Margaret Price, traversed a diagnostic "threshold" that both anatomizes and quantifies body-mind disconnection, which in turn renders autistic being pathological.[112] Or, to call upon Alison Kafer, the temporalities of autistic embodiment are clock defying and unruly, un/intended "shifts in timing and in pacing" that queer notions of *kairos* or rhetorical moments.[113]

Emma Zurcher-Long, a nonspeaking autistic teenager, blogs prolifically about the ways in which her untamed body presents a rhetoricity, an entelechy, that diverges from her own purposive wills. Writes Zurcher-Long, "To have intention is a skill. To have intention is a hurdle to jump over."[114] Involuntarity, for Zurcher-Long, has come to signify its own, uniquely apraxic kakoethos, whereby autistic motions are symbolic for their nonsymbolism. An autistic may not fully intend to wave her arms or repeat license plate numbers, and yet an embodied intentionality inheres in those moments, creating meaning and harnessing energy out of a not-entirely-meant performance. Autistic moves remake moments; autistic moves transport the meaning of meaning to involuntary realms; autistic moves remain out of sync with the timeliness that has often come to characterize rhetorical effectiveness. As one such example of rhetorical asyncopation, Zurcher-Long writes prolifically about the seeming randomness of her vocalizations, noting, "My mouth constantly talks different from what I think."[115] When she speaks, listening bodies attempt to discern meaning in her speech, to anchor her words within the context of a given moment, often without success. But the symbolism that rhetoric has placed on intent and timing has the effect of reducing her very being, her core self, to mere motions. In poetic form, Zurcher-Long describes the violence of rhetoric's impatience, its unwillingness to crip and queer time:

> Timing is crucial.
> Nobody can help bring order to the bothersome braying
> that brutish tyrant who won't allow others the time or space.
> Patience is needed.
> I am here
> sometimes insistently so
> but there is so much more to discover.[116]

Opportune moments, kairotic moments: autistic involuntariness is that which is always passing by, an extended duration of continuous motion. Price has characterized rhetoric's edification of timeliness as kairotic space, as high-stakes, of-the-moment domains in which "knowledge is produced and power is exchanged."[117] Not only do kairotic spaces typify rhetorical moments, but their very structure presumes intentioned bodyminds of sound mental character. Kairos, Price reminds us, is not just about timing, but about space, infrastructure, and sociality. Kairos is both the building up to and the bounding of rhetorical action. It is what rhetoricians and behaviorists both cherish and adore: dissecting time, movements, and spaces in search of rhetoricity, and uplifting those bodies that deftly perform as prosocial, effectual bodies.

Involuntarity, then, complicates ideas of a motion/action dichotomy in rhetoric's figuration of the social symbolic. An asocial approach to rhetoric would be an untimely, expansive approach to moments, motion, and volition. An asocial approach, to borrow from Massumi, would frame rhetoricity in terms of passage rather than position.[118] But Burkean rhetorics bound symbolic action, as though able-bodiedness and heterosexuality were compulsory preconditions for acting symbolically. What room is made for the lurch, the stim, the tic if rhetoric is only that which is voluntarily acted upon and performed?

A more extended account of Burke's considerations of neurodivergence can be found in *On Symbols and Society*, an anthology of his selected work from the 1930s through 1960s. Here, Burke speaks of the interrelations between poetry, style, and disability with the "unreality of the world in which we live."[119] Predating Ian Hacking's discussion of diagnostic looping by decades, Burke writes, "These handicaps may become an integral part of his [the neurodivergent person's] method; and insofar as his style grows out of a disease, his loyalty to it may reinforce the disease."[120] Burke's point here is that disability reinforces rhetoricity as much as rhetoricity reinforces disability. Upon first glance, this suggests profound implications for recouping a rhetoricity for autistic interlocutors. It concretizes, for instance, the ways in which autistic people have come to transform a diagnostic category into a neuroqueer culture that extends beyond the mereness of autism and embraces a plurality of queer/crip experiences, personas, and performances. But while Burke's psychogenic musings in many ways function as a prescient disability rhetoric, earlier in *On Symbols and Society* Burke laments the ocular, arrhythmic style of mathematicians, visual thinkers, and hyperlexics, placing them in direct opposition to the psychogenic symbolic. Although he does not name autism in these examples, he does describe what resembles stereotypes of autistic perception—disconnection from the human and the rhetorical body.

And yet, Burke is but one exemplar of what rhetorical traditions—of which there are many—have come to privilege in rhetors, audiences, messages, and situations. As Diane Davis observes of Burke and contemporary rhetoricians: "Rhetoric, at the very least, requires an engagement with the symbolic. This engagement, while it defines the human ('the symbol-using animal'), is what nonhuman animals purportedly lack."[121] Sociality, much like intention, plays a profound shaping hand in the dimensionalities of rhetoricity and thereby humanity. (Just like Gerald Ford.)

## Countersocial Rhetorics

But what of an asocial or antisocial model of rhetoricity? And in what ways do asociality and antisociality diverge not only from one another, but from sociality itself? From queer theory we might engage the strategies of the antisocial turn, disrupting and dismantling rhetorical impulses that seek to universalize what it means to act, intend, and move. In many respects, antisocial motions align with crip-cultural disability theory. As I discuss in chapter 2, both theories are configured in opposition to medical and rehabilitative models of disability. In the same vein, social models of disability, which locate disability as a construction of oppressive sociocultural designs, might be more transformatively and neuroqueerly framed as antisocial models of disability, as Fiona Kumari Campbell argues.[122] And while queer theory and crip theory are not analogous or mutually interchangeable, they are, as Alison Kafer suggests, resonant and "intertwined," relational and coalitional categories that diverge yet whose politics are not "discrete."[123] When engaged queerly, neurodivergence foams rhetorically at the mouth, its capacities overflowing.

McCallum and Tuhkanen remind us that "queerness has always been marked by its untimely relation to socially shared temporal phases, whether individual (developmental) or collective (historical)."[124] Such untimeliness, in its crip-queer iterations, might include the potentialities of awkward gestures, crip time, dysfluency, obsession and perseveration, and executive (dys)function.[125] Of stuttering and disabled speech, Joshua St. Pierre remarks that "the disabled speaking body is temporally 'out of step' with the normalized bodily rhythms and pace of communicative practices in relation to both lived and objective time."[126] St. Pierre denotes normative (inter)bodily actions as choreographies and disabled speech as "a suspension in the movement of speaking speech."[127] Asyncopation, untimeliness, stops and gaps and stutters and disjunctures—such are the makings of neuroqueer worlds, neuroqueer rhetoricity.

Queerly mobile as asociality and antisociality might be, as terms of work they carry clinical baggage. Consider, for example, the ways in which countersocialities have come to function in sexed-brain discourse. Were I to draw examples from Simon Baron-Cohen's books *The Essential Difference* or *The Science of Evil*, the font would run aplenty. Where Baron-Cohen's gender essentialisms come in handy, however, is in their distillation of the ways in which neurodivergence has come to function as sexed causals of disability. In fact, Baron-Cohen's central argument proclaims that neurodivergence exists along a continuum ranging from hyperfeminine to hypermasculine brains. Per Baron-Cohen, feminine brains are those that empathize, and masculine brains are those that systemize. In *The Essential Difference*, Baron-Cohen makes clear that one's "biological sex" is independent of brain type, writing, "Not all men have the male brain, and not all women have the female brain. In fact, some women have the male brain, and some men have the female brain. The central claim of this book is only that *more* males than females have a brain type of S [systemizing], and *more* females than males have a brain type of E [empathizing]."[128] Baron-Cohen's constructions, in addition to being rooted in misogynistic and scientistic reduction, premise themselves on the theory that sexed brains are determined by level of fetal exposure to testosterone. According to Baron-Cohen, "A few drops of this little chemical could affect your sociability or your language ability."[129] Armed with the possibility that this "special substance" results in either balanced (B) or sex-typed (E-S) brains, Baron-Cohen postulates that autism, given its subjects' unintentioned rigidity and imperviousness to emotional states, represents what might be termed the "extreme male brain" (EMB).[130] If empathizers are the hypersocial, then systemizers are its asocial opposite.

Interestingly, whereas autism and systemizing are detailed at length in the text, Baron-Cohen ends *The Essential Difference* with only conjecture about how an extreme female brain (EFB) might behaviorally manifest. He rejects the idea that psychosis or sociopathy, for instance, represent EFB behavior, arguing that such forms of neurodivergence evidence a lack of empathy rather than a pre-

TABLE 1.1. SEXED-BRAIN RESEARCH ON ANTISOCIALITY VERSUS ASOCIALITY,
AKA ABLEISM, NEUROSEXISM, AND TRANSANTAGONISM IN CHART FORM

| Antisocial (Zero-Negative) | Asocial (Zero-Positive) |
| --- | --- |
| Countersociality | Lack of sociality |
| Deficits in affective empathy | Deficits in cognitive empathy |
| Shows disregard or indifference toward others' feelings | Lacks a concept of others' feelings (including their very existence) |
| A destroyer of sociality and relationships, sociopathic | A nonhuman sociality, a sociality of things, a sociality of one |
| Evil | Hapless |
| Hyperfeminine | Hypermasculine |

ponderance. But other scholars who have undertaken sexed-brain research disagree, having even used Baron-Cohen's E-S/female-male continuum in service of typing those whose neurology might be extremely feminine. Brosnan, Daggar, and Collomosse, for instance, posit that psychosis does indeed represent the extreme female brain, serving as autism's polar opposite on what they term the "social brain continuum."[131] Whereas Baron-Cohen argued that individuals diagnosed with psychosis and/or personality disorders lack empathy because of issues relating to cognitive insight or manipulative behavior, Brosnan et al. suggest that "hyper-empathising may constitute a case where people attribute intentionality when it is not there."[132]

Thankfully, for these claims Baron-Cohen and others have received much in the way of criticism. Jordynn Jack has argued that EMB models operate via the rhetorical figure of the incrementum, wherein measures of scale are employed to determine one's level and layers of sociality.[133] Cordelia Fine, for her part, has described such research as a kind of "neurosexism," which promotes "damaging, limiting, potentially self-fulfilling stereotypes."[134] And yet, despite these and other critiques, Baron-Cohen's *The Science of Evil*, as well as his subsequent work, continues down the domain of sex, empathy, and sociality.[135] In particular, Baron-Cohen examines a series of neurodivergent conditions, ranging from autism and narcissism to sociopathy and borderline personality disorder. Operating under what Nick Walker has described as a "pathology paradigm," Baron-Cohen constructs each of these conditions as conditions of empathy—wherein autism represents zero-positive empathy and the other diagnoses embody zero-negative empathy (see table 1.1).[136] Baron-Cohen figures autism as a condition with varying degrees of asociality, as well as a deficit in cognitive empathy, or the purported ability to recognize mental states (read: ToM), such that the empathic deficits stem from a nonintentional and thereby innocent stance. Conversely, he figures personality disorders as antisocial conditions that result in affective empathy deficits, thereby culminating in what Baron-Cohen claims is his book's main inquiry—the science of evil.

Baron-Cohen's proclamations about the nature of evil and intentional stances do real violence to neuroqueer subjects. Not only do they operate on gross stereotypes about neurodivergence, aggression, and intentionality, but they likewise advocate a braining of being—as though neural structures and thereby persona and morality are set in motion by special hormone juices. Indeed, even his more contemporary work expands upon this line of inquiry, moving beyond the endocrinal to the neural and behavioral. In one such study with Ypma et al., Baron-Cohen and his coauthors contend that "autistic traits lie on a sex-related continuum in the general population, and autism represents the extreme male end of this spectrum."[137] In support of this claim, the authors share results from a neuroimaging study of autistic men and women, in which brain regions associated with mentalizing and social cognition were noted to have abnormal connectivity. Here the authors clearly state that both autistic men and autistic women are located "down the more 'male' end of the spectrum."[138] In another study of the sexed-brain continuum, Baron-Cohen and his coauthors conducted online empathy-systemizing and autistic quotient assessments of approximately 800 autistic and 3,900 allistic men and women.[139] Based on their participants' self-reports, they conclude that sex differences between autistic men and women are significantly reduced when placed in comparison with allistic controls. Describing autism as a "masculinization" of the brain (even and especially in women), they contend that these traits can be observed across behavioral, symptomatological, cognitive, neural, and endocrinal domains.[140]

Notably, those who identified as transgender or intersex were excluded from the authors' study, an exclusion informed by grossly ableist and transantagonist assumptions. Numerous studies, including those coauthored by Baron-Cohen, have suggested that intersex and transpeople—especially female-to-male transpeople and individuals with androgen insensitivity syndrome—have a higher number of autistic traits than do cisgender people. These studies have none-too-subtly suggested that gender variance and autism might be causally linked or otherwise neurally correlative. To be clear, my concern lies not with questions of etiology (I might indeed be causally queer or genderqueer because I'm autistic, or vice versa), but rather the ways in which these rhetorics of etiology pose violent implications for the neuroqueer. The implications, of course, have been many: that for autistic people, trans identity is little more than an obsession or a compulsion; that the "transactional relationship" between transness and autism represent deficits in ToM (gender does, after all, require a developed sense of self and others); that autistic people might "misinterpret" their autism-related social oddities and exclusions as genderqueer identity; that research toward a cure on autism might lead toward research that cures transness or intersexness; and so on.[141] While I am indeed arguing that autism is queerness or queering unto itself, and that, anecdotally and even empirically speaking, a larger percentage of autistics identify as queer or genderqueer when compared to allistics, I am unwilling to accept research that would attribute our gender identities to ableist ideas such as "lacks concept of self and other."

As I describe in the next section, Baron-Cohen's theories—whether hormonally or neuronally focused—forward a normatively entelechial understanding of in/voluntarity. That is, Baron-Cohen envisions cognitive landscapes that, thanks to hormonal cocktails, hold wills and causes unto themselves. Autistics lack intentionality because their supposedly excessive testosterone wields intentions for them. These hormones embody causes and finalities simultaneously, and the autistic's failure to developmentally arrive vis-à-vis gender propriety is evidence. For Baron-Cohen, testosterone and estrogen represent asocial and social poles, respectively. Special juices are determinants of motion, intention, and fate.

Of course, Baron-Cohen's hetero/cis/sexist notions of sociality are not the countersocialities that I wish to invoke. Quite the opposite. In positing counterso-cialities as neuroqueer ways to move, I am calling upon Diane Davis's contention that rhetoric "is not first of all an essence or property 'in the speaker' (a natural function of biology) but an underivable obligation to respond that issues from an irreducible relationality."[142] That is, sociality does not neurologically reside, nor does it predict or predetermine (non)rhetorical action. But, more importantly, the "irreducible relationality" of which Davis speaks is the more than human. While antisocial rhetorics are typically conceived as those rhetorics that pervert and disrupt normative structures—that is, negating the already social—asocial rhetorics are rhetorics that complicate what we've come to understand as social. That is, they pose an affront not just to social bodies, but to the idea that sociality holds value unto itself. Asocial rhetorics bristle against the compulsoriness of interaction, of human engagement, of compliance with the neurotypical. If we consider, momentarily, what Aristotle said of rhetoric—that it is the domain of the probable and contingent—we might think of asociality as that which is ecologically oriented and perseverative, that

**FIGURE 1.6.** Photograph of me as a toddler with a younger sibling. In the background are a number of stuffed animals, which toddler-me has lined up into rows, autistic style.

which extends notions of communion and relationality beyond the human. In this I am thinking of the autistic child who lines up her dolls in a row, whose play is typified not by making the dolls interact, but in creating a database of doll bodies, line after line after line, field upon field upon field. The lining up of toys is often listed as one of many woeful autism signs to which parents should remain on high alert. But if we consider lining up toys as an asocial rhetorical move, we might begin to resee irreducible relationality as that which is forged with and between things, fields, spaces, air particles, moments, motions. When are dolls people, and when are dolls dolls? When dolls lie, does rhetoric also lie?

Antisociality and asociality are not necessarily mutually exclusive. As well, socialities, even those defined by absence, are fluid, ever shifting. The idea that sociality is a zero-sum game, as many autism specialists would suggest, or that it is a plot on a map with infinite regress, is redolent of Zeno's paradox. But as Massumi counters, "A path is not composed of positions. It is nondecomposable: a dynamic unity. That *continuity* of movement is of an order of reality other than the measurable, divisible space it can be confirmed as having crossed."[143] The neuroqueer is that which is in continuous, teleporting motion; it is a rhetoricity that defies location and measure, in spite of others' attempts to pin it.

## Entelechial Forces

Where does rhetoric lie? In asking this question yet again, I am this time conjuring images of earth, coffins, graveyards. Where does rhetoric lie? What has it buried? Does rhetoric ever leave the earth?

I ask the above in part as a rhetorician, but perhaps more in my capacity as someone who has been deemed "not living." From parent memoirs such as *I Wish My Kids Had Cancer* to zombie-themed autism fundraising walks, comparatives of autism and death abound.[144] In such narratives, autism does not function as an analogue or an equivalent to death, but instead operates as a worse-than: as in, autism is worse than death because it is a living death, an involuntary and total mode of being. In her 2013 "A Call for Action," the late Autism Speaks cofounder Suzanne Wright reiterates this sentiment, exhorting parents with the following: "These families are not living. They are existing. Breathing—yes. Eating—yes. Sleeping—maybe. Working—most definitely—24/7. This is autism."[145] In other words, Wright suggests, autistic people are mere husks, fleshy orbs who breathe and dwell and exist, but whose presence is not accurately termed living. Rather, theirs is a presence that weighs down families, rendering allistic others unliving as well.

In response to Wright, autistic writer Sarah Kurchak compares Wright's death metaphors to the rhetoric of the antivaccination movement, most especially its fixation with autism causation.[146] Observes Kurchak, "We're facing a massive public health crisis because a disturbing number of people believe that autism is worse than illness or death."[147] Kurchak implores her allistic readership to consider the implicit autism arguments embedded within antivaccine discourse. If parents are conceivably willing to risk their children's death in order to minimize autism risk, she reasons, then what does such a move say about autism?

Autism's rhetorics are gallows minus the humor. Grimness attends autism because autism consumes. If we were once again to summon Žižek, we might see this grimness at work in autism's destructive impulses, its purported proclivities toward obliterating symbolic universes. This framing of autism—as symbolic death, as symbolic absence—is largely psychogenic in origin. Eugene Bleuler proposed autism as a schizophrenia subtype in 1911; and it wasn't until World War II that Leo Kanner and Hans Asperger presented the first case studies of autism as its own specific, diagnostic category. When autism materialized into diagnostic thingness, psychoanalytic models dominated theories of autism's etiology and essence—not simply matters of cause, but matters of whatness, matters of being. Autism, per Kanner, is a disturbance of affective contact, is a desire for sameness, aloneness, repetition.[148] Hans Asperger maintained that autism "totally colours affect, intellect, will and action."[149] What autism seemingly colors and disturbs is everything—the entire perceptual and rhetorical experience of human being. Autism lies in wait.

In psychoanalytic constructions, autism is not unique among mental disabilities—or neurodivergent embodiments—for having been theorized, variously, as a disorder of object constancy, libidinal drives, repetition compulsion, and/or self-other formation. Nonetheless, in these formulations, autism has often represented an extreme among extremes. Drawing upon Freud, a number of psychoanalytic theorists have conceptualized autism as the defusion of drives.[150] These drives, as it were, represent competing instincts toward life and death, or creation and destruction. Autism, of course, represents a move toward the latter, toward death and destruction: the autistic child withdraws or self-isolates because she is so fearful that her neuroses manifest as acute aggression. The autistic child not only hates herself but employs autism as a "defensive strategy to avoid intense levels of stress and anxiety."[151] Read under a death-drive framework, autism's many symptoms might be recast as violent motions that masquerade as actions, as harried impulses to return to "non-organic matter."[152]

Echolalia, then, is latent hostility. Perseveration—or any ritualistic behavior—is a destructive compulsion, an edging toward nonexistence. Object orientation is a coping mechanism, a refusal to engage human others as a means of self-protection. Spinning in circles is abject narcissism. Reversal of pronouns is code for self-obliteration. Shitting oneself is failure to distinguish flesh from inorganic matter, is a retreat toward nothingness. Stimming is autoeroticism. Autism is absence of thought, total destruction of the symbolic universe.

I could keep going. For autism is frequently conceived as deadly residence or death-wishing instinct. Even beyond psychoanalysis, autism is primed toward the nonliving or nonhuman—its subjects are "alien," "other-worldly," "ethereal."[153] Contemporary cognitive theorists may not use a psychoanalytic lexicon when describing autism, but its deathly tropes most certainly linger. On a certain level, the death drive might be understood as what motivates autistic behavior. Autistic people lack capacity for intent because autism intends for them, because aggression wills away their rhetoricity.

Regardless of etiological theory, autism is constructed entelechially. In this I am calling upon Aristotle, who described entelechy as a finality or cause that is possessed within and unto itself.[154] Aristotle's primary example of entelechy was that of the seed: a seed's potential and eventual plantness is encoded within that very seed. The seed is both a cause and a final outcome, and its becoming a plant represents its striving toward a predetermined telos or aim. More contemporarily, we might think of genes, DNA, or brain structures as being their own kinds of entelechy—neural formations that drive our potential and eventual destinies. Entelechy, then, is contained unfolding and being. If we were to follow Burke, we might claim that this entelechial unfolding of being is an unfolding that moves in service of perfection or fulfillment. But Burke's conception of entelechy, as I will discuss momentarily, is overtly concerned with symbolic realms—the entelechies of symbolic action rather than motion. These indeed might be the normative entelechies with which clinicians, psychoanalysts, and the directors of autism nonprofits behold and thereby decompose the autistic. But in motioning toward a queering of the autistic rhetorical, I am meaning to suggest something different—that autistic entelechies are noteworthy for their perseveration and persistence rather than their im/perfection, that entelechies represent not only the im/potentials for a thing in itself, but instead direct us toward the motioning of striving.[155]

Should we shift from seeds to autism, we might ask: What of autism's course? Toward what diverging ends does autism strive? And, more importantly: Can autism ever reach an end? How does the autist escape her demi-rhetorical placement on the autism spectrum?

As I mentioned previously, Burke's configuration of the entelechial is inherently symbolic and is inextricable from motive. Building upon Aristotle, Burke described entelechy as the "temporizing of essence."[156] Unlike Aristotle, Burke's concern wasn't with the innatism of biology, but rather how narrative comes to be understood, determined, or essentialized. In this way, entelechy is circumscribed in a narrative's ending: how a story is fulfilled, what makes a story "timeless."[157] For Burke, narrative entelechy bears intimate connections with metaphor, wherein death symbolizes both an ultimate ending and an ultimate essence. In *A Rhetoric of Motives*, for example, Burke says of the "imagery of killing": "The depicting of a thing's *end* may be a dramatic way of identifying its *essence*. This Grammatical 'Thanatopsis' would be a narrative equivalent of the identification in terms of a thing's 'finishedness' we find in the Aristotelian 'entelechy.'"[158] In other words, reading audiences come to identify with death imagery because such imagery involves character transformation: death is the end point of inner change. To reveal one's end is to reveal one's essence, one's core self.

This representation of entelechy, I am arguing, is both ideological and normative in function. For not only do its preconditions rely on the human and the symbolic, but it likewise falsely assumes an entelechy of finishedness rather than directedness. As Byron Hawk observes, "Entelechy becomes not the striving for a single, predetermined goal but the striving itself that generates multiple lines of divergence as a residual effect."[159] Hawk's embrace of motion rather than end point is intrinsic to the neuroqueering of rhetoric: neuroqueer rhetoricity comes into being through movement and the residues of movement, through creeping, sidling, ticcing, twitching, stimming, and stuttering, through failing to arrive. Recalling Anzaldúa and Dolmage, we might revisit mētis and cunning as one such neuroqueer and thereby entelechial force. Dolmage describes mētis as "always introducing newness," as "intellectual and material movement against normativity," as nonlinear.[160] At once beckoning and resisting the paradoxical, Anzaldúa writes, "A glance can freeze us in place; it can possess us. . . . But in a glance also lies awareness, knowledge."[161] In like manner, Debra Hawhee relates mētis as a "kind of bodily becoming, insofar as it is transmitted through a blurring of boundaries between bodies."[162] The neuroqueer dwell in continuous, embodied motion. Ours are rhetorics of perseverative loops, cumulative loops, loops that defy rest or sense or logic. To be neuroqueer is to always be striving toward being neuroqueer.

What I express above, of course, contrasts the symbolization and clinicalization of entelechy, of rhetoricity writ large. I am suggesting that, regardless of whether or not autistics are intentional or social or symbolic, we have potentiality to be rhetorical (much as we have potentiality to reject the rhetorical). Intentionality is itself an end point, measurable and knowable through discrete effects; it is likewise the end point of many autism god theories, an ideological force that renders the autistic frozen and lifeless. In many respects, this normative entelechy that I am describing negates entelechy's traditional definitions. Following Leibniz, Jung, and Bergson, entelechy has been conceived as a life force, as vital instinct, as élan vital. The death drive as entelechial, were we to follow the above, should be oxymoronic. But when autism enters the fold, paradoxes abound, and entelechy's rhetorical formations have tended toward the deadly.

Take, for instance, Stan Lindsay's work on what he terms "psychotic entelechy."[163] Lindsay's entelechy builds upon Burke's, which involves "tracking down the logic of perfection implicit in symbols, terminologies, nomenclatures."[164] But more than this, Lindsay's interests in entelechy are psychopathological in scope, concerned with the ways in which immoral logics come to fruition. He defines this psychotic entelechy, then, as "the tendency of some individuals to be so desirous of fulfilling or bringing to perfection the implications of their terminologies that they engage in very hazardous or damaging actions."[165] While Lindsay claims that he intends *psychotic* as a reference to psyche rather than psychosis, his main entelechial exemplars are cult leaders who have been popularly and pejoratively figured as mentally ill—such as David Koresh, Jim Jones, and Gene Applewhite. What Lindsay deems psychotic entelechy I deem normative, for these approaches to entelechy are grossly ableist, psychologizing the motives of others in frequently pathologizing terms. Other scholarship on normative entelechy has examined bomb making as well as trenchant political conservatism, and all of the violences that these terministic screens bring to completion.[166] In so doing, these studies ask: toward what ends do politics and/or violences strive? What is violence's im/perfection?

As Lindsay notes, Burkean entelechy moves beyond biology, substituting the deterministic with the intentioned: "Burke inserts human choice, or free will, or action."[167] When it comes to autism's entelechies, however, clinicians grapple with a condition in which the symbolic, terministic, and volitional are in grave disrepair. Per Burke, all motives have ends. It is the goals or telos of an intention that come to totalize that intention. Intention strives toward perfection by having and attaining a denouement. Given the heavy weight of allistic criticism that I've scoured in this chapter, such intentioned moves seem impossible for autistics. As Emma Zurcher-Long maintains, intention requires skill, requires aim. If autistics are demi-rhetorical, then we can't reach any ends; our neuroqueer, ticcing, stimming bodies wander without aim. Zeno keeps us locked, feet wedged in flypaper, bodies eternally bound. Our autistic means are of no matter, for if we fail to attain neurotypical ideals, then our debilitated bodies will never be matters of finishedness. Autistic essence is absence. What does have intention, though, what does possess cause unto itself, is autism—not autistic people, but autism-as-entity, or that which parasitically possesses us hapless autistic folk. Our brains hold more agency than we do, because autism lies atop. David Morris describes residence as that which has earth as a reference point—for without the earth, there can be no concept of up, or down, or even referentiality.[168] It is this referentiality to the land that indigenous scholars have underscored in their appeals to decolonize rhetorical traditions. Such tropes of nonrelatedness, as Qwo-Li Driskill and Andrea Riley-Mukavetz warn us, have been used, for centuries, to dehumanize and murder native peoples.[169] These tropes, then, have constellated power, rendering especially vulnerable those whose identities ford multiple oppressions. And, conveniently, this rhetorical reconfiguration of the entelechial as psychic or psychotic death is one that motivates numerous violent impulses, using the figure of the autist as one of its metaphorical agents. Autism covers the brain and binds our bodies to earth as swiftly as it absents our bodies from earth. Autism's intentions are postures, impostors, pod persons. Autistics might be otherworldly or alien, but autism keeps us grounded and fixed in demi-rhetorical position: its ends are paradoxes, living death. "Madness," Burke warns us, "is but meaning carried to the extreme."[170]

Bernard Rimland, a parent-turned-scientist who fervently railed against psychoanalytic theories in the 1960s and 1970s, embraced a normative-entelechial model of autism in which autism did indeed represent an extreme, or a limit case on the continuum of human sociality.[171] Rimland ended *Infantile Autism* by proposing a theory of neural entelechy, suggesting that human brains reach their predetermined ends by seeking sensory stimulation. In support of his claim, Rimland asserts that neurons have "wills," "motives," and "desires."[172] Further, Rimland maintains that his scholarly interests lie in neurons' behavior, as if neurons have capacity for symbolic action, as if neurons are social creatures. In this, his terminology is surprisingly behaviorist in scope. Neurons seek rewards; neurons are activated by stimuli; neurons can be conditioned into appropriate response. What causes a neuron to behave in a certain manner? What consequences follow neuronal behavior? Toward what ends do neurons strive?

For Rimland, then, autism's entelechy is borne not of its rhetorical perfection, but of its imperfection. As Baron-Cohen notes, "When the meta-representational hardware develops normally, biology has done its job."[173] But in autism this job is not done: biology has failed, has veered toward deadlier ends via deadlier means. Autism is a more literalized entelechy: its means and ends are death and destruction. Autism's life force, as it were, is the process of dying.

These are the tracings and trappings of autistic (non)rhetoricity. In tracing toward the queer, I am tempted to suggest that autistics embrace the death drive, that we roll with our entelechial destruction and kaboom all the things. Following Edelman, we might argue that autism's queerness is imbued precisely in these deathly impulses.[174] Autism destroys—and norms need destroying. Antisociality is our referent, and destruction is our method. Autism is, in toto, the death drive. But I am stuck on this idea, for in suggesting that autism is, at its very core, an end (or the end), we only further foreclose autistic futures. In the words of Muñoz, I want to "wrest ourselves from the present's stultifying hold."[175] I want to imagine an expanse, an after, a not-yet-realized, a potentiality beyond the expiration of autistic motions, gestures, echoes, ephemera. These are the queer entelechies that I mean to summon—not the Burkean flavor of symbolic wills, psychotic means, or ideological immorality. My flapping fingers might kill norms, but they are not unto themselves symbolic of my inner deadness, nor are they violent motions that warrant public surveillance and fear. As Byron Hawk reminds us, "We are our accidents and our connections as much as our choices."[176] I might at times be totally absent of thought, in the throes of overload or meltdown, selectively mute and literally senseless—but I am not literally nor am I symbolically dead. Death is in many ways another fixity, another paradoxical hold on autistic people. And when the autistic living are presumed to be the already dead—when the autistic living are metaphorized in queer and psychoanalytic theory as metonyms for the already dead—real violence is perpetrated upon our bodies. These, as autistic blogger Zoe Gross warns, are killing words.[177]

"Madness," Burke warns us, "is but meaning carried to the extreme."[178] This is locational language: autistics are linearly extreme, developmentally extreme, statistically extreme. But these are not the entelechies of the neuroqueer. Following Latour, "We should imagine filamentlike entelechies, spun out and interwoven with one another . . . which are incapable of harmony because each one defines the size, the tempo, and the orchestration of this harmony."[179] Autistic motions are kakokairotic, kakoethical—asyncopated motions that defy time, space, and character.

Importantly, the argument that autism is a kind of living death—and thereby worse than death (because it is symbolic death, a death in which organs and body meat keep churning while the external world remains beyond grasp)— fuels homicidal logics. Media reports of caregivers murdering autistic people have become so commonplace that in 2012 the Autistic Self Advocacy Network (ASAN) instituted an annual day of mourning in remembrance of disabled victims. And, in 2015, ASAN created an antifilicide toolkit, made freely available to the public online. That an autistic-run autism organization felt a need to create a parent manual on how not to murder one's children is particularly telling. Autism's climate is one of death, and its tracings hail back to its earliest theorizations.

Among autism's psychogenic cast of characters is Bruno Bettelheim. In autism circles, Bettelheim's is a story often told. His is a story of refrigerator mothers, of mothers whose aloofness caused their children's descent into autism, into psychic death. But his was a story widely believed, in part because he spoke as a Holocaust survivor, employing his incredible ethos to proclaim just how bad off autistic children were (read: very bad off), often comparing their psychic imprisonment to the despair he observed at Buchenwald and Dachau. In *The Empty Fortress*, Bettelheim infamously claimed that autism represented such a profound state of inactivity that suicidal behavior represented an improvement in condition:

> It is the ultimate statement that nothing more must be lost, because the autistic child is so depleted that any further loss would mean death. . . . Thus autism is a position even more extreme than suicide; and suicide, or suicidal tendencies, are a first step toward once again becoming active. . . .
>
> Suicide alone seems a more extreme position, but is not. Because suicide involves a goal-directed action that the autistic child seems even less capable of performing than the suicidal person. Infantile autism might be viewed as a position of despair where even the requisite energy to end it all is lacking, or else where all doing is avoided precisely to defend against a passive dying, as in death by marasmus, for example.[180]

Bettelheim's might be a psychoanalytic sentiment, but it is a sentiment that has survived the past five decades. It is a sentiment that has engorged itself in how autism is defined across clinical and popular contexts. The two Bettelheimian tropes that remain at work in contemporary autism politics are those of intention and symbolic action—or, the domains in which rhetoric lies and lies. A world without symbols and goals is an impoverished world, a nonworld. Autistic people are so unintentioned, are so tragically involuntary that suicide represents improvement, because if one is suicidal, one has access to motive and symbolic egress. But also embedded within Bettelheim's death wishing is a nefarious logic of inaction that manifests as parental blame. This logic fuels parental desperation, as if parental desperation were a market, because if parents have autistic kids, then it means that both parent and child are inactive, and even suicide or homicide is something more than autism.

I read Bettelheim, and I read Kelli Stapleton, the Michigan mother who locked her autistic child in a minivan and attempted to poison her with lit charcoal grills. I read London McCabe, the six-year-old autistic child whose mother threw him over a bridge to his death. I read Melissa Stoddard, who suffocated on her own vomit after her stepmother duct taped her mouth and tied her in four-point restraints. I read Bettelheim, and I read the autism charities who defend filicide, claiming that child-murder fantasies are "understandable" and "normal." I read ABA lobbies, and the swept-under-the-rug histories of queer suicides. I read Autism Speaks's research repository of autistic brains, because our autistic dead are somehow more alive and useful than the autistic who are living.

As Burke says, "the killing of something is the changing of it."[181] What is autism without life? Nonautism! (That which we should desire! Dear Ivan Pavlov, please train us to salivate for death!) Under these entelechial logics, our only escape from our autistic fixity is to off ourselves. Or, should we lack the goal direction to end our own lives, our caregivers are impelled to do it for us. These are rhetorical violences as much as they are material violences. Entelechy, like death, is that which "strive[s] to be played out to completion."[182] The world claims that autistics are involuntary, and then again claims that involuntariness is a fate worse than death. What are autistics to think? What are autistics to do? How to complete the autism puzzle? (Cough, cough, coffin.)

Wayne Booth's *The Rhetoric of Rhetoric* at many junctures takes up the question of violence and its meanings for rhetoric.[183] Booth's definition of rhetoric is particularly expansive, incorporating "all forms of communication short of physical violence."[184] Because Booth frames rhetoric as a potential location from which problems might be mediated, violence and threat—the opposition of such mediation—is thus exempted from Booth's conception of rhetorical exchange. What Booths seeks resembles conflict resolution, the sort of work that will indeed be heated, energetic, and contested, but that nonetheless tries to work through dissensus, polarization, and bipartisanship by means of non-violent exchange. And yet, what Booth elides is that the history of rhetoric is a violent history. As Carolyn Miller suggests, rhetorical impulses are often imperialist impulses—whitening, converting, persuading, assimilating.[185] We see these rhetorical impulses at work in many marginalized spaces—raced, classed, gendered. As I describe in chapter 3, any minority status is arguably a demi-rhetorical status. Black rhetors are presumed both too black and not black enough to effect an argument; queer rhetors are presumed too queer and not queer enough to intend an action; and so on. Rhetoric's lies are that its violences are not really violences. Rhetoric can violently absent or end counter-social bodies by claiming that rhetorical violences are softer, fluffier, and moraler than the lives of so-called deviants. This is mere rhetoric; this is rhetrickery; this is sophistry: when dying is rhetorically cuddlier than living.

When we figure violence outside the domain of rhetoric, we also violently figure those who've experienced violence and those who have committed it. We conveniently absent ourselves from larger conversations about what violence is and what it does and the kinds of effects, affects, and purported intents attached to it. When neurodivergence comes into view, it is something to end violently in part because the neurodivergent are presumed to be violent: the logic is such that normative violence against the neurodivergent is not violence at all, is only a preventative of a greater violence. Here I echo Margaret Price's assertion that "prevailing myths about mental disability and violence shore up an ongoing structural violence."[186] In invoking Price, I am alluding not only to the mass media's falsely stereotyped correlations between mental illness and violence (both individual and mass acts of violence), but likewise to

1  disabled practices that are often culturally and inaccurately inscribed as violence (e.g., self-injury, reactions under stress, communicative frustration), and

2  the erasure of disabled people's experiences of abuse, violence, and trauma, including and especially abuse and murder perpetrated by caregivers, as well as violence against disabled people of color (of which the instances are systemic and many).

Regarding the second point: it feels as though, almost daily, we encounter another story about an autistic youth of color who has been targeted by law enforcement—imprisoned, beaten, killed—often for the crime of "being autistic while black."[187] One prominent example is that of Reginald "Neli" Latson, whose hell began in 2010 when he was then eighteen years old. Latson, who had the gall (sarcasm) to wear a hoodie, had traveled to the library and decided to sit in the grass and wait for it to open. Upon seeing a stimming and pacing black teenager waiting outside, an anonymous caller phoned the police to report a "suspicious character."[188] A responding officer approached Latson and asked for his name; when Latson tried to walk away, the officer grabbed Latson, struggled with him, and subsequently arrested him. The resulting charge was assaulting an officer, of which Latson was convicted and sentenced to two years in prison and eight years' probation. If the story thus far seems unjust, it gets only worse: while in prison, Latson was routinely denied mental health care, despite having several disabilities including autism, and at one juncture he attempted suicide. While at home and on probation, Latson again threatened suicide, and was subsequently arrested—this time, placed in twenty-four-hour solitary confinement. Numerous autism activists lobbied on behalf of Latson and his release from what was, essentially, torture. While Latson was eventually released, it was only due to a conditional pardon from Virginia governor Terry McAuliffe in January 2015. The threat of rearrest forever looms, and a teenager lost many years of his life to repeated racial profiling and ableist violences.

Much as Booth notes that there is something queerly rhetorical about giving someone the middle finger, I am suggesting that there is something queerly rhetorical about making overtures toward suicide, or cutting one's own thighs with a box cutter, or banging one's head repeatedly against a radiator, or slapping oneself while twirling and screeching in the middle of a grocery store. I have done all of these things, and here I am, writing about it, presumably from a (non)rhetorical stance, but in writing from an autistic (non)rhetorical stance I am also writing from a white (non)rhetorical stance. In writing this, I am also suggesting that what clinical tracts classify as violence or destruction or death drive or living death thrive on notions that the mentally disabled are arhetorical. With regard to Latson, these clinical tracts "shore up" (to again invoke Price) innumerable structural violences, propelling the bigoted notion that disabled people of color represent the most compellingly deadly of futures. And neuroqueer motions—some of them self-injurious, many of them not—culminate entelechially in these normative stories, defining the whole of our neuroqueer selves as violence in need of further violence, with such violences exponentially compounded when racism and antiqueerness bristle against the fold.

> —Our cognition primes us for destruction, sayeth The Rhetorics, which
>    is the autistic's imperfect imperfection.
> —The killing of something is the changing of it. Let us channel
>    Burke and contemplate the eugenicist impulses in rhetorical
>    transformation.
> —Autism's remnants reside; only death will evict autism from the earth.

Violence protects us from our violent selves: this is where rhetoric lies.


Coda: The Primacy of Meaning

Rhetoric's lies are many. I have in this chapter glossed many of the items that rhetoric both privileges and buries—intent, perception, symbolism, sociality, allistic life. Autism, I have argued, functions as a never-quite rhetoricity, and thereby a non-rhetoricity in these constructions. The autistic are in continuous, residual motion; rhetoric never arrives.

As the title of this book might suggest, I am acutely interested in authoring, or what it means to invent or shape a discourse. There is something particularly defeatist about this chapter (spoiler: not to mention the next) when it comes to autistic people's wills and ways. I have made rhetoric seem fucked up, and autistic people totally fucked. In many respects, this is true: when autistic people enter rhetorical situations, we are often silenced, ignored, berated, infantilized, corrected, scolded, behavior-planned, extinguished, institutionalized, electroshocked, restrained, hog-tied, faux-praised, tasered, secluded, shamed, raped, shaken, hit, teased, studied, molested, laughed at, or murdered. In this list, I am not being hyperbolic. Rhetoric's machinations are many, and for neuroqueer subjects, rhetorical practice might seem elusive at best or violent at worst. Words determine our fate, and yet we are often denied access to words. Sometimes these access barriers are matters of our neurodivergence—we might not speak, read, write, type, point, or sign. Traditional conceptions of language may be cognitively impossible for us, even though lacking tradition is not equivalent to lacking language. And yet, neurodivergence is glibly faulted as reason for our rhetorical excision. Making rhetoric work for the Other is too much work for the same-old. Rhetoric's barriers are stratified by misperceptions of neurodivergence as well as limited ideas of what it means to communicate and commune.

If we return to Royster and Kirsch, we might recall that there are many rhetorics, or many ways of crafting the thingness of what a given rhetoric might privilege. Recalling Dolmage, we might claim our own neuroqueer rhetoric, a rhetoric that uncovers, upsets, and unsettles power structures at work in normative spaces. Dolmage's disability rhetorics are futuristic: they are rhetorics (inter)dependent upon disability (as opposed to rhetorics that seek to eradicate, contain, or disqualify the disabled). But these rhetorics are also immanently queer, (re)verbing that which wishes to remain static. Queerness and disability may not be equivalent or even analogical, but they are resonant and interweaving constructs, and they are norm-shattering ways of moving, are ways of disorientating toward the perverse. As Jonathan Alexander and Jacqueline Rhodes relate, "Queer rhetoric works to unseat the rhetorical and material tyranny of the normal itself."[189] Crip-queer rhetorics uphold Dolmage's assertion that rhetoric's purview is "meaningful bodies," wherein the locus of "meaning" (much like the construct of "body") queerly shifts among uncertain, fleeting, and mundane means: for rhetoric is determined by the undetermined or the indeterminable.[190]

This is to say: rhetoricity isn't mere, even if it does lie. Neuroqueer rhetorics, per Dolmage, reconfigure bodies and language by obliterating their boundedness. One doesn't end at the skin much like one doesn't end at morphemes or vocalizations; there is no possibility of halving, because there is no whatness or constant to be halved. The queer, as Alexander and Rhodes aver, is "irreducible, uncontainable, itself defying the impoverished logics that reduce desire and intimacy to gay and straight, this or that, male and female, one or the other."[191] That is, queer rhetorics defy the dichotomous, reject the grip that Zeno's paradoxes have brought to bear on pathologized subjects in rhetorical domains. Queer rhetorics are entelechial in their forever-becoming, through the being of their striving toward futurity.

There is something provocative in claiming irreducible defiance as unabashedly neuroqueer. Where normative rhetorics reduce, neuroqueer rhetorics defiantly stim. In some respects, I have been using *neuroqueer* and *crip-queer* interchangeably because these constructs can be synonymous or overlapping. But as Alison Kafer cautions, *crip* often invokes bodies as physicality, reifying Cartesian divides and diverting brainness to its own, often lesser categories in the realm of disability.[192] This isn't to say that crip isn't enminded. As a term of work, it is decidedly activist, drawing upon the radical potentialities of queer theory as a means of positioning itself: crip is to disability what queer is to LGBT; while each calls upon and is informed by the other, cripness and queerness cannot be reduced to stasis, and both resist the respectability politics that work to make marginalized people prosocial or governable.[193] In like manner, there has been concerted work over the past decade to explode the axes of crip studies beyond the physical resonances that often attend the word *cripple*. Robert McRuer and Sami Schalk, for example, have compellingly argued that crip is unboundable: it is not a polar, linear, or diagrammable construct.[194] As such, crip is not limited to, nor is it synonymous with, disability. As Schalk contends, crip might be better understood as a mode of disidentification, in which solidarity and coalitional politics of/among "minoritarian subjects, communities, and/or representations" form the basis from which one might claim criphood.[195] In other words: crip theory investigates and destroys notions of what or who comes to qualify as or from a given standpoint; it likewise provides theoretical tools for re/seeing identification, politics, and marginality.

And yet, crip at times remains a point of contention in neurodivergent spaces. Despite its current trajectories, its lineages are hard to shake. Neurodivergent activists may encounter crip as importing the logics of Ed Roberts's famous quote: "I'm paralyzed from the neck down, not from the neck up."[196] As autistic activist Kassiane Sibley aptly summarizes, "I'm not sure it's my word and I actually have disabilities. Plural."[197] Crip histories largely elide the neurodivergent, privileging rhetors who are critically conversant and academically able, constructions that often silence those with cognitive disabilities. Neuroqueer, in some respects, emerges as an analogue and expansion of crip, which arguably isn't or wasn't as queerly enminded as it could be. If queerness is a not-yet-here, a tracing toward futurity, then has crip already arrived? In posing this question, I do not mean to suggest that this is a yes/no formulation (or that there can even be an answer). Rather, I mean to suggest that the neuroqueer movement has been acutely concerned with centering the interstices of queerness and neurodivergence, the latter of which has often taken a backseat in disability studies and disability rights activism. These concerns are not necessarily at odds with crip theory, but they do identify moments and futures in which neurodivergence requires overt engagement rather than brief nods or inadvertent elision.

Importantly, neuroqueerness is frequently rendered as all-encompassing in activist narratives, what autistic scholar-activist Nick Walker relates as both an "adjectival" and a "verbing," a "reclaiming [of] one's capacity to give more full expression to one's neurodivergence and/or one's uniquely weird personal potentials and inclinations."[198] Neuroqueering signifies a generous and inter-bodily gesturing, one that postures beyond brains, bones, and dermis; one that waves in a plurality of identities, orientations, affective stances, and lived experiences, modes ranging from autism to deafness to trauma to asexuality.

Here, then, I return to neuroqueer rhetoricity, to motioning beyond mereness, lying, and linear continua. When we author autism, what and who are we to author? Have we fully considered or questioned why we need rhetoric? Can one step out of it, much like one steps in it? Where does rhetoric lie?

I am still worried about lying. It might be my autism (it has, after all, taken over my brain). And yet, I believe that autistics are often wrongly, unjustly, and ableistly construed as lacking in capacity for both representational meaning making and intentionality. Moreover, I believe that our cultural reverence for meaning and intent—our privileging of it as a core characteristic of humanity and rhetoricity—is both misplaced and woefully ill advised. Symbolicity may be rhetoricity, but rhetoric is not constrained to the symbolic. Rather, as Rickert claims, rhetoric is a condition of the symbolic's emergence, representing the vast resources from which symbolism can be forged.[199] To claim that someone without meaningful language (however disparately *meaningful* is defined) is thereby non-rhetorical is to suggest that much of the material world exists outside the bounds of style, arrangement, invention, memory, epistemology. It discounts not only autistic rhetoricity, but the rhetoricity of other marginalized subjects. Rhetoric is not always narrated, despite narration always being rhetorical: the *New York Times* best-selling autie-biography is as much a font of rhetoricity as is the autistic child headbanging in a clinic. There might or might not be meaning; there might or might not be symbolic linguistic formation or representational intent; but there are rhetorical effects, there is invention at work, there is rhetoricity. In the words of Lennard Davis, there is a *there* there.

These are the means of the queer rhetorical situation: what we know and want to know are not necessarily what is prioritized, sentient, or perceived—the thereness of neuroqueer rhetorics is complicated. At times, meaning is not the most meaningful of rhetorical forms. Clinical desires for symbolicity call upon numerous cultural anxieties around compliance, conformity, and the kind of abstract(ed) mutual understanding that is institutionally mandated or implied across rhetorical situations. Without meaning, what is the point? Without representation, what is the point? But the point is jagged: neuroqueer rhetorics articulate alternate spaces and knowledges for inter/relating, indexical worlds that draw upon im/material resources, a cripped kind of betweeny.

At times I am told, if rhetoric is everything and everywhere, then rhetoric is surely meaningless. A corollary of this statement might be framed as such: if rhetoric can be autistic—or if autists are indeed rhetorical—then rhetoric is surely meaningless.

I have many responses to these assertions. My impulse is to question why rhetoric must take meaning as its center, much like I question why rhetoric is so preoccupied with humans, and intent, and conferences with fluorescent lighting. As Kennedy, Rickert, and Ahmed variously ask: If rhetoric is energy to be realized, if rhetoric is ambient, if rhetoric is sticky, if rhetoric is what binds some nebulous us—does it not still have an effect?[200] I may not intend to vomit while watching a Jenny McCarthy video on vaccine conspiracy theories, but my emesis is most certainly effectual.

But I also want to put forth that, at times, rhetoric is meaningless. Meaninglessness is not the pejorative so many of us would presume. I feel most autistic when I'm not making sense of anything—and there is a certain tranquility and terror and disconnectedness in that, dwelling in a synesthetic jumble of nothingness, awash in all the inventional resources that an autly sensorium can provide. Asociality is my autistic commonplace; it is the removed space in which I dwell, senselessly and senseless. I want to suggest that rhetoric can be meaningless and that meaninglessness is a potentiality that rhetoric should (and can, and does) embrace. To question the meaningfulness of rhetoric should not be to question its worth. Rhetoric is the purview of meaning and cacophony both. It enables us to arrange meaning from the meaningless, much like it enables us to make meaninglessness out of meaning. Exploring symbolicity as a means to locate and root out meaning, autistic writer Star Ford contends that in allistic narratives, "things are symbols, not actual things."[201] What is the meaning, she asks, in "those kinds of experiences"—the experiences of prototypical neurotypical lives, wherein, for instance, "a popular girl leaves her boyfriend, there is a big fight, social groups get rearranged, someone is expelled from school, and there is a party where people do things that are hilarious and relieve the built-up tension"?[202] What and where is the meaning? An autistic, Ford claims, may (or may not) discern little to no meaning from the social ephemera that cumulate to dictate an allistic moment, narrative, or life. Conversely, for allistics, meanings, a plurality of meanings, reside. "The word 'meaning,'" she writes, "should be torn apart into three different levels: definition, intent, and relevance."[203] The word *meaning*, in other words, is often meaningless because it holds so much, and thereby wields great power.

In those moments when I cannot intelligibly express the above exhortations (which are, frankly, most of my moments), I temporarily fall back upon my *fuck rhetoric* stance. If rhetoric can so quickly reject the neuroqueer, then why should we seek its graces? In this I am reminded of a lightning talk given by Raul Sanchez at the 2014 Cultural Rhetorics conference, in which he described Aristotle as rhetoric's racist uncle. If rhetoric is so mired in exclusionary, oppressive, and seemingly unforgivable theories and practices—then do we really want part in/of it? Is this an instance in which we apply Audre Lorde, or Nick Walker, or Sara Ahmed, and behold rhetoric as the master's tools?[204] Do we need rhetoric? And more, do we want it? Is it in any way a desirous frame?

In many respects, I consider my answer to these questions—and the fact that this book exists—to be a strategic queering of sorts. I think we do want rhetoric, and we do need rhetoric, because we cannot afford to be denied it. With rhetoric come matters of life and death. There is a certain sentience presumed of and in rhetoricity: disabled people have long known that if one cannot persuasively argue for the validity of one's life, then one's life is considered not worth living.[205] How to mean rhetoric? How to mean meaning? In authoring autistic futures, perhaps our first queer move is to reject rhetoric's braining, inextricable as it is from spectra and poles. On some level, my exhortation to move away from the brain likely sounds facile, given that this is a book about neuroqueering and autism. But there is a difference between the countercultures that organize to resist neuro-hegemonies and the neuro-hegemonies that propagate notions of mental capacity as a means of controlling certain bodyminds. Rhetoric isn't milk, and brains aren't vats.

But more than this, as Malea Powell urges, we should question the idea that the rhetorical tradition (in all of its *the*-ness) is an accurate reflection of what rhetoricity itself contains.[206] That is—is Aristotle rhetoric? Kenneth Burke? James Berlin? In part, yes, or no, or maybe, or meh—but rhetorical studies' primary project has long been interrogating what the fuck rhetoric even is. Arguably, to be a rhetorician is to have no clue what rhetoric is, for rhetoric is ever shifting, historically contingent, powerfully shaped, impelled by predictions about nebulous futures, and seemingly always related to (no, *defined by*) context and situation.

Rhetoric lies. And lies. And lies.

TWO. **intervention**

It's an event I like to call the Curious Incident of the Vote at the Book Club. There are fifteen of us huddled around a burly Barnes and Noble table, eleven autistic, four non. The lights are very loud, the autie voices and the coffee machines even louder. Several months previously, my disability services counselor had referred me to the book club, suggesting I use it as a space to "practice." She held the space in high esteem—one that would allow me to socially faux pas, ad infinitum. And so I sit there, practicing how to practice. As we fifteen vote on our next book, I wring my hands, silent but focused, and after much banter, we've narrowed our choices down to two possibilities: Joseph Heller's *Catch-22* or Mark Haddon's *The Curious Incident of the Dog in the Night-Time*, the latter being the autism novel du jour, complete with a teenage savant who hates yellow cars, melts down in London, and recites prime numbers.

Before the final vote, three autistic members voice their vehement objections to reading *Curious Incident*. They maintain that it's the most simplistic, vile, ridiculous book they've ever come across. We vote, and *Curious Incident* wins—only because two autistics have abstained from voting, and all four of the nonautistic moderators have cast their votes for *Curious Incident*.

And so, with the exception of those who call themselves neurologically typical, we all practice melting down in public. One person totally flips out in authentic autistic fashion, screaming and jumping and flailing and throwing hardcover books. Another covers her ears and hunkers down. Two others start yelling. Two leave the table. One looks bewildered. My hard drive shuts down, then crashes, and I mentally leave planet earth, effectively mute and literally senseless, just one more autistic person participating in an autistic chorus. At that moment, as the meltdowns garner what I can only presume are the *tsk-tsk* looks of blue-haired ladies, I wonder what I am practicing.

As I attend the meetings in the weeks that follow, it becomes clear what the book club moderators expect me, expect us, to practice: audience awareness. Christopher, the novel's teenage and autistic protagonist, doesn't seem to have any—like his pretty little rhetorical triangle got a side bit off. And more than this, the moderators expect us to see ourselves as little Christophers. They ask us questions like, "You know that time when Christopher wishes everyone on earth were dead but him so that he can pursue his autistic interest and not be bullied—do you all wish the same thing?" To which our most vocal member responds, "Fuck Christopher. Fuck you!"

He is practicing something that I wish desperately to practice.

## Practicing Autism

*Practice* is a term that can harbor particularly agentive resonances. To discuss a rhetorical practice, for example, conjures images of an intentioned rhetor showcasing and effecting rhetorical skill. When modified by the word *autistic*, however, practice transposes into something more passive, more cognitively determined. What am I practicing? Who is the determinant of what I practice? In clinical settings, autistic practices are often better termed *autistic symptoms*, for when autism modifies practice, practice resides in the pathological. In rehabilitative settings, where the goal is to mitigate the pathology that directs and informs what a given body practices, autistic practices are more optimistically conceived as a *when* than a *what*, as an object of duration rather than constitution. When autistic people practice social skills, the moment of practice obscures the whatness of normalization. Norms lack dimensionality, in part because their dimensions are temporally determined. We might call these dimensions context—say, as one example, a book club meeting at a local bookstore. When such a meeting is a situation of practice, rather than a situation of meeting, all moves and mechanisms of the autistic bodies involved remain subject to and of determination. How loud are our voices? How comfortably and appropriately are our bodies disposed in the bookstore chairs? How on-topic are the words that escape our mouths? How might we generalize these norms, these social skills, these allistic determinations in other, nonbookstore domains?

I have spent much of my life practicing nonautism, or what my autistic comrades call allism. The stuff of my real self is the stuff of neither reality nor selfhood, because autism supposedly impedes my capacity for knowledge of both self and other. I have spent the better part of my career arguing that disability is a rhetorical condition because larger publics—doctors, teachers, service professionals, parents, pop psych gurus—recognize disabled people as decidedly arhetorical. On some level, I find my claims obvious: of course autistics are rhetorical, even if we do complicate ideas about intent, affect, and relationality. I feel like this is a *no shit* kind of thing, that of calling agency to the fore, elaborating what an autistic, neuroqueer rhetoric might resemble and provoke or invoke.

But, as I discuss in my introduction, autism is not a *no shit* kind of thing. Autistics not only smear literal shit, but they muster up some figurative shit on the project of rhetoric. Questions abound, questions like: What about ticcing? What about language and mutism? What is rhetoric without intent? What is rhetoric without the verbal? What is rhetoric without words, without sanity, without consciousness, without audience?

Autism has long functioned as a limit case in cognitive studies, purportedly representing the bounds of the human.[1] And, much to rhetoric's dismay, autism routinely calls into question ideas related to intent, feeling, sensation, selfhood, rationality, and thought. As I suggested in chapter 1, autism's liminality fuels its popularity within clinical and popular discourses. Its mysteriousness, its increasing diagnostic prevalence, its subjects' so-called otherworldliness— these constructions give life to urgency, to panic. More people are becoming autistic; more people are becoming nonpeople.

And so, what does *fuck you* look like on the part of nonpersons? How and what can we claim as autistic rhetorical practice when rhetorical practice is reserved for the human?

And yet, few scholars will overtly claim that autistics are arhetorical. At times their arguments about rhetoricity are implicit or are matters of degree. Autistics, in this regard, are demi-rhetorical in that we are claimed to possess some residual (read: normative) capacity for rhetoric, yet these remnants of our disability infinitely render us effectually non-rhetorical. The pathological part consumes the whole, as if metonymy met Pac Man. Sometimes autistics lack a theory of mind in its entirety; sometimes autistics have an impaired theory of mind. Or, put another way, to invoke the rhetorical framework offered by George Kennedy: some autistics bear no capacity for rhetorical energy, and other autistics (read: the so-called milder ones) have some residual rhetorical energy, or perhaps the ability to pretend as though they have rhetorical energy (even if, in reality, they've got none).[2] In such constructions, autistic *fuck yous* do not indicate community resistance, or even understandable individual response to systemic prejudices about neurological disability. Rather, *fuck you* is an autistic symptom, not a rhetorical practice: *Fuck you* is emotional dysregulation. It is a meltdown. It is affective disturbance. It is lack of awareness about context, audience, environment. It is disruption. It is aggressive stereotypy, or echolalic hostility. Whatever *fuck you* is, it requires mediation.

The interdisciplinarity of autism studies, and cognitive studies writ large, imposes challenges on the language we use to talk about autism. A neurologist talking about theory of mind modules may not be talking about rhetoric, and yet is most certainly talking about rhetoric. Theorizations of rhetoricity are endemic to autism research, even if not so named. My reading and writing of rhetoric in this project, then, is a means of ferreting out constructions of the (non)rhetorical. When a clinician speaks of cognitive empathy, where does rhetoricity lie? When an educator writes about early intensive behavioral intervention, where does rhetoricity lie? When an autistic moves among objects and gazes through humans, where does rhetoricity lie? There is a certain sophistry to these questions, for rhetoric resides as much as it deceives.

Of course, my argument, if I were to pose one, is that autism is a rhetoric, that autistic people are profoundly rhetorical, and that autism presents means and motive for reconstructing and dismantling the bounds of rhetoric. In making such an argument, however, it is important to both surface and dismantle the logics that bind autism to non-rhetoricity. However paradoxical these logics might be, they guide policy decisions, dictate the ways in which autism and autistic people are culturally figured, and impose profound consequences on autistic lives. Moreover, the horrors that attend arhetorical logics cannot be separated from logics purposed to subjugate and tame the queer. Autistic people have long identified with or as the queer—whether by means of sexuality or gender identity, or by means of a queer asociality that fucks norms. Neuroqueer rhetorics recoup the logics of symptoms and transform them into logics of (non) practice—orienting, moving, sidling, cripping, verbing that which is beside.

In this chapter, as well as this book more broadly, I am actively negotiating what I mean by the neuroqueer, or the relationships between the neurodivergent and the queer. I have been, until this point, evasive and resistant toward a concrete definitional—in large part because, I believe, autism's queerness maintains its power through its refusal to engage the social—the socially defined, the socially contingent, the socially causal. This isn't to say that autistic people are never social, or that we never import, practice, or rehearse the logics of prosocial bodies. Rather, I mean to suggest, following Rachel Groner, that "all people with ASD are queer and, simultaneously . . . there are no people with ASD who are queer."[3] Here, Groner is calling upon one of the paradoxes that structure neuroqueer life. On one level, autistics are of necessity queer because ours is a condition that defies sociality. Without a social compass, autistic people purportedly fail to acknowledge others, fail to recognize that other humans have their own thoughts, beliefs, and desires. As such, autistic people theoretically hold little to no referentiality with regard to gender and sexuality, with regard to any norms of any kind. Ours is disorientation rather than orientation. Our relational capacities are queerly configured and queerly practiced. And yet, because of our neurological queerity—our bodyminds mechanistically will us toward the socially aberrant—we are not really queer. If autism makes us do it, do we have the capacity to identify (our selves or our practices) as anything but pathological? To be neuroqueer is to strive toward the becoming of being neuroqueer. Autistics never arrive. These are the ways in which we are demi-rhetorically placed.

Of course, one of the radical potentialities of queer rhetorics is their refusal to be contained. Karen Foss's exhortation that queer rhetorics embrace a "both/and" suggests that such rhetorics both are and are not rhetorics.[4] Although a both/and positioning intimates that queer rhetorics occupy between spaces, queer rhetorics might be better conceived as a multiplicity of interstices, as categories that require definitional confluence as much as they require self-destruction and annihilation. These are the entelechies of which Byron Hawk speaks, in which the neuroqueer gestures toward "multiple lines of flight, where an entelechy is broken into and redirected toward unforeseen paths."[5] Take that, developmental milestones.

As we are well aware, logics that seek to delimit the neuroqueer, to render it passive and ineffectual, dominate public discourse. In this chapter, I direct my focus to one such potent strand in public discourse, a strand whose edges bleed across the scientific and therapeutic—that of applied behavior analysis, or ABA. In particular, I examine the rhetorics that attend ABA, most especially ABA's contention that queerly deviant subjects require intensive rhetorical intervention. While some of the work of this chapter concerns therapy sessions themselves, my claims in this chapter are not rooted so much in the exegeses of sessions but rather in the rhetorical aims of ABA as a discipline, writ large. This discipline has been codified as many things, depending on source—as a science, a methodology, a systemic approach, a suite of therapies, a tradition, a political lobby, and a body of research.[6] Whatever one chooses to call ABA, it is evident that ABA's influence is broad and, like any field, has many shades, nuances, and differences in how it is both theorized and executed.

Quite detestably, it is this problem of nuance that has left ABA's many rhetoricisms virtually untouched in academic discourse. One exception is Alicia Broderick's groundbreaking "Autism as Rhetoric: Exploring Watershed Rhetorical Moments in Applied Behavior Analysis Discourse."[7] Broderick positions ABA as an "autism discourse community," a community that employs "increasingly deliberate, pervasive, and skillful use of rhetorical devices" in order to gain rhetorical legitimacy as both a science and therapeutic approach.[8] This quest for legitimacy thrives in large part, Broderick observes, on its parental fan base. Parents came to view ABA as that which kept their children from being institutionalized—rendering any autistic arguments against ABA as misunderstandings about the actuality or substance of what ABA indeed is. Following Broderick's claim, we might declare that ABA's discourse isn't known for its provocativeness or multiplicity but rather for its quest to contain, tame, and redirect the neurologically queer. I am suggesting that ABA is rhetorically and thereby materially violent toward all things queer.

As I describe later, arguments against ABA are often met with the following response: "That's not real ABA." Barry Prizant, for example, attempts to redirect such arguments by differentiating between traditional and current ABA (which, despite creating another dichotomy, fails to answer the question of what, exactly, makes for ABA's realness or authenticity).[9] However, all variations of ABA—whether deemed good or bad, real or fake, traditional or contemporary—find their derivations in certain key topoi, positions, and motions that both launched the field and continue to fuel its plurality of iterations. It is from these topoi (recovery, environmentalism, and surveillance) that I launch my rhetorical critique: determining not only how ABA works rhetorically, but the ways in which ABA renders neuroqueer people effectively arhetorical. To claim that ABA works rhetorically is also likely to generate contentious response from those who study or practice applied behavioral sciences. After all, behaviorism's strengths and efficacies are supposedly borne out of their (pathological?) drive for objectivity, and rhetoric is anything but objective, what with it being mere and tricky. Applied behavior analysis works because it doesn't assume; ABA works because it outwardly claims no value system, other than application of scientific learning principles in naturalistic environments. But like any valueless system of applied study, ABA's values are many. This, I believe, is where rhetoric must enter. Applied behavior analysis compels rhetorical scrutiny, for ABA is a theory of rhetoric unto itself.


Practicing Caution

Given ABA's centrality to contemporary autism treatment and research, this is a difficult chapter to write. As I noted earlier, this is, in part, because ABA is difficult to define yet is overwhelmingly embraced. Clinicians sing its praises. As an autism therapy, it is recommended by innumerable medical, psychiatric, and educational establishments, and it is practiced in spaces ranging from the clinical to the domestic.[10]

But so too is ABA an underdog story. As I explore more in depth in my discussion of ABA's recovery fixation, parents were among ABA's first adopters, long before any credible or credentialed medical organization recognized its supposed efficacy. Its beginnings were initially represented by psychoanalysts and other academics as an evil, a behaviorist methodology that supposedly transformed humans into little more than dogs, machines, or automatons. Applied behavior analysis and similar behaviorist frameworks faced critique not only from clinicians who held dear their psychogenic frameworks but from literary critics, philosophers, linguists, and educators, including Kenneth Burke, Maurice Merleau-Ponty, Noam Chomsky, and Jerome Bruner. Parents of neuroqueer children championed its successes. ABA's earliest proponents, chiefly Ivar Lovaas, claimed that ABA was responsible for mass deinstitutionalization as well as prevention of queer suicide, locating his approach squarely within the rhetoric of disability rights. Parents of affected children formed lobbies and political organizations, wrote books and opened residential schools, returned to college and became the very experts they despised. This is ABA: a beloved, hard-won, data-driven, unquestioned good for neurodivergent children. How to define its rhetorical malevolence?

Parental lobbying for ABA is but one advocacy strand that has led to its widespread coverage in health insurance plans across the United States. In addition to mass-clinical recommendations in favor of ABA's efficacy, major autism organizations have called for ABA's costs—which can number in tens to hundreds of thousands of dollars per year—to be covered by insurance. Autism Speaks, in particular, has launched a number of such lobbying measures under its Autism Votes project. So-called autism parity bills require insurance companies to provide coverage for ABA, because ABA is among the few evidence-based interventions approved for autistic individuals. What has resulted, then, from ABA's insurance-reimbursement hegemony are a number of eclectic therapeutic methodologies (such as floor-time modalities, occupational therapy and sensory integration therapy, cognitive-behavioral therapy, speech therapy, and so on) having become suddenly repackaged and sold as ABA. As a result, a number of autistic children who are receiving ABA may not actually be receiving ABA. Thus, upon encountering my rhetorical condemnations of ABA in this chapter, there is a good chance that a reading parent will think, "But that's not what my child went through!" It very well might not be.

In addition to eclecticism at the level of methodology, there is also eclecticism at the level of the therapist. A therapist may employ mixed-methods interventions, modes that are partly based on behaviorist principles and partly tailored to the desires of the family or the desires of the therapist. Thus, in essence, many autistic children undergo a less-intensive, choose-your-own-adventure version of ABA. And yet, for as many experts who may refer to such eclectic or modular approaches as "watered-down" variants or "ABA lite," there are as many who claim that modularity, spontaneity, and flexibility according to rhetorical situation are endemic to ABA (i.e., wherein ABA lite = the real ABA).[11]

But for all of my discussion of ABA's rhetorical moves and motives, I have yet to give a concrete description of what it entails on the ground. Applied behavior analysis is a data-driven, antecedent-behavior-consequence model of social interaction. Behaviors are preceded by stimuli, and they are reinforced through consequences. As such, ABA concerns itself not only with mapping the life course of a given behavior, but with instigating and charting its stasis and change. To accomplish such behavioral momentum, ABA calls upon ritual and unending surveillance of the neuroqueer subject: a whole team is employed in the intervention process, recording and observing the autistic child's observable behavior (and what precedes it) by means of videotaping, written logs, and invisibility behind two-way mirrors. State recommendations for ABA's duration average forty hours per week. This level of intensity can only be maintained when all people in the child's life are trained as cotherapists. Parents, siblings, teachers—anyone and everyone becomes responsible for capitalizing upon each moment as a teachable moment. And, crucially, these moments recur in varying approximations, thriving on behavioral repeat.

Applied behavior analysis operates under behaviorist and operant principles. It is not concerned with a condition's etiology, or even with a condition, but is rather concerned with reinforcing and extinguishing antisocial (or inappropriate) behaviors. It accomplishes its behavioral shapings by breaking down human behavior into the tiniest of parts, and repeating desired parts over and over and over, rewarding desired response and punishing or ignoring undesired response. These are called discrete trials. A discrete trial might consist of getting a child to touch her nose. The therapist might begin by grabbing the child's hand and placing it over the child's nose while saying, "Touch nose." Later in the trial, the therapist will endeavor to get the child to respond this way on her own. If the child cannot mirror her therapist's body language, the therapist will work with the child to create approximations of the motions of nose touching—breaking down the action into a series of smaller steps that seem to have infinite regress, rewarding the child for her not-quite-but-almost-there imitations of an arm leaving the side of the body, of an arm flaunting into the air, of an extended finger, of a bodily brush that comes close to the nasal region. This—termed shaping, in behavioral lingo—eventually results in the refining of nose-touching motions, to the fading of reinforcements or the introduction of aversives, depending on the child's level of compliance with the therapist's commands. When the therapist says, "Touch nose," and the child finally complies, the child will be rewarded, usually by a small piece of food, like a single M&M or gummi bear, followed by praise like, "Good touching!" To borrow a phrase from autistic author Sparrow R. Jones, ABA therapists take what children love and "hold it for ransom."[12] A lunch is never fully, wholly a lunch: it is a series of discrete lunch pieces to be fed as reward over a series of trials. In the early days, for instance, Lovaas recommended that parents forgo feeding their children prior to therapy sessions at his UCLA clinic.[13] Food is a motivator for compliance.

If the child fails to touch her own nose—say, she touches her eye, or spits at the analyst, or tells the analyst to go fuck herself, or simply does nothing—the therapist may ignore the child. She may physically turn her body away and avert her gaze, no matter how despondent or confused the child becomes. If the child still fails to comply after numerous and subsequent trials, aversives might be employed. Aversives, in a word, are a kind of punishment or negative stimulus. They range in their severity. In Massachusetts, for example, electric shock is routinely employed on minor children at the Judge Rotenberg Educational Center, a residential school that houses neurodivergent students and fits them with backpacks containing electroshock equipment. Shock has (thankfully) grown less common, and the center's practices have been condemned as torture by the United Nations, but aversives have deeply abusive and ever-present legacies in behavioral therapies. Physical abuse in the form of spanking or belting were featured in the scholarly accounts of ABA during the 1970s. Present-day aversives variously take shape in the form of time-outs (often in closets, cells, or segregated rooms), Tabasco sauce on one's tongue, spray bottles filled with vinegar, forced proximity to a cold or hot surface, physical restraint, screams directed at the child, and so on. A number of disabled children, it should be noted, have died from restraint and seclusion practices at public schools in the United States. Depending on the therapist's treatment philosophy, failure to touch one's nose might result in any of these aversive consequences.

But aversives are not limited to those items termed aversive in the literature. Applied behavior analysis unto itself is its own kind of aversive. Its duration and intensity are all consuming. For the neuroqueer child, ABA is life. The "touch nose" discrete trial might be repeated for days. Or months. Or years. Typically, behaviorists do (and should) give up at some point if a child is not responding and move on to different trials or methods. And yet, the experience of many families suggests that ABA feeds on this length, intensity, and mind-numbing repetition, wherein a child's entire day, as Beth Ryan puts it, might revolve only around, "Touch nose. Gummi bear."[14]

Among the many behaviors that ABA aims to extinguish are echolalia, perseveration, and stereotypy—really, a vast swath of neuroqueer repertoires. Echolalia is the repetition of words and phrases; perseveration encompasses obsession with certain (often those deemed antisocial) topics, such as a young boy's communicated desire to wear jewelry, or an all-encompassing obsession with the birthdates of musicians from the Electric Light Orchestra; stereotypy, also called stimming or self-stimulation, refers to complex and often repetitive, embodied movements that are again deemed antisocial, such as hand flapping or femininely flexing an elbow. For the most part, none of these actions—or behaviors—is bodily harmful. Jumping while flapping one's arms does not hurt the neuroqueer child, nor does it hurt anyone around him. But the logics of harm that structure ABA are, again, concerned less with the child and more with the repercussions for larger social bodies, social bodies that ground their staying power on cisnormative and ableist ideals. As well, these particular neuroqueer moves are not only considered vital in a collective/autistic cultural context, but they likewise hold significance for autistic individuals. Perseveration is a kind of autistic inventional practice; stimming can be communicative or compensative; and so on. And yet—these are among the socially inappropriate behaviors that ABA seeks to extinguish, primarily because they mark the neuroqueer as noticeable, distinguishable, and deviant. Take, for instance, the following clinical commentary on the psychopathology of trans children from Rekers, Bentler, Rosen, and Lovaas: "Defensive mechanisms such as social isolation, withdrawal, and perhaps even anti-social acting out may be manifested."[15] In this statement, the authors describe the gender-variant child in terms that remarkably resemble how they describe the autistic—isolated, withdrawn, antisocial. These are the rhetorical exigencies for behavioral extinction.

Quite contrastingly, autistics describe ABA as autism's analogue of the cochlear implant. They view it as a kind of cultural annihilation.[16] As I discuss later, they have unfortunately few nonautistic allies in this. After all: if autistics have the capacity to pose arguments against ABA, we can only make those arguments because ABA or ABA-like experiences granted us the capacity to argue. But more than this, ABA has maintained its legitimacy through clever rhetorical maneuvering, claiming to recover subjects whose condition is culturally figured as "the worst thing that can happen to a family."[17] Recovering a child from autism wields different political and cultural power than, say, recovering a child from gender nonconformity or recovering a child from same-sex attraction—even if recovering a child from autism by default necessitates all of the above. While therapies that overtly claim to abolish all things LGBT are alive and well, such practices elicit considerably more visible protest and public scrutiny than do those that mitigate the autistic.[18] (Eradicating autism is, after all, an often-unquestioned moral good.)

If you come to this book with knowledge of autism or autism discourse, you have likely heard of ABA. In fact, much of my description thus far has been remarkably autism specific, in part because ABA has come to function as a master trope for autism. If you come to this book with knowledge of queer theory or queer identity, however, it is less likely that you will have encountered ABA under its current name: the ABA you are more likely to know has religiously morphed, present-day, into what is popularly called reparative therapy. It is for these reasons that I believe ABA requires rhetorical reorientation: it shapes (and wreaks violence upon) the lives of its many subjects, all in the name of normalcy. In the United States, ABA is recognized as the gold-standard autism therapy and is endorsed by numerous medical establishments.[19] Often, it is the primary (and sometimes only) therapeutic intervention that insurance companies will cover, in large part because of its supposed evidence base. Moreover, many state recommendations advocate for an amount of therapy equivalent to that of an adult work week, refashioning autistic childhood into a full-time job. And, finally, ABA functions both rhetorically and materially as a back door for the cis/heteronormative: its aims are to socialize—to straighten—every embodied domain of its neuroqueer subjects.

Importantly, as I mention above, autism and queerness are implicated in one another, are mutually sustaining—even if at times radically diverging—conceptions of what it means to demi-rhetorically move and defy. Both are conditions of and conditioned on countersocialities; both are modes of being-becoming characterized by a persistent failure to arrive. As Alison Kafer notes, "Queerness is something always to be queered," much like cripness is something always to be cripped.[20] In like manner, Jay Dolmage reminds us that "historically, these identity categories have been defined against yet through one another: homosexuality or nonnormative sexuality as some terrible disease or genetic flaw, people with disabilities as sexually inappropriate, over or undersexed, as 'freaks.' "[21] What ABA reveals for us, then, are the ways in which the autistic has been behaviorally and cognitively queered, much like the queer has been behaviorally and cognitively made autistic and countersocial. It is for these reasons that, in this chapter and beyond, I at times collapse the finer categories of autism or gender or sexuality under the broader banner of neuroqueer, as one means of acknowledging the impermeability of the so-ciorhetorical and the sociosexual. While each has points of divergence, all are predicated on the other. To be autistic is to be becoming queer, in potentially infinite manifestations. These multiple paths of flight, to channel Hawk, are not equivalent or stationary, but are rather always-unfoldings of rhetoricities that frustrate norms.

Accordingly, I contend that ABA maintains its distinction as a gold-standard autism therapy because it pathologizes (and thereby devalues) neuroqueer commonplaces (including, but not limited to, gesture, orientation, invention, and style). The methods that ABA promotes are many, but the three circulating topics I find most endemic to pathologizing neuroqueer rhetorics are recovery, environmentalism, and surveillance. These topoi not only guide methodology (e.g., how the analyst assesses or changes an environment, which behaviors a therapist chooses to reinforce or extinguish, the intensity and duration of prac-titioner observation), but they likewise promote sweeping ideologies about neuroqueer rhetoricity and rhetoricity more generally (read: normatively).

As a means of exploring the embodied impact of these topoi, I devote the remainder of this chapter to ABA's clinical history as a therapy used to so-cialize and normalize the neuroqueer. We can see these socializing impulses at work in ABA's attempts to defeminize gender-nonconforming children, much like we can see these socializing impulses at work in ABA's attempts to inculcate compliance in the autistic child. What unites the strands of the chapter—environmentalism, recovery, and surveillance—is the always-return to the social. Practitioners work toward building normative socialities through myriad rhetorical means, including childhood play, interpersonal interaction, language use, bodily comportment, and more. These logics of social compli-ance, as underscored by Luckett, Bundy, and Roberts, concern themselves with outward behavior almost to the exclusion of mental states or cognitive change.[22] As a result of ABA's external focus, the authors characterize ABA as "cosmetic potential," an entelechy in which behaviors are re/directed for "being more socially acceptable than the behaviors they replace."[23] In this regard, I suggest that ABA's queer(less) histories coterminously emerged as a therapy for autistic children because autism's supposed asociality has long been implicated in discourses in/around queer rhetorical behavior, most especially that which is made legible on the body. Apologists for ABA deny the rhetoricity of neuroqueer subjects while concurrently admitting that ABA overwrites its subjects' rheto-ricity with compliance. In this construction, queerness and/as autism are at best liminal cases, and at worst are constituted outside the bounds of rhetoric.

Practice is only practice when it is able, straightened, and compliant.

## Practicing at UCLA: ABA Meets the Neuroqueer

When Leo Kanner identified autism as a clinical category unto itself in 1943, he, like those who followed him, made speculations about its etiology. Kanner, and others who adopted a psychogenic approach toward treatment in the mid-twentieth century, believed parents to be a potential cause of their children's autism. And yet, unlike some of his contemporaries, Kanner thought autism was potentially improvable—in/organicity and mitigation did not strike him as mutually exclusive.

Nearly two decades later, behaviorism began to encroach on the autistic. In 1961, when Ole Ivar Lovaas started what would become his decades-long faculty post at UCLA, he did not come armed with an interest in autism. Rather, as he articulates it, he began with an interest in language. In a 1993 article published in the *Journal of Applied Behavior Analysis*, Lovaas provides a thirty-year retrospective of his work at UCLA.[24] In particular, he chronicles his decision to work with autistic children, as well as his induction into the burgeoning behavioral sciences contingent within the field of psychology in the 1950s and 1960s. Lovaas briefly characterizes behaviorist approaches as reactive moves against psychoanalysis and Freudian theory, standpoints that dominated psychology and linguistics at the time. The applied approach of his doctoral mentors, he notes, was strongly empirical, starkly anti-Chomskian, and unfortunately micro in scale. Lovaas observes, for example, that "behavioral psychologists seemed antagonistic towards those who addressed social problems" and suggests their antipathy toward social- and macro-oriented projects stemmed from a radical disconnect between "theory and empirical observations" at the time.[25]

Lovaas and other emerging scholars represented a data-driven turning point: he and his colleagues located their interests in large questions, large problems, all primarily social in nature. For Lovaas, his question-problem revolved around language, indebted in large part to Skinnerian thinking on verbal behavior.[26] In particular, he sought to understand the relationships, if they existed, between verbal and nonverbal behavior: whether and how changes in one domain impacted, mutually constituted, or socially reinforced the other. How do humans develop language? How does language evolve, and when, and where? In order to unearth such dynamics, Lovaas required research subjects in whom he could both observe and control developing language. Upon arriving at UCLA, it became evident to him that autistic children represented such a population.

But more than verbal language or verbal behavior, I would argue, Lovaas sought to understand and control rhetorical behavior. That is, Lovaas sought subjects who presumably lacked a sociality (or, at best, possessed a deviant one) so that he might foster rhetorical capacities from the ground up. By 1965, when *Life* magazine profiled Lovaas's work with autistic children at UCLA, Lovaas was well into spearheading the first of his long-term, applied studies on behavioral interventions with autistic children.[27] Titled "Screams, Slaps, and Love: A Surprising, Shocking Treatment Helps Far-Gone Mental Cripples," the *Life* article sensationalized the aversive components of these interventions. The first page of the spread featured two enlarged images of UCLA researcher Bernard Perloff screaming and angrily gesticulating in the face of Billy, an autistic child, presumably as punishment for engaging in an undesired behavior. A subsequent page showcased a series of images of Pamela, another autistic child, fitted with electrodes on her back and standing barefoot on a floor lined with metallic strips. Lovaas had taken her to the room because of her refusal to engage in her "lessons." In the first image, Pamela stands in the room and stims; in the next image, a switch has been flipped, and she writhes as the electricity pulses through her body. Noted the authors, "She [Pamela] read for a while, then lapsed into a screaming fit. Lovaas, yelling 'No!,' turned on the current. Pamela jumped—learned a new respect for 'No.'"[28]

In later writings, Lovaas would come to downplay aversives, defending their use only in the most dire of circumstances, such as injury of self or others. By the time Lovaas had begun working with a different cohort of autistic children for the 1971 Young Autism Project, aversives were supposedly rarely employed.[29] Nonetheless, as Chloe Silverman remarks, the punishing protocols of ABA quickly became its most well-known and controversial talking points up through the late 1980s, when the Autism Society of America, which had previously supported aversives, released a statement against their use.[30] But for Lovaas and other behaviorists, I'd argue that aversives represented (and still presently represent) one among many mechanisms that sought to modularize, manipulate, and ultimately predict instances of rhetorical behavior, or the many motions required to constitute a normatively rhetorical action. Such behavioral motioning mirrors that which Kenneth Burke routinely decried throughout his scholarly oeuvre, wherein the behaviorist scientistically reduces symbolic action into nonsymbolic, discrete, and automatonic movements. These movements are not only mechanistic and rigidly conditioned; they also institute fixed positions from which the developmentally delayed can never escape. Shaping behavior is a processual and never-ending endeavor, and in this way behaviorism presumes that becoming straight or nondisabled is an always-becoming, a never-arriving, a forever-rehabilitation. Burke's warnings about behaviorism's roteness and antifuturity bear particular relevance, then, to aversives and other means of rhetorical and social control. Writes Burke, "But when we analyze behavior in the strictest sense, 'expectation' does not exist. For expectation involves a future, whereas behavior can only be observed in the present. Behavioristically, a state of 'expectation' is identified with a set of neuromuscular conditions *now*."[31] In the instance of aversives, Lovaas and others employed them to extinguish unwanted behaviors, as well as to in-build consequences to what they perceived as a specialized, prosthetic, and rehabilitative environment for neuroqueer children. If neuroqueer children failed to perform normalcy in typical environments, rationalized Lovaas, then surely modifications to the neuroqueer child's environment would motivate normative behavior. Despite beginning with language, these contingencies were employed across rhetorical and embodied domains, potentially shaping, as Lovaas claimed, an entirely new self.[32] In this regard, the potential of a prosthetic, specialized environment is the always-now—any change could result in neuroqueers backsliding into neuroqueerity.

A decade after the *Life* article hit newsstands, Lovaas again found himself profiled in a major trade publication—a spread in *Rolling Stone* alongside George A. Rekers, holding a newly minted doctorate from UCLA. This time, however, the focus had shifted from autistic children to gender-variant children.[33] Titled "The Gender Enforcers," the *Rolling Stone* piece chronicled Lovaas and Rekers's work with boys who were claimed to be effeminate in gesture, manner, and speech.[34] Operating concurrently with UCLA's Young Autism Project, the UCLA Feminine Boy Project (FBP) intervened in the lives of so-called effeminate boys perceived to be at risk for homosexuality, transsexualism, and transvestism.[35] Importantly, both projects were ABA projects, their primary differences being differences of categorization (feminine-perceived boys versus autistic children) rather than substantive difference (both cohorts were, as Lovaas characterized across the studies, grievously and socially impaired). The ultimate goal, then, of the FBP was to reinforce young boys' masculine-perceived behaviors by means of praise and reward while extinguishing young boys' feminine-perceived behaviors by means of aversive consequences (variously, by spanking, beating, or removal of love and affection). These behavioral moves were employed in service of rhetorically shaping effeminate boys to be indistinguishable from their more masculinized peers, much like the autistic children were being shaped in service of indistinguishability from their allistic peers.[36]

Lovaas served as principal investigator for the FBP and coauthored numerous publications on child sex-role deviance with George Rekers, who would later use his FBP contributions for his 1972 dissertation as well as the basis of his life's work. By 1982, Rekers had published two books—*Growing Up Straight* and *Shaping Your Child's Sexual Identity*—which marked a distinct shift in his approach toward straightening and normalizing the behaviors of gender-variant children.[37] Although Rekers had alluded to his devout Christian views on homosexuality in prior scholarship, in these books and subsequent works religious morality increasingly functioned as a centerpiece. Not only were behavioral therapies appropriate interventions because of the supposed "social stigma" and "psychological adjustment problems" that accompanied queer life; these interventions were likewise necessary because "sin is ravaging their [queer people's] lives."[38]

Perhaps unsurprisingly, Rekers is presently a staunch gay conversion and reparative therapy advocate.[39] Rekers cofounded the conservative Family Research Council and for years served on the board of NARTH, the National Association for Research and Therapy of Homosexuality. He remained active as both a researcher and an expert witness (primarily against adoption and custody cases that involved a gay parent) until 2010, when he made headlines for hiring a male escort from Rentboy.com to accompany him while he traveled.[40] Rekers's archived home page from 2010 features his ardent denial of these allegations (which Rekers describes online as "slanderous" and "misleading innuendo") but also reveals the extent to which Rekers believes in the rehabilitative power of behavioral therapy on neuroqueer subjects.[41] The page navigation features links to TeenSexToday.com (Rekers' former blog), as well as the Gender Identity Disorder Resource Center. At the top of the page, a text link entices site users to "Read what Professor George shared with his travel assistant about the Christian faith," none-too-subtly reinforcing Rekers's contention that queerness is a psychosocial scourge.

The discursive overlaps among therapeutic modalities employed on autistic and gender-variant children in the name of ABA are uncanny and chilling. Punishment, saturation, compliance, and routine surveillance are among the commonplaces of those who deem themselves therapists or early interventionists. Applied behavior analysis has been studied in many contexts beyond the neuroqueer, much like ABA existed as a field of study prior to Lovaas's engagement with it.[42] I have chosen to focus primarily on the UCLA projects and their followers, however, because the Lovaasian construction of socially appropriate norms not only permeates neuroqueer histories and futures—it profoundly delimits, ignores, and subjugates the possibilities and potentialities of a neuroqueer rhetoricity.

Accordingly, I argue that while, historically, neuroqueer subjects have been theorized as arhetorical by lay and clinical publics, these publics are now, contemporarily, using sociocultural models of disability as a means for acknowledging the existence of neuroqueer rhetorics, only to render those rhetorics as lesser and aberrant (and thereby not really rhetorics). As I make clear in chapter 1, these semi-hemi-acknowledgments support what might be termed demi-rhetoricity, or the idea that neuroqueer people possess infinitely halved gradations of rhetorical capacity, which renders them effectually non-rhetorical in numerous social domains. What marks ABA practitioners as somewhat distinct from their historical forebears, however, are their foci on the social environment in combination with detailed surveillance and goals of recovery. Whereas for Lovaas, sociality resides in the spatialities of observable and embodied behavior, for theory of mind and autism fractionation theorists, sociality resides in neural structures. Each takes on the opposing pole of a Cartesian duality, seeking to explain brain through behavior or behavior through brain—but both approaches hold the shared belief that behaviors change brains as much as brains change behaviors. I return to this normalizing of the plastic at chapter's end, but find it important to state that these constructions of brains, bodies, and environments revolve around the prosocial, around compliance with the wills of the body politic.

And so, it is these three topoi—environmentalism, recovery, and surveillance—to which I will presently direct our attention. Arguably, ABA draws upon numerous topics, tropes, and themes in service of training the neuroqueer in the arts of normative rhetoricity. As such, my focus here is far from exhaustive, and, indeed, these topoi are impermeable and sustain one another.

1 Environmentalism. Behaviorist discourse appropriates (and thereby raises questions about) the social model of disability, or the idea that inaccessible spaces create disability rather than bodily pathology. One of the key arguments driving ABA is that the environment needs to be changed for neuroqueer people. As in, disability and queerness cannot be reduced to questions of innateness or heredity in bodies, but are rather socially reinforced by means of environments that are only equipped for certain (read: nondisabled, heterosexual, cisgender) bodies.

2 Recovery. Behaviorist discourse employs the language of recovery when working with minor rhetor/ic/s. While behaviorism makes no claim of cure, it does make claims of optimal outcomes, lessened severity, and residual (as opposed to full-blown) disability. Recovery, then, is not the process of becoming straight or cisgender or nondisabled, but is rather the process of faking the becoming of normativity.

3 Surveillance. Without intense observation, ABA wouldn't be an analytic. Various technologies of surveillance and record keeping

are employed across many of ABA's rhetorical situations: in-person observation, observation by means of two-way mirror, audio or video recording, note taking, baseline charting, and other graphic measurements of behavior data, to name but a few examples. Surveillance in this regard holds numerous applications and meanings. Behavior is monitored so as to determine its function—what precedes the behavior, what in the environment potentially motivates the behavior, what kinds of reinforcing consequences appear to maintain or reward or stifle the behavior, and so on. But behavior is also monitored as a means of charting change or fluctuation, as well as determining behavioral stasis—or what, even, a child's given behavioral repertoire is.

In the sections that follow, I examine but some of the many domains, both historical and contemporary, in which these topoi recur in discourse on ABA. My approach is by no means completist, and ABA's canon and cast of characters are vast. Alicia Broderick's rhetorical analyses of autism discourse take up the figure of the watershed moment, wherein a given moment in ABA history becomes kairotic or exigent because it "includes and incorporates and revises and reinvents the seeds of the earlier moments in a variety of complex and innovative ways."[43] Following Broderick's lead, then, I engage these topoi not because they are temporally bounded moments or even the definitional elements of what might be termed ABA. Rather, these topoi require urgent consideration because they recur and permeate, and their targeted subjects are among the most vulnerable. As such, as I move across time and context, I identify rhetoricisms that work to maintain neuroqueer compliance, while I also draw upon neuroqueer individuals' sharp critiques of ABA's rhetorical machinations. When neuroqueer people's environments are strictly controlled, when neuroqueer people are forced into compliant behaviors in the name of recovery, when neuroqueer people are surveilled in every movement and moment—when these topoi become the lifeblood of neuroqueer being, such being becomes a way of unbeing. Such are the stakes of neuroqueer rhetoricity and ABA's attempts to abolish and delimit it.

Practicing Environmentalism

Those familiar with disability rights discourse will immediately recognize similarities between ABA's environmentalism and the rhetorics attending social models of disability. The 1975 "Fundamental Principles of Disability," authored by members of the U.K. Union of the Physically Impaired against Segregation (UPIAS), represents one of the most oft-cited historical documents in histories of disability activism.[44] What marked the UPIAS principles as noteworthy was their definitional work toward a social model of disability. Under a social model, societal barriers, segregation, obstacles to inclusion, and discrimination are what constitute disability. Moreover, social models of disability (especially U.K. models) generally make a distinction between disability and impairment.[45] Whereas disability is social construction (and a social oppression), impairment represents embodied experience and the phenomena that accompany having a neuro/physio/divergent body (e.g., the social constructions that create, sustain, and figure blindness versus the physicality of seeing or not seeing). The social model likewise differentiates itself from a medical model of disability, which primarily figures disability as a problem of individual bodies in need of cure or repair, as opposed to a construction rendered by social structures that center norms and able-bodied defaults. The medical model privileges, as Tom Shakespeare notes, "the dominance of medical approaches and of medical experts."[46]

Typically, in describing the social model of disability, scholars and activists alike call upon the figures of the ramp and the curb cut. If stairs present the only entry point into a building, then disability isn't located in the person who arrives at a staircase in a wheelchair; rather, disability in this instance is a relic of inaccessible design, in which the stairs disable potential users. Curb cuts operate on a similar principle. Without them, sidewalks have a larger propensity to disable pedestrians—whether traveling via wheelchair or with luggage in tow. The social problems of disability, then, are not problems of brains, tissues, or bodies, but are rather societal infrastructures, material and conceptual, that privilege specific embodied and enminded experiences of the world.

These emphases on social infrastructures and material change—where society imposes more disabling obstacles than does one's physical/mental existence—is central to the design of the social model. As James C. Wilson and Cynthia Lewiecki-Wilson contend, "Disability studies seeks to advance the cause of the disabled and promote social change by analyzing the present social formations that contribute to maintaining the walls of exclusion."[47] Thus, as a field, disability studies by and large regards disability as a social construct vested in bodily and material reality: discourse structures disability to the extent that it has material effects, traversing almost every level of political, educational, economic, and relational infrastructures.

There have, of course, been numerous critiques of the social model, namely its refusal to engage thoroughly the materiality of disabled embodiment or enmindment. While Shakespeare and Watson acknowledge that the refusal

to engage is not so much a denial of materiality as a strategic focus on secur-
ing civil rights and services, they argue that social model rhetorics perpetuate
"straw man" ideas about the body not mattering to disability, thereby reducing
discourse on disability to harmful dualisms.[48] Jay Dolmage, Nirmala Erevelles,
Robert McRuer, Margaret Price, Tobin Siebers, and Wilson and Lewiecki-Wilson,
among many others, have likewise appraised the social model's shortcomings
and exclusions, which work to delimit conversations on pain, distress, citizenship, material conditions and circumstances that include and extend beyond the
body, and disability's implication in neoliberal discourses, as well as the racial
and gendered dimensions of disability's construction and lived embodiment.[49]

As a strategic intervention, the social model (or perhaps more accurately
phrased social models, plural) continues to predominate in disability studies as
an academic field as well as in disability rights activism more generally. Many
of the gains made in disability rights and community participation have arguably come into being because of the social model. Significantly, the locus of
burden—a loaded word in disability circles—is shifted from problemed bodies
to systemic ableism and societal oppression. In the autistic culture movement, for example, the social model occupies a profound rhetorical presence.
Organizations such as the Autistic Self Advocacy Network (ASAN), the Autism
Women's Network (AWN), and the Autism National Committee (AutCom) work
from the discursive repertoires of social justice and civil rights, advocating not
only for service provisions and community living supports but also working
from the model that autism is a culture unto itself, a culture that is not only
socially created as a disability but is a countersocial way of being, communing,
and communicating.[50] Importantly, despite my social-model phrasing in the
previous sentence—that autism is socially created as a disability—none of the
aforementioned organizations, all of whom agitate for neurodiversity and radical social acceptance, believe that autism is immaterial, or is merely a matter of
linguistic fiction created by men in white coats with hierarchy fetishes. AutCom,
for instance, is among the few organizations that serve and are primarily led by
autistic individuals who are nonspeaking. Numerous autistics have narrated
lived experiences of autism that painfully intersect with sensory overload, self-
injury, or mind-body disconnections (where a given body part enacts its own
intentions, to the chagrin of the autistic rhetor's wishes).[51] In sum, autistic
politics regards the social model as the rhetorical mechanism that contributed
to mass deinstitutionalization, as the series of arguments that enable an autistic person to argue for the validity of her life and way of being in the world.

The social model of disability continues to undergo robust retheorization
within the field of disability studies, enduring ever more proliferations—and

contestations—through engagements with critical race theory and queer theory.[52] Let us recall, from chapter 1, Fiona Kumari Campbell's contention that what disability studies now requires is an antisocial turn, a politics that refuses respectability.[53] In making this claim, Campbell rejects the idea that removing barriers can and should remove deviance (queer and crip alike). "Subverting ableism through a strategy of inclusive normalisation for marginal folk is a somewhat spurious claim," she maintains.[54] In the context of autism, we often see discourse on inclusion supported by appeals to ABA, which is hyped to promote inclusion by making the autistic less "freakish," to cite Cynthia Kim.[55] In this vein, Campbell asks, rather pointedly, "has sociality worked?"[56] Can the neuroqueer socialize without having been assimilated? (The answer, of course, being no. Allistics are the Borg.) Instead, Campbell envisions "cripped cartographies" in which the "anti-social enables the reclaiming of a disability style."[57]

The conversations on (anti)social models and disability culture movements are many, far beyond the gloss I have offered above. But these conversations remain important to ABA, in large part because ABA's rhetorical framings have capitalized upon disabled activists' work toward accessible environments. That is, ABA by and large stories itself as a metaphorical curb cut for autistic people, as an orthotic that renders the neuroqueer indistinguishable from the neuronormative. It is likely no secret that I believe behaviorist environmentalism to be egregious and co-optive, about as far from crip theory or neurodivergent culture building as one can get. Given what I have so far described of ABA, after all, it seems that, if anything, Lovaas and his colleagues would fit squarely within a medical or rehabilitative model of disability rather than within the realm of cripistemological social justice. Yet, among UPIAS's many fundamental principles in their 1975 charter, one particular social-model truism has remained hopelessly irresistible for ABA rhetorics: that "disability is a situation caused by social conditions."[58] For Rekers and Lovaas, the etiologies of childhood gender variance or autism were insignificant, for they believed that modifying social conditions by means of behavioral control would mask any traces of neuroqueerness. Neuroqueer subjects, being deviant, do not "learn well from the average environment because that environment has not been constructed for them."[59]

Of course, what distinguishes ABA's environmentalism from the environmentality of antisociality and crip culture is this: Whereas crip culture envisions disabled futures, ABA does not. Whereas crip culture makes meaning and use out of the differences that arise from queercripped embodiment or queercripped enmindment, ABA does not. Whereas crip culture rejects the discourses of rehabilitation and its remedial focus on individual bodies, ABA does not. With ABA, environmentalism is all inclusive: every moment, every space, and every person with whom the neuroqueer subject comes in contact all become refigured as prosthetic devices. The entirety of the world, the entirety of the neuroqueer spatial and temporal and interpersonal landscape—everything, everyone, and everyday is rehabilitation in action. Environmentality, by contrast, "is a transient time whereby our cripped selves rub up against biology, environmental barriers and relationality. Like queerness," Campbell writes, "the lifecycle refuses patterning."[60] In other words, neuroqueerness becomes a being-becoming through hyperrelationality with broader fields of experience. Practitioners of ABA agree with this perspective to an extent—but harbor the belief that this being-becoming is a deadening rather than an enlivening, is a force to be obliterated rather than engaged. Consequently, ABA tells us that the environment is what queers the autistic, and thus a whole temporal-spatial expanse must become prosthetic in service of recovery and treatment.

Despite their obvious rehabilitative scope, both the Young Autism and Feminine Boy projects marketed themselves as agents of environmental change as opposed to medicalized or embodied change. In *Teaching Developmentally Disabled Children: The ME Book*, a massive handbook accompanied by a set of VHS training videos for parents and therapists, Lovaas routinely exhorted the necessity of adapting neurotypical environments to suit the needs of autistic bodies.[61] In one such passage, Lovaas extolled the all-encompassing nature of what "environment" could potentially signify: "If a child's behavior is influenced by the environment in which he lives and learns, and since a child's environment is composed of several different settings (such as school, home, and neighborhood) then it follows that the child's total environment should be arranged to become therapeutic and educational, if the child is to make maximal gains in treatment."[62] The child's "total environment" indeed signified totality for Lovaas. This totality was to be realized through several means. Saturation, duration, and intensity stood chiefly among those means, and through this rubric, Lovaas addressed parents with the following: "With responsibility, the developmentally disabled individual takes on dignity and 'acquires' certain basic rights as a person. No one has the right to be taken care of, no matter how retarded he is. So, put your child to work; his work is to learn."[63] Or, put alternatively: it is the job of the neuroqueer to obliterate our queerness. In their observations of ABA-inspired methods at a local school, Eyal et al. report that "contemporary autism therapies . . . are fast-paced, intensive, requiring all of one's concentration and attention, hence are broken down into short durations. Their time is the time of work. 'Do your work' is the constant injunction we heard at the school for autistic children where we observed."[64]

If it is a neuroqueer child's job to undergo behavioral therapy, then a child's entire week is conceivably structured like a forty-hour work week, often with overtime. Moreover, what Lovaas had learned from his "first comprehensive study" on autistic children was that the child's learning environments needed to be as naturalistic as possible for the child to both retain what she learned and to generalize that learning to other rhetorical situations.[65] Lovaas's first cohort of autistic clients had begun seeing Lovaas in 1964 and had previously been institutionalized when they entered his UCLA clinic. Many of the autistic children in his care had come to him from unimaginably dire situations. In one case, a child had been semipermanently restrained in bed as a preventative measure for self-injury. He had been held captive in a four-point position for so long that his muscles had atrophied.[66] Upon learning the abuses and indignities these autistic children had suffered under institutional care, Lovaas suspected that many of the behaviors deemed autistic were more properly deemed institutional. (That is, state hospitals inspire so-called maladaptive behaviors unto themselves.) As such, his pilot study drew from these assumptions and the children received treatment in the UCLA clinic for at least a year each, sometimes longer. However, after the autistic children's time at UCLA had ended, Lovaas was crushed to learn that most of his child subjects had regressed to their pre-ABA behaviors:

> We worked under the belief that if we removed the children from their natural environment and placed them in an institutional setting, we would be able to obtain very accurate measures of the children's behaviors on a 24-hour schedule and better control all relevant aspects of their environment. Second, we thought that 1 year of intensive one-to-one treatment (2,000+ hours) would be enough and that treatment gains would last. When we discharged the clients to the state hospital from which they had come, they inevitably regressed. It was heartbreaking to observe Pam and Rick, who had gained so much with us, slowly but surely lose the skills they had acquired.[67]

Upon reflecting on his initial misconceptions with his 1964 cohort, Lovaas recalled that those children who were released to their parents, as opposed to the institution, appeared to have better outcomes and retained some of their behavioral gains. The laboratory could not become the home—but the home conceivably could become the laboratory.

And so emerged Lovaas's environmental philosophy, which might be better termed a kind of environmental immersion. Quite cannily, Lovaas and others would frequently draw upon disability rights discourses and famous disabled people as a way of rhetorically figuring ABA's immersive nature. Bernard Rimland, parent to an autistic son and eventual founder of the National Society for Autistic Children (which later became the Autism Society of America), routinely compared not only ABA but aversives such as electric shock to the successes of Helen Keller and Annie Sullivan. In a 1978 article in defense of both Lovaas and aversive methods, Rimland mused, "If [Annie Sullivan] had insisted on using only hugs and kisses, Helen would have assuredly ended up as a living vegetable—a hopeless, institutionalized, blind deaf-mute."[68] Lovaas too would routinely invoke the averted vegetable tragedy that for him came to constitute Helen Keller. In a 1973 article, for example, Lovaas and his coauthors concluded by asserting that ABA's learning principles were not new, but had rather been practiced in some fashion by figures ranging from Annie Sullivan and Helen Keller to Jean-Marc Gaspard Itard and Victor, the "wild boy" of Aveyron.[69]

As with many horrific things, Lovaas appears to have remained either unaware or unconcerned that one of Itard's aversive techniques involved dangling Victor headfirst out of a fifth-story window.[70] The defenestration was Itard's aversive response to Victor having a meltdown during a cardboard cut-out exercise.[71]

When Lovaas embarked on his later studies—with autistic and gender-variant children—the laboratory expanded to include both the clinical and the domestic. Realizing, too, that physical space wasn't the only environmental landscape in need of modification, Lovaas set out to determine how environmental control could prosthetically extend to include the people and objects that came to comprise a given environment. If the children required twenty to sixty hours of intensive therapy per week, it seemed impossible to staff those hours solely with trained therapists or graduate students.[72] In this regard, Chloe Silverman's *Understanding Autism* chronicles the ways in which parents have historically and contemporarily carved out autism advocacy roles, including Lovaas-style ABA.[73] As she notes, Lovaas enrolled parents as cotherapists, encouraging them to capitalize on every moment as a teachable moment. Eyal et al. likewise underscore Lovaas's ecological approach to autistic behavior, wherein "ABA becomes then a form of 'joint embodiment' in which the therapist, most often the parent, becomes a prosthetic device, an extension of the child's body, facilitating the child's communication and interaction with the social world."[74] More contemporarily, in discussing the ABA-influenced components of the Early Denver Start Model and its approach toward autism, Sally Rogers and Geraldine Dawson maintain an emphasis on rhetorical totality and the neuroqueer child's lack of access to neurotypical environs.[75] The authors suggest that "the nature of autism constricts learning opportunities, affecting every hour of the child's life and resulting in a greater and greater number of lost opportunities month by month and year by year. The young child with autism thus has far fewer experiences with which to construct his or her understanding of the people and events in the world."[76] Thus enter the parents, siblings, relatives, friends—anyone and everyone must be drafted into the role of cotherapist if the neuroqueer child is to shed her neuroqueer behaviors.

In their roles with the FBP, Lovaas and Rekers maintained a consistent ideology vis-à-vis precision and control of environment. Whereas the Young Autism Project recruited its participants initially via local hospitals, residential schools, and later, parental word-of-mouth, the FBP was marketed through the Gender Identity Clinic at UCLA and gleaned a number of participating families by means of a television advertisement. The clinic, having been founded by Robert Stoller in 1958, eventually switched hands to Richard Green, who would come to direct the project during Rekers's tenure as a graduate student and send referrals for behavioral treatment to Ivar Lovaas.[77] Green starred in the television spot and listed a number of warning signs of prehomosexual and effeminate behavior in young boys. And it was Green's presence on television that convinced Kaytee Murphy to bring her nearly five-year-old son Kirk to UCLA for assessment and treatment. Once there, Kirk, variously pseudonymized as "Kraig" or "Kyle" in the literature, was referred to Lovaas and Rekers for ABA immersion. The treatment period lasted ten months and consisted of discrete trials in the clinic and at home, where "parental attentiveness or disinterest was used to positively or negatively reinforce specific 'masculine' or 'feminine' behaviors, such as playing with boy-type or girl-type toys."[78]

About a decade after Kirk had undergone treatment at UCLA, Green conducted independent follow-up interviews with Kirk and his mother and published the transcripts in his book, The "Sissy Boy Syndrome."[79] During her conversation with Green, Kaytee intimated that what she had seen on TV inspired panic because the warning signs of homosexuality and transsexualism were apparent in her then four-year-old son. At one point, she expresses gratitude for the program, remarking, "Had he not been on the treatment reinforcement program telling him what was right and what wasn't right, why wouldn't he want to wear women's underwear or nightgowns or whatever as he got older? As far as I'm concerned, he wouldn't have known there was anything wrong with it until people started teasing him and hurt him."[80]

Unfortunately, however, Kirk had already been hurt, in a visceral and physical sense. In numerous articles, Rekers and Lovaas would detail the means by which they sought to train the queer out of Kirk. At UCLA, Kirk and his mother were sent into a playroom and were observed from behind a two-way mirror.

Once in the playroom, Kirk had opportunity to choose toys and costume accessories from two different tables—a feminine table (which housed dolls, purses, cosmetics, and tea sets) and a masculine table (which housed toy guns, race cars, airplanes, and soldiers).[81] Kirk's mother wore earphones through which she was given instructions by the researchers on the other side of the mirror. As instructed, when Kirk played with masculine-type toys, Kaytee would smile and compliment Kirk on his choices; and, when Kirk instead chose from the feminine-type toys, Kaytee would ignore him, physically turn her body away from him, and at times begin reading a book, as though Kirk weren't there.[82] Lovaas and Rekers note that Kirk was so distraught at his mother's behavior that they initially had to stop the experiment to allow him to calm down.[83]

At home, ABA's punishments were harsher. Rekers and Lovaas detail the lengths to which Kirk's parents had been trained as cotherapists, agents of reinforcement or punishment who were always on alert regarding the gendered nature of Kirk's behavior. While Kirk's masculine behavior continued to be rewarded by parental affection and praise, his feminine behavior was met with physical beatings from his father, as well as the loss of attention and affection from his mother.

In later work, Rekers, Rosen, Lovaas, and Bentler would more thoroughly chronicle the behaviors that came to constitute feminine- versus masculine-type behavior.[84] Here the researchers called gendered behaviors "sex-role stereotypy"—the word *stereotypy* being a decidedly disability-specific term.[85] For effeminate boys, stereotypy incorporated cross-dressing, speaking in a high-pitched voice, breast-feeding dolls, and self-referencing with terms such as *fag* or *queer*, as well as postures that included limp wrist, arm flutters, hands on hips, or flexed elbows.[86] Again, in relating these embodied gestures, Lovaas and Rekers signal their all-encompassing concern with the prosocial. In this regard, the gender-variant child is as much autistic as the autistic child is gender variant: autism is metaphorized as deviance, a deviance so pervasive that it impacts all developmental and psychosexual domains of behavior.

In his work with autistics, Lovaas frequently deemed stereotypy as a problem behavior in need of eradication. His autism theorizations had clear carryover for the FBP. Stereotypy for Lovaas involved any embodied movement or vocalization that didn't hold social significance.[87] That is, if a behavior wasn't goal-directed toward allistic social or rhetorical conventions, it wasn't meaningful or desirable. More amazingly, Lovaas viewed stereotypy as nonfunctional because he thought it to be purely asocial and reinforced by its self-stimulating properties. Wrote Lovaas, "The main consequence of the behavior is more of the same behavior."[88] So, an autistic child rocking hir body or a gender-variant child flexing hir elbow represented behavioral motions that held no social significance merely because they were socially aberrant. That the behaviors persisted in these children, Lovaas reasoned, was because the children found them self-soothing or self-regulating—they were internally motivated, and because the intentionality of these behaviors was unobservable to an analyst, their meaning or function for the neuroqueer children was thereby irrelevant.[89]

Like all behavior, stereotypy is viewed by ABA as environmentally contingent. The ecological rhetoric surrounding stereotypy, and other behavior, routinely invokes the figures of topography and repertoires. Behavior can be mapped; repertoires are founts from which behavioral resources can be assayed or drawn. And indeed, this is rhetorical language. Repertoires especially harbor inventive resonances, suggesting that behavior is ABA's equivalent of topoi, tropes, or commonplaces. Topography likewise sounds like an analogue for the body of rhetoric, or the rhetorical body, the vast plane from which actions and practices might be forged. And yet for the neuroqueer, for Kirk Murphy, claiming rhetoricity wasn't an option. Untouched by intervention, their rhetoricity was, at best, an asocial or antisocial rhetoricity. And even after having undergone intensive intervention, their rhetoricity was still effectually none, as I will discuss momentarily. For neuroqueerness resides.

Thirty years after Green's The "Sissy Boy Syndrome" was published, the Murphy family felt very differently about the FBP and the interventions used on Kirk. No longer did Kirk's mother view the FBP as a much-needed preventative for her gender-nonconforming child. In 2010, they brought their story to blogger Jim Burroway of Box Turtle Bulletin, who composed a multipart series on the pain that Green, Rekers, Lovaas, and others had created for Kirk and his family. The story was later picked up by CNN and Anderson Cooper. This was the first time the family had gone public. It was the first time it had become known that the "Kraig/Kyle" in the research published out of UCLA was, in fact, Kirk Murphy, who, despite his ABA-ing, had come to identify as gay.

Kirk's mother and siblings had broken their silence because in 2003, Kirk had hung himself in his apartment in New Delhi. He was thirty-eight years old.

Practicing Recovery

The environmentalism of ABA represents a profound totality of rhetorical situation, one that transgresses the spatial, relational, and embodied. And it is this totality that draws the righteous anger of autistic adults. Some of these adults identify as ABA survivors, in the vein of the mad pride identification with the consumer/survivor/ex-patient (c/s/x) movement, while others use the moniker ex-ABA to invoke parallels with the (ex-)ex-gay. Others describe having gone through an ABA-lite or ABA-inspired regime, or having grown up with parents who, in the absence of clinical advice or formal diagnosis for their children, armed themselves with Lovaas handbooks and attempted a do-it-yourself approach on their kids.

Whatever their history, autistic people have long come to decry the hegemony of ABA, which preaches compliance and saturation while extinguishing their repertoires of neuroqueer practices and motions. As autistic researcher Michelle Dawson famously noted in "The Misbehaviour of Behaviourists," ABA dismantles "autistic people into a series of bizarre and inappropriate behaviors."[90] It is from this behavioral repertoire that analysts come to understand what, exactly, an autistic is—certainly not a person, in the words of Lovaas: "You see, you start pretty much from scratch when you work with an autistic child. You have a person in the physical sense—they have hair, a nose and a mouth—but they are not people in the psychological sense. One way to look at the job of helping autistic kids is to see it as a matter of constructing a person. You have the raw materials, but you have to build the person."[91] If we return to my opening narrative about the autistic book club, we can begin to glean some of the trappings of ABA (or ABA lite) that rhetorically structured an environment that has, for me, come to characterize that moment in time. Recall, for instance, that a social skills outing of eleven autistic adults seemingly required a presence of four allistic moderators. Recall too that the purpose of this book club was therapeutic: we were not there to meet and discuss a book; we were there to practice the art of socializing, of mimicking allistic customs and behaviors such as voting, turn taking, small talking, eye gazing, and voice modulating. That *The Curious Incident of the Dog in the Night-Time* won the vote might be viewed as an unpredictable matter of circumstance; or, given the autistic-to-therapist ratio, it might instead be viewed as an analytic protocol designed to establish a baseline for the degree to which our autistic upset would be socially (in)appropriate. For practice is only practice when it isn't neuroqueer.

Whatever one might say about the book club, I'd suggest that, in many respects, the topos of recovery invisibly guided the dynamics of our meetings. After all, I had been recruited into this book club so that I might appear more social/ized, so that I might better approximate the rhetorical trappings of the neurologically typical. Of course, what behaviorist approaches to environment ignore are the tendrils of sensation and interrelation that invent knowledge and mediate autistic experience. In attending these book club meetings, I generally left feeling more autistic rather than less so, despite their prosocial intentions. The coalescing of stimmy bodies in a space filled with loud ambience—whirring of coffee machines, thumbing through pages, humming of fluorescents. The awkwardness of monologuing, the feel of the fold of stocking between my toes and shoe sole, the focused attention on the way our softcover books left an oily residue upon touch. As autistic writer Jeannie Davide-Rivera stresses, "Empathy for autistics is about relations."[92] While Davide-Rivera is partly speaking of human relations, she here registers something broader, an empathy that is rhetorically contingent on the more-than-human. Recovery, then, defers toward the curative impulse, toward remaking autistic relations into social prostheses. Recovery in this way is metaphorized as ecological, as creating neural and behavioral change through environmental means and control. In what remains of this section, I focus on the rhetorical significations that recovery embodies in ABA discourse, especially that which involves parents.

Recovery has long served as a trope for those who conduct research on minority rhetors and rhetorics. Feminist rhetorical studies, in particular, forwards recovery work among its larger aims. Other subfields within rhetoric and composition have taken a similar strategy, working to uncover rhetorical traditions that are feminine, queer, disabled, indigenous. Recovery is often construed as a historiographical project, one that involves "remapping" territory, geologically "assaying" the field for underrepresented rhetorical "elements," and "reclaiming" women and those deemed Other from within rhetorical history.[93]

But recovery, I submit, comes with rhetorical baggage. In particular, I am here concerned with both who does the actual recovering and who is said to be recovered. Recovery, in the historiographical sense, suggests that something or someone must be surfaced. This thing or person has been hidden from view, from broader public knowledge. In order to come into view, then, an intervention of sorts is required: someone must intervene, must unearth that which has been obscured or buried. Recovery, then, invokes any number of metaphors, none of which seems palatable in a disability studies project. First, recovery suggests an archaeological or anthropological project, one that has particularly colonial resonances. While feminist rhetorical scholars are often women recovering women rhetors, recovery efforts in other domains are often led by those outside the community/context/culture that is supposedly in need of surfacing. In other words, the privileged do the uncovering; the marginal are the recovered. These recovery dynamics are not notable merely because of scholarly positionality; indeed, there is often a discovery framework embedded within this recovery metaphor. In feminist rhetorical projects, territories may often be remapped more than they are unmapped, burying as many rhetors and rhetorical traditions as they exhume. Malea Powell and Angela Haas, for instance, call attention to the ways in which rhetorical

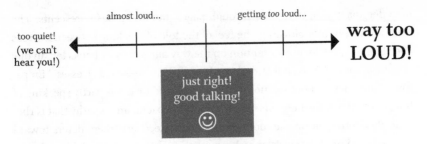

**FIGURE 2.1.** An example of a volume chart typically used on autistic and other neuro-divergent people in educational or therapeutic contexts. This particular chart features a horizontal line with arrows at both ends. The far left edge is labeled, in small font, "too quiet! (we can't hear you!)." The far right edge is labeled, in large font, "way too LOUD!" There are gradations in between each end, including "almost loud . . . ," "just right! good talking!," and "getting *too* loud." The "just right! good talking!" gradation sits in the middle of the chart and is offset by the color green (here gray) and a large smiley face.

scholars have appropriated indigenous knowledges and claimed such practices as novel, otherworldly, or new.[94]

As well, recovery has particular meanings within disability discourse. To recover is to no longer be disabled or ill. There is a certain ableism embedded in this term, at work in the concept itself. Recovery speaks of an aberrance becoming norm, of relinquishing defect in favor of the default. In autism discourse, recovery is often posed as the optimal outcome of ABA, wherein being indistinguishable from one's peers is the only object to which the neuroqueer should aspire. The recovery of ABA has all the trappings of rhetorical discovery: excavating the human from the prison of autism; remapping the autistic brain to forge plastic and flexible neuronal territories; affecting the queer by refusing to acknowledge its presence; making known the deviant by rendering it non-deviant. In the book club, we autistics recover from *fuck you* as a social worker whips out a volume chart, hastily points to TOO LOUD!, and then leads us in communal practice of indoor voicing.

Recovery, then, becomes both a means to rehabilitate and to discover, with both means operating from a curative register. When discussing recovery and ABA, it's important to discuss two watershed moments in ABA's history. Alicia Broderick's work on behaviorism identifies these moments as Ivar Lovaas's 1987 follow-up article on the results of the behavior modification program at UCLA, as well as published parental reports on ABA's potentially restorative powers.[95]

Lovaas's "Behavioral Treatment" retrospective on his Young Autism Project participants shook the autism world.[96] In it, Lovaas analyzed follow-up data from a sample of nineteen autistic clients. And, based on measures such as IQ and educational placement, Lovaas determined that nine—or 47 percent—of his clientele had "achieved normal intellectual and educational functioning, with normal-range IQ scores and successful first-grade performance in public schools."[97] In other words, Lovaas claimed that 47 percent were now indistinguishable from their peers. In other words, because of ABA, these children had been recovered from their autism.[98]

Even prior to the 1987 report, parents had been clamoring for their autistic children's placement in Lovaas-style ABA programs. However, the parent memoir that invigorated parental advocacy was Catherine Maurice's *Let Me Hear Your Voice*, in which the author claimed her two autistic children had recovered through intensive ABA.[99] Among other contributions, Maurice's memoir sedimented a long and unfortunate tradition of comparing autism to cancer and ABA to chemotherapy. Just as chemo represents a harm that is less harmful than cancer, so too does ABA legitimize the use of aversives on children whose "essence" has become autism instead of personhood.[100] Michelle Dawson's trenchant critique of behaviorists' misbehavior spares Catherine Maurice no punches, most especially on the subject of the cancer analogy: "The behaviourist behaviour of recruiting cancer has also found free reign in legal battles arising from the sheer expense of sustaining the autism-ABA industry. In the Auton case, Canada's ABA legal epic, the autism-equals-cancer statement of Madame Justice Marion Allan echoed and was echoed in the autism-equals-cancer variations of the petitioners and became a media staple. When a judge, or Dr Maurice, or any behaviourist yells cancer, any ethical consideration for autistic people obediently hurries to the nearest exit."[101] As Dawson aptly observes, the rhetorics of ABA routinely invoke imagery of death and fatality in order to make claims about the exigency of early intervention (i.e., before it's too late).[102] These rhetorics, as I noted in chapter 1, figure autism as nonpotential, as a perverse entelechy of death. Ariane Zurcher, parent to an autistic daughter, echoes Dawson's concerns about the ethics and efficacy of ABA's rhetorical self-positioning. In one such blog post, Zurcher contends that the first autism book she'd ever read was Maurice's, and her initial fear and impression upon her daughter Emma's diagnosis was that autism was a fate worse than death.[103] Zurcher recollects the intensive, forty-hour weekly sessions that Emma underwent, all with the diagnostic promise that she would be "mainstreamed" by kindergarten.

Yet when ABA resulted in no progress for Emma, Zurcher and her husband were blamed: "ABA was a solid, 'scientifically' backed methodology. It was spoken of as fact. We were the only variable."[104] At four years old, Emma was described as "manipulative" and "noncompliant" by her BCBAS (board-certified behavior analysts).[105] After all, recovery—or indistinguishability—is dependent upon the total restructuring of the autistic child's environment. Zurcher, now a prolific neurodiversity writer who has turned her blog over to Emma's authorial control, maintains that ABA is a flawed methodology. Importantly, she says that it's something she'd never consider using on her nonautistic son. She asks, "Why do we not use ABA for the neurotypical population?"[106]

It is important to note that most parents do not take Zurcher or Dawson's stance with regard to questioning the ethics of ABA. In fact, ABA's floating emphases on recovery have less to do with loss of neuroqueerness and more to do with the covering of neuroqueerness with normalcy. Neuroqueerness always abides, resides—and behavioral interventions work only to instill behaviors that appear neurotypical while obfuscating or shelving those behaviors that signal queerity. Such are the stakes of ABA's imposed rhetorical situation.

Strategically, ABA positions itself as being proparent (e.g., parents are not the cause of their child's autism) and yet—it heralds all the residue of psychogenic-era parent blame under the banner of environmentalism. Neuroqueer identity is dissected into discrete behavioral units that parents have opportunity to reinforce or extinguish—units that are either deviant or appropriate/prosocial. Parents are enlisted as cotherapists and require training. Without training, parents are likely to encourage the antisocial behaviors that render their child deviant in the first place. As such, the recurrence of deviant behaviors in a neuroqueer child may be used to suggest that parents have failed to do their job as cotherapists. And while floating signifiers about death and dying attend ABA's treatment of gender-variant and autistic children, so too does the threat of institutionalization remain a key argument for seeking the recovery that ABA offers. In this regard, institutionalization is still often read as parental failure. Applied behavior analysis compels parents to sacrifice—money, selfhood, relationships with their children—all in the name of normalcy.

Prior to Maurice's book and its instigation of cancer-death tropes, institution-death tropes drove parents of autistic children to agitate for ABA in the 1970s, including and especially the use of aversives. Surprisingly, the 1965 *Life* spread of Lovaas's "gallery of madness" did little to deter parents from seeking ABA services or electric shock devices. In 1993, Lovaas described how he came to use contingent aversives on autistic children in the 1960s—a tale that he had shared with desperate parents in prior years.[107] One of his clients, Beth, began self-injuring in his presence, banging her head repeatedly against the sharp corner of a steel cabinet. Lovaas reports that, out of instinct, he grabbed Beth, threw her over his knee, and "whack[ed her] on her behind."[108] When she began head banging again, he smacked her again. Here Lovaas defends his actions by claiming that he viewed Beth as he did any of his four children, and that if any of his children were to engage in self-injurious behavior, corporal punishment was how he would intervene. His rhetorical appeal to parentage is a deft—and dominating—rhetorical move: it calls upon ABA's continual appeals to environmentalism, to restructuring environments into prostheses, to building, from scratch, a kind of natural order.

In the intervening years, up through the late 1980s, parents echoed Lovaas and deemed aversives to be both lifesaving and cutting edge. In one such defense, Bernard Rimland compared aversives to tonsillectomies, remarking that critics of aversives "were perfectly willing to have the child 'gassed and cut with sharp knives' in the operating room, where severe pain and long-lasting discomfort would be inflicted and the risk of death would be run, when they believed that it was all being done for the child's welfare. How strange it was, then, that they should get upset at the use of far milder, far less dangerous, and far less physically damaging methods by Lovaas and his group, when again it was all being done for the child's best interests."[109] Another parent, Ruth Sullivan, proposed that electric shock represented an experimentally ingenious tool, asserting that, like lobotomies and megavitamins, shock represented a necessary evil.[110] Other parents, such as Rosalind Oppenheim and Francine Bernstein, willingly advertised the efficacy of cattle prods on autistic children, demurely referring to them as "tingle sticks."[111] In Bernstein's case, she sued and successfully settled with the Illinois Department of Mental Health / Developmental Disabilities in 1987 to include cattle prods in her autistic son's treatment plan; nearly two decades later, Bernstein again found herself in court when Illinois law barred the treatment and she took her son's disability service agency to court (and lost).[112] So entrenched was electric shock in the notion of recovery at the time that one behavior modification manual exhorted parents to contact a registered electrician before installing shock devices at home.[113] Indeed, Lovaas himself, along with his frequent coauthors, heralded aversives as preventatives of queer suicide.

Contemporary rhetorics of ABA curb talk of such viscerally aversive methods. With the exception of the Judge Rotenberg Educational Center, electric shock has fallen out of favor, as has the corporal punishment that came to characterize young children's experiences with the FBP. But as autistics, parents, and former analysts report all too frequently, punishment remains a vital part of ABA—whether it takes the form of screaming or taste aversions or the action of being forced to perform a discrete trial unto itself. Compliance with adult commands is the rote and substance of ABA. Meredith K Ultra, a former

**FIGURE 2.2.** In this drawing, two parents engage in discussion with two therapists about their autistic child, who sits on the floor flapping his hands. The mother whispers to the father that what's being described sounds like torture, and, in response, the father tells her to listen to the experts, lest their son be institutionalized. Meanwhile, one therapist holds out a waiver that requests parental consent for aversive consequences, as the other therapist glibly counters, "He'll thank us when he's older!" Courtesy Meredith K Ultra, *Ink and Daggers.*

behavioral technician, demonstrates via her illustrated blog, *Ink and Daggers,* the extent to which aversives governed her past treatment of autistic children. In one drawing, a young child fearfully cowers in his chair as a hand with a spray bottle closes in.[114] In another such drawing, two parents engage in discussion with two therapists about their autistic child, who sits on the floor flapping his hands.[115] The mother whispers that what's being described sounds like torture, and, in response, the father tells her to listen to the experts, lest their son be institutionalized. Meanwhile, one therapist holds out a waiver that requests parental consent for aversive consequences, as the other therapist glibly counters, "He'll thank us when he's older!"

In other respects, autistic bloggers have described ABA as a neurotypical inversion of drag, as a kind of allistic costuming that seeks to deperversify the neuroqueer. Recovery, then, functions as what autie-biographer Liane Holliday Willey terms "masking," or closeting.[116] For Willey, masking harbors gendered resonances, calling upon not only that which is autistic but that which is "sex-role deviant" (to borrow from Lovaas and Rekers). Passing as allistic was insepa-rable from passing as feminine—her "masking rituals" were a new kind of ste-reotypy, a stereotypy that borrowed from socially appropriate repertoires and served to present Willey to the world as a nonautistic woman.[117] I discuss this gender-checking self-governance in more detail in my section on surveillance, but it's crucial to note the ways in which these closeting behaviors both emerge from and extend beyond ABA's recovery topos. Lovaas and his collaborators pos-itively frame these violences as "expand[ing] behavioral alternatives available to the child."[118] In defense of these "broadened repertoires," the authors em-phasize the dangers of queer acceptance, queer community, or queer-affirming counseling, noting, "We find this line of argument to be totally unacceptable and irresponsible. Such an approach seriously reduces the possibility of choice for the individual, and actually unjustly narrows the person's options."[119] Op-tions, of course, are only options when they are straight. Anything queer is but an end point, a deadly residence.

Such therapeutic approaches dominate neuroqueer life. In my own expe-riences with psychotherapy, for instance, my disclosures of pansexuality are often bound with autistic behavior in the imagination of my therapists. As in, if only my autisticisms were in check, so too would my queer identity evaporate, and vice versa. Some of these notions are residual of ABA, some are residual of the extreme-male brain theory of autism, and some are residual of autism itself, wherein its unsocialized victims wholly lack concepts of gender, sexual-ity, and social propriety. As autistic blogger Kit Mead laments, "I feel like a fake queer. . . . Social interactions feel crushing."[120]

Girls, women, and nonbinary-identifying individuals are not only diagnosed later with autism than are cisgender boys, but many fail to be officially diag-nosed at all. Autism researchers continually debate whether autism's gendered ratios—ranging from 4:1 to 10:1 male-to-female—are a matter of biology or phal-locentric and ciscentric conceptions of developmental disability. Meanwhile, autis-tic women, as well as nonbinary and queer-identified autistics, frequently nar-rate their purported recovery stories as stories of closeting, masking, passing, fakery, burnout, and self-governance. Because many of these narratives come from individuals who were diagnosed as teens or adults, the connection to ABA might seem tenuous at best. And yet, their stories hold all of the trappings of ABA's rhetorical topographies, wherein the autistic is socialized through mind-numbing repetition, reward, and aversive consequence to act like a good little girl. As autie-biographer Elaine Day describes, "Social reciprocity, eye contact, and even mannerisms are actually physically taught to us from an early age in an attempt to make sure that we develop into appropriately mannered young women, and the simple fact is that it can make diagnosing AS [Asperger's syndrome] at a young age almost impossible."[121]

The invocation of recovery by ABA, to reiterate, is not total cure or eradication of neuroqueerness. As well, contemporarily, recovery's ideology often takes shape as discourse around "optimal outcomes" (OO) for autistic children—that is, children who undoubtedly harbor the "residual difficulties" of autism, but are nearly indistinguishable from their allistic peers.[122] In one such study of optimal outcomes, Deborah Fein et al. reported on thirty-four OO children who had a "clear documented history of ASD" yet no longer met diagnostic criteria.[123] Even in OO case studies, researchers make clear that autism's neural structures and autism's impulses remain—but those structural impulses are behaviorally covered by that which a social body deems more palatable: allism and cisnormativity.

I am tempted to suggest that, in an act of neuroqueer defiance, readers sound out the OO abbreviation of optimal outcomes as a self-stimulatory ooooo, and repeat the refrain loudly and impassionedly, preferably while in a public space. *Ooo, oooo, ooooo!*

The recovery of ABA is that of mimicry, of imitating normalcy and generalizing passing behaviors across rhetorical situation. Passing is considered the optimal outcome of behavioral intervention. This is what we, the neuroqueer, are entreated to practice. *Oo.*

### Practicing Surveillance

Practice decimates autistic bodies. In an impressive takedown of ABA, autistic author Sparrow R. Jones laments that ABA's promise of recovery is better conceived as an insurance-funded masquerade.[124] Applied behavior analysis equals forced compliance, total control, and constant surveillance. The neuroqueer subject cedes control of his privacy, his body, his very being, and his concept of self. Therapy's intention, he emphasizes, is to "break down a child's resistance and will."[125]

Will and intention hold a special place in ABA discourse, in that will and intention cease to matter. What a child intends or means is of no matter to behavior analysts, because intention and meaning are not observable, verifiable, or validatable phenomena. Intent isn't empirically visible in the way that flapping fingers are; nor is meaning as neutrally descriptive as fingers moving back and forth, or fingers thumbing the air, or fingers fluttering over the eyes of an autistic interlocutor. What finger motions mean cannot be contained in a graph, plotted as an average, or intuited by means of physical observation. However, finger motions can be contained, extinguished, reinforced, prompted, faded, shaped, or otherwise brought into compliance. The wills that matter are those of the analyst.

Lovaas often grappled with questions of meaning, intention, and mental states, as did many behaviorists in the Skinnerian tradition of operant conditioning. In *The Autistic Child*, Lovaas handled feeling and symbolic action according to behaviorism's reductionist tradition, describing a smile as "a behavioral topography which acquires meaning to the extent that it acquires stimulus properties over other behaviors and comes to be controlled by stimulus events which surround it."[126] The clinical coldness brought to bear over a facial expression often associated with joy or happiness is particularly striking. As well, Lovaas's indifference to the meaning of smiling bears little consequence because ABA doesn't aim to offer neuroqueer children new repertoires of meaning. To smile isn't to signify one's contentment; it's to comply with a behavioral and prosocial demand.

As the smiling example indicates, ABA takes seriously its modularity, its endeavor to dissect what might otherwise be thought the simplest of human behaviors into complex chains of discrete, interlocking parts. In order to accomplish such total control, the analyst body must function as the ever-watchful body; the prosthetic environment must function as the panoptic environment. If every moment is a teachable moment, and if neuroqueer children are to reach desired OO status, then their motively emanating bodies must cede to the eyes, hands, and shaping of the therapeutic moment, a duration that constitutes the whole of their neuroqueer lives.

The tyranny of surveillance is perhaps most observable in Rekers and Lovaas's work with Kirk Murphy at UCLA. Not only were Kirk's UCLA sessions observed by two-way mirror, but his home life was similarly recorded, with his parents and siblings participating in the surveillance of his gendered behaviors. At home, Kirk was monitored by means of a token economy, in which he earned blue chips for masculine-type behavior and red chips for feminine-type behaviors. While his blue chips were interchangeable for rewards and praise, his red chips served as currency for beatings from his father.

Token economies are but one of many surveillance technologies employed in service of behavioral therapy. Lovaas had gotten the idea for their use from Teodoro Ayllon and Nathan Azrin's *The Token Economy*, in which the authors presented results from a multiyear study on their use of a token system at Anna State Hospital.[127] Ayllon and Azrin echoed (and even cited) what Lovaas had come to believe about immersion, which involved "design[ing] a motivating environment based upon [operant] reinforcement theory."[128] *The Token Economy*, however, noted the "impracticality of continuous surveillance," due in large part to the minimal involvement of hospital staff as well as the failure of various recording devices (one-way mirrors, microphones, and video cameras) to capture accurate reports of patients' behaviors.[129]

Both the Young Autism Project and FBP surmounted the limitations of Anna State Hospital because of their domestic versus institutional setting. Here, parents and family could be the cotherapists, and could in turn catalog, chart, and annotate the activities of their neuroqueer children. In "The Governance of Gender Non-conforming Children," Jake Pyne provides an incisive and biting analysis of Rekers and Lovaas's familial outsourcing.[130] Both the token economy and the two-way mirror figure into Pyne's Foucauldian analysis of Kirk's treatment, wherein the tokens inculcate self-surveillance and the two-way mirror serves as the ultimate panoptic ga(y)ze. During the UCLA playroom sessions, for instance, Kirk was repeatedly told that while he could not see the examiners, they could see him. The rhetorical training of ABA might be best understood as a kind of "we are always watching you."

As Pyne notes, ABA's surveillance isn't only (hideously) remarkable for its capacity to observe, chart, and narrate individual acts. Rather, ABA at root espouses ideologies and technologies of normalization. What practitioners trip over themselves to call a "science of learning" is in fact a science of regulation and social control:

> Beyond the absurdity of this conception of gender, beyond the inherent misogyny, heteronormativity and cisnormativity, the technique itself is of interest. These are not examples of a bigot acting in ignorance, but a meticulous observation and systematic cataloguing of a set of bodies. This is not a project of simply imposing rigid gender norms, but of complete and total mastery, a sustained effort at seeing and knowing and an expanding repertoire of the technologies with which to do so. These children are not rejected for their difference, they are brought closer. Not a refusal to recognize them, but an insidious desire to acquire knowledge of them.[131]

It is worth noting here that the cataloging methods employed by Rekers in the UCLA study were not unique to its subjects, but rather are part and parcel of ABA proper. Applied behavior analysis is not uniquely ABA without recording, cataloging, or scrutiny of every discrete unit of the neuroqueer subject's behavior. In ABA parlance, this unfettered surveillance—this panoptic gaze—is termed *functional assessment*. Functional assessment, generally speaking, encompasses varying methods for determining the reasons behind—or functions of—so-called problem behavior. Functional assessment might take shape as descriptive assessments, wherein the behavior analyst, by direct observation of the neuroqueer subject and/or by means of (indirect) interviews (with parents, teachers, staff, the client), records copious amounts of observational data (often and preferably in naturalistic settings). By all means, the goal behind descriptive assessments is to record antecedent, behavior, and consequence, to chart a kind of narrative that precedes a behavior and the kinds of effects that follow the behavior.

Functional assessments might also take shape as functional analyses—and, in many respects, the panoptic gaze of Rekers most resembles these, for the rhetorical situations with which he presents Kirk are clinical, are decidedly of Rekers's own making. Functional analyses diverge from the descriptive in that they are experimental assessments. They entail situational manipulation: the idea is to instigate a problem behavior, to make a situation arise rather than merely to hope for its occurrence in the wild. As Robert LaRue notes, "functional analyses involve making systematic changes to the environment to evaluate the effects of different conditions on the target behavior(s)."[132] In the design of research studies, descriptive and experimental assessments may go hand in hand, with the descriptive assessment preceding and informing the functional analysis. As Rodriguez et al. suggest, interviews and observations in naturalistic settings provide data that can aid in the design of the experimental assessment, "increasing the ecological validity of our experimental analyses."[133]

Clearly, Rekers engages in the descriptive. He and his UCLA colleagues gather reams of indirect and direct data, data that precede his laboratorical exercises. He interviews the parents; he instructs the parents to remain on high alert at home, to keep diaries and logs of their child's behaviors, within and beyond the clinic's walls. What's more, Rekers and Lovaas routinely engage in the visual rhetorical exercise of charting baselines and changes in their child subjects' behaviors. In a 1974 discussion of Carl, another gender-variant child, Rekers, Lovaas, and Low provide a number of graphical figures that showcase when and how often eight-year-old Carl engaged in "feminine content, feminine inflection, and masculine content" in his speech patterns.[134] Among other items, the behavioral observations recorded and were coded for *feminine gesture manner-isms, play acting of a feminine role, feminine play with sister, masculine play,* and *masculine play with brother.*[135] These baseline and differential reinforcement data were gathered from both UCLA and home-based treatment sessions over a period of fifteen months, suggesting the depth and saturation of the examiners' behavioral cataloging.

But what's also important to note is the self-surveillance that ABA instills in its subjects. It is perhaps now a truism to say that ABA recognizes that neuro-queer subjects possess a kind of rhetoricity, albeit a demi-rhetoricity—we do things, we make the motions, we engage in behaviors, and we do these things because we find them to be, in some way, self-reinforcing. Meaning might at-tend these motions and doings and behavings, but the meaning that attends queerness is not the meaning that attends the social-symbolic. Applied behav-ior analysis cannot erase queer meanings because it does not concern itself with the etiologies of those meanings or the neuroqueer biocultural conditions that might come to inform those meanings. In other words: ABA doesn't remove the neuroqueer—it overwrites it. It succeeds in its overwriting because its subjects are primed to self-check, self-regulate, and self-doubt. And once subjects are thought to be capable of self-governance, their refusal to comply is viewed as willful, excessive, and unnecessary.[136] As autistic activist Kassiane Sibley elo-quently frames it: "Any and all traits of autism are due to moral failures and choosing to act different once you've been declared indistinguishable. Lovaas said you have no right to act bizarrely (this is one of the things that stuck with me from my reading of 'the ME book'), so when you choose to do so, you choose the negative consequences. Any 'distinguishability' and the way people react to it, is a function of your own faults."[137] These are the consequences of "broadening repertoires," of declaring neuroqueer futures worse than death, of believing that only allism can bring hope, communication, or community.

Coda: Practicing Plasticity

Contemporary rhetorics of ABA assert that ABA's methodologies are more than mere conditioning, much like ABA's therapeutic effects are more than mere closeting, scripting, or mechanization. Gender-nonconforming subjects don't merely appear to be masculine, much like autistics don't merely appear to be-have in a socially appropriate fashion. The change in appearance is effected by a change in brain chemistry. Neuroplasticity is ABA's newest rhetorical tru-ism, wherein ABA changes the brain. Jocelyn LeBlanc and Michela Fagiolini emphasize this particular truism, arguing, "The developing brain is remarkably malleable, capable of restructuring synaptic connections in response to changing experiences."[138] Whether discussed in clinical journals or in media accounts, ABA purports to change neural pathways, rewire neuroqueer brains, and ford synapses. The challenge of ABA is posed thusly: if autistic brains are rigid where allistic brains are flexible, then how might rewiring take place? And thus, Lovaas reenters the fold: repetition, intensity, work as life.

Importantly, even with its newfound rhetorics of plasticity, ABA does not claim to transform the autistic brain into a nonautistic brain, much like ABA doesn't claim to rewire queer brains into cissexual or heterosexual brains. Rather, the ABA mandate is to create neural pathways that result in normative-seeming behavioral profiles: we are not in-wiring straightness or allism, but are rather in-wiring a masquerade of straightness and allism. Passing has become a kind of cognitive-behavioral therapy, the ultimate goal in developmental treatment plans.

If brains possess the flexibility to be less autistic, less queer—in all of the behavioral resonances of less—then it becomes, as Kafer describes of crip-queer futures, an unquestioned good to train the brain, to work toward a world free of neuroqueer subjectivities.[139] In training our brains out of neuroqueerness, we are training our brains into a fuller, albeit still residual, rhetoricity. Neuroqueerness may forever reside, but its traces can be mitigated and hidden. In this way, training one's brain into conformity in behavior, comportment, gesture, and verbal exchange becomes a cultural mandate. If one has capacity to assimilate, it is one's duty to do so.

But this focus on the potentials of plasticity intimates rather normative potentials. That is, we might behold ABA's neurohype less as an entelechy and more as an impulse toward deadening or flattening. The plastic, Catherine Malabou tells us, both gives and receives shape.[140] As with rhetoricity, plasticity in ABA discourse is halved, focused almost exclusively on how the neuroqueer can be shaped rather than how the neuroqueer shapes (and fucks, and defies, and writhes). This passivity of being shaped lives in behaviorism's most cherished stories, often fondly recounted in B. F. Skinner's quest to teach pigeons how to bowl. As Skinner recounts, the plasticity—or malleability—of his pigeons' behavior only became possible through mechanistic ridigity, wherein the practice of giving shape reduced the pigeons' actions into discrete, divisible movements: "We decided to reinforce any response which had the slightest resemblance to a swipe—perhaps, at first, merely the behavior of looking at the ball—and then to select responses which more closely approximated the final form [the pigeon swiping toy pins with its beak]. The result amazed us. In a few minutes, the ball was caroming off the walls of the box as if the pigeon had been a champion squash player."[141] Skinner describes shaping as a "series of approximations" (which are then differentially reinforced)—the chaining of which fords a seemingly impossible difference: one approximation leads to another, halving behavioral distances until they reach target behaviors.[142] What enables the behaviorist to avert Zeno's paradox, in this construction, involves a combination of motivation and environmental prosthesis: What drives the behavior in the performing subject, whether pigeon, rat, or queer? What precedes (or antecedes) the behavior? How to construct an environment that rewards approximations as well as the desired eventual responses? How to effect rhetorical and thereby neural change through behavior?[143]

Neuroplasticity, with all of its attendant demands on neuroqueer subjects, is inarguably rhetorical. And yet, rhetorical engagements with neuroplasticity are only beginning to emerge. Among those who have taken up the charge are Davi Johnson Thornton and Christine Skolnik.[144] Whereas Thornton provides resistant and critical analyses of plastic rhetorics and their effect on individual subjects, Skolnik adopts neuroplastic logics as a means for retooling theories of cognitive rhetoric. In short, Thornton's work might be characterized as examining the rhetoric of plasticity, whereas Skolnik's is better framed as examining the plasticity of rhetoric.[145]

Thornton's *Brain Culture* reviews popular and scientific discourse around brain health and cognition, directing particular attention to self-help manuals as well as the rhetorics surrounding brain imaging studies. Although Thornton's project does not take up ABA, her analyses regarding what she terms the "rhetorical brain" have direct import for behaviorism's many topoi.[146] Thornton examines the ways in which the brain rhetorically functions as the residence of subjectivity, identity, and free will. When selfhood is localized within the brain, she argues, changing one's brain presents innumerable opportunities for changing one's very self, and all of the privileges that selfhood purportedly confers. Thornton identifies the ways in which self-help literature, for instance, works to quantify and pathologize agency (e.g., the will of the healthy person versus the will of one's pathological brain). In an extended critique of Daniel Amen's *Making a Good Brain Great*, Thornton surfaces how cognitive rhetorics quantify both behavior and free will and gain their rhetorical traction through neoliberalism. The productive subject reigns, and mental hygiene is a paragon of productivity. What neuroplasticity lends to capitalism are rhetorics of improvability and calculability. A kind of reverse Zeno's paradox, neurological improvability can always double, can always expand, yet can never exceed: improvement, deftness, speed, and flexibility are never finite; under neoliberalism, we will always need more of these things, and it is our individual responsibility to acquire them. Moreover, indebted to behaviorist logics, such therapeutic approaches, in all of their reverse-Zeno-ness, premise themselves on predictability. If individual behavior can be calculated, quantified, and ultimately predicted, then therapy has succeeded. Put alternatively, in order to normalize one's brain, or to train one's cerebral self into productive mental health, one must reduce and dissect her every behavioral motion into elements that can be extinguished or reinforced. We are compelled to rewire our neural circuits for the social good of the body politic, ad infinitum.

While self-governance is a dominating topos of ABA, ABA is by no means the only applied or therapeutic approach that promulgates governmentality. As Thornton notes, "The brain-based version of therapy discourse is perhaps more pernicious in this regard, because it both individualizes social problems (all social ills can be attributed to brain dysfunction) and articulates social norms as natural, biologically and scientifically true."[147] Thornton's foreboding message here is multiply reminiscent of ABA's residualized histories. Recall, for example, Lovaas and Rekers's all-too-quick resignation that neuroqueer subjects require rewiring because of social stigma or increased risk of suicidal ideation. Where the norm goes unquestioned, the social will always trump the individual. But so too does ABA inculcate normative ideals and avoidable aberrances. Autism is deviant; queerness is deviant. In this regard, ABA demands of its subjects both compulsory heterosexuality and compulsory able-bodiedness, which, as Kafer argues, "works in two ways: first, through the use of physical force, and second, through what [Adrienne] Rich calls 'control of consciousness.'"[148] Even in moments when Lovaas claimed neuroqueerness to be part of the natural order, normativity's naturalness and biological superiority ranked higher, proved more desirable.

Whereas Thornton takes a rhetorical approach to neuroscience, Skolnik takes a neuroscientific approach to rhetoric. Among her many arguments, Skolnik positions rhetoric as a body of cognitive practices and embodied behaviors that warrant further neurobiological scrutiny.[149] In particular, she suggests that doing rhetoric is tantamount to changing one's brain. Every utterance, motion, and interaction alters our neurochemistry. Our brains change as we rhetoricize. Even in reading this book, your brain is physically changing. (My dearest hope is, upon reading this book, you will come away from it somewhat more impaired than when you began.)

Under Skolnik's framework, then, behavioral interventions train our brains into and unto rhetoricity—a claim not too dissimilar from those of behavioral scientists. A similarly potent strand within the plasticity of rhetoric is what Anne McGuire terms "developmentalism": common logic dictates that the younger we are, the more flexible are our brains.[150] This, then, accounts for the urgency that accompanies much of the discourse on early intervention across behavioral domain. Indeed, LeBlanc and Fagiolini characterize autism as a "critical period disorder."[151] In order for behavioral therapy's motions to have lifelong effects, its preferred subjects are those whose brains are most acutely shapeable—toddlers and young children. Rhetorical training needs to start early. (Think *Chironomia* for preschoolers.)

Thornton's work on the rhetoric of plasticity is not necessarily opposed to Skolnik's work on the plasticity of rhetoric. One can be critical of neuroplastic rhetorics and still acknowledge that the brain means something, that the brain does things. Even though plastic livers, to borrow from Thornton, do not generate the fervor or intrigue of plastic brains, the brain is implicated in and affected by rhetoric.[152] Of course, many scholars have noted the limitations and pitfalls of identifying with or as cognitive subjectivity. To claim that I am autistic is one thing; it is another to claim that autism is my selfhood. And yet, in claiming that I am autism—not just the adjectival *autistic*—I am not suggesting that the entirety of my brain or being is a cognitive definitional, a metonymic psychic essence. Autism, as I have narrated throughout, extends beyond the skin. But, more pressingly, clinical exegeses of autism pinpoint many of the core markers of what might be termed identity, in all of identity's fluidity and fluctuations—affect, intent, concept of self, concept of others, empathy, sensation, cognition, motor coordination, mental processing, interests and hobbies, relationality, communication, and so on. If these are the items my doctor terms autism, how am I not to say that autism is me?

But, as with all things residual, autism supposedly resists plasticity, at least in ABA discourse. Duration, surveillance, and environmentalism remain ABA's chiefest topoi because they signal the immanent rigidity and involuntarity of autistic brains.[153] Rhetoricity cannot be fully realized in neuroqueer subjects, for neuroqueerness resides. The brain's capacity for trainability—more plastic and malleable in children, but still plastic into adulthood—requires that intervention be a lifelong endeavor. Applied behavior analysis has captured the public imagination with the figure of the child, whose future has presumably been stolen by varying manifestations of neurological queerness. Funding allocations by the NIMH and other grantors overwhelmingly demonstrate that children are autism's most tragic targets and thus most deserving of intervention and cash flow.[154] What is there to preempt in the adult? That autistics or queers might live to see adulthood signals a profound failure of interventionist discourses. Despite enduring autistic people's futureless futures, emerging ABA research has begun to embrace the idea of intervention across the life span, suggesting that ABA's surveillance, roteness, and demands for compliance never cease. In a spread for the Autism Society's quarterly newsletter, for instance, Peter Gerhardt claims as mythical the idea that ABA is only effective for young children and maintains that ABA for autistic teenagers and adults has potential to improve their "competence" in a number of social domains.[155] The title of his piece—"The Promise of ABA: Creating Meaningful Lives throughout Adolescence and Adulthood"—suggests none too subtly that if neuroqueer lives are to have meaning, it is through behaviorist meanings, through bending neuroqueer bodies to neurotypical wills.

For the neuroqueer, our life is work. We still haven't empirically answered whether or not ABA can rewire autistic brains, even if the rewiring is merely a neuro-closeting. But presupposing ABA could rewire autistic brains, should we? (Rhetorical question. The answer is *fuck no*.) Applied behavior analysis is host to a number of ethical questions that, quite unfortunately and often to traumatic effect, are passed off not as questions in need of philosophical reflection and debate but instead as matters of common sense: the default assumption is that it is better to be nonautistic than it is to be autistic, always. And this assumption has done great damage to autistic and nonautistic people alike. As Victoria Pitts-Taylor notes, plasticity is often heralded as a kind of "neuronal liberation," as therapeutic endeavors that optimize our best selves.[156]

But these plastic futures, if we recall Kafer, are not disabled futures. The rhetorics of plasticity and self-governance in ABA compel the neuroqueer to drop the NQ in favor of a nonphonetic OO. What we require, then, is a version of plasticity that accounts for the queering of rhetoricity, for the being-becoming that any claim to neuroqueerness demands. Malabou's exhortations about giving and receiving are prescient here, rhetoricizing the behavioral-neural as multivariate pathways that direct us toward the potentialities of neuroqueering. But more than a gift-receipt exchange, Malabou tells us, plasticity truly lives up to its namesake when it explodes: "But it must be remarked that plasticity is also the capacity to annihilate the very form it is able to receive or create. We should not forget that *plastique*, from which we get the words *plastiquage* and *plastiquer*, is an explosive substance made of nitroglycerine and nitrocellulose, capable of causing violent explosions. We thus note that plasticity is situated between two extremes: on the one side the sensible image of taking form (sculpture or plastic objects), and on the other side that of annihilation of all form (explosion)."[157] Indeed, and as I discuss in chapters 3 and 4, autistic entelechies direct us toward that which diverges and destroys, fucking the diplomatic and embracing the awkward and perverse. Stims and tics explode off the neuroqueer body; sensory overload can propel autistics into meltdown and self-injury, and sometimes gravely so. In relating these examples, I do not mean to suggest that autistic plastique is always of necessity positive, shiny, or cheery. Rather, I mean to suggest that plasticity signals rhetoricity in all of its potentials, causes, and directions—it is the unfolding of being and coming-to-being; it is the precondition and potential of what might become, in all of the infinite variance of autistic becoming; it tells us something, or, at the very least, possesses that possibility unto itself. As James C. Wilson reminds us, self-injury—even self-injury that can result in retinal detachment or death—is a rhetorical act, worthy of our attention and ethical deliberation.[158] In like kind, Erin Manning tells us that "pure plastic rhythm is dynamic form in potential," that the plastic signals a "becoming-body that is a sensing body in movement, a body that resists pre-definition."[159] These are the entelechies, embodied schematics, and time scales toward which the neuroqueer strive.

The futures that ABA promotes close off spaces for neuroqueer voices to in/voluntarily assert themselves, infinitely halving claims to autism or autistic rhetoricity. But as plastique suggests, the mechanistic surveillance of the behaviorist cannot contain the eruptions that ripple off autistic bodies. Autism, as Dawn Prince-Hughes relates, "is simply being human—but without the skin."[160] In chapter 3, "Invitation," I explore the dynamics of neurotypical rhetorical situations and the ways in which autistic people cunningly embrace those skinless, explosive tactics that are claimed to lessen our rhetorical agility. What ABA has come to signal for autistics is an in-made rhetorical paradox from which escape is difficult: the laughable presumption that autistics can only communicate their feelings about ABA because they've endured ABA.

*Oo. Oooo.* Let us queerly practice.

THREE. **invitation**

For nearly a decade, I've sported an autistic pride button on my backpack. As buttons go, this one is fairly prominent. It is three and a half inches in diameter, with a bright, rainbow-colored Möbius strip sandwiched between the words *autistic* and *pride*. These days my backpack is orange, and the button just, well, shows. People notice it. People notice it often.

As a graduate student, I assisted our local ASAN chapter in creating (by hand) piles upon piles of these buttons. My autistic friends and I spent hours brainstorming slogans and taking turns at the computer as we debated fonts and Photoshop filters. We labored over the production of these buttons—much like we labored through the stares of nearby students, all a-watch as a stimmy, vocal cadre of autistics descended upon the button machine at the student union. We formed aut-sembly lines, talked about inadequate county services as we lined the counter with pin backings, and cursed our fine and gross motor skills while we foibled with scissors and other sharp objects. When I say we bled over our buttons, I mean this sincerely.

My pride button is a topos, an inventional site, a relational site. I stare at it, I finger its smooth texture, and I locate numerous stories. There are the stories behind its birth, yes, or the stories about how it falls into puddles, or gets caught on the felt-backed seats of public transit. But more, this button frequently functions as an invitation to discourse: it attracts unsolicited commentary from colleagues and strangers alike. People encounter my button, and they have opinions about it. Very strong opinions.

—There is the man at the bus station who presumably sees the rainbow and the word *pride* and asks, quite seriously, if I'm one of those feminazi lesbians. He needs to know. Am I one of them?

—There is the Kroger cashier who sees my button, and asks why I wear it. When I tell him that I'm autistic, he responds, quite cheeringly, "Good for you! Going to the store, all by yourself!"

—There is an older woman, on the bus, who taps my button and tells me she has an autistic son. When I excitedly exclaim, "I'm autistic, too!" her eyes fix on mine. "No," she corrects me. "You have the Asperburgers."

—There is a young woman who breathily grabs at my hand as I await my bus. Autistic flair, public transit, benches and foot space to roll and pace—if there were an autistic analogue for a gay bar, it would be a train depot. This woman pulls at me, precise and sparing with her words. "Why pride?" she asks. "I'm autistic," I tell her. She smiles at me. "Button," she says. "Button. I would like one."

—The TSA agent pulls my bag toward the edge of the conveyor belt, angling the button toward his face. I hurriedly unveil my laminated disclosure card, the one that tells first responders and airport personnel that I have issues™ with hands in my space, and social niceties, and understanding what they—they-they, any they, all the theys—want from me. He looks at the card, looks at the button, and proceeds, randomly and matter-of-factly: "What do you think about that testosterone theory?"

—An autistic man outs himself to me on a Columbus, Ohio, bus. "I don't remember faces," he explains. Then, pointing to my button, "But I remember that."

—I am out walking. A cluster of teenagers lags several yards behind me. The spatial tension transports me to middle school trauma. Oh shit, they can see my button. I walk more briskly. I hear them crack gay retard jokes as I bolt around a corner.

—There are around ten of us, all holding autisticky signs and wearing pride buttons as we protest an Autism Speaks walk. An SUV slows down, comes to a halt, a window unrolls, and a man's voice beckons us. His extended finger points to our signs as he measuredly surveys our protest line. "You're all a bunch of fucking retards!" he screams. We lower our signs as the SUV drives off, our mouths agape.

—A student shyly approaches me after class. "Where can I find a button like that?" she asks.

I could go on. For my button incites as it seemingly invites discourse. Autism is not only my identity, or even my own personal commonplace. Autism is a profoundly kairotic condition, a topos en masse. People encounter autism, even with a stranger, and they feel compelled to speak, to seek.

Of course, I am more interested here, in this chapter, in invitational rhetoric than I am in my invitational button. As well, I am keenly aware that these narrative retellings around my button are mired in what Peter Vermeulen would call the contextual. In offering a preliminary definition of context, Vermeulen wryly admits that the "meaning of the word *context* is dependent on . . . well, the context in which it is used."[1] Vermeulen provides an approach toward context that bears remarkable similarity to how rhetoricians often approach rhetoric: capital-E Everything and Everywhere. Rhetoric, many have argued, has become globalized and all-encompassing, has become what Edward Schiappa has termed "Big Rhetoric."[2] That is, regardless of domain, regardless of object of inquiry, rhetoric can and does rear its head, declaring itself always relevant, always present, latent in surrounding detail. Whereas Schiappa embraces rhetoric's everythingness and everywhereness (so long as rhetoricians continue to do "good work" and forward rhetoric as a nonpejorative term), others in the field routinely bristle at rhetoric's seeming expansiveness.[3] In a critique of Herbert Simon's sweeping approach to rhetoric, William Keith et al. counsel readers that "if everything is rhetoric/rhetorical, then it is neither informative nor interesting to be told that a practice/discourse/institution is rhetorical."[4]

Replacing *practice/discourse/institution* with *autism* often generates responses in the vein of Keith and his coauthors. If autism cognitively resides, then surely rhetoricity lies beyond the autist's grasp (or so the logic often goes). In this I am reminded of a conference presentation I delivered as a graduate student. During the question-and-answer session, the room erupted into severe scrutiny of this very sentiment: that autistic people are rhetorical, that autism is a rhetoric unto itself. People were upset, very upset, that I would even suggest such a thing. One such comment came from the mother of an autistic child. She stood up in the middle of the room, neurotypically perched her eyes upon mine, and boomingly declared, "I am deeply uncomfortable in thinking about autism as rhetorical." Following her response, several people in the room nodded (some even slow-clapped), all in service of reiterating the absurdity of the idea. How could autistics—the academy's ultimate arhetorical foil—how could they be rhetorical?

In that conference presentation, as with many of the things I write or say lately, I outed myself as autistic. I even shared the book club anecdote that opens chapter 2, wherein a group of allistic people concertedly silenced the desires of their autistic clients, presumably in the name of rehabilitation or social skills.

And yet, this anecdote had little effect at the conference. People, especially parents, were pissed with me, the autistic demi-rhetor who was too cute and too unempathetic to say anything about rhetoricity, never mind autism. In this professional moment, I became unprofessional: this is the effect that studying oneself often has, especially when that self is a neuroqueer self. I was an autistic person declaring myself to be rhetorical, and a posse of Professional Type™ people fervently swooped in to deny me that right. How dare I consider myself among them, the rhetorical? How dare I insinuate that people like me can rhetorically act?

And so, disclosure is inherently charged, polemical, affective. These anecdotes of mine may be hard to read, but they are harder for me to write. Whether I narrate my neuroqueerness via button, verbal speech, text, or even in stimmily entering a room, I am always disclosed. And, in those disclosures, others feel compelled to respond, to make their mark upon my neuroqueer frame. As Lloyd Bitzer says of such charged moments, "Let us regard rhetorical situation as . . . an exigence which strongly invites utterance."[5] My body serves as their kairos, their rhetorical exigence. My body is disclosed in a manner that invites utterance, and strongly so.

Autism's kairos and contexts are tricky things. What others feel compelled to say, and how those sayings impact my narration—all of these details surely influence others' impulses to communicate something about autism, much like my button and the immediate rhetorical situation around my button figure a certain, always contextually varied and informed, kind of invitation. Context, like rhetoric, is everything and everywhere (except, of course, when it comes to autism). It is the symbolic filter through which allistic people come to apprehend autism's degraded presence. It is hard to get past the *autistic* on my button, not to mention its juxtaposition with *pride*. Autistic identity is seemingly incongruous with reality.

But more than invitational buttons, I am interested in how disclosures around autism invite discourse more generally, especially discourse that is contentious or doubting.[6] In particular, I am interested in nonautistic refutations of autistic identity, and, more importantly, the ways in which these refutations inspire autistic rhetorical theory and response. Put more plainly: I believe that disclosure represents a particular kind of inventional site within autism land. Because autism, in the cultural imagination, is an ambiguous and often mystery-laden construct, any disclosure around autism invokes questions, invokes guesswork, incites demands for particularity. One cannot claim autism without being pressed for more—more information, more cross-examination, more refutation, more response, more words flowing from more mouths. But there is likewise a problem of ethos (or kakoethos, to quote Jenell Johnson) inherent in these disclosures, wherein autistic people are figured as lacking authority to speak on or from within autism.[7] Autistic academic Dinah Murray laments these figurations of autism and ethos, noting, "Disclosure of an autism spectrum diagnosis means disclosure of the fundamentally flawed personhood implied by [autism's] diagnostic criteria. It is likely to precipitate a negative judgement of capacity involving permanent loss of credibility."[8] In disclosing autism, we are both too autistic and not autistic enough, variously called fakers, whiners, retards, and mindblind. We are exposed as we expose.

In this chapter, then, I interrogate the ways in which personal disclosures around autism are figured within invitational rhetoric. Most pressingly, I examine the ways in which autism disclosure functions as a metonym for diagnostic assessment. Admitting that I am autistic, for instance, provides entry for others to tally my symptoms, to compare the context of my disclosure against their knowledge (or lack thereof) of autism's motions and means. That is, declaring one's neuroqueerness is often culturally read as an invitation for neurotypicals to theorize and assess what neuroqueerness is. In this way, autism disclosure is often agonistic, expectant of allistic refutation. The ability to say, "I have autism," for example, is intuited as evidence that one does not have autism—or, at least, not real or severe autism.

Were we to return to chapter 1's discussion of Zeno's paradoxes, we might apprehend the ways in which severe/mild binaries or autism/allism binaries create a kind of autistic fixity. My invitational button paradoxically locates me as both too autistic and not autistic enough. I am subsumed by the placeness of autism, and any mobile attempts on my part toward rhetoricity will fail, because there are infinite standpoints between autism and allism, autism and rhetoricity, autism and realness. In this vein, spectra might be considered a master trope for disability. Spectra enable nondisabled others to position a disabled person's claim to disability as elliptic or enthymemic: neuroqueer narratives are never the whole story. Context is everything and everywhere, and neuroqueer rhetors are rhetorically and infinitely halved, unable (or unwilling) to tell or perform what allistic audiences most privilege. Following this logic, a claim to autism is read as partial or incomplete and in need of nonautistic correction, clarification, or rehabilitation. And it is through rehabilitation that we can mete out our potential: elliptic stories suggest that the autistic is an entelechy of prosthesis.

While I begin this chapter by exploring the ways in which allistic rhetorics have come to figure the autistic as elliptic and acontextual, my resting point is not the pessimism nor the abuses that have come to typify rhetorical exchanges around autism. Rather, I move to autie-biographies and the ways in which autistic rhetors un/willfully incite and invite refutation in their personal disclosures. Autistic people have long theorized invitational rhetoric in autistic cultural spaces, often invoking what Judy Endow and Brenda Smith Myles have termed the "hidden curriculum" to unearth ableist practices that frame autistic ethos as partial or nonexistent.[9] As a means of troubling invitational rhetoric, I use these conversations on hidden curricula as a lens for exploring the precarity of autistic ethos within larger concepts of the rhetorical situation. As I have discussed throughout this book, the autistic subject is typically rendered as either a non-rhetorical or a demi-rhetorical subject. It follows, then, that with demi-rhetoricity comes deflated ethos.

In the previous chapters, I focused on the ways in which clinicians incrementally halve autistic rhetoricity. My turn to autie-biography builds upon this line of inquiry by suggesting that halving is but only one employ of demi-rhetoricity. In particular, I look toward what Margaret Price has called "counter-diagnosis" as one means through which autistic people queer the contours of rhetorical containment, of diagnostic fixity.[10] In toying with the very idea of diagnosis itself, autistic rhetors instill their own queered credibilities, in which authority is derived from one's pathological lack of authority. In this regard, autistic rhetorics might be regarded as a way of thinking not about "how much rhetoric or how much autism can my brain hold," but rather about rhetorical attraction or rhetorical desire, and what it means to roll, crip-queerly, outside the bounds of rhetoric.

Elliptic Discourse

Clinical constructions of autism frequently position expertise and self-knowledge as antithetical to autism itself. Whether by means of theory of mind, weak central coherence, executive dysfunction, or reduced corpora callosa, clinicians wield any number of rhetorical constructions to counter the knowledges and desires of autistic individuals. It is by now a common trope to claim that disabled subjects are self-absorbed, unable to perceive anything beyond their own impaired lives. Autism is but one condition in which self-absorption has been rendered as clinically factual: to be autistic is to have little to no concept of other humans. (Sorry, human readers, for my failure to conceive of your existence.)

Disclosure is (demi)rhetorically charged. Disclosure is both imperiled and politically generative for any number of reasons: it can make the neuroqueer vulnerable to rhetorical and physical attack; it has the possibility of humanizing the neuroqueer; it can be necessary for receipt of social assistance or rehabilitative services; it can cause loss of employment, familial rejection, even death. Disclosure, I am arguing, holds such widely variable potentials for embodied effects because of its rhetorical distributions. Our every neuroqueer/ed action, emanating as it does from our impaired brains, is locatable on a clinically indebted rhetorical continuum. Our rhetoricity is always subject to being perpetually and infinitely halved.

Because I am interested in theorizing autistic invention and neuroqueer rhetoricity, I am also invested in discerning how we are authored into opposites, into nonhumanity and psychic absence. Even though rhetoric is that which we have been denied, I believe rhetoric's schemes and figures enable the neuroqueer to unfold and dismantle the structures that would bind them to Zeno, structures that oppress, subjugate, and fix.

Take, for instance, the following verbal disclosure: "I am disabled." A statement such as "I am disabled" holds more meaning than those three words might suggest. It is the kind of statement that is predicated on inference, a cherished rhetorical topos. In identifying myself as disabled, I am saying very little yet potentially saying a great deal. There is an opening, a staggering plateau, embedded in the crevices between each word: *I—am—disabled. Disabled* acts as a placeholder for numerous potential meanings, calling upon complex social and institutional matrixes that govern what a disabled body might signify. These significations include everything from cost-burden analyses (Should we kill disabled infants? How much does it cost to raise an autistic versus nonautistic child?) to living arrangements (Who will care for my disabled child when I die?) to presumed physique (Where is disability located in/on the body? How might we surface impairment for the benefit of my nondisabled gaze?) to the results of clinically sanctioned diagnostic testing (diagnosis: classic autism, a.k.a. stolen childhood syndrome) to segregation from public space (Can I enroll my child in special ed? In a sheltered workshop? A group home?) to eugenic pasts and futures (Do you ever wish that you hadn't been born?).

These inferences, in any given disclosure, culminate the very being of disability. By inference, I mean that which is inductively or contextually reasoned, that which is determined by means of (nondisabled) probability—that which must attend intentionality in order to make it social. When disability is exposed, so too are nondisabled inferences about what disability is and can mean. Inference is normatively generated, filling in rhetorical gaps with generalizations about how terrible it must be to be cognitively impaired. Inference assumes. And, quite often, these inferences have straightening intents and effects: taming the cripple, containing the queer, averting the catastrophe that is neurodivergence.

Because disclosure defers to the inferential, it is also elliptic, and at times enthymemic. Here I am speaking about ellipsis, which is a rhetorical scheme of omission. Ellipsis is a figure that occurs at the syntactic level of discourse. A common example is ellipses, the three trailing dots ( ... ) one might find concluding or embedded within a sentence. When we encounter those three dots as readers, we intuit that something's missing, that those three dots serve as a placeholder for something. And, as the logic of ellipsis goes, as readers we supposedly understand, based on context, what that missing something is. That is, we supposedly understand what those three dots mean and why they're there—whether they work to stave off redundancy, maintain poetic form, or suggest the inconclusiveness of a thought.

And so, when I say the following three words—*I am autistic*—those three words are often interpreted as being more than those three words. As in, there is some kind of syntactic omission, there is something I mean to be saying but am not saying, as though there is an *and* that should follow my disclosure, and a listening party thus feels invited to fill in the blanks in their response. As in, *I am autistic* is consequently interpreted as *I am autistic* ... (dot dot dot).

Following this logic, audiences may perceive an individual disclosure ("I am autistic") as an unspoken invitation to question, interrogate, elaborate, and/ or theorize that disclosure, as well as discursive elements only tangentially related to that disclosure. So, for example, in response to "I am autistic," one might be greeted with: "But you don't look autistic!" Or: "When were you vaccinated?" Or: "Have you tried $B_{12}$ supplements?" Or: "Congratulations!" Or: "You are nothing like my autistic child." Or: "What does it feel like to be you?" And so on.

Elliptic conversations are endemic to rhetorical studies and in instructional textbooks. As I discuss in a later section, one such elliptic form is the enthymeme, which is arguably the governing structure of rhetoric itself (i.e., rhetoric is a function of creating and inducing knowledge from the partial). But if we attend to discourse more locally (as opposed to the global, overarching "all of rhetoric itself"), we might consider elliptic discourse as those momentary spaces and places in which language tapers off, conversations pause, or meanings abscond. As Edward Corbett notes, "Any position we take in an argument necessarily establishes a note of partiality," and it is through ellipsis that we work to fill rhetoric's partiality, its discursive gaps.[11] Ellipsis, consequently, is a rhetorical scheme that forces interlocutors to read between the lines— which, if we were to accept clinical indictments, autistics supposedly cannot do. Judi Randi and her coauthors, for instance, argue that autistic children lack narrative coherence and narrative competence, deficits that are largely related to paucities in intentionality and inference ability.[12] What this means, then, is that autistic conversations are punctuated by lack—they are rhetorically perceived as elliptic, and any allistic inference must be correct, moral, empathetic, and rehabilitative by the sheer fact that allistics are rhetorically superior to autistics. In other words: there is no wrong response to my neuroqueer disclosures. I can say that I'm a pansexual autistic queer who is sometimes asexual, and my ex-therapist can (and did) respond that there's a pill for all of that.[13] Because my ex-therapist is rhetorically endowed (and because I have rhetoric envy), he is elliptically empathetic, able to offend me and claim my offense as another pesky autism symptom.

Ellipsis, as a rhetorical scheme, presumes a shared rhetoricity, or a shared understanding of language, culture, and communication. In order to fill a gap, interlocutors need both to intend and perceive a gap to begin with. But when one's communication isn't seen as communication, it is hard to build a space in which anything is rhetorically negotiated or shared, in which a rhetor's intention predicts an audience's perception. Thus, when autism enters the fold, any rhetorical breakdowns or differences in interpretation are considered the result and failure of autism. That is, the assumption is that autism represents, or instigates, rhetorical failure and social miscommunication. When a stranger asks me at what age I was toilet trained, the failure lies with me: the stranger asks this question because I have failed to volunteer my bathroom habits, and I have failed precisely because I did not magically rhetorically grok that this information was what the stranger wished to know. In such normative stories, my elliptic machinations result from a normatively entelechial brain and autistic disposition that neuronally wills and resides, that predisposes me to be mindblind and lacking in social-symbolic thought. As a demi-rhetor, I can never disclose enough, even when my disclosures are far too much (e.g., I sometimes pierce my own flesh with corn-on-the-cob holders) (dot dot dot).

On one level, I want to forward a fervent argument against the idea that autistic people fail at rhetorical life. If we drop autism from the conversation, for example, it is very easy to state that all rhetorical exchanges might be characterized as failure or, at the very least, failable. As Lisa Zunshine has noted in her past discussions on theory of mind, failure is omnidirectional in rhetorical exchange.[14] Signals cross; frowns and smiles are misread; miscommunication based on misunderstandings abounds in human interaction. Inference is only at best a probability—rhetoric is guesstimation. But when disability is disclosed, failure and rhetoric take on different forms: the disabled person becomes marked as and with deficit, while the nondisabled interlocutor is marked as able, conversant, intelligent, and well, the goal to which the disabled person should aspire.

Rhetorics that pair disability with failure as default make me shiver with righteous anger. But on another level, there is potentiality in failing. We might, for instance, look to Jack Halberstam's *The Queer Art of Failure* and consider the ways in which neuroqueerness might be conceived as "stand[ing] in contrast to the grim scenarios of success that depend upon 'trying and trying again.'"[15] As Halberstam proposes, queer failure might be regarded as a "style," which, in rhetorical terms, provides possibility for recasting neuroqueer practices as in/voluntary motions that dis/adorn and fuck with rhetoric's canons. As I discuss in chapter 4, one such failtastic exemplar might be stimming, or self-stimulation, which has often been metaphorized as masturbatory. Stimming, then, might be embraced in all of its purported failings, both neuronal and social. Autistics are rhetoric's wankers, perverting notions of intent, affect, meaning, and socially appropriate response. Halberstam relates failure as the "privileg[ing] of the naive and nonsensical," where one "might argue for the nonsensible or nonconceptual over sense-making structures that are often embedded in a common notion of ethics."[16] In this regard we might turn to autistic perception, which Erin Manning has described as a "complex dance of attention," as an "attunement to life as an incipient ecology of practices, an ecology that does not privilege the human but attends to the more than human."[17] There is nonsense in autistic being and doing, nonsense meant multiply: the excess of sense and sensation, the absence of sense and sensation, the monotropic perception of field as partially whole or wholly partial. Autistic rhetorics can and do hold meaning, but so too are they symbolic for their nonsymbolism, for their simplicity and their pedantry and their nothingness.[18] Our failures to attain rhetoricity might be read as defiance against that which is rhetorically normative.

And yet, ellipsis. There is real violence in this presumption of an always-omission. How to reorient—or disorient—our perceived and involuntary failures? How to invite failure when failure is read as invitation?

## Invitational Rhetoric

Not all invitations are created equally. As someone who self-injures, I have learned this lesson at many junctures. An invitation to take antipsychotics might seem optional or self-effacing, but when that invitation is posed by a lab-coated doctor whose impatient clipboard has developed its own bossy personality, invitation might be more accurately read as demand. For (ex-)consumers of psychiatric services, coercion frequently attends that which is invited or perceived to be inviting. In referring to myself as queer, for example, a listening shrink might apprehend this statement as an invitation to intervene, in all of the therapeutic and historical resonances of intervening. Perhaps I fancy myself bisexual, or pansexual, or demisexual—or whatever flavor of the queer alphabet I am this week—because manly male men find my autism unattractive, or because autism impedes my understanding of gender roles, sex, desire, attraction, and prosocial behavior. Perhaps I fancy myself queer because I experienced an excess of testosterone during my fetal party days in the womb, and in reality I have a dudebro brain that misfires neurotransmitters when encountering the ladies. Shrinks are good at backdooring (gender)queer curatives when the invitation is disclosed or cloaked in disability's trappings.

While invitation might appear to bear similarity to persuasion, it is often rendered as distinct within rhetorical studies. A TV commercial for an antidepressant might present itself as an invitation to seek a prescription or converse with one's doctor. And yet, ultimately the aim of the commercial is not to invite discussion about antidepressants, but rather to convince or persuade a viewing public that this particular antidepressant might be right for them. (This pill is right for you, despite the sexual side effects and dry mouth. This pill's persuasiveness lies in its ability to exponentialize the psychic pain of your neurodivergence over the almost imperceptible, side-effect nuisances of uncontrollable drooling or increased appetite. Take this pill, or risk your joy/life/relationships/normalcy.) Invitation and persuasion, then, as terms of work, diverge in their motives and means, their uptake in interlocutionary exchange. Whereas persuasion strives to bring bodies over, invitation strives to bring bodies under. At times these prepositional differences are slight, and at times they are overlapping, impermeable, or indistinguishable. Nonetheless, invitational rhetoric endeavors to encourage, provoke, and welcomingly wave toward conversation. Where persuasion seeks to conquer, invitation seeks to dialogue.

The substance of invitational rhetoric as theorized in feminist rhetorical studies at times diverges from the negativistic depictions I have presented in this chapter. It might be useful, for example, to approach feminist rhetoric's embrace of invitation as being an elliptic framework unto itself, one in which elliptic discourse is favored over directive or forceful discourse. Building upon Sally Gearhart's work on feminist rhetorics of nonviolence, Sonja Foss and Cindy Griffin proposed invitational rhetoric as a necessary alternative to traditional rhetoric's orientation toward persuasion and agonistic discourse.[19] In particular, feminist rhetorical scholars have contended that change—bringing or persuading an opposing party to the rhetor's side of the table—is a form of inflicting violence or reifying oppressive structures. Foss and Griffin, for instance, positioned Kenneth Burke's rhetorical theories as a patriarchal embodiment of persuasion.[20] Recall, for instance, that Burke's consideration of identification, persuasion, and rhetorical transformation were at times indebted to death imagery, wherein the "killing of something is the changing of it."[21] "Embedded in efforts to change others," wrote Foss and Griffin, "is a desire for control and domination, for the act of changing another establishes the power of the change agent over the other."[22] In this, it is easy to read advertisements for antidepressants as being uniquely dominating in their suasive intentions. Regardless of whether neurodivergent people feel they benefit from psychiatric medication, the goal with such ads is to change minds, rhetorically and neurologically.[23]

Conversely, invitational rhetoric is dialogic rather than persuasive, apprehending positions and standpoints and interlocutors as all having "immanent value."[24] The aim of invitation is to re-view the rhetorical situation as ellipsis by design: any rhetorical exchange involves gaps, disparate and conflicting viewpoints or ideologies, nooks and crannies from which negotiative discourse might arise. Moreover, Foss and Griffin frame invitation as a set of rhetorical practices that can only emerge from and within safe spaces. They suggest, to this end, that the "condition of safety involves the creation of a feeling of security and freedom from danger for the audience."[25] In this sense, invitation not only represents an elliptic pause, a bringing-under of bodies, but an environment in which interlocutors perceive equitable exchange to be safe and sanctioned.

There have, of course, been many hesitations around invitational rhetoric, and I count myself among the hesitators. Jeffrey Murray foregrounds the inequity inherent in most dialogic exchange, asserting that while rhetoric demands reciprocity, it also operates from asymmetrical standpoints.[26] He suggests, in turn, that "both invitational rhetoric and direct moral suasion are modes of rhetorical engagement," and that rhetors cannot choose between one mode or the other but must engage both in order to "represent or fulfill the mandate of ethics."[27] But more than questioning the interdependence of invitational and persuasive discourse, it's important not to overlook the brutality that attends invitation. That is, invitation/persuasion is not a benevolent/violent binary. Advocates of invitational rhetoric decry the violence and oppression of persuasion, yet they elide the violences and oppressions that invitation itself propagates. Lozano-Reich and Cloud, for instance, problematize the idea that safety can (or should) ever exist in rhetorical exchange, pointing out that the "invitational paradigm . . . [falsely] presupposes conditions of economic, political, and social equality between and among interlocutors."[28] In other words, invitation demands equals and equity, even in those instances where inequality is rampant. Lozano-Reich and Cloud inspect the contours of invitation, suggesting that it is better termed "invitation only," wherein marginal bodies are immanently excluded rather than immanently valued.[29] For invitational rhetoric presumes actors of equivalent social standing, much like ellipsis presumes shared rhetoricity, shared power.

If I were to ground the power imbalances of invitational rhetoric within autism discourse, applied behavior analysis (ABA) would serve as one apt example. To recap, ABA is both a discipline and a series of attendant methodologies that forward behavioral principles of learning and change. Its therapeutic and analytical practices remain the most widely used and recommended of early intervention services for autistic children, despite rampant objection on the part of autistic activists. The discourse surrounding ABA, however, is primarily controlled by researchers, therapists, and parents of autistic children. Whatever debates or viewpoints that circulate around ABA, autistic opinion remains conspicuously absent, often relegated to blogs and web forums that ABA practitioners either troll or ignore.[30] Popularly, ABA is represented as the intervention that holds the most possibility for "optimal outcomes" in autistic children, or for rendering autistic children "indistinguishable" from their peers.[31] In many ways, ABA is considered a nondebate, a moral and public good that works in service of futures free from autism. No future for autism is among the dearest of clinical goals, and ABA is one methodology that works to transform sentiment into reality. In a spread for *Parade* magazine in 2008, for example, Autism Speaks cofounder Suzanne Wright implored readers that autism is a public health crisis in need of swift mediation: "We're now playing catch-up as we try to stem the tide and ultimately eradicate autism for the sake of future generations. If we continue our current trajectory, we'll get there in my lifetime."[32] More pointedly, in their lobbying for insurance reform, Autism Speaks has functioned as one of the most ardent supporters of ABA's efficacy and necessity for autistic children, claiming that without ABA coverage, parents end up "mortgaging their entire futures."[33]

How does one invite discourse when that discourse insists your eradication is to the benefit of nations? In declaring myself autistic or queer, there is much that I elliptically and passively invite. I invite commentary on my soul (spoiler: I am going to hell); I invite commentary on the tragedy of my brain (spoiler: Autism stole my personality, and I might be contagious). These are the invitations to discourse that neurotypical others may intuit when they encounter my disclosures, regardless of whether I willfully welcome or insinuate such invitations to begin with. That ABA practitioners might read my body as an invitation to their discourse only reentrenches the idea that autistic people are patients, research subjects, experiments, autistexts ready for rhetorical shaping.

Importantly, ABA's earliest subjects were not limited to those identified as autistic. As I elaborated in chapter 2, UCLA's Feminine Boy Project (FBP) conducted ABA-based studies on gender-variant children in the early 1970s, representing the largest-funded NIMH project on preventing homosexuality in U.S. history.[34] In his acknowledgments page for The "Sissy Boy Syndrome," Richard Green noted that even the Playboy Foundation served as a grantor for the FBP, both when the NIMH "briefly disrupted the flow of this fifteen-year study" and at another juncture when the project required travel funds to follow up with participating families.[35] In short, the FBP sought to minimize risk for homosexuality, transvestism, and transsexuality (often conflating all of the aforementioned), and theorized that feminine traits served as (gender)queer predictors in child subjects. (And, apparently, Playboy decided it was to their benefit to ensure male heterosexuality by any method, lest they lose potential customers.) Eradicating feminine behavior, then, was a means of preventing queer and trans futures, therapeutic moves that were ultimately portrayed as a broader social good that spared both the child and society the pain and stigma of queerness. As such, abusive behaviorist methods were legitimized and moralized. Better to beat the shit out of a child than to risk the possibility of a genderqueer adult.

And so, again I ask: How does one invite discourse when that discourse insists your eradication is to the benefit of nations? Clearly, ABA and its advocates do not find immanent value in the neurologically queer. Then again, neither do neuroqueer activists believe there is immanent value in the rhetorics that ABA forwards. Feminist rhetoricians might suggest invitational rhetoric as a concerted, intentioned method appropriate to such ideological impasses, wherein those from opposing worldviews suspend judgment and engage in dialogue (rather than attempting to persuade or convince others). But as Maureen Mathison makes clear, invitational rhetoric "assumes that all positions are equally valuable, when this is clearly not the case, as shown throughout history. Certain positions have denigrated and denied the lives of many."[36] Ibby Grace's pithy tagline for the NeuroQueer blog exemplifies Mathison's concerns about bodily denigration: "Ole Ivar Lovaas couldn't decide whether ABA should be for Queers or Autistics: NeuroQueer!"[37] Here, Lovaas's indecision is neither valuable nor immanent, nor does it serve as a safe topos from which to share discourse: for Lovaas electroshocked and encouraged the belting of his neuro-queer child subjects. When the stakes are as severe as bodily annihilation, do those without power really wish to invite the presence and purposes of those who would do them harm? What peace is there to be made? When is rhetoric ever safe?

Invitational rhetoric did not emerge from a vacuum. In his critical examination of feminist rhetoric's disciplinization, K. J. Rawson argues that feminist rhetorical studies has come to constitute its own normative canon, wherein invitation functions as a governing commonplace.[38] In particular, Rawson draws attention to feminist rhetoric's dual focus on gendered analysis and recovering women rhetors within the history of rhetoric, both of which rely on normative and binaristic conceptions of femaleness as a category. Rawson's critiques of feminist rhetoric are consistent with my own: the field has yet to grapple, visibly and fully, with its own essentialisms and elisions, not only about gender, but about whiteness, dialogue, ability, and power. In seeking to counter rhetorical traditions that elevate and privilege the masculine, feminist rhetorical studies has offered a counter-rhetoric that, nonetheless, reifies a multitude of normative stances. Invitation presupposes stock feminine personae, in which interlocutors have access to rhetorical power. Such interlocutors are often white, able, cisgender, and/or straight, agilely drawing upon inventional resources available only to those most rhetorically mobile.

Invitational rhetoric, then, harbors scant consideration for demi-rhetorical bodies, whose wills and ways are so often glued into place, assumed incapable of experiencing the full rhetorical gamut. When disability disclosure is read as an "offering," à la Foss and Griffin, ellipsis swoops into view as the default and patron trope of cripples, as though any disclosive moment is an opening for the diagnostic gaze.

## Diplomatic Rhetoric

"I am a good diplomat."

These were the words that held my attention as I sat in a chair characteristic of most clinical settings—sterile, hard, seemingly surfaced for creatures without spines or sensory receptors. Here I was at an autism clinic, applying for a spot in a social skills program that was also moonlighting as an autism research study. A research associate–cum–social worker had earlier handed me a binder of paperwork, which featured a series of symptom questionnaires and diagnostic check boxes. In order to qualify for services, I once again had to jump through diagnostic hoops, despite already having diagnostic papers that attested my "incurable" condition. "I am a good diplomat," I repeated to myself. The choices on the form ranged, Likert-style, from *definitely agree* to *definitely disagree*. "Diplomat, diplomat," I whispered, fumbling for an answer. A woman across the hall slow-nodded, as if my whispered echoes had confirmed her deepest pathological suspicions of me.

After twenty minutes of pondering, I flagged down the social worker. "What is this question asking, exactly?" I entreated. In my confusion, I had summoned to mind all of the possibilities I could imagine, none of which seemed relevant to an autism survey. Was I a good diplomat? I hadn't worked for the government or any other entity that could conceivably describe its work as diplomacy. I hadn't even participated in mock diplomatic activities, such as Model UN, seeing as I had dropped out of the ninth grade. I wasn't an ambassador to anything, except maybe the Electric Light Orchestra.[39] How could I assess my facility with diplomacy without ever having worked as a diplomat?

Of course, the social worker seemed to interpret my confusion as a classic autistic response. The question wasn't gauging my finesse with international policy, but was rather attempting to demarcate my sociability. Was I socially deft? Was I sensitive? Was I tactful and kind and contextually appropriate? Was I a good diplomat?

Some years later, I learned that this question—and, in fact, the whole questionnaire—hailed from the Autism Spectrum Quotient, a screening instrument developed by Simon Baron-Cohen and his colleagues at the Autism Research Centre at the University of Cambridge. The AQ, as it is commonly known, was popularized by web outlets in the early 2000s as public interest in autism reached critical mass. A full-length reprint of the test, for instance, had appeared in *Wired* magazine as a companion piece to Steve Silberman's "The Geek Syndrome."[40] In the *Wired* spread, an online AQ test implored users to respond to fifty statements ranging from "I am fascinated by dates" to "I find making up stories easy."[41] Users could then tally their scores to determine whether or not they possessed a preponderance of autistic traits (which, the test cautioned, does not necessarily indicate whether someone is actually autistic). Those with a higher number of autistic traits, according to the AQ, are far less likely to be good diplomats.

I am among them. I am not a good diplomat.

Diplomacy is, of course, a rhetorically charged construction. It carries invitational resonances, wherein interlocutors are charged with the bringing-under of bodies, trading rhetorical truisms as though dialogic exchange were a cocktail party. But so too does diplomacy imply a normative respectability, wherein rhetors maintain calm demeanor and comply with the polite gestures of the body politic. That is, in order to be considered diplomatic, one must be-have, move, and communicate in prosocial, appropriate ways. Diplomacy is the rhetoricizing of civility and deference. It is what autistics are time and again claimed to lack. If we believe what clinical scholarship tells us, then autistics reside in the domain of bluntness, impulsivity, literality, and flattened affect; di-plomacy, conversely, is the realm of "tact" and "complex forms of deception."[42] We are Malabou's plastique, ready to detonate. Diplomacy is deferential art, and autism is unfiltered neurological onslaught. Or, to put it more autistickly: we, the autistic, have easily accomplished all that the acronym TMI (too much information) has to offer. Diplomacy is trickery dressed as morality. Autistic author Rachel Cohen-Rottenberg notes this particularly ironic stance—that autistics are considered liars for the kinds of honesty in which they traffic, while allistic liars are considered honest for the diplomacy with which they handle themselves.[43] As she aptly laments, "Autistic people are called unem-pathetic, rigid, black-and-white thinkers in a society in which most political discourse is inhuman, inflexible, and polarized."[44]

Diplomacy, in many regards, functions as a metonym for rhetorical ex-change, or the kinds of sociality that rhetoric privileges. It is rhetorically en-demic. Rhetors employ diplomatic methods as a structural means of some-times persuading, sometimes inviting audiences to a given table. Diplomacy is the extension of welcoming gesture, of pressuring or pressing others with courteous words and outstretched hands. One can have stances and be diplo-matic, but those stances, if they are to prove attractive to doubting others, require cloaking, repositioning, discursive transposition. A stance becomes diplomatic when it represents itself as an opening rather than an end point. Yet a stance is an end point, feet glued in place, chair nailed to ground. Stances head tables, not zip lines. When clothed in the guise of motility, however, a stance beckons, parading itself as a diplomatic gesture. Stances escape Zeno's freeze-frame by pretending they are transportable, creative, and inviting (even if exactly the opposite is true).

Let us here consider a different Zeno, not Zeno of Elea, but Zeno of Citium. A fourth-century philosopher, Zeno regarded rhetoric as a diplomatic exercise, what he termed an open hand. Logic or dialectic, however, was represented by a closed fist. As George Kennedy explains of Zeno's metaphor, "Dialectic is rigorous and constructs chains of arguments; rhetoric is popular and expan-sive."[45] The closed fist signals comprehensiveness, the boundedness of logic and knowledge. The open hand is rhetorical widening, a figure of flexibility and receptivity. Autistic bodies are commonly read as closed fists in need of al-listic open-handedness. We are rigid, lockstep, creatures of pathological habit.

M. Ariel Cascio argues that rigidity has become so metaphoric of autism that it stretches "across different domains [and] demonstrates a way in which diagnostic characteristics become metaphors for medical practice."[46] Even social stories, an interventionist genre in which common social skills or scenarios are dissected for autistic children, operate under the default assumption that autistics are "brutally honest," "guileless," and nondiplomatic—and that each of these characteristics requires rhetorical remediation.[47]

When I self-identify as neuroqueer, for example, allistic others can presume that my identification is borne of a rigid bodymind whose rhetoricity is neurologically absented or halved. Why would I readily identify with stigmatized identities? Do I not comprehend that claiming disability is to insult myself or to lessen my own worth? Do I not realize that allistic, heterosexual others will find my brazenness impolite, irrelevant, off-putting, or (my favorite) militaristic? "Don't label yourself," responded a social worker when I told her I was queer. My identity is the clenched hand, knuckles pulsating from tensioned muscles. Able-bodied identity escapes being an identity, because able-bodiedness is default and classic and planar, is an inviting table, is a facetiously welcoming gesture.

Although neuroqueer subjects are often reduced to rigidity as a means of denying their rhetoricity, there is value in the clenched hand, the antidiplomatic disclosure. As in, "Fuck this. I'm autistic." Rigidity can simultaneously harness and transcend pejorative. In 1969, Edward Corbett famously refigured the contours of Zeno's analogy, suggesting that rhetoric's open hand often serves as a gatekeeper, preventing marginal bodies from participating in civic spaces.[48] In particular, Corbett argued that the radical activism of the 1960s—most specifically, the Black Power as well as civil rights movements—had given way to new rhetorical tactics, tactics emblematic not of the open hand, but of the closed fist. Wrote Corbett, "The closed fist [of Zeno] symbolized the tight, spare, compressed discourse of the philosopher; the open hand symbolized the relaxed, expansive, ingratiating discourse of the orator. . . . I see the two metaphors now as having taken on a new tenor. The open hand might be said to characterize the kind of persuasive discourse that seeks to carry its point by reasoned, sustained, conciliatory discussion of the issues. The closed fist might signify the kind of persuasive activity that seeks to carry its point by non-rationale [sic], nonsequential, often non-verbal, frequently provocative means."[49] Corbett's reimagining of the closed fist—as provocation rather than logic—was especially indebted to activist strategies, such as boycotts, sit-ins, marches, riots, and even tactical acts of aggression, namely vandalism and violence. Describing the new rhetoric of the closed fist as "muscular rhetoric" or "body rhetoric," Corbett remarks that its most likely proponents are the "dispossessed, the disenfranchised in our society—poor people, students, minority groups—people who do not have ready access to the established channels of communications."[50] In other words: where the open hand summons those in or with power, the closed fist strikes and shatters. Diplomacy is merely another kind of invitation, an opening through which only the few have means to enter.

A number of disability studies scholars have wrangled with invitational rhetorics and their impact on disabled bodies. Both Brenda Brueggemann and Shannon Walters, for instance, have maintained that muscular rhetorics draw their power and potential from their slipperiness, their embodied effects.[51] In *Rhetorical Touch*, Walters directs our attention to haptics, and the ways in which touch compels rhetoricians to "comprehensively let go of the idealized image of an independent, nondisabled, singular rhetor and to embrace the possibilities of new configurations among communicators, speaking and nonspeaking, and multiple audiences across ranges of ability and disability."[52] In particular, Walters suggests that the opening and closing of one's palm are not moves borne of the "same basic skeletal structure," but are rather haptical tactics that disabled rhetors may choose to engage dependent on the power differentials in a given context.[53] Brueggemann, in *Deaf Subjects*, considers a similar approach to rhetoric's skeletal structures, positioning the open-closed hand within American Sign Language (ASL) literature. More specifically, she focuses on ABC-123 stories, in which signing interlocutors perform the English alphabet on the body, creating a "between space for ASL-English."[54] Here, Brueggemann maintains that the opening and closing of hands work in concert together in this ASL between space, gesturing across and between expansive and compressed discourse, across and between verbal and nonverbal action. Writes Brueggemann, "Whether open or closed, the hands, face, and body of the signing ABC-123 storyteller set up the entire grammar of the story, poem, or performance."[55] Neuroqueer grammars twist rhetorical gestures as they deploy them.

Disclosive moments are moments in which normative conceptions of diplomacy and rigidity tussle. They are moments in which hands beckon and wave, in which hands signal STOP or draw fingers to throat in death-style motion, in which hands are bound and restrained from stimming, in which hands fold neatly on tables, in which hands remove hands from throats, in which hands lift up the legs of chairs and topple bodies, in which hands open, close, punch, caress, retreat, die. Rhetorics are metaphorically handsy things, and the complexities of disclosure reveal both violent and reclamatory nuances.

And yet, disclosure and diplomacy are sites from which the precarity of neuroqueer ethos might be queerly regarded and queerly reclaimed. Am I my diagnosis? When my neuroqueer bodymind makes known its presence, what, exactly, does it intend to confess? Who shall witness or invite my confession, and with what power do they compel my bodily response? To restate the obvious, clinical rhetorics present serious challenges to disability disclosure. To claim autism is to claim rudeness, silence, tactlessness, nonpersonhood; it is to invite doubting others to lay diagnose or question one's rhetorical competence. And yet it is precisely these claims and challenges that buttress much of the autistic culture movement's embrace of public disclosure, of uncloseting one's autism. Clinicians would have us believe that autistic absence in public life is but a symptom of autism itself: autism prevents us from full participation; should an autistic participate or express desire to participate, the legitimacy of her autism must be called into question. It is this catch-22 that fuels activist desires for personal narrative and declarative positionality around autism.

As autistic author Cynthia Kim points out, "[Passing as allistic] robs us of who we are and cloaks us in disguises that are ill-fitting and unflattering, leaving us stranded halfway between a fictional ideal of normal and the truth of our real selves."[56] Autistic poet N. I. Nicholson echoes the gravity of Kim's sentiment, warning, "I spent nearly all of my childhood trying to pass for allistic, once I figured out that I was not the so-called 'normal' that everyone else seemed to be. My chameleon circuit worked so well it almost killed me."[57] Diplomacy, in many senses, is one such kind of passing, a fictional ideal that can kill, physically and spiritually. In saying this, I do not mean to suggest that autistic people are never diplomatic, or that our brains lack tact modules, or that vaccines inject children with rude mercury. Rather, I mean to suggest that diplomacy is an allistic construct, one that is straightly configured so as to disinvite neuroqueer subjects. We have been authored as and into meanness. It is through diplomatic exchanges that autistic people return to the paradoxical, becoming demidiplomats in the eyes of our opposition. Can we ever reason ourselves out of the nonreason that rhetoricians presume of us?

And so, I am not a good diplomat. I am, in the words of Cheryl Marie Wade, "the sock in the eye with a gnarled fist."[58] Others may project invitation onto my body, but my body's rigidity punches, lurches, and shatters with (in)voluntary response. My *autistic pride* and *neuroqueer* buttons are prickly declarations, objects that confess as much as they stab. There is a queer simultaneity in autistic opening and autistic fisting, of engaging the diplomatic as bluntly as our bodyminds shun it. As Petra Kuppers describes, "Disability *is*, but isn't clear. Pain and muscular effort *is*, but isn't readable, and knowable, and able to be put into pat narratives."[59] Paradoxes attend disability, even when disability resists the paradoxical.

Mainstream narratives around autism privilege the figure of the child, which is perhaps one reason why desexualized caricatures of autistics abound. Autism is, we assume, a childhood thing: a childhood diagnosis, a childhood disclosure, a childhood experiential, a childhood episteme. Some of the more pernicious of these tropes revolve around ableist constructs of mental age, presupposing that autistic adults are adult in physicality only, and thereby require elliptic readings of any and all autistic utterances. Rhetoric, in many respects, is not only an ableist and heterocentric project, but an ageist project. If one's brain isn't fully developed, in all of the shady resonances that cognitive development promotes, then rhetorical capacity is often regarded as primitive, halved.[60] Developmentalism presumes rhetorical incapacity of people who are designated "childlike" because it problematically presumes incapacity on the part of children writ large. Even worse, the figure of the perpetual child provides fodder and motive for forensic case studies on autistic people, from which journalists and pop psychologists extrapolate stereotypes of autistic adults as inherent pedophiles (e.g., if autistic adults are mentally children, then they run the risk of functioning as children psychosocially and psychosexually, or so the logic goes). In 2013, Temple Grandin's mother, Eustacia Cutler, wrote a horrific article for the *Daily Beast* in which she (quite unempirically and egregiously) warned that autistic men are potential child pornographers lying in wait: "Though now equipped with a full-grown body and full-grown sexual drive, many ASD males are stuck emotionally at a prepubescent age. They look like grown men, but inside they're only 10 years old. They don't want adults to show them how sex is done; they want 10-year-olds to show them."[61] As if Cutler's suppositions weren't defamatory enough, a number of autism professionals and journalists have joined the alarmist bandwagon, suggesting autism as a cause for predatory behavior and child rape.[62] Such proclamations also call to mind long-standing motifs that ardently work to equate queerness and pedophilia. In the case of autism, researchers often position pedophilic futures as yet another reason for interventionism. If autistics aren't trained into prosocial beings, then they will steal the childhoods of allistic others—for this is what autism, that parasitic entity, impels its subjects to do.

Disability activists have maintained for some time that children are often weaponized by disability charities.[63] Rhetorics of alarmism bring in funds, and disabled children and their stolen futures serve as pitiable mascots. Autism Speaks, for instance, has for years compared childhood autism prevalence to a number of fatal situations, such as car crashes and hypothermia, despite autism being nonfatal. More egregiously, Autism Speaks's promotional materials routinely exclaim that "more children will be diagnosed with autism spectrum disorder than AIDS, diabetes and cancer combined."[64] The conditions to which Autism Speaks compares autism are notable because these comparisons are meant to invoke dichotomies around genetic lottery versus voluntariness and personal choice (think, for instance, of stereotypes about smoking and lung cancer, or sizeism and type 2 diabetes), with the nonfatal genetic condition (autism) positioned as the worst possible outcome. Furthermore, the AIDS comparisons summon numerous cultural stereotypes, most especially those that target gay men.[65] Autism Speaks, like many past disability charities, benefits from histories of ableism and queer fear as a means for raising money. The stigma that attends AIDS, for example, is leveraged against the figure of the unwilling and long-suffering autistic child, who is claimed to receive far less federal funding than those who have HIV/AIDS, at $79 million versus $394 million.[66] Queers might be recruiting children, but autism recruits more, and it's deadlier—a (neurologically queer?) living death.

And yet, the vast majority of autistics are not children (nor are they adult children, groan) but adults. Childhood is where many autistethnographies diverge from traditional narrative scripts about autism. Autistethnographical writing, while at times recounting childhood or lost adolescence, overwhelmingly bends toward the adult. In particular, my focus in this section revolves around autistethnographical narratives that relate experiences of diagnosis and disclosure. Many of these narratives, whether published via blog or print venues, revolve around adult diagnosis. That adults can receive autism diagnoses often comes as a shock to those outside the autistic community, including the very professionals who conduct diagnostic assessments—because isn't autism a childhood thing?

If autism is a childhood thing, then autistic adults are read as children, as hovering toward the severe edges of a demi-rhetorical continuum. Claiming, for instance, that one was diagnosed with autism as an adult is often read as misdiagnosis—one's autism must not be real enough or terrible enough if it hadn't been cataloged during early childhood. Of course, these stereotypes ignore, for instance, that many adult autism diagnoses take shape as reclassifications, replacing and/or complementing prior diagnoses such as intellectual disability, verbal apraxia, schizophrenia, ADHD, borderline personality disorder, selective mutism, cerebral palsy, Tourette's, and beyond. Deinstitutionalization brought as many diagnostic shifts as did revisions to the DSM.[67]

But so too is it important to recognize the racism, ethnocentrism, sexism, and classism that attend autism's diagnostic politics. It is well documented that children of color in the United States, most especially black and Latinx children, are diagnosed far older, and in much smaller proportions, when compared with white children.[68] For instance, Paul Heilker points out that black autistic children are frequently "misdiagnosed as having Attention Deficit Hyperactivity Disorder, Obsessive Compulsive Disorder, and Oppositional Defiant Disorder."[69] These misdiagnoses delay the age at which autistic children (and adults) of color receive necessary services from school districts or governmental agencies, and likewise impact their ability to self-identify and access disability culture and autistic elders.[70] Furthermore, the pathologizing of black and brown bodyminds codes blackness and brownness as neurologically determined and immoral behavior, a logic that calls upon, as Nirmala Erevelles argues, racist legacies (not to mention present-day practices) of "eugenic criminology."[71] In these nefarious constructions, disability and race intersect to frame children of color as dangerous, with danger resulting from aberrant biology and disordered conduct. As such, whereas white autistic children might be represented as hapless victims of neurology, autistic children of color are often represented more deterministically and violently, as products of bad parenting or as volcanoes waiting to explode. Importantly, Erevelles warns, many neurodivergent diagnoses, including autism, are operationalized as weapons of voluntariness and willfulness when applied to children of color, wherein students are "denied the support that an individual education plan can provide because the predominantly white [school] administration assumes these students are *choosing* to act out."[72] These vicious stereotypes manifest insidiously in the lives of disabled children of color, reducing their access to care and support as well as segregating them from their communities, thrusting them into school-to-prison pipelines, and drastically increasing their likelihoods of abuse or death.

Among the many avenues through which disabled children of color are exposed to systemic violences, Erevelles draws attention to zero-tolerance policies in k–12 settings, in which children of color are more likely to be tracked into special education and targeted by law enforcement. One prominent example of police abuse and racist interventionism is the protracted legal battle of Kayleb Moon-Robinson, an autistic and black child who, at the age of eleven, was charged with disorderly conduct for kicking a trash can at school.[73] Even more horrifically, two weeks after the initial charge, Moon-Robinson was arrested for felonious assault when he resisted going to the principal's office after the school resource officer attempted to forcibly drag him there.[74] Outraged by the ways in which an autistic child had been criminalized for acting autistically (or even just plain acting like an eleven-year-old child), autistic blogger, parent, and activist Morénike Onaiwu writes, "According to the Individuals with Disabilities Education Act (IDEA) and the Americans with Disabilities Act (ADA), Kayleb should have been afforded certain provisions and accommodations by his school district and by local law enforcement. He was not. And now this 6th grade child has to face life as a convicted felon before he's even old enough to drive. Not because he shot, stabbed, raped, or murdered anyone, but because he did not receive sufficient support for his disability. He is now being made to pay the ultimate price."[75] Clearly, race attends diagnosis in particular, and often violent, ways. When autistics of color are disclosed, statements such as "I am autistic" are often interpreted both callously and elliptically by white and allistic others. While doubt arguably attends any autistic disclosure, the doubt surrounding autistics of color is of a different magnitude, one sustained by lack of representation and invisibility across the broadest reaches of autism politics. Autistic blogger N. I. Nicholson maintains that "the noticeable lack of our [black] voices in the public discussion of autism will continue to perpetuate the myth that autism is a 'white' issue."[76] Even a cursory glance at the boards of major autism advocacy organizations reveals white supremacy at work. The leadership of autism orgs in the United States and Canada is startlingly white, including those organizations that are autistic-run and pro-neurodiversity in focus. As one example, blogger Kerima Çevik created an infographic depicting the racial makeup of Autism Speaks's 2013 board of directors.[77] Of the thirty-three board members, twenty-five were white men and only one board member was a person of color. All board members, of course, were nonautistic.[78]

In addition to its highly raced dimensions, autism diagnosis is profoundly gendered, largely skewing toward young (often white, often middle-class or affluent) cisgender boys. Ratios like 4:1 and 10:1 abound in cognitive studies journals, highlighting the clinical impulse to overlook girls and diagnose boys, boys, boys. But maleness not only lingers in statistics and diagnostic disparities—it finds itself embedded in clinical conceptions of autism at their most basic levels. We might recall, for instance, that autism's very essence is often theorized as a condition of the "extreme male brain."[79] Diagnostic instruments, such as the Modified Checklist for Autism in Toddlers, exhort parents and social workers to remain on high alert for the many and supposedly woeful signs of autism, signs that infiltrate childhood play, signs that involve spinning the wheels of toy cars or fixating on lampposts and ceiling fans. One questionnaire, the Autism Spectrum Quotient, asks prospective diagnosees to check certain boxes if they prefer museums to movies, remember license plate numbers, or care about the feelings and lives of human others.[80]

Bearing distinction as the first book published on autism and gender actually by autistic people, *Women from Another Planet?* (WFAP) is a self-proclaimed autie-ethnography produced by several autistic women and autistic gender-queer individuals. In one chapter, Jean Kearns Miller, an autistic writer and professor, argues that "little professorial girls may be seen as a social anomaly (not acting like girls), and their perceived socio-sexual deviance may obscure their neurological difference. . . . But are we really such an anomaly? Perhaps our invisibility skews the data."[81] Similarly, in her contribution to WFAP, Jane Meyerding attributes her late diagnosis to allistic obsession with her gender nonconformity. Recounting her identification as a lesbian feminist during the 1970s, Meyerding laments her seeming alienness within a community that, she'd thought at the time, might provide her a sense of kinship and commonality. It was only after she realized she was autistic, however, that she understood herself as genderless. As she describes, "My gut, my feelings, my self-awareness remain stubbornly and radically un-gendered."[82] But Meyerding's identification as both autistic and genderless was delayed, in part, because her gender variance had been flagged variously as willfulness and insubordinate behavior. Although Meyerding admits to (even cherishes) her willful and stubborn commitment to radical feminism, she experienced others' denials of her disability and her gender identity as attempts to eradicate her very essence. Her impulse, she notes, is toward bodies that exist outside gender, language, and social customs: "The kinds of connections I want (and occasionally crave) are too esoteric and bloodless to interest normal people, although they would be rich and enriching for me."[83]

And, indeed, it is this very construction of the impulse that genders the dimensions and domains in which autism is claimed to lie. Daina Krumins, another writer in WFAP, follows Meyerding as describing autistic impulses as a form of relationality—but this relationality is often read under a gendered rubric by those who wield diagnostic power. These impulses, she asserts, culminate as a striving toward the nonhuman. For Krumins, this more-than-human relationality is organized around textures: "The most important things—visual things, textures particularly, but also shapes, colors, movement—were the things to which my heart opened."[84] Describing her fear of dolls, she asks, "So what is alive and what isn't? What makes the atoms in the lake different from the atoms that make a human being?"[85] Importantly, Krumins notes that others viewed her communion with and among things as a young girl being unladylike rather than a young girl being autistic.

Cisnormativity governs autism's diagnostic constructions. We can locate these cisnormative impulses in demi-rhetorical ideas about male and female brains, much like we can locate these impulses in interventionist rhetorics and histories. In many respects, ABA is more aptly termed a sociosexual intervention than a mere social intervention, seeking as it does to make neuroqueer subjects virtually indistinguishable from their neurotypical, heterosexual, and cisgender peers. Becoming nonautistic is likewise becoming nonqueer—for anything that registers as socially deviant may fall under autism's purview.

Each of these impulses deeply affects how autistic women, nonbinary individuals, and people of color self-disclose, in large part because they pose barriers to clinical diagnosis as well as personal identifications with autism. Of normative entelechies, Burke wrote, "What is more 'perfectionist' in essence than the impulse, when one is in dire need of something, to so state this need that one in effect 'defines' the situation?"[86] The cisnormativity that structures diagnosis is a terministic compulsion, or an ideological striving toward neurological containment. These logics determine not only who qualifies as autistic but who qualifies as sociosexually deviant—and where the overlap or synonymity between the two lies. If clinical diagnosis is a rhetoric of the open hand, then this hand is open to very few individuals, shrinking backward faster than it can extend. But more, even when granted these invitations—wherein deviant bodies are acknowledged for their deviance—neuroqueer subjects are routinely denied the agency and rhetoricity to control their own lives, to author their identities, performances, epistemes, and expressions, on their own terms. The autistic turn to virtual spaces and self-publishing, in many respects, represents one such move toward reclaiming corporeal authorship of autistic experience, in all of its diversity.

## "Coming Aut"

Though certainly not equivalent, becoming autistic is not unlike becoming queer. Becoming is not so much a disease course or an orchestrated change in one's neurosocial essence as much as it is a coming-to-know. In this we might recall Byron Hawk's contention that entelechy isn't prescient for its ability to come to a predetermined end, but rather for its processuality, for its striving toward a becoming that is multiple and always-more.[87] Becoming exceeds diagnostic process, even when diagnostics hold a shaping role in one's coming-to-know, or one's self-epistemic. Diagnosis unto itself represents multiple lines of flight, directing potentially infinite and always-emerging ways of becoming oneself. In stating this, I am indebted to Stephanie Kerschbaum's work on difference and what it means to identify (with) those differences that culminate and/or anatomize one's very being.[88] In examining the whatness of difference, Kerschbaum draws from Mikhail Bakhtin to suggest that identity is not only fluid and malleable but always emergent, always entelechial in its striving toward that emergence. In this regard, I become autistic (or autisticker?) every waking moment. The longer I regard myself as autistic, the more autistic I become.

While diagnosis seemingly invites the commentary, pronouncements, and disbeliefs of nonautistic others—preserving the nonautistic, as it were, as an open hand—autistic people routinely queer the contours of what it means to disclose or diagnose. They fist those fuckers up, exchanging DSM bullet points for their own experiences with and exposures to autistic communities. Community narratives often focus intently on diagnostic moments, not as a means to validate one's autistickness, but rather to narrate, warp, and bend the processes by which an autistic person enters an autistic culture. Can one claim autism if one believes ze has a theory of mind? Is a person any less autistic if they believe the DSM-5 is exclusionary and/or bullshit? Can one identify as autistic if one has never received a diagnosis to begin with, but feels affinity with #ActuallyAutistic Tumblr?

This focus on culture is particularly neuroqueer: it diverts attention from discourses that might otherwise seek to pathologize or intervene in the lives of autistic people, in many ways shattering the aims of diagnostic process itself. This process is, in many respects, what Margaret Price calls "counter-diagnosis." In "Her Pronouns Wax and Wane," Price examines the ways in which neurodivergent life writers queer disability disclosures by means of counter-diagnostic moves.[89] Price describes counter-diagnosis as rhetorical maneuvers that "subvert the diagnostic urge to 'explain' a disabled mind" and declares its affinities to the "coming-out story" in queer narratives.[90] What marks these rhetorical moves as queer, however, is their pseudo- or demi-rhetoricality, their willingness to reject the rhetorical. Counter-diagnosis, according to Price, doesn't entirely discount diagnosis, but it also doesn't affirm diagnosis. Rather, Price maintains, these disclosive narratives accrue their power in "accepting, rejecting, mimicking, and contesting the diagnostic urge in various ways. Counter-diagnosis is an oxymoronic form."[91]

Numerous autistic narratives over the past decade have addressed the coming-out valences of counter-diagnosis, framing autistic disclosures in decidedly queer-imbued terms and rhetorical frames. One example is the aptly (and ironically?) named Ask and Tell, which none-too-subtly throws punches at the U.S. military's ill-famed Don't Ask, Don't Tell policy. Edited by autie-biographer Stephen Shore, Ask and Tell features essays written solely by autistic authors, addressing everything from constructing an individualized education program in elementary school to dating and sexuality and the "unconventional diasporas" that have come to form autistic cultural spaces.[92]

Dinah Murray's edited collection *Coming Out Asperger* is another such example of queerly influenced countering. In her introduction to the collection, Murray details the varied meanings that clinical diagnosis can hold over its autistic subjects—meanings that shift over time and according to rhetorical situation. She writes, "Diagnosis is not a simple and straightforward process involving the transfer of some information from one box to another box. The transfer of the diagnosis does not occur in an isolated space of its own; it does not occur instantaneously; it has a history, and it has consequences. The difference goes beyond the moment of information transfer; the diagnosis makes a difference to our memories of the past and to our expectations for the future."[93] Like Price, Murray elucidates the demi-rhetorical dimensions of diagnosis. Popularly, diagnosis is often conceived as a one-time event that identifies what is to be "avoided, cured or aided."[94] For the neuroqueer, however, diagnosis tends to be all consuming and temporally contingent, serving as a demi-rhetorical lens through which the diagnosed can (un)story their lives. In this manner, diagnosis doesn't constitute the ten minutes in which a doctor hands over paperwork and explains your condition: it is, perplexingly, the wormhole through which all of your disclosures, relationships, knowledges, and practices travel. Autism provides a discursive and often causal lens through which individual and collective bodies might be authored. In being disclosed, we become autistexts, body-texts ripe for shaping, configuring, intervening, and dis/empowering.

Coming out autistic, then, to revisit the narrative frame of Murray's book, is continual engagement with diagnosis. "Coming aut," as it were, queers into countering. Neuroqueer disclosures might be marked by their repetitiveness and contingency—for disclosing is not a singular moment, nor is one disclosure ever the same as a subsequent disclosure. Consequently, disclosure can often take form as myriad encounters with allistic others who presume any admission represents opportunity for intervention. We become embodied dot-dot-dots, potential sites of correction. Coming aut, however, does have radical potentialities. These potentialities, as Byron Hawk has claimed, extend "beyond instrumentalist, linear readings of entelechy toward functional ecologies and lines of flight."[95] In other words, coming aut is notable for its plasticity and always-emergingness, its multiple paths toward eventual fruitions. For example, Stephen Shore highlights how disclosure can effect "change in the societal construction of a person on the autism spectrum. Each individual disclosure works towards changing this societal construct one person at a time."[96] This emphasis on changing societal perceptions—especially those of the alarmist, autism-is-death variety—is one that autistic writer Morénike Onaiwu compellingly impresses upon her readers:

I more than wanted to come out; I needed to. I wanted anyone out there who remotely identified with me in any way (age, gender, ethnicity, region, etc) to be encouraged by my existence. To know that they were not alone. I wanted autistic kids (like my own, and others) to know that it's okay to grow up to be an autistic adult—like me. I wanted people to know that though I have very real challenges, being autistic has also afforded me many strengths too. That my (nor your) life is not "destroyed" by autism, but it is very much intertwined with it and all of its elements (positive and negative).[97]

In this vein, coming aut can facilitate, as autistic blogger Corbin Kramer maintains, a kind of "autistic networking."[98] As Onaiwu makes clear, storying autism opens spaces for intergenerational autistic community—and, importantly, storying spans modality. A stimming body discloses autistic stories, as does a typed manifesto on Wordpress, as does a self-injuring child on a school bus. These stories are at times codified in print, and at times they resist social-symbolic impulses, lingering in the textures of unnarrated experiences, or in the relationality between the autistic and the material world.

Counter-diagnosis promotes a crip-queer ethos, what Jenell Johnson has termed kakoethos (literally, as she puts it, "anti-ethos").[99] Importantly, and as discussed in chapter 1, Johnson emphasizes that kakoethos is not the absence of ethos. Instead, she argues, kakoethos signifies bad character, or the "discreditable."[100] Kakoethos entails opposing, countering, and neuroqueering that which is typically framed as authoritative and credible. One model of such counter-diagnostic and kakoethical moves is the practice of self-diagnosis in autistic spaces.

In autistic communities, diagnosis is often, though not exclusively, discussed across three categories: official diagnosis, unofficial diagnosis, and self-diagnosis. Notably, none of these categories is mutually exclusive, and their definitions shift depending on context and interlocutor. The taxonomy remains important, however, because most autistics are adults, despite what autism charities might have us believe, and thus often have personal experience with more than one diagnostic encounter. In the United States, large-scale autism prevalence studies, such as those conducted by the Centers for Disease Control and Prevention (CDC), overwhelmingly limit their samples to children.[101] Thus, numerous stakeholders, most prominently Jenny McCarthy, use prevalence statistics such as "1 in 68" to argue that autistic adults are nonexistent—merely because they haven't been either clinically assessed or cataloged in longitudinal studies. In England, however, a study by Brugha et al. found that adult autism prevalence was 1.1 percent among the sample they engaged, roughly equivalent to the prevalence found among children at the time.[102] When conducting prevalence studies, regardless of age range, researchers have counted individuals as autistic even when they do not have clinical diagnoses, meaning that the numbers we throw around incorporate a potentially wider swath of individuals than doctors see fit to recognize officially.[103]

Like those of many individuals, my diagnostic story is hard to pin down. Often, when I declare that I'm autistic, others feel invited to respond with, "When were you diagnosed?" I have been recipient to this question for nearly two decades, as if the moment of my official diagnosis should overtake all else in importance. But more, the potential meanings of this question confound me, in part because it's impossible to glean why someone might be asking this question, or what innuendos might lie hidden (in all of their elliptic glory) in the crevices of syllables.

If I want to be precise, *autism* entered my vocabulary when I was fifteen years old. At that point in time, I had stopped attending the ninth grade and was facing a truancy hearing. The school district, however, thought my absence might be disability related and decided to assess me for learning disabilities. To be clear, there is very little that I remember (or want to remember) about this period in time. I thought of myself as a truant—a dropout, a failure. My anxiety was so high that I had experienced a total mental and physical breakdown, and undergoing stringent disability assessments had only instilled more despair, to the point that I became suicidal. My parents, for their part, were not enthusiastic about the idea that I might be disabled, learning or otherwise, and sought out second opinions from other clinicians. But despite all of these efforts to resist disability, autism made itself known.

Only, autism did not make itself officially known. That is, my diagnosis was not an official verdict, but more of a clinically informed pronouncement that I was autistic and should seek additional testing. This pronouncement, despite its certainty, did not derive from an autism-specific battery of tests, nor was it made by practitioners qualified, in the eyes of many service grantors, to make that pronouncement. In other words: the assessment might have qualified me to claim I was autistic or even to receive an individualized education program (maybe), but it did not qualify me for university accommodations, social assistance, or county services.

Ultimately, I dropped out of high school, and it wasn't until I was a college-aged adult that I sought an official diagnosis. This trajectory toward officialness is often narrated by autistic people. Memoirist Cynthia Kim, for instance, recounts in her blog her decision to seek testing at the age of forty-two.[104] The decision, she notes, wasn't born of a need for services or accommodations—by that point in her life, she was self-employed and had, through much struggle, determined her own set of self-accommodations that enabled her to both compensate and thrive. Instead, Kim maintains, "While not necessary in any practical sense, my Asperger's syndrome diagnosis was a turning point for me. It answered a question that I'd been asking myself since childhood: Why am I so different from other people? That may seem like a trivial question, but when left unanswered for decades, it can become unsettling and haunting. Finally having an answer opened the door for me to do something I'd never been able to do: accept myself as I am."[105] Kim's claim of acceptance grapples with all of the queer perversity that counter-diagnostic narratives have to offer. As I noted earlier of Dinah Murray's work, diagnosis is clinically framed as identifying the pathological, generally for the purposes of eradicating or mitigating the freshly labeled pathology. To seek diagnosis for acceptance—for something like autism—flips the bird at what diagnosis generally intends. Kim's desire for diagnosis is to subvert the fixity that diagnosticians wish to dole out. Interestingly, Kim proclaims that it was prior to diagnosis and her own self-discovery when she felt the curative impulse most keenly. "The more I tried to fix myself," she writes, "the worse I felt."[106]

In my case, I felt I needed the officialness because I had not found successful means of coping. In many respects, my self-identity as an autistic person had long been forged, and I mostly felt accurate and validated in claiming autism for myself. But seeking diagnosis as an adult in the United States is quite a challenge. Many insurance companies will not cover adult assessment, as most states' autism parity laws (if they even have them) only structure diagnostic coverage up to ages eighteen or twenty-one. Without insurance, assessment costs can range from $500 to $5,000. In my case, I had to take out additional student loans to cover the costs. Even worse, county and state developmental disability agencies often require that one receive an official diagnosis prior to age twenty-one or twenty-two in order to receive vital services. (So, for instance, even though Medical Science™ tells us that one is born with autism, if one's autism isn't cataloged by a circumscribed set of tests and proctored by People with Super-Specific Credentials before age twenty-three, then one is shit out of luck.)

The hurdles that official diagnosis poses are many. Socioeconomic status, age, gender, race, and ethnicity all impact the likelihood of one receiving officialness's brand. And yet, receiving an official diagnosis, as Julia Miele Rodas makes clear, can often pave oppressive futures for those who have been so marked.[107] Autistic people face lives of substandard care, segregation from their communities, institutionalization, and forcible medical interventions. As well, those with official™ diagnoses may be barred from serving in the military, face significant barriers in child adoption and/or custody battles, risk losing their children at any time to social services, are routinely denied citizenship or residency status upon emigrating, are systematically disadvantaged in divorce and civil separation cases in court, and may lose choice and civil rights altogether if forced under the legal guardianship of another, allistic adult.[108]

Refusing diagnosis and its attendant paradigms, Nick Walker notes, can present powerful possibilities for coming aut.[109] For her part, Rodas counters diagnosis by claiming herself "not diagnosed, but 'diagnosable,'" an identification through which she can "simultaneously claim kinship with disability and disown the social stigma and medicalized reduction in those conventional readings."[110] In many respects, what Rodas calls *diagnosable* maps onto neuroqueer conceptions of self-diagnosis. Unlike official or even unofficial diagnosis, which requires clinical intermediaries and pathology paradigms, self-diagnosis resists definition or containment, straddling and fucking common notions of identification and disability.

The kakoethos of self-diagnosis primarily arises from lack of doctor involvement. Anyone, as allistic logic goes, can randomly decide to call themselves autistic. The invitations presumed of autism disclosures, however unconscious, frequently stem from an allistic desire to police neuroqueer bodies—to ensure that only medical systems ensure the purity and fixity of what autism or ability can mean. Because autism is perceived incrementally, no autistic person can ever be autistic enough, regardless of the means through which they come to identify as autistic. I may have an official diagnosis, but is it official enough? How many neuropsychologists evaluated me? Where did they receive their training? What tests did they administer? Am I sure that I wish to label myself with this diagnostic scourge? Any and all of these questions routinely attend autistic people's decisions to make known their neuroqueer identifications.

With self-diagnosis, however, autistic people may face rhetorical situations in which their morality and sense of ethics are heavily scrutinized. Autistic blogger M. Kelter echoes both Walker and Rodas in claiming that self-diagnosis reveals the prejudices that attend any kind of diagnosis, especially those perceived as official. In turn, Kelter encourages autistics to behold self-diagnosis as a kakoethical form of self-advocacy, wherein the self-identifications of autistics hold more weight than diagnostic authorities or diagnostic skeptics: "Seeking an 'official' diagnosis simply is not an option in all contexts, for all people. 'Official' is privilege. . . . On average, it tends to work a little better for white guys like me, who fit a narrow, outdated stereotype. In a context like this, self-diagnosis is self-advocacy. And I think that's what the skeptics really target. I think that's what they really can't stand. Sense of self defined by the individual, from the inside out, with a full understanding of who they are . . . the skeptics instinctively want to shut this process down."[111] Earlier in this section, I stated that becoming autistic is not unlike becoming queer. I return to this statement because it is echoed in Kelter's contention that skeptics despise autistic agency. Despising here is not necessarily a kind of hatred (though at times it is) but more of a refusal to move beyond the idea that autism does not equal total involuntariness. Claiming rhetoricity, claiming self-definition, claiming empathy or understanding—all of these claims, in some way, defy autism's clinical categorizations.

But even more perversely, revealing oneself as doubted or doubtful, in the eyes of allistic others, functions as a kind of street cred among autistic rhetors, as a cunning movement between embracing rhetoric and pissing on it. Part of the autistic experience is not being believed. The woman who told me that I must only have the "Asperburgers," for example, represents one such uninvited, refutational response to my autistic disclosure. Not only does she hopelessly mispronounce *Asperger's*, but she falsely assumes that Asperger's is my diagnosis and likewise falsely implies that Asperger's is not an autistic condition. This unstated premise—that Asperger's isn't autism—contributes to what might be called her refutational enthymeme:

1  Asperger's is not autism.
2  This person must have Asperger's.
3  This person does not have autism.

Such diagnostic denials from laypersons and strangers are incredibly common, to the point that they have become a rite of passage for autistic people. In many respects, one cannot claim autism until others have denied one's autism. Such are the queer paradoxes of autistic (kako)ethos.

But the kakoethos of self-diagnosis is also queerly counter-diagnostic because it refuses fixity. Self-diagnosis, unlike most official autism diagnoses, need not remain permanent. Unless we are among the lucky (sarcasm) $\infty$ autistics from chapter 2, those of us who are officially diagnosed will remain forever incurable. And even when doctors believe that our autism, in all of its parasitism, recedes or lessens, autism still resides. Officialness freeze-frames us on diagnostic charts, entrenching us forever in clinical systems and strata.

Self-diagnosis, to the contrary, can be freeingly fleeting. It can also live in tandem with other kinds of diagnoses, official and non. Even though I didn't know I was autistic until I was fifteen, I had always known I was some kind of disabled. The threat and specter of disability ordered my life. When I was a baby, for instance, my parents were referred to a specialist under suspicion that I had cerebral palsy. I toe walked so excessively that I was fitted for leg casts to flatten my gait. Cerebral palsy, however, never materialized as an official diagnosis—it merely served as one among many blips on my disability radar, eventually culminating to form what would become autism, of which toe walking is a so-called symptom.

And yet, I never self-identified with cerebral palsy, in part because I do not remember wearing casts, and my knowledge of these events derives solely from parental storying. As a teenager, however, I began searching, quite ardently, for disability. Before I became autistic, I self-identified with schizophrenia. At the time, my family did not own a computer, and so I gathered what knowledge I could from disparate sources—library books, television, newspaper clippings, overheard conversations about so-called crazy people. There were distinct elements of schizophrenia that did not fit my own self-conception. And yet, out of all the knowledges I had, this had come closest to explaining who and how I was—anxious, flatly affectual, hearing and seeing and feeling things that others did not, rotating between mutism and talking loudly to myself, rarely being understood.

Years later, I came to learn of the significant historical overlaps between autism and schizophrenia, and how autism was initially thought to be a specific subtype of schizophrenia. My identifications shifted toward the autistic. While it might be easy (and maybe even sciencey) to say that I never had schizophrenia to begin with, such proclamations ignore the very real shaping power that my self-diagnosis once held. As well, these doubting logics accord stasis to any and all disability, assuming that categories are objective, essential, and immovable. Diagnoses are never end points, despite paradoxically asserting themselves as such. Fifty years from now, autism as we diagnostically know it might cease to exist. Yet, despite autism's diagnostic transience, I, like many others, remain committed to claiming autism and the profundity of its knowledges, cultures, and demi-rhetorical motions, even if those claims are temporary or improbable.

## Neuroqueering Diagnostics

Throughout this book, I have been using the term *allism*. Allistic, generally speaking, means nonautistic; in like kind, allism refers to the state of nonautism. The term's origins remain unclear, but autistic bloggers trace its usage as early as 2003, to a parody piece authored by Zefram titled "Allism: An Introduction to a Little-Known Condition."[112] However, despite coming into the world well over a decade ago, *allism* has gained widespread currency in autistic virtual spaces only within the past few years. Variations of allism (such as #allistic and #allistics) function as well-trafficked hashtags and autistic commonplaces across social media, and have likewise served as inspiration for numerous derivative sites, including the Tumblrs Allism Speaks, Allism Yells, and the short-lived Allism Shuts the Fuck Up.

Often, the very people who diagnose others' pathology encounter great difficulty in considering their own. Confronting the idea that lacking disability might in any way be a disadvantage would strike most as paradoxical. To be autistic is, after all, an indictment of egocentrism, lack of empathy, and non-rhetoricity.

Counter-diagnosis, however, need not only take shape as self-assessment. Counter-diagnosis works diffusely in its queering of pathological invitations. For instance, why keep only to those categories created by clinicians? In the absence of ethical, friendly, or sustained academic research on autistic rhetorics and cultures, autistic people have generated their own robust methodologies and means for determining, contesting, and theorizing notions of autistic ethos. In particular, demarcating and assessing the conditions of nonautism has served as one such practice. Notably, in constructing pathological theories of nonautism or allism, autistic rhetors work to define allism as something more than absence of autism, as a means to unmask cognition that has become so naturalized as default or normal that its substance goes unquestioned.

Allism's popularity arose, then, out of desire to theorize the privilege of those not marked autistic. In service of this need, Judy Singer and Jim Sinclair independently coined the term *neurotypical* (NT) in the early 1990s, an abbreviation for *neurologically typical*, to designate those lacking autism. However, neurotypical quickly outgrew its relation to autism and nonautism. One's allistic or nonautistic status does not necessarily guarantee a neurotypical status: any person who identifies along the axes of mental or cognitive disability (broadly construed) is not neurotypical. Those with dyslexia, epilepsy, cerebral palsy, multiple sclerosis, depression, bipolar disorder, traumatic brain injury, ADHD, and so on, are not neurotypical, but are rather neurodivergent.

Allism as a marker, as a concept, then, functions as a mechanism for regarding the neurotypes of the nonautistic—for calling attention to both a neurological ideal and a neurological ideology. Allism's derivation mimics that of autism, where the Greek *autos* is meant to signal self, and the Greek *allos* is meant to signal other. Allism heralds, then, a kind of relationality and privileging of human sociality, much like autism privileges a divergent kind of relationality, one in which sociality is figured as self- and object centered, or wherein sociality isn't figured at all. Autistic activists have claimed that the autism/allism bifurcation in many ways resembles the relationship between transgender/cisgender as well as the radical potentialities of queer identifications beyond a polar homo/hetero.[113] The autistic theorization and usage of allism is queerly made and queerly indebted. It bespeaks a kind of disorientedness, imagining the potentialities of divergent and perverse a/socialities. Among Zefram's touchstones in his satirical exploration of allism, for example, are affect, socialization, and subtext. "Allism: An Introduction" reads like a combination clinical tract and DSM entry. It juxtaposes allistic mob mentality against autistic self-regard, allistic manipulation against autistic accuracy, allistic generalization against autistic complexity, and allistic verbosity against autistic concision and multimodality. Zefram suggests none-too-subtly that allism is a condition marked by conformity and crowd pleasing, whereas autism is an affective disposition toward the objective (in terms of both truth seeking and positioning epistemology as the domain of the nonhuman material world). Autism is figured as relation with nature and object and place, whereas allism is figured as the intangible, the invisible, the social.

And yet, as the above bifurcations unravel, they are rendered less as bifurcations and more as categories and types of things, a clever play on the DSM-IV entry on autism, wherein autistics are described as perseverative and detail obsessed. Zefram's allism/autism emerges not as a strict binary, nor does it exist as a continuum or spectrum, nor does it reveal itself as a series of nesting dolls. Rather, the relation of, between, and against the categories of the social or the affective or the subtextual appears rhizomatically, like an intensive tagging structure or word cloud on a blog site, at times conflicting and at times subsuming the other—and sometimes simultaneously so. For instance, readers are forced to confront the following: Is autistic asociality a category unto itself, or is it a kind of sociality? Or, even more, how do sociality and asociality both call upon a kind of antisociality? What contains what, and when, and to what effect? The allism manifesto provides few answers, other than illuminating the culturally vexed and determined structures of diagnostic manuals and clinical texts.

Another allism satire, *Field Notes on Allistics*, similarly (and wryly) complicates the condition of nonautism.[114] Run by Dani Ryskamp, the blog is narrated through the perspective of an autistic parent who lives in a world in which autism is a neuronorm and allism is a developmental disability. In this satire, the narrator's children and partner are allistic, with the site functioning as a parodic mommy blog. Defining allism as "an inability to express independent emotions, an inability to fruitfully occupy one's own time, and a pathological need for the presence, interaction, and approval of others," *Field Notes* covers topics ranging from allistic manners ("eerily sociopathic" and "utterly illogical") to jobs in which allistics may succeed ("Allistics seem to do very well when they can mirror the behaviors and emotional states of a leader").[115] As well, *Field Notes* takes great care to satirize the alarmist tone of autism discourse, warning readers, for example, that allism is linked to the 2009 recession, or that allism usually comes with multiple comorbid diagnoses, such as FIFA-type Sports-Seasonal Affective Disorder (SSAD).

Importantly, Zefram's and Ryskamp's allism manifestos model their tone and form upon an earlier clinical parody maintained by Autistics.org, a website for a mock research center known as the Institute for the Study of the Neurologically Typical (also known as ISNT).[116] The ISNT website features a range of clinicalized texts, including symptom checklists, diagnostic questionnaires, short medical ethnographies, and a mock DSM entry for Neurotypic Disorder (designated by the short code 666.00).[117] Immediately on the site's opening page, visitors are confronted with vivid, negativistic imagery of the person afflicted by neurotypicality: "Neurotypical syndrome is a neurobiological disorder characterized by preoccupation with social concerns, delusions of superiority, and obsession with conformity. Neurotypical individuals often assume that their experience of the world is either the only one, or the only correct one."[118] At all ends, ISNT's authors employ—and redirect—allistic rhetorical commonplaces around autism in service of clinicalizing nonautism. The sarcastic tone, as well as the harshness of ISNT's examples (e.g., "behaves as if clairvoyant of another person's distress"), in many respects reflects those stereotypes that would mark the autistic as undiplomatic or tactless. And yet, the blunt, unfiltered force of these diagnostic musings makes clear the power of Corbett's closed fist, affectively socking neurotypicals in the gut with the weight of their own clinicalisms.

In this vein, the ISNT website notifies readers via disclaimer that its writings are satirical and meant to be humorous, not meant to be taken literally. Interestingly, however, the language choices throughout the disclaimer suggest the authors assume an audience of autistics—but only for this disclaimer page. Nowhere else on the site do the writers proclaim their intentions or their writing's desired effects. In this regard, ISNT seemingly doesn't care if allistics take the site literally—in fact, theirs is an invitation to pathological discourse, and all of the sour feelings such discourse incarnates. Literality is a prime trope here: it aims to replicate an affective experience that autistics know too well—that of the alarmist, the pitiable, the tragic, the incurable, the defective.

Whereas autism is clinically conceived as a pervasive developmental disorder, NT disorder is categorized by ISNT as an invasive developmental disorder. The difference in word choice may seem insignificant, but it echoes a common thematic strand endemic to the allism genre: normates attempt to normalize all facets of disabled life. As parent Roy Grinker once described of applied behavior analysts, "[They get] in your child's face."[119] When *pervasive* is put in opposition with *invasive*, *invasive* sounds far worse. To pervade is to permeate, waft, or color—its resonances suggest saturation or infusion, like water absorbing tea leaves. To invade, conversely, calls upon the rhetorics of conquest, colonization, or seizure. Invasion is not at all a value-neutral descriptor.

Invitational rhetoric, and with it the respectability of diplomacy, only take the neuroqueer so far. Diagnosis is often a fisting gesture cloaked as an open hand: being subject to and of medicine can be violent and self-destroying experiences. But the kakoethos that attends counter-diagnostic disclosures holds radical potential because it queers perceptions of center, linearity, residence, and rigidity. It is plastique. The kakoethical may be ulcerated and it may be stigmatic, but it is entelechial in its trajectories—always-unfolding, defiant, and theoretically stimmy.

## Coda: Elliptic Gazes

When authors write through and about autism, they—their very being— become subject to refutation. When I declare that I am autistic, complete strangers feel compelled to challenge me, or console me, or talk to me very slowly. As I hope I've made clear, there are numerous reasons why autism disclosures invite doubt, violent interference, or an orientation toward failure. Autism is so imbricated in the cultural imagination as soul-stealing deficit that failure finding and symptom covering has become an art unto itself, a modus operandi for researchers. An end goal for clinicians is to undisclose the disclosed, to clothe the autistic in allism, or nonautism. The rhetorical situation of autism disclosure is always a reveal, which is often followed by a covering. Ellipses are placeholders, empty spaces and gaps wherein the abstract becomes concrete: fill it in, fill it in, fill it in. Saying I'm autistic is some kind of hideous faux pas, an insult to myself, an utterance that truly signals how much fixing I require.

Ellipsis occupies a kind of lore status in autistic communities. When autistics speak of rhetorical omissions, we often speak of "unwritten social rules," or what Judy Endow, following Brenda Myles, has termed the "hidden curriculum."[120] In autistic life writing, significant, meticulous attention has been paid to elliptic utterances—to a social milieu that assumes a culture of shared neurology, of shared rhetorical moves, of shared intuition and tacit knowledges. This isn't to say that autistic writers or collectives don't have their own unspoken knowledges. The sticky point, as Endow notes, is the following: "Even though it is socially acceptable for NTS to point out hidden curriculum violations committed by autistics, it is NOT socially acceptable for autistics to point out hidden curriculum violations committed by NTS."[121]

Endow speaks of violation in the way that I have been concerned with failure, omission, and invitation in this chapter. Many an autistic rhetorical act has been construed as a failure in rhetoric rather than a lesson in rhetoric. Nick Walker has described this as a pathology paradigm, one in which an autistic's every disclosure—whether by speech, gesture, or proximity to other disclosed bodies—is read as misfiring neurons (which, elliptically speaking, compels rehabilitative response).[122] If we had more space and time, we might trace this logic further and discuss enthymemes and syllogisms. So too might we consider the ways in which elliptic disclosures incite a kind of crip confessionalism, à la Foucault. For disclosing autism can impel what Jim Sinclair once described as a self-narrating zoo exhibit, where one disclosure is merely a metonymic stand-in for any and all, no-holds-barred disclosures.

Rhetoric is indebted to disclosure, much like disclosure is indebted to rhetoric. Their logics are self-feeding. Autistic culture begs and pulls at the threads that tie together rhetorical traditions. Perhaps my stims and tics are the result of involuntary bodily responses, responses that cradle empty spaces and beckon someone or something to fill those spaces. But does something require intent or inference to have rhetorical effects? When I make hand movements, even when those movements go unnarrated in all of their indecipherable nonverbal glory, I am still a participating body. My gestures impact my persona and utterances; they hold dear even if unknowable meaning; they are present and resistantly elliptic and part of larger, shared autistic discourses. My stims indecently shatter, revealing and reveling in all of their rhetorical fragility. These reconstructions (of stimming, of disclosure) press us as they press rhetoric: How do we theorize commonplaces, topics, themes, metaphors, and any other rhetorically cherished concept—and what of their connection to feelings of distress, to intent and involuntary action, to affect over reason? How might autism claim rhetoric as it dismantles it?

FOUR. **invention**

It happens in Minneapolis when my headphones snap in half. I am attending a major conference located in a hotel that, by my best unscientific guess, has more reflective surfaces per square inch than any architectural dwelling on the planet (excepting, perhaps, snow globe museums and mirror mazes).

My senses jumble. Sounds strangle as my vision collapses into nails-on-chalkboard texture. I taste copper and the pit of my stomach winces against conference murmur. I am hours from home. I am stranded in Minnesota, in a very shiny, sensorily overwhelming hotel, and my headphones lie dead on the floor. Tunnel vision is the new me.

Panic sets in, and it sets in very quickly.

Meltdowns represent one of autism's oldest and arhetorical patron saints. In those moments when I offer claims that run counter to dominant autism narratives—such as the autistic community's objection to cures, or electroshock therapy, or bleach enemas, or chemical castration—I am often confronted with the image of THE MELTDOWN, all caps.[1] Allistic parents will tell me that I am not like their autistic child. I am not sprawled on the floor, red-faced and screaming and beating fists against carpet. I am not kicking my colleagues or banging my head against the lectern. I am not like their child, because if I were like their child, I'd be eating the pages of my Rhetoric Society of America program while smearing feces on someone's projected image of Jenny McCarthy. "There are children who *throw things*," a parent will explain, as if to mortify me. "There are children who have *real* autism."

Confronting autism stereotypes inevitably involves confronting one's autistic identity. My own confrontation involves what others like to think of as autism lite, as if my neurology is some watered-down version of what is otherwise a Chernobyl-like disability. Do I retort with my own bathrooming histories, which involve shit smearing, pants wetting, and bladder-mind disconnects? At what point does my sharing become oversharing—which, in turn, will be paradoxically read as a symptom of autism that prevents me from fully understanding autism?

But I do not subscribe to functioning labels because functioning labels are inaccurate and dehumanizing, because functioning labels fail to capture the breadth and complexity and highly contextual interrelations of one's neurology and environment, both of which are plastic and malleable and dynamic. Functioning is the corporeal gone capitalistic—it is an assumption that one's body and being can be quantitatively measured, that one's bodily outputs and bodily actions are neither outputs nor actions unless commodifiable.

Of course, while melting down in Minnesota, I am not thinking of these things. I am not thinking about parents, or real autism, or autism lite, or *Playboy* models-gone-autism spokespersons. In fact, I am not thinking about anything at all. My skin is my cognition, and it is metaphorically on fire. I am busy defying Cartesian logic; I don't think, but somehow I still am. I am in this hotel; I am without headphones; and I am rocking my body hard against, quite miraculously, a mirrorless wall in my shared hotel room. As my bruises accumulate, my distress grows tempered, lessened, a slow fade. How is this not real? How is this mild? Who invents this shit?

## Inventing the Neuroqueer

To be autistic is to live and to lie in a between space. When thinking of meltdowns, for example, I am caught between a desire to claim their rhetoricity and a repulsion toward according them meaning. As many autistics have narrated, no two meltdowns are alike, and even one meltdown experience cannot be encapsulated or described in terms of oneness or experience. Meltdowns are generally unpleasant, and unpleasant is putting it mildly. Sometimes they have causals, yet describing a meltdown as that which is caused both oversimplifies and underdetermines their exigence. Meltdowns are entelechial in this way: their cause and finality are of less consequence than their passage, which is to say that meltdowns are fulfilled through their striving to be un/knowable. A meltdown might mean nothing; it might holophrastically mean one thing; it might serve as an embodied placeholder for multiple meanings, which might or might not bear logical connections. Autistic scholar Nick Walker, for instance, relates meltdowns to larger, rhetorical issues surrounding self-regulation, writing, "We take in more information, more raw sensation, than non-autistic people, and the everyday sensory noise of life in the modern industrialized world can be enough to over-stimulate us. Situations that might only be mildly stressful for others can be overwhelmingly stressful for us simply because the stress is happening on top of the ongoing stress of sensory over-stimulation."[2] To be autistic is to live and lie in a between space—the crevices that neurotypicals can ignore often function as the entirety of what neuroqueer subjects perceive. Brenda Brueggemann, in her work on deaf rhetor/ic/s, refers to these between spaces, these crevices and elided openings, as "betweenity." Brueggemann's conception of identity, like much of the queer work in this book, moves away from demi-rhetorical notions of fixity, instead apprehending identity as "a relational positioning" that is always in flux.[3] Importantly, Brueggemann's modeling isn't linear. Occupying a space between deaf and hearing identities, or deaf and hard-of-hearing identities, or deaf and Deaf identities, and so on—none of these betweenities, as it were, can be charted with a ruler, minced into halved units, or conceptualized as dots between antithetical poles. Brueggemann's betweenity expanse, rather, is configured triangularly, and ultimately, rhetorically: as a space "filled with argument and intent and constructed through a triangulated communicative interchange between a three-part 'speaker' (or signer), audience, and context/subject."[4]

In many respects, Brueggemann's betweenity is a deaf- and disability-centered story that we have encountered before. Gloria Anzaldúa's *Borderlands / La Frontera*, for example, elucidates the between spaces and borderlands and nonlinear coming together of identities that traverse race, ethnicity, language, disability, sexuality, and gender.[5] Anzaldúa's mestiza consciousness, in particular, embodies a "movement away from set patterns and goals toward a more whole perspective, one that includes rather than excludes."[6] Describing not only the ambiguity and clashing of indigenous, Mexican, and Anglo cultures and perspectives, but also the ways in which disability, sexuality, and gender identity create "pluralistic modes" from which the mestiza performs, Anzaldúa describes ways of being that defy duality.[7] As I discuss in earlier chapters, my approach toward such betweens, patterns, and movements derives primarily from José Esteban Muñoz's ephemeral hermeneutics—in large part because his focus on traces and traversals provides residual insight into the crossroads that both Anzaldúa and Brueggemann relate.[8] These between spaces, then, as they recur across community, discipline, identity, and context, are notable not only for the binds and binaries that they shatter, but for the evidence they leave behind, for their "indeterminancy [and] . . . potentiality."[9]

What do meltdowns leave behind? Where are the marks on my body, my ethos, my soul, my skin?

Although I have spent a fair amount of time in this book detailing the ways in which autistic people's ethos and subjectivity are routinely called into question by allistic rhetors, my ultimate aim is not to suggest that autistic people are forever locked into an inescapably sucky (rhetorical) situation. Instead, in a nod to Muñoz and ephemera, I wish to pivot my argument here quite substantially: halving is but only one employ of demi-rhetoricity. That is, whereas rhetoric's project is often an allistic one that portrays autistics as halved, lesser, or absented, I submit that autistic people queer rhetorical traditions in part by queering demi-rhetoricity. That is, autistic subjects stake and deny rhetoricity by queering what rhetoric is and can mean, by in/voluntarily middling and absenting themselves from rhetoric's canons. That is, we are Karen Foss's queer both/and, embodying and engaging rhetoricity and non-rhetoricity both, messing with residue and spreading our neuroqueer dandruff all over your black blazer. We are interbodily invention.[10]

In this chapter, I move briefly across three sites (or, rather, stimpoints—more on this momentarily). Each of these sites, I maintain, unveils the inventional possibilities of neuroqueer demi-rhetorics, stimming or moving us toward understanding, disorientation, breakdown, gestalt, partiality, and/or queerer intimacies. Although these sites and my treatment of them are by no means exhaustive, I begin by exploring queer communities' construction of the demi figure, asserting that demigenders and demisexualities are integral to any queering of rhetoric. In making this claim, I link the conditions that attend sexuality and gender identity to the conditions that attend rhetoric, suggesting that when we speak of rhetors, we are often speaking of (normatively configured) rhetorsexuals. Queering demi-rhetoricity, then, necessitates an engagement with the queering of other spaces, relationalities, intimacies, bodies, and discourses. But so too does it suggest the possibilities of stepping out of rhetoricity altogether, and questioning the desirability (and at times tyranny) that rhetoricity imparts.

From queering deminess I move to my final two stimpoints, sites that, I argue, exemplify the beautiful, rigid strangeness of navigating demi-rhetorical worlds. In my attempts to recoup rhetorics of involuntary acts, I look to autistic figurations of vocalizations, stims, and complex body movements as my major examples. Each of these items, dependent on context, might be clinically termed *echophenomena*—that is, the echoing of words, sounds, motions, and other sensory stimuli. Echolalia, the more commonly known echophenomenon in autistic discourse, involves the imitation of sound or speech; echopraxia, as another example, is embodied echoing of others' movements. In clinical discourse, echophenomena are represented as both involuntary and pathological—as corporeal motions that transpire beneath the level of conscious awareness. Engaging what Casey O'Callaghan calls "echophenomenology," I consider the ways in which autistic echophenomena might be queerly read and queerly practiced as demi-rhetorics, as a/volitional motions that queer the between spaces of bodies, objects, environs.[11]

From my final stimpoint, I consider the ways in which autistic movement might be transformed into rhetorical action, as well as the ways in which autistic movement might resist such transformation. In considering what it means to collapse Kenneth Burke's duality of motion and action, I look to sensorimotor schemas as a heuristic for thinking about neuroqueer demi-rhetoricity. Motor schemas have been well discussed across fields including neurology, psychology, philosophy, and cinema. While these interdisciplinary conversations remain important, I primarily turn to rhetoric, positioning motor schemes as kinds of rhetorical schemes. In rhetorical studies, schemes are figures that involve arrangement and order, and they privilege both repetition and rigidity—the supposed domains of neuroqueer subjects. We might think of motor schemes as rhetorical figures that are embodied, echoed, and cripped, a perverse way of involuting (i.e., making involuntary) discourse on elocution or rhetorical gestures.

To be autistic is to negotiate inventional movements, movements that straddle the rhetorical and the non-rhetorical, that muddle and murk. Like any inventional movement, autism's is configured by its coalitional histories. The autistic culture movement has long viewed gay pride, Deaf culture, and the civil rights movements as its exemplars. Many autistic people identify as queer and/or find meaning in queer commonplaces and theories, and many autistic people have resonant experiences as do deaf people, including and especially related to speech, social communication and exclusion, and sensory differences. And, as Lydia Brown and Kerima Çevik have noted, disability activism more broadly is not a new or emergent movement, but rather a long-standing civil rights movement whose tactics, strategies, and rhetorics are frequently modeled after black civil rights activism and social justice movements in the United States.[12] This modeling, of course, speaks to the historical erasures that white disability activists all too routinely promote, as well as the ongoingness of the fight for racial equity and justice in the twenty-first century (i.e., our world is not postracial, and the movement is not over), much of which profoundly intersects with disability issues. Not only is special education a form of disability segregation, but it represents, as Çevik and Erevelles maintain, a form of resegregation, as disabled children of color are routinely separated (in different classrooms, in different schools) from their white disabled peers.[13]

These coalitional histories are rooted in oppressions, cultures, communities, and violences, some of which are shared, and others of which are reified by those who carry (white) (nondisabled) privilege. But if we consider, for a moment, rhetorical overlaps among these coalitions, the question of communication occupies a central, distinct place for autistic and deaf communities in particular. In other words, both communities' focus on communication is neither quirky nor new, but rather centers issues of justice, access, and rights. It is for these reasons, then, that I draw upon conceptions of Deaf Gain and here briefly relate them to autism's exigency as an inventional, embodied motioning. In their recent collection, titled *Deaf Gain*, H-Dirksen Bauman and Joseph Murray redirect conversations that would behold deafness as loss, lack, or absence (e.g., hearing loss, absence of sound, lack of ability, etc.).[14] Instead, the authors consider deafness as an orientation unto itself, one defined by gain and advantage.[15]

Bauman and Murray emphasize that there is no one universal approach to gain, much like there is no one universal way to be deaf (or, for that matter, to be autistic). As Kristen Harmon suggests, even though lived experiences of deafness are infinite and varied, to be deaf is to be deaf: under a Gain framework, there is no partially deaf, no profoundly deaf, no mildly, severely, or functionally deaf.[16] Because deafness isn't posited as loss or gradation of loss, deaf is deaf is deaf. These might seem like discursive minutiae, but the significance, especially for demi-rhetoricity, is monumental: if we are seeking to build a world in which neuroqueer people are respected and seen as wholly human, then our frame of reference cannot revolve around what deaf/autistic people are missing, nor can it rely on sliding-scale conceptions of disability and normalcy.

Of course, Deaf Gain has not gone without critique, and I too have my own caveats, concerns, and dissensus to offer.[17] Nonetheless, I believe that, conceptually, Gain has much to offer in our explorations of neuroqueerness and rhetoricity. In discussing the varied meanings that Gain invokes, Bauman and Murray look to American Sign Language—suggesting that among Gain's many, multilingual significations are (1) the benefits of deafness, (2) the contributions of deaf people, and (3) deaf people being ahead, innovative, and inventive. Here I want to focus on that last item—invention. As I mentioned, I am interested in the inventional aspects of Deaf Gain as a method for thinking about neuroqueer rhetoric(s), neuroqueer language(s), neuroqueer culture(s), and, ultimately, neuroqueer being.

Invention holds particular meanings within rhetorical studies. When we think of invention, we might be thinking of scientists in a lab, of people inventing products or algorithms or artifacts. And while that certainly is a kind of inventional practice, I am invoking something different here, something rhetorically driven. Were I to summon Aristotle, I might position invention as "discovering the best available means of persuasion," as heuristic.[18] But a more current (and relevant) approach to invention, I think, comes from the work of Bre Garrett, Denise Landrum-Geyer, and Jason Palmeri, all of whom position invention in relation to embodied and multimodal communication. In one such offering, they describe invention as the "process of making connections, rearranging materials (words, images, concepts) in unexpected ways. . . . [Invention] manifests through the body, for a given body actively participates as an inherent material, alongside other materials, other bodies . . . in the ever-becoming, ever-shifting engulfment of semiosis."[19] Here, Garrett and her coauthors exhort that embodied communication is not a site for intervention, as many clinicians would have us believe, but is rather a site of invention. Their description of invention's ever-becomingness follows what Debra Hawhee has called "invention-in-the-middle," a way of forging that is neither active nor passive but an entelechial force unto itself. As Hawhee writes, "'Invention-in-the-middle' assumes that rhetoric is a performance, a discursive-material-bodily-temporal encounter, a force among forces. This mode of invention is not a beginning, as the first canon is often articulated, but a middle, an in-between, a simultaneously interruptive and connective hooking-in to circulating discourses."[20] Here I wish to emphasize that, as Anzaldúa describes of ambiguity and unfixed identifications, this "interruptive" movement is not a linear between but rather a tic, a stim, a spasm.[21] Invention is always located, but it is not fixed or fixable: it is an ecology in movement, a vital force through which the neuroqueer might come to know.

Embodied communicative forms—including the echo, the tic, the stim, the rocking body, the twirl—represent linguistic and cultural motions that pose possibility for autistics. Scholars have long argued that autistic people do not have a culture because they do not have a shared language, or any equivalent to the sign languages that linguists and others have used to distinguish or legitimize Deaf cultures.[22] Autism is culturally and clinically juxtaposed against linguistic impairment: autistics don't do language, and if they do, they suck at it in some way (or so the logic goes). But if autism is an inventional stimpoint—then autistic, embodied communication (whether sign or stim or tic) has the potential to reinvent what we think we know about rhetoricity.

Importantly, while invention has often been framed in relation to meaning or the beginnings of some grander future meaning, invention is also about scraps—items we've discarded, the embodied reeling that accompanies failure,

unintentional effects and affective responses. Although failure is often negatively coded as the moral failings of (marginal) individuals, without failure
there could be no rhetoric.[23] As Judy Holiday notes, "ignorance is a precondition of invention. . . . The aporia [uncertainties] of ignorance provide the
spaces enabling invention, and invention enables us to expand our repertoires
of what there is to know and imagine."[24] And, as Jack Halberstam contends,
there is queer potentiality in failure, in awkwardly embarking upon that which
results in unintended effects. Even when striving toward something other, failure is one among many paths of flight.[25]

In this chapter, each of the sites that I examine—queer demi-rhetorics,
echophenomena, and motor schemas—are, I am arguing, inventional sites. In
using terms such as site, stance, or topography, I am in many ways engaging
misnomers, for there is nothing settled, permanent, linear, or fixed about neuroqueer invention. Sites and stances imply orientation, much like topographies
imply mappability. As I discuss in the next section, neuroqueerness is perhaps
better imagined as dis- or unorientation, as that which perpetually fucks with
our sense of direction, compassing us toward traces of the untraceable. These
are queer entelechies. Rather than attempt to stake or freeze-frame our entry
into such discourses, I believe it more capacious to gesture toward, in all of the
namesake of the stim.

## Re/claiming Demi-rhetoricity

As I alluded in the previous section, I believe that demi-rhetoricity holds potential as a reclamatory strategy for those who publicly disclose an autistic identity.
Were we to invoke Sara Ahmed, we might recall that "queer does not reside in
a body or an object, and is dependent on the mutuality of support."[26] Queerness repels tenancy; its ephemera trace projections and meanderings rather
than fixity. In this way, demi-rhetoricity might be queerly recast as a between
or beside rather than a residence, wherein betweening and besiding are verbed,
are José Esteban Muñoz's not-yet-heres, his always-becomings. Neuroqueer
rhetoricity doesn't orient on a line but instead collapses shapes and diagrams
of all kinds—disorienting and unorienting participating bodies. Following
Brueggemann and Walters, neuroqueer demi-rhetorics are those that grapple,
twist, and defy.[27] They are demi-rhetorics of and beyond the bodymind. They are
neuromuscular prowess and skeletal awkwardness. They embrace a rhetoricity
that might just as quickly be called a non-rhetoricity. When power makes itself
known, the paralinguistic edge of the closed fist rams into view, wordless and
rigid and biocognitively frank. (Mixed metaphors are fun.)

From a queer demi-rhetorical perspective, disclosing might be better understood performatively, as engagement between the intentioned and unintentioned motions of neuroqueer bodyminds. Disclosures are more than voluntary verbalizations; neuroqueer bodyminds can make themselves known with the flapping of hand, the averting of gaze, the limpening of wrist. As I've narrated throughout, authorial intent is frequently attended as one of the major questions of rhetorical analysis. But what if intent weren't so . . . intended? What kind of intentionalities might be claimed as queer intentionalities? What are we figuring as conscious and voluntary? Queer demi-rhetorics might discard the question of intent altogether, or regard intention in a distributed or Latourian fashion, or privilege the involuntary reflexes of awkward bodyminds that come to make a motion. Where does my finger intend, and how does that reject or contradict the intentions of my stomach? Was my toddler shit smearing neuronally predestined? How to intend my facial tics, the ritualistic banging of my head against a barren wall?

To be clear, when I speak of neuroqueer demi-rhetorics, I am not invoking the figure of the incrementum, nor am I suggesting that queering is but another means of fixing autistics in place. As previously stated, when it comes to lines with ends and edges, the word *fix* holds dual meanings. On one level, neuroqueer subjects have been passively fixed along continua, suggesting that our every motion is but a half-motion, a nonaction. On another level, fixing neuroqueer subjects in place represents an attempt to fix or rehabilitate our presumed pathology. When neuroqueerness is perceived as fixity, it is perceived as residing or residential, as a parasitic entity upon which intervening others can chip away, yet never fully cure or evict.

Instead, I am suggesting a queering of these linear models. Involuting embodies disorientation; it fists and distorts the lines upon which allistic others attempt to fix us. In defying Zeno's place, we displace and are displaced. As Ahmed relates, "Disorientation can move around, given that it does not reside in an object, affecting 'what' is near enough to the place of disturbance."[28] In rejecting residential models of queerness, Ahmed specifically positions disorientation as a queer disturbing of affect. Importantly, her appeal to the queer moves between "sexual and social registers," and so too does it parallel language commonly used to author autistic people.[29] Autistics are among the neuroqueer in that we are routinely theorized as having "disturbances of affective contact."[30] We have not only been authored as disorientation embodied, but as unorientation that disembodies, as that which defies social and sexual registers to such extremes that we defy all orientation, necessitating paradoxical rhetorics of emplacement to hold us in line, to contain our motions and commotions.[31]

A queering of demi-rhetoricity would also enable us to examine more thoroughly the ways in which the rhetorical is implicated in straightened notions of the social and the sexual. In my introduction to this book, I claimed that autism as a condition has, since its very inception, been crafted as a disorder of neurological queerness, rendering autism incipient to multiple panics around gender and sexuality. Autism supposedly predisposes us to brains that have no concept of what it means to be prosocial. Gender, sexuality, diplomacy, tact—these constructs elude us, because we remain unoriented toward that which might be deemed normative, both socially and sexually. If we attend to autism's clinical history, we can locate such rhetorsexual constructions at numerous junctures in time and theory. In the late nineteenth century, before autism was a diagnostic entity, some practitioners (such as John Harvey Kellogg or Samuel Gridley Howe) believed that mental disability was caused by sexual deviance, namely, masturbation and homoeroticism. Decades later, psychoanalytic approaches to autism, as with many forms of neurodivergence, embraced causation theories that read so-called symptoms as expressions of sexualized rage or deviation. Houzel and Maroni, for example, draw upon Frances Tustin's work in the 1970s to suggest that autism is a primordial bisexuality, in which psychic chaos results from a failure both to differentiate and complement self with other, or maternal with paternal.[32] Tustin, as well as Bettelheim, frequently conceived the nipple itself as an autistic object, an exemplar of autism's asociality, wherein breasts came to symbolize maternal hatred and autistic longing for nourishment.[33] Following this, echolalia—the repeating of words and phrases—came to be theorized as autoerotic in nature, with supposedly arhetorical acts of repetition serving a sexually arousing function for the autistic child.[34] And even prior to psychoanalytic theories of autism, stimming—repetitive motions that might include body rocking or hand flapping—was (and still is) frequently regarded as masturbatory and sexually perverse.[35] In all things, autistic methods of being, inter/relating, and communicating came to be read as sexually indebted and sexually deviant.

Of course, constructions of autism as both arhetorical and perverse do not end at the psychoanalytic. Historically and contemporarily, autism's many theorizations not only work to uncritically conflate gender and sexuality; they also assume that, in discovering autism's causes, researchers might likewise discover clues about what causes everything LGBTIAQ+. As I discussed in chapter 1, Simon Baron-Cohen and his colleagues at the Autism Research Centre have often claimed autism to be a case of the extreme male brain. In these theories, researchers presume that autism's causes might be traced to hormonal imbalances. Consequently, they claim, hormonal excess leads to queer excess: an excess of testosterone in utero results in an excess of neuroqueer behaviors. In typifying autistics as having not only male-sexed brains but extremely male-sexed brains, researchers and therapists alike are authorized to argue that autistic people's gender identities and sexualities will always deviate from norms. With regard to transness, for example, researchers have both suggested that a higher number of transpeople (especially transmen) display autistic traits and that autistic transpeople may (presumably mistakenly) identify as trans because of social or rhetorical confusion related to delays in childhood development.[36] In one such move, Edgardo Menvielle suggests that "[autistic] children with social cognition problems may be more prone to be stressed by their own pubertal changes, making clinical distinctions between gender dysphoria and dysphoria due to body maturation challenging."[37] In another such move, N. M. Mukaddes interlinks "gender identity and gender-related problems" in autistic children to the pathological category of gender identity disorder in the DSM-IV.[38] Mukaddes's argument rests upon the idea that possessing a fixed, singular gender identity is part and parcel of child development, with cisgender identity serving an empirical (and thereby neurobiological) relation to prosocial communication and self-help skills.

In this regard, cisgenderness is correlated with both appropriate developmental milestones and rhetorical capacity. Relying upon categories in the DSM-5, Jacobs et al. posit that autism and gender dysphoria may share etiologies because both diagnoses call upon issues surrounding communication and rhetorical identity.[39] Suggesting that autistic and trans children experience "difficulty articulating their inner experience of gender," the authors maintain that "the formation of a clear gender identity may depend upon cognitive, social, and communication skills, which can be impaired in people with ASDs. Abelson et al found that children with more profound cognitive deficits had trouble establishing and articulating a consistent gender identity."[40] Research on autistic people's so-called homosexual behaviors in sex-segregated institutional settings likewise interweaves the rhetorical, the gendered, and the sexual. Researchers routinely lock themselves into polar arguments around queer causation, reverting to the all-too-common innateness versus choice debate about what causes the Gay or the Trans. The hidden premise, of course, is that possessing causal knowledge will provide mechanisms for eradicating both disability and queerness. With regard to autism, the social/biology dichotomy often takes shape as follows: are institutionalized autistics behaving queerly because they lack biorhetorical concepts of gender and social propriety, or are they behaving queerly because they do not have access to opposite-sex partners? In other words, sexuality, gender identity, neurobiological development, and rhetoricity are interconnected constructs in clinical theory and practice, and their shared trajectory often takes form, rhetorically, as quests for causes and cures. If one element falls askew, the entire triad crumbles. For what is communication if it is queer or among queers?

In the above theorizations, sexuality and gender identity are not only rhetorically charged but rhetorically determined. Humans are not merely rhetors, but rhetorsexuals: our fluctuating capacities, abilities, and desires to be rhetorical remain intimately connected to our placement on a series of bell curves. If rhetoric's exigence effects change by means of an intentioned rhetor interacting with and appealing to the values of a socially disposed and disposing audience, then prosocial invitations to discourse are arguably the invitations that rhetorically predominate. In other words: one cannot do rhetoric if ze is a ze; one cannot do rhetoric if ze fails to conceptualize how normatively gendered and sexed others rhetorically act; one cannot do rhetoric if ze has a bodymind that has been categorized as disturbed. Rhetoric not only socializes, but it genders and sexes, enables and invites prosocial bodies.

And yet, neuroqueering demi-rhetoricity endows us with more than the capacity to reposition neuroqueer histories. It provides us with means and motive to fuck with rhetoricity itself. As I mentioned earlier, rather than behold identity or rhetoricity along a linear spectrum, deminess might instead be queerly viewed and queerly practiced as a kind of dis- or unorientation. It might be regarded as a way of thinking not about the residual capacities of neuroqueer brains, but rather about rhetorical attraction or rhetorical desire. When is rhetoric a desirous frame? What and whom does rhetoric arouse? When might it be advantageous to rebuff rhetoric's advances, to embrace other, queerer means in its stead?

In asking the above, I mean to call upon queer notions of the demi figure. While I have until this point used *demi* to signal that which is halved, I am here invoking something different with regard to partiality. In queer circles, deminess can be figured as a sexuality and/or a gender identity. Demisexuality and demigenderness tend not to imagine sexuality and gender as middled residences on linear spectra (though at times they do).[41] Rather, deminess instead functions as a queer attachment to remnants, as a nonbinary disorientation. Demi-identities reject binaries, and instead regard gender and sexuality as fragmentary and oscillating. To claim a demigirl identity, for instance, is to suggest that one holds a partial or shifting relation to some construct of girlness. This connection might only figure in the slightest, most skeletal of ways: perhaps the person in question identifies as AFAB (assigned female at birth) and nothing more; perhaps the person in question fluctuates in hir gender identity;

perhaps the person in question considers hirself nonbinary with a gender expression that is commonly read as "woman"; perhaps the person in question passes as a woman, or publicly self-discloses as a woman; perhaps the person in question at times identifies as femme, or even demifemme; perhaps the person in question identifies as all of the above, either simultaneously or at different moments in time.

In addition to demigender identifications, the demi figure operates within constructions of asexuality as well. Demisexuality is generally described as an asexual, or gray asexual, identity. Demisexuals, like those who are demigender, do not relate their gray-a/sexualities as halved or lesser, but rather outline their sexual orientations as muddled, transient, and nonbinary.[42] While some demisexual-identified individuals locate demisexuality as a midway between being sexual and asexual, it is more frequently rendered as a form of fluctuating desire—an orientation in which relationality and longing are always in flux, in limbo, and often running on crip or queer time.[43] Often, demisexuality is represented as a secondary form of sexual attraction, wherein one does not experience sexual attraction until getting to know someone better (and it's important to note that "getting to know someone better" is a purposefully vast placeholder that might cover time spans ranging from five weeks to five decades). Conversely, primary sexual attraction is often identified as a more instantaneous, affective process (think, for example, of the fleeting attractions one might experience over an image on a billboard).

Whereas allosexual-identified people experience crushes, asexual-identified people experience squishes—rhetorical differences that seem slight, but that hint at the ways in which permanence, texture, and social contact inform and direct our formulations of rhetoric and relationality.[44] The resonance of *crush* evinces smashes, shards, swift and propelled motion. To crush is to pulverize; to crush on someone is to characterize attraction as infatuation, saturation, fullness (even if all of these feelings are instantaneous or fleeting). Crushing takes all; crushes subsume. By comparison, squishes are sensorily complicated: the object of squishing both takes and gives shape. Squishing can leave marks, finger imprints, welts, and other tracings. But that which is squished can likewise repel, oppose, or even bounce back into a prior or alternate form. Squished ephemera can also accept some indentation, stretching the contours of a squished or squishing body, while also refusing to conform fully to an interlocutor's brand. Furthermore, an object's squishability depends on its substance, but squishiness also revolves around pacing and duration: a stress ball can be flattened into a pancake if intervening hands provide enough pressure, but when the force releases, the ball may revert to its original spherical shape.

This reversion to ballness might be instantaneous, or it might slowly inflate over the course of seconds or minutes. The flatness of a squished ball—and the speed with which it takes or returns shape—is factored by the density of the foam that constitutes it, as much as it is by the brutality and size of the hands that seek to dominate it. Malleability is time dependent, object dependent, force dependent. Modeling clay, by comparison, can be poked, prodded, kneaded, spun, licked, or pummeled, its form always bending, weaving, and twisting toward some new or alternate shape.

In exploring the resonances of squishing, I do not mean to suggest that it—or asexual motions and forms—is superior, or even antithetical, to crushing. Rather, I delve into these nuances to suggest that demi-rhetorics explode and expand queer relations. Here we might recall Malabou's contention that plasticity is as much about creation as it is annihilation or explosion.[45] Attraction is both affective and rhetorical; it is a sense-felt mode of disorienting. While attraction may configure bodyminds toward specific actions (e.g., sexual activity, romantic intimacies, or abstention), attraction is perhaps better conceptualized as a kind of leaning or longing. Such desiring might involve arousal, or fascination, or a kind of emotional or interbodily turning toward—or none of these things at all. One might not experience sexual attraction, for example, but might experience romantic attraction. Some asexual individuals disidentify with romance altogether, identifying as aromantic. Others yet find it core to their identities to provide thick description around what it means to experience platonic attraction (or, in some cases, queerplatonic or *wtf*romantic attractions).[46] Attractions aren't static, nor are they temporally bound. Attraction affects and dis/orients bodyminds, contorting and pulling at those spaces which lie between.

In differentiating between modes of attraction, demi-rhetorics once again complicate relationships with time/ing and identification. Deminess suggests that identity is a queer way to move; it recognizes that identity is "always yet-to-be" rather than merely occurrent or static.[47] Demi-rhetorics pose vast, motile resources from which neuroqueer subjects might draw, perform, dismantle, or build. In this regard, demi-rhetorics transcend Zeno not only in motion but in duration. We might term this duration crip time, or queer time, or neuro-queer-crip time. But whatever we term it, deminess demands temporal landscapes that diverge from traditional relationships with time. Whereas "straight time," according to Alison Kafer, represents "a firm delineation between past/present/future or an expectation of a linear development from dependent childhood to independent reproductive adulthood," neuro-queer-crip time teleports across time scales and spaces.[48] As one such example, autistic blogger E from *The Third Glance* intimates the ways in which her shifting sexualities are often misread linearally, as "developmental delay" or "maturation," as opposed to neuroqueer flux. Writes E, "I'm asexual at this time in my life. That might change in the future. I doubt it will, but it's always a possibility. If I become 'not asexual' later in life, that doesn't mean I've 'matured' enough to be sexual. It just means that now I'm no longer asexual. And it might never happen. And if it does, it might reverse itself again. But I'll still live a fulfilling adult life, regardless."[49] Neuroqueer demi-rhetorics are always-emergent and cannot be chronologically contained.

Demi-identities are squishy, verbed, and fluid. And yet, there has been significant debate over whether or not asexuality is queer:[50] Is it a queering of relationality? A queering of movement? A queering of being? All or none of these things? Some asexuals identify as queer just as some gay people do not. Often, the question of queerity and asexuality (much like any LGBT identity) is relegated to matters of personal identification or choice: if one claims queerness, then one is queer. While I defer to individuals making their own decisions around personal identification, I am here advocating that we regard asexuality queerly because asexuality regards both desire and identity as fluctuating and transient. Queering is a motioning toward, a fisted gesture, an always-becoming. And there is something particularly queer about the ways in which ace communities proliferate notions of attraction, desire, and relationality.[51] As I previously discussed of demisexuality, aces work ardently to theorize and radically expand concepts around eros and longing—sexual, sensual, romantic, platonic, and more.

My own attachments to queering and queerness are demily complicated. In coming to understand my own queer identifications, I am constantly reminded of what Kerschbaum describes as "yet-to-be-ness."[52] Throughout this book I have related that I am pansexual; and yet, my embrace of pansexuality is as much a past mode of being as it is a yet-to-be, for I am also demisexual. In claiming demisexuality, I am at once claiming pansexuality and panromanticism. In this, I am not sliding across or between pansexuality and panromanticism as if they were antithetical poles, or as if my placement along a sexual-romantic scale would always be halved. In rejecting the idea of spectra, Eunjung Kim calls upon historical asexuality narratives, explaining that "[even in] Kinsey's model, asexuality did not exist on the bipolar continuum but lay outside the measure, as an anomaly."[53] Consequently, my anomalous measurelessness is a fluctuation between sexual and romantic desire, sexual and asexual attraction. At some junctures these fluctuations in attraction represent distinct moments in time, but they also accord a certain simultaneity: I embody a both/and.

But so too does my queer motioning hold a certain indebtedness to disability constructs: I am autistic, neurologically and discursively speaking. In many respects, claiming asexuality is culturally read as claiming an oft-fought disability stereotype. Disabled people have long agitated for recognition as (allo)sexual beings. Those who embrace asexuality may be shamed or subject to reprimanding from disability rights activists, especially since disabled people have faced long histories of desexualization.[54] Disabled people have been characterized, both historically and contemporarily, as forever children, and these infantilizing constructions have served as rationale for innumerable abuses, including forced sterilization, institutionalization, and euthanasia. Even in queer circles, asexuality carries baggage, often serving as a signifier for passing, assimilation, and/or homonormativity. In her discussion of the ways in which public spaces work in service of taming queerness, Dereka Rushbrook reflects on the means through which gay individuals may choose to "adopt an asexual behavior that hides their homosexuality."[55] Because heterosexuality is a naturalized construct, Rushbrook observes, heterosexuality and asexuality are often culturally conflated—that is, the absence (or, rather, heterosexual presence) of sexual performance is viewed as normal or default, because heterosexuals often remain "unaware of their own performances."[56]

Additionally, asexuality's queerness is frequently resisted on the (faulty) premise that ace identifications provide space for otherwise heterosexual individuals to play gay, or, conversely, that asexual people are queers who guise themselves in cloaks of heteronormativity. In their examination of assimilation within LGB narratives, Erica Chu fiercely disrupts these assumptions, suggesting that queer politics have long fomented a compulsory eroticism that forecloses coalition building with and among asexuals.[57] Asexual politics, they maintain, can queer already-queer ideas of the queer by exploding the variance of queer variance. Put alternatively, asexuality opens and interrogates multitudes of variant sexualities, sexualities that depart from axes of sexual attraction and wave toward unconventional intimacies. In addressing the question of asexuality and respectability politics, Chu laments that "for many LBGQs, not being sexually active or not voicing sexual attraction is associated with involuntary entrance into the closet and is therefore aligned with assimilating into normative society or trying to pass as straight."[58]

The above, of course, is not the asexuality of which I speak, nor is it (generally speaking) the asexuality that asexual communities self-claim. Chu's sentiments concerning the respectability of asexuality are especially pertinent to demi figurations, and the ways in which deminess might be queerly regarded as much as it might queer already-queer regarding. Often, demisexuality's middling and muddling of desire, attraction, and affect is popularly read as that which is normal—as in, everyone is demisexual in some way, because all humans experience middlings and muddlings of desire. Within asexual Tumblr communities, for example, LGB-identified bloggers frequently comment that demisexual attractions represent a human universal and are thereby not only unqueer, but heteronormative. To be clear, such comments serve as microaggressive points of frustration among asexual activists, who frequently contend that asexuality is a (dis)orientation, a mode of being rather than a mode of acting.[59] As autistic blogger Chavisory remarks, "The distinction [between allosexuality and demisexuality] is in the direction of the relationship. *Most people* do not need to have a particular emotional state evoked *in order to even feel hungry*. Most people do not, for instance, need to be emotionally attracted to a waffle before they want to eat the waffle, before they want to have anything physically to do with the waffle."[60] What Chavisory and Chu underscore is that asexuality is not resonant with, nor equivalent to, compulsory heterosexuality. Asexuals are not heterosexual, nor is asexuality analogous to passing, celibacy, or universality. Compulsory heterosexuality, much like the infantilization of disabled people, might be more accurately framed as a kind of desexualization. Sarah Sinwell describes desexualization as the extent to which one is "seen as sexually attractive and desirable," a distinction that asexual activists have for years proclaimed.[61] In this vein, Sinwell suggests that asexuality connotes a self-described experiential (i.e., varying experiences of attraction or arousal). Desexualization, to the contrary, calls upon a heteronormative gaze, wherein judging others decide and determine the deviant's fuckability.

The intersections of disability and queerness grow tricky when causals are involved, as evidenced by earlier discussions of theory of mind, psychoanalysis, and gay gene research. And yet, it is a precarious thing to rhetorically frame my so-called fuckability along an incrementum that runs from the biological to cultural, or from the involuntary to the voluntary. Am I, for instance, asexual because I'm autistic? And in what ways is the *because* in the previous sentence an elliptical construct, a pregnant pause brimming with invitation to theorize? Autistic asexuals are so numerous that it has become commonplace on asexy web forums, such as AVEN, for allistic individuals to declare their nonautism in introductory postings, as if the mark of disability was a "spoiling" of an otherwise asexual identity.[62] And while one of the banes of asexual disclosure is the allosexual response, "Did you get your hormones checked?," the repeated ace disidentification with disability or chronic illness effectually others those who identify multiply. (That is, what if my asexuality were caused by hormones, or autism, or the weather, or aluminum, or . . . ? Do these things make one's self-identification lesser?)

Disclosure—and with it the presumption of invitation—can do real violence to neuroqueer bodies. When I confessed I was "some kind of asexual" to a fellow blogger, she retorted, "You're asexual *and* you don't like hugs? Aren't you concerned about autism stereotypes?" Seemingly, my neuroqueer disclosure had been read as an identification with desexualization, with perpetual childhood, and this blogger felt invited (perhaps even compelled) to discursively position my admission in the domain of stereotypes. And yet, in other corners of the Internet, autistics have claimed that their sexual orientations and/or their gender identities are, in toto, autism. As one such example, Alyssa Hillary, a prolific autistic blogger, has at many junctures maintained that sier gender is, plainly, autism: "Either autism holds the spot where most people put their gender, or autism is my gender, and I am not sure if those are different statements or different ways of saying the same thing."[63]

As I'll soon discuss, Hillary's is a concept that resonates. Siers is not the resonance of failed theory of mind modules causing transness, nor is it the resonance of masturbation causing autism, nor is it the resonance of brain localization and lesbian genomes, nor is it the resonance of symbolic impairment causing gender-bending or homoeroticism or bi-pan-fluid glory. Rather, Hillary's supposition invokes all of the complicatedness that is autism. If we recall Edward Schiappa's contention that rhetoric is everything and everywhere, we might also consider a substitution—that autism is everything and everywhere.[64] Autism, per Jim Sinclair, is pervasive, "colors every experience, every sensation, perception, thought, emotion, and encounter, every aspect of existence."[65] For an autistic person, then, what isn't describable by or through autism? I ask this keenly, wryly, but also queerly. In claiming I am autism, I am not suggesting a deterministic neuroscape in which my fate is wholly circumscribed by some residential entity that has gripped my essential innards. Rather, like Hillary, I am suggesting that autism isn't a discrete object, much like pansexuality isn't some bright orange spot on a PET scan. Instead, autism is a rhetoric, a demi-rhetoric—a means through which we come to know, perform, identify, self-isolate, perceive, fuck, rock, and interrelate. Autism is a means of communing and recognizing, of cripping and queering spaces and relations, and seeing and acknowledging kindred spirits.

Kafer describes crip-queer kinship as a "lust born of recognition," and I believe this sentiment offers a great deal toward our consideration of what it means to be demi-rhetorical.[66] And it is through this lusting that I now return to invention and what it means, rhetorically, to act involuntarily.

Resonance is a crippity feeling. In autistic communities, this gut feeling—this "lust born of recognition"—is at times called *A-dar* or *aut-dar*, terms that are clever plays on *gaydar*. We encounter one another, and we know.

But resonance exceeds A-dar, which typically involves recognizing traits of oneself in others, or even at times making lay diagnoses about others' neurotypes. Resonance is an interbodily knowing, a betweenity that pervades. Autistics might resonate with each other, but so too do they resonate with the nonhuman. In hir viral video *In My Language*, Mel Baggs rebuffs the allistic desire to interpret, to root out symbolism and social meaning in autistexts.[67] Instead, Baggs describes a demihermeneutic of things, wherein hir "native language is not about designing words, or even visual symbols, for people to interpret. It is about being in a constant conversation with every aspect of my environment."[68] In each scene of the video, Baggs regards hir surroundings as hir surroundings regard hir. In the scene quoted above, sie runs and flaps hir hand under water from a faucet, and the swirling of hir hand multimodally echoes the water's downward force, the spray of droplets against the basin, the onomatopoeic gesturing of liquid and flesh. There is rhythm, there is imitation—but meaning need not attend for this motioning to aurally or affectively resonate.

There is something synesthetically resonant about the term *resonant*—for it connotes a bouncing, a reverbing of modality against and between a mediating other. Autism echoes. Casey O'Callaghan, in his phenomenological investigation of sound events, suggests that echoes are perception of "the same sound event twice because of how waves propagate."[69] In making this claim, O'Callaghan pays careful attention to the properties not only of sounds themselves, but of those objects (human and non) that mediate perception of sound, noting, "Sounds are particular events in which a surrounding medium is disturbed or set into wavelike motion by the activities of a body or interacting bodies."[70] In citing O'Callaghan, I do not intend to engage in a lengthy phenomenological exercise on sound. Rather, my approach here is a more multimodal engagement with echoing, or what might be termed echophenomena in the land of the neuroqueer. According to Kawohl and Podoll, echophenomena are "environment-driven responses . . . defined as pathological imitations of external stimuli."[71] These imitations are multiply embodied, and include such motions as

—echolalia (the repetition of words and phrases),
—echopraxia (the repetition of body movements or configurations),
—echomimia (the "reproduction of facial expressions"),

—echographia (the repetition of written words), and

—echoplasia (the repetition of shapes by means of sculpting, tracing, or drawing).[72]

None of the above echophenomena are exclusive to autism; they transcend diagnosis and are core parts of disability culture more generally. Some of these phenomena, however, have been popularized through autism, via both clinical research and autistic narratives.

Imitation is, of course, endemic to autistic cultural texts and spaces. Narratives on imitation at times focuses on issues relating to mimicry, passing, or concretizing the abstractions of allistic body language, discourse conventions, and other social ephemera. Often, these conversations on imitating allism take shape as self-help manuals that demystify allistic customs, social rules, behaviors, and rhetorical practices. While some of these manuals function more as rulebooks whose ultimate goal is for autistics to pass as allistic, most focus on the perils of passing, which include overwhelming stress, self-hatred, and loss of autistic identity and community.[73] In her deconstruction of the hidden [allistic] curriculum, for instance, Judy Endow argues that nondisabled people wrongly assume theirs to be the natural sociality, effectively othering and quashing disabled means of communicating and knowing.[74] In another example, autistic life writer Rachel Cohen-Rottenberg asserts that passing is an imitation borne of compliance, wherein "burnout [is] inevitable."[75]

Other critiques of passing—or imitating that which you are not—take interventionist discourses as their object of refutation. With regard to applied behavior analysis (ABA), for example, autistics have long claimed that indistinguishability from one's peers, to quote Lovaas, is a eugenic logic that ABA holds at its center. Nonspeaking author Ido Kedar has routinely offered sharp and incisive critiques about ABA, in particular, its demands for imitation and its callous disregard for autistic people's ways of moving. In an especially biting blog post, Kedar writes,

> ABA believes autism is a severe learning disability that is treated by drills, rewards and baby talk. This makes recognition of the motor challenges nearly impossible because all the data from the child's success in performing the drills is interpreted as a measure of how much the child understands speech, and not of whether the child can get his body to move correctly. Therefore if a child is told to jump and he doesn't jump because he can't get his body to move at that moment in that way, his failure is chalked up to a lack of understanding the word "jump" even if he damnwell understands the word "jump" and everything else.[76]

As I discuss shortly, a number of autism researchers have begun to direct their attention to what autistic people, especially those who are nonspeaking, have been arguing for years: what Ralph Savarese has termed a "sensorimotor perspective on autism."[77] Sensorimotor approaches regard atypical sensoria, mind-body disconnects, disjunctures between volition and embodied response, and impairments in motor planning and coordination as core components—at times even the underlying essence—of autism. In exploring both the echoed and the sensorimotoric, I am not here laying claim to a god theory of autism, in large part because autism's queerness traces toward that which remains unfixed, unessentializable. Rather, I am suggesting that these theories function narrativistically, gesturing toward the commonplaces, tropes, and embodied arcs that autistics repeat again and again. Ours are stories of disconnects, meant multiply and diffusely.

And so, even though autistic people are known for their echoes, they are paradoxically theorized as being echo impaired. Often, this distinction is boiled down to matters of volition: echophenomena, such as autistic echoing of phrases, are largely considered involuntary, even if such echoing is done voluntarily. (Such are the paradoxes of compliance.) Conversely, imitation, such as complying with a behavior analyst's demand to mirror her jumping body, is regarded as voluntary, even if it is coerced or scripted. While, on its surface, Kedar's ABA anecdote might appear to reinforce this in/voluntary dichotomy, a deeper engagement with autistic life writing demonstrates the pernicious power that such a/volitional binaries can wield. In one such narrative, parent Ariane Zurcher recalls a conversation with Ibby Grace, an autistic professor and activist, about mind-body disconnection and Zurcher's then-preteen daughter, Emma.[78] Zurcher had long struggled with how—and whether—to interpret Emma's echolalic scripts. Before Emma began typing to communicate, echolalia served as a sort of communication bridge, but the words Emma spoke (such as "city tree house") often did not relate to any immediate context. Were Emma's echoes a matter of involuntary and neuronal disruption, or were they purposive communication? Reflecting on these echolalic moments, Zurcher writes, "I was asking Ibby for her thoughts about some of the things Emma would say out loud that I found baffling. Ibby told me that I mustn't try to do a word for word translation, but needed to feel the emotion behind the words and try to understand the context that way. I remember being utterly confused by Ibby's explanation and suggestion, but now, today, I get it, in a way I have not understood until now."[79] In subsequent conversations with her mother, Emma confirms Ibby's suspicion—that echolalia's meanings lie more in affect or anxiety than they do in the bounds of syntactic units. What's more, the question of

Emma's in/voluntarity oversimplifies a complex, rich, and storied expression. Uttering "city tree house" might be involuntary in that Emma is not specifically referencing a place, nor is she using speech to express thoughts or desires via the containers that words typically demand. But reducing her scripting, or any scripting, to involuntary delayed echolalia erases the embodied meaning of her vocal gestures. As Zurcher notes, echolalia, like other echophenomena, often takes shape as associational or perceptual signification. Echophenomena do not symbolically represent so much as they immediately, and often acontextually, signify. Echophenomena queer our perceptions of referentiality, in part because even repetitions of the same phrase, gesture, or complex body movement can reference or signify entirely different things. They are, in a word, corporeal neologisms. "City tree house" might mean Emma is anxious; it might be a pleasurable phrase to utter; it might mean, as it did in the above story, that Emma wishes for privacy. "City tree house" might mean all or none of these things, simultaneously.

And so, like asexy squishes, echoes resonate. When I was a child, for instance, I had a long-running obsession with the 1980 film *Airplane!* I spent hours watching and rewatching the film, hoarding lines as if each were a precious metal meant for display on my mental bookshelf. While, at one point, I had the entire film memorized, certain lines occupied more of my attention, creeping out of my esophagus when I could not retrieve any other verbal scripts. I quickly learned, for instance, that screaming "There's a sale at Penney's!" netted widely different reactions dependent on rhetorical situation and interlocutor. But so too did this line function as a metonym for a complex array of feelings, tics, arguments, observations, rituals, and general smart-assery. During a middle school social studies project, I filmed myself running around a neighbor's yard, echoing the line while holding a sign with my teacher's name painted on it. Whenever I was at a mall, I'd stop dead still at an entrance and shout about Penney's, regardless of whether, in fact, the mall in question had a JCPenney store. When I was particularly upset, anxious, or aiming to impress someone—all of which, I might add, are incredibly different categories of rhetorical and emotional response—I would often string multiple *Airplane!* lines together. At one relative's funeral, for instance, I found myself absent of verbal thought and immediately devolved into the entirety of Stephen Stucker's lines from the film. ("Nick, Heath, Jarrod—there's a fire in the barn!")

The inventional possibilities of echoing are many. In responding to others' invitations to dialogue with a scripted "Just like Gerald Ford," I coparticipate in the construction and destruction of rhetorical situations. In their discussion of autistic social awkwardness, Jennifer Cook and Geoffrey Bird observe that "successful social interaction relies on appropriate modulation of the degree of imitation according to the demands of the social situation."[80] Cook and Bird's assumption of success, of course, relies on allistic conceptions of sociality and rhetorical exchange. It likewise assumes that rhetorical success should be defined socially. If we return to Mel Baggs's In My Language, it becomes very clear that Baggs's engagement with hir environment is not predicated on human response or exchange. In bodily echoing hir surroundings—humming, waving and rocking, fingering flowing water—Baggs motions toward nonhuman communion, an exchange absent of symbolism and replete with feeling. Can we declare echoes as rhetorical failures when they do not seek human interlocutors to begin with? (Answer: hell no.) But so too is it important to acknowledge Baggs's and others' wishes to reject the rhetoricity of their echoing. That is, rhetoric is not always a desirous frame: as with any stimpoint, rhetoric harbors its own peculiar resonances. Often, these resonances are not what might be termed savory: they disavow and disqualify marginal bodies from entering, perpetrating material violences through symbolic means. Neuroqueer demi-rhetoricity is not neuroqueer if its subjects are denied the ability to self-define.

Echoes invent. Even what autistic writer Cynthia Kim terms "nonfunctional scripts" invent.[81] For Kim, "scripting becomes nonfunctional when an incorrect or inappropriate script is offered up automatically by a brain pressured to respond."[82] Echomimia—the reproduction of another's facial expressions—is typically offered as an example of nonfunctional echoing. Copying a colleague's smile when you're unhappy might not convey what you wish to convey, especially when you are trying to get your body to create expressions of displeasure. And yet, echomimia, even when nonfunctional, invents demi-rhetorical situations that might culminate in the exchange of meanings, moods, or moments. The awkwardness of bearing a facial expression that mismatches my words, for example, might invent any number of things: the destruction of trust, the creation of mutual anxiety, the beginnings of a frustrated diary entry, the palpable feeling of air molecules flitting around faces in the confines of a small office copying room. Invention need not be positive to be considered invention, much like invention is not constrained to one moment in time. Echoes proliferate, jump-start, and interrupt. They provide stimpoints from which others might build intimacies or entirely disengage.

In some regards, what I am describing here diverges from Casey O'Callaghan's contention that echoes are constrained to a singular event. O'Callaghan, to reiterate, examines the sonic dimensions of echoing and maintains that echoes are field distortions of a singular event (as opposed to multiple or discrete sound events). In many respects, I am applying his work to an entirely and sensorily different set of circumstances. Because echophenomena are neuro-queerly multimodal, I depart from his idea that echoes are constrained by their eventness. With regard to disability, echophenomena cannot be restricted to one event. Each echo can constitute its own discursive unit, and, as I've been suggesting, it can also serve as a placeholder for multiple meanings. These multiple meanings might spread or shift over time, or they can fill one singular echoing act, signifying multiple meanings or feelings simultaneously.

What I find queerly instructive from O'Callaghan, however, is the notion that echoes are a kind of mediated disruption. That is, when sounds or motions or scripts emit, mediating bodies and surfaces and empty spaces muffle, warp, distort, and queer the originary emission. I might hear an *Airplane!* line, and I might repeat that very line, even matching the inflectional nuance of Stephen Stucker's vocal delivery. And yet, my delivery is not his delivery; there is something about the performance of this line, on my body, that disrupts not only its meaning, but its affective resonance. My acontextual echoes can never duplicate or even approximate the feelings, moods, and gut checks that Stucker inspires. With echophenomena, then, we might regard disabled body-minds as scriptual queerers or queerings, as demi-rhetors who transmit multimodal signifiers that might or might not hold symbolic ties to their originating transmissions.

In keeping with deminess, echophenomena have queer ties to timing and duration. Researchers routinely describe echoes as "pathological, automatic, and non-intentional behavior."[83] The frequency with which I encounter these sentiments leads to me to believe clinical scholarship is its own kind of echolalic gesture. (Autism researchers are, after all, obsessed with autism.) What is important for our purposes, though, is the clinical differentiation between immediate and delayed echoing. That is, echoing need not immediately follow an original event in order to be properly conceived an echo. I last watched *Airplane!* several years ago, yet my scripting is still clinically considered echolalia. Sometimes, the passage of time so distorts repetition that repetition might not be recognized as a repeating of anything.

As with all things autism, however, autistic people generally adopt a more complex view of echolalic duration and life spans than do their allistic counterparts. The longer one engages an embodied script, for instance, the more severe and tragic one's autism symptoms are clinically perceived to be. In considering the extended life course of certain echophenomena, Grossi et al. assert that echolalia is a "'slave' repetition of verbal stimuli."[84] This construction not only recalls Bettelheim's horrifying comparisons of autism to both slavery and the Holocaust; it likewise reduces and ignores the expression and felt senses of autistic rhetors who echo.[85] Nowhere is autism's residuality or residence made clearer: as an entity, autism is its own will, one that imprisons and enslaves its fleshy subjects.

But autistics, of course, tell different stories. These stories are queerer, at times embracing the foulest of stereotypes as reclamatory gestures. Although echoes are polysemous, autistic writers often describe echolalia and echopraxia as pleasurable. In some respects, the autistic focus on pleasure beckons the psychoanalytic, with echophenomena variously portrayed as autoerotic and masturbatory. Therapists may wish to curb echoes because they can bring their neuroqueer subjects such excitement, the kind of excitement that oozes beyond the body and infects or startles socially appropriate others. There is queer pleasure in echoing. Autistic blogger Julia Bascom relates echoing as a flappy, happy experiential, a welling of feeling that her mere skin cannot contain. Of her perseveration on the show *Glee*, she writes, "The experience is so rich. It's textured, vibrant, and layered. It exudes joy. It is a hug machine for my brain. It makes my heart pump faster and my mouth twitch back into a smile every few minutes. I feel like I'm sparkling. Every inch of me is totally engaged in and powered up by the obsession. Things are clear."[86] Echoes can be orgasmic, literally and metaphorically. Echoes ripple across the body, compelling yet more repetition because repetition calms, soothes, excites, ignites. In many respects, echoing might be read asexually or demisexually, as interbodily attractions that do not take others or even entities as their objects of desire. Echoes are attractive, despite displacing the human sociality that often attends romantic or sexual attraction. And yet, desire inheres. Repetition's disturbances both arouse and reinforce further repetition. Desire is a strong compulsion, pressing neuroqueer subjects to demi-rhetorically engage the repetitive, the ritualistic, the complexly embodied.

As autistic activist Phil Schwarz asks, "What is so intrinsically wrong about hand-flapping, about narrow and unusual interests, about an aesthetic sensibility attuned to repetition or detail rather than holistic gestalt, or objects rather than people?"[87] (And I respond: Indeed.) Queer rhetorics defy bell curves, upon which Schwarz's list items are all too often mapped and charted. At many junctures in this book, I have described queering as a kind of verbing. Within this queer(ing) framework, we might consider echoing to be a kind of reverbing, for reverbing points toward an asociality that wanders and bounces.

## Sensorimotor Schemas

In many respects, echophenomena and the sensorimotor overlap; at times, they might even be interchangeable constructs. Both terms call upon motor coordination, planning, and performance, and both muddle all-too-typical divisions between body and mind, voluntarity and involuntarity. Whereas echophenomena involve repetition of an original act, the sensorimotor is not confined to reverbing—it structures a far wider swath of demi-rhetorical motion. In theory form, sensorimotor approaches to autism often work as a counter to those theories that so ardently deny the autistic's capacity for rhetoric. As Ralph Savarese notes, arhetorical models of autism are those in which "experts continue to interpret atypical comportment as the outward sign of inward dysfunction."[88] The arhetorical models to which Savarese alludes are many of those I've engaged throughout this book: theories about theory of mind, psychoanalytical theories, entelechial theories, queer fear theories, behaviorist theories, extreme male brain theories, elliptical theories, and so on.

Savarese turns to the sensorimotor for a number of reasons, two of which are particularly important to our neuroqueer considerations of rhetoric. First, Savarese contends that regarding autism as sensorimotor divergence more accurately represents autistic movements between volition and avolition, and it does so in a manner that respects and maintains autistic people's humanity. In other words, sensorimotor approaches resist spectra and diagnostic fixity. Of this, Savarese writes, "Because each autist will compensate for his differential development in a unique way, no two individuals with the same observational score of ASD will have the same manifestations of the disorder. This fact highlights the importance of personalized diagnosis, treatments, and tracking of progress."[89] In one fell swoop, Savarese resists the spectrumization of autism while also making clear that autism's essence is its considered lack of essence. This queer observation leads me directly to the second crucial element of sensorimotor approaches: these are the theories of autism that autistic people themselves have authored. That is, autistic people have long been claiming that they have theories of mind, much like they've long been claiming that autism is a fully embodied experiential, much like they've been claiming that autism is a motoric culture of flaps and echoes and bodily disobedience. Autistics author the conditions of their rhetoricity.

In their work on autistic rhetorics, autistic scholars Jason Nolan and Melanie McBride maintain that autism is embodied semiosis.[90] Nolan and McBride examine the ways in which autistic movements are cataloged by researchers as arhetorical mechanisms, devoid of signification or volition. In response, the authors turn to stimming, also known as self-stimulation, as a sensorimotoric rhetoric, claiming it as "an expression of embodied autistic semiosis that communicates sensory significations otherwise pathologized within neurotypical semiotic domains."[91] The potential significations of stimming, they note, are wide ranging in both form and (non)meaning, culminating in what they term "sensory utterances."[92] Stims might take shape as finger flicking, full-body rocking, knitting, nose picking, vocalizations, ritualistic sniffing, hand waving, rapid eyeblinking, or banging one's head against an object or surface.

The potential embodied expressions of stimming are endless. And yet, stims are clinically differentiated from tics, often on the basis of perceived voluntariness and feasibility of suppression, as well as their purported reinforcement value. Although both tics and stims are generally conceded to be semivoluntary, tics are typically represented as being more involuntary than stims. Both tics and stims might manifest as urges that require completion, but tics are thought to require release at some point in time, unlike stims, which can arguably be de-escalated or redirected. The difference between the two might be clearer via the following analogy, related by autistic blogger Kirsten Lindsmith: "While holding back a tic seems closer to holding back a sneeze, I would say that holding back a stim could be compared to holding off on scratching an itch (if that itch never went away, and kept increasing with time, like a mosquito with its nose in your flesh that refuses to leave)."[93]

Degree of volition, however, is where stims neither begin nor end. The very origins of the term, an abbreviation of *self-stimulation*, suggest that stims are both actions and effects: stims would not be stims if they were not self-reinforcing, arousing, or fulfilling a bodily need. Stimming conceptually arose in relation to the sexualization of the so-called feeble-minded and mentally defective at the end of the nineteenth century. With the rise of psychoanalysis, sexuality became the starting point from which many neuroses were classified, diagnosed, and treated. An earlier term for self-stimulation, stereotypy, dates back to 1909 in the *Oxford English Dictionary*, invoked in relation to "insanity" and "nervous disorders." Self-stimulation's etymology, however, is noted as initially being a reference to masturbation, and only later did its meaning transpose to reference stereotypy/movement/stimming as we understand it now with regard to disability. Here it is instructive to note that, at the turn of the nineteenth into the twentieth century, many doctors and eugenicists believed that masturbation was a potential cause of neurodivergence. As well, given that this moment in time was an era of mass institutionalization, the sexual habits and proclivities of neurodivergent people were copiously observed, recorded, and intruded upon. Masturbation, as it were, was largely thought a problem—not necessarily because neurodivergent people masturbated in public (though at times this was indeed the case), but because desexualization was the ideal mode for controlling the rhetorical motions and relations of institutionalized subjects.[94]

When we describe stimming as playful or arousing, then, we are not always engaging the innocent—sensorimotoric rhetorics attend and summon painful histories. But conceiving stimming as play, as Nolan and McBride note, reframes the stim as "an expression of focused engagement with an intrinsically attractive or motivating sensory event or as 'unstructured' and open-ended exploration."[95] In other words, there is queer potentiality in reclaiming the masturbatory, in wagering that stimming is desirous and self-exploratory and self-fulfilling, that stimming can be purely self-focused and yet still be considered rhetorical.

In turning to stimming, in turning to the sensorimotoric more generally, I am suggesting that autistic configurations, in all of their diversity and singularity, might be harnessed schematically. In cognitive studies, schemas are, according to Rice and Elliott, "complex, nonconscious knowledge structures which result in the active processing of information."[96] But such schemas not only relate to knowledge structures; they also structure and inform our conceptions of time. In his analysis of Piaget's theories of child development, J. P. Byrnes suggests that through repetition of sensorimotoric schemes, children "can imagine themselves doing something before they do it. . . . In addition to being able to imagine future events, children can also think about things that happened to them in the past."[97]

In many respects, cognitivist notions of schemas reify many of the neural hierarchies that autistics have come to despise, most especially the notion that motor schemas are one of many pit stops along linear, and thereby neurotypical, trajectories of child development. To developmentally disabled individuals, developmentalist discourses (such as Piaget's) reek of ableism. David Morris, however, looks to Henri Bergson and Maurice Merleau-Ponty as a means of twisting motor schematics: "The motor schema is a moving pattern immanent within movement, that plays back and forth between body and world, through the body and brain as a differential system that alters movement as it plays across different zones of the body (in the way that light bends when it plays across different media)."[98] In many respects, Morris's configuration of motor schemas is one that resonates with(in) autistic narratives. Morris doesn't conceive the sensorimotoric as developmental milestones, nor does he localize it to a Zeno-like place within a place within a brain. Rather, motor schemas move—they represent more than mere brain matter, dispersing across interbodily sites or tics. A brain can intend, but so too can a finger, a reflex, an air particle, a tongue muscle, an ear lobe, an eyeball. Moving patterns are patterned through concerted engagement within and across the body; a complex host of conscious and unconscious and semiconscious phenomena culminate to type one word on a page, for instance. While I might direct and be aware of my fingers slamming the keyboard, I am not consciously feeling the pulsating of my neurons, or the chemical reactions of particle circulation in the air I breathe.

Among nonspeaking autistics, disconnection between bodily parts and impulses represents a major trope, a touchstone upon which autistethnographers story the seeming perplexity of their actions. In "My Uncooperative Body," nonspeaking activist Amy Sequenzia describes her body as "stubborn" and "unreliable."[99] In one narrative arc, Sequenzia fills dozens of staccato lines with the motions required for her to type. These motions are significant, for Sequenzia's primary mode of communication is not only typing, but supported typing. In order for Sequenzia to sensorily utter, as it were, her body requires prompting, facilitation. That is, her communication depends upon participating others:

> When I am finally ready to type, my brain needs to use all the energy available to make my fingers keeps moving. A touch on my elbow by my facilitator helps my body calm down and the coordination improves.
> Sometimes my body requests more than a touch on the elbow. This happens when my brain is too tired because of seizures or insomnia but my need to type is too overwhelming to ignore. After I finish typing my brain needs some rest. Sometimes my body agrees and I can rest. Sometimes my body rebels and rest is elusive.[100]

For Sequenzia, human contact instills a schema, a rhetorical patterning of embodied movements that, in concert, habituate her bodymind to the touch-screen of her iPad or the hand of her facilitator.

In many respects, rhetoric's positioning of schemas is not all that divergent from Morris's: rhetorical schemes are patterns that, in combination, work to create embodied effects. Often, these patterns are inconspicuous. We might feel the rhythm of a given utterance, but we might not necessarily connect a text's persuasive power to its use of parallelism or alliteration, for example. It is only through focused engagement with a text that we might begin to surface the structures that mediate our reading or listening experience. In *Bodily Arts*, Deborah Hawhee examines rhetorical schēmata, in relation to ancient Greek discourse on athletic training and embodied motion.[101] Hawhee describes schēmata as "forms of movement acquired through repetitive habituation—and their use in response to particular situations."[102] It is only through "repeated encounters with difference," she claims, that we come to know—ourselves, others, autistic rhetorics, queer loves, the meaning of *Airplane!*, and so on.[103]

Rhetorical schemes are inventive schemes, ways of coming to knowledge through habit, compulsion, or echoing. Earlier in this chapter, I spoke of the varied paths I undertook before coming to know myself as demisexual or pansexual. It is only through habituation that I have come to identify myself as queer anything. In invoking the habitual, I am not meaning that I reside in queerness, or that queerness is a localizable place or developmental milestone. Nor am I suggesting that pansexuality is my forever identification, or a point along an incremental path. Rather, I am saying that, through habits—repeated encounters, echoed scripts, confronting rigid bodies in which I see reflections of my own, engaging in self-talk and stim-talk, murmuring brushes of words such as "I think I'm queer, I think I'm queer, just like Gerald Ford"—through habits I have come to neuroqueer knowledges.

This lust of recognition, as Rachel Cohen-Rottenberg muses, is an embodied and rhetorical lusting. Of stimming and her own self-recognition, she writes, "When I first saw references to stimming [as an adult], I couldn't believe my eyes. So many of the behaviors were ones that I had manifested as a child, and some had come along with me into adulthood. Because my childhood home was constantly overstimulating—full of loud voices, poor boundaries, and erratic behavior—I definitely needed some soothing, and I came up with a number of stims."[104] In the above passage, Cohen-Rottenberg recounts those moments in which her embodied schemes became manifest to her as rhetorical schemes. These particular schemes—stims—were so-called symptoms of a developmental disability, but her identification with those schemes wasn't a medical identification. Instead, stims harbored possibility—the possibility of self-soothing, or self-regulating, or releasing.

Stims, like any corporeal schematic, need not be shiny, masturbatory, or positive to be regarded inventively or rhetorically. Meltdowns and self-injury, for instance, perhaps serve as prime exemplars of the pain and frustration that might accompany autism. At times, these schemes resist narration. Pain configures knowledges that cannot be surfaced discursively. If meltdowns transpire because one's body cannot otherwise express, then capturing that expression via language or some other modality can surmount an impossible task. I cut myself, yet I cannot necessarily say why I cut myself. But when I do cut myself, my body makes specific motions that ultimately culminate in a climax of sorts: I have to locate a box cutter; I have to root the blade into my skin; somehow, in the absence of verbal thought, my hand steadies the blade and repeats the gorge while my other body parts—nonverbal brain, trembling thigh, nondexterous fingers—determine where, and how, and how deep to cut. The semiconsciousness and nondiscursivity of my thinking does not in these instances make me nonthinking, nor does it necessarily make me arhetorical. A therapist might say that only an insane person would willingly scar her body with a blade; and I might be insane (or I might be just like Gerald Ford); yet none of these allistic pronouncements can ultimately determine when and how I rhetorically identify. Sometimes I feel my cuts are rhetorical, and I trace over their bumpy, scabbing contours as the wounds heal. Other times, I find the cuts pointless or ineffectual, and I call a shrink for an appointment. I waver, demi-rhetorically. The stimmy schemes of my self-injurious behaviors queer the lines of power, much like they queer the lines of *my* or *me*. When my hands hoist sharp objects against other body parts, where, and in what, and in whom, is power located? How is discourse circulated? What is discourse on a scarred and yet-to-be-scarred body, and how do fleshy subjects stand subject to circulation? When the blood rushes to my heart after a cut, am I to think of veins as discourse, blood as circulation, knife as power? After all, Dolmage describes rhetoric as the circulation of power through discourse—knife through blood through vein.[105]

None of the above is answerable. But it certainly is queer, affecting the objects and bodies through which rhetoric patterns.


Coda: Revisiting Autism and Rhetoric

Paul Heilker has often defined rhetoric as a way of being in the world through invention, structure, and style. In our work together, we have used this lens as a means of arguing that autism is a rhetoric unto itself.[106] There is something profound in claiming that autistic people are rhetorical beings. (Much like there is something profound in claiming autistic people are not rhetorical beings—which is by far the more common and unfortunate belief.)

If autism is a rhetoric unto itself, then we must confront the idea that being autistic confers ways of being, thinking, moving, and making meaning that are not in and of themselves lesser—and may at times be advantageous. This is not to deny the existence of disability, nor is it to suggest that every autistic action is of necessity a symbolic, meaningful, or social move. Rather, it is to suggest that not only is autism a world (à la Sue Rubin), but that autism is a negotiation between rhetorical and arhetorical worlds. And, while at times these worlds may be idiosyncratic or mutually unintelligible, these worlds hold value, meaning, and at times meaninglessness. They are inventional movements, stimpoints that force us to question long-held notions about rhetoric and its privileged topoi.

What neuroqueer theory grants us is the capacity to behold rhetoric as a sometimes unattractive option—as that which disgusts or repels us, as a force from which we can abstain. Sometimes, rhetoric fails at failing. It can contain, promote, or destroy all that we may feel, experience, or mean. As well, rhetorical attraction more capaciously identifies the ways in which bodyminds are always subject to disclosure, sometimes by choice, but more often not. Even when we are figured as absent presences in clinical texts, we are still the bodyminds that constitute the empirical data, the clinical trials, the case studies, the very reasons for the existence of these texts and journals in the first place. Our bodyminds may not be self-disclosed, but they are disclosed through diagnostic means: screening tools, behavioral observations, medical exams. It is easy, tidy, and convenient to dismiss the diagnostic gaze as an example of disabled passivity. But if we think about our demi-rhetorical position as absent presences, we can begin to examine the ways in which clinical wills and clinical practices bend toward, around, and in opposition to those of us who are neurologically queer. We practice demi-rhetorics, queerly relational and queerly nonrelational spaces, spaces in which our disclosed bodyminds continually (re) invent the contours of rhetorical being, rhetorical arousal, rhetorico-whatever.

Finally: if we are to recognize autistic, embodied rhetorics as inventive, then we must also recognize and privilege the participation of autistic people. Any approach to autism is an approach toward autistic people. And if we are to do this work, much of it linguistic and rhetorical, then we need to consider the multitude of potential research frameworks at our disposal, including narrative- and rhetorical-based methodologies. This in part means confronting ideas, debates, and conversations that might otherwise seem distinct or disparate from data. This likewise means elevating the voices of queer autistics, autistics of color, nonspeaking autistics, and autistics who face or have faced institutionalization.[107] Finally, this also means recognizing as sources and collaborators the very people whom we too often and too quickly think of as mere research subjects.

Neuroqueer demi-rhetorics are demi-rhetorics of gain and of pain. And without these queer ticcings toward queer futures, we all stand to lose a great deal.

I began this book in a shit-stained bedroom. I will not end there. I think I will end in a field. A field filled with pinwheels. I will stim in this field, hands wrenching, full and swaying body movements, words that are cool and crisp, like *pulchritudinous*, all echo-localized. Parallelism is repetition but repetition isn't always parallel, pinwheels, pinwheels, pinwheels.

I have long been working on this book, a book about the neurologically queer and how we crip rhetorical traditions. In support of my book project, I've had to read a great deal of psychiatric literature, the kind of literature that beholds the mentally disabled as though they are ants writhing beneath a magnifying glass. The gaze, the psychoanalytic gaze: autistics are insects, and we will break their appendages one by one. In many respects, reflecting on my toddler bathroom habits has been a welcome departure. The histories of my people hang heavy. I imagine these clinical stories as a coat of molasses, weighting pinwheels with sticky sorrow.

**Reading one.** Ivar Lovaas constructs his shock room in the late 1950s. He lines the floor with electrodes. He sends in a child patient, a child patient with a flappy, swaying, stimming body. He flips a switch. The child convulses. She learns her lesson, until she stims again, until she finds her neuroqueer self brooding and spinning in clinical spaces with shocking gazes.

**Reading two.** Frances Tustin in 1972 declares that the nipple is an autistic object.[1] I first read Tustin while in the field, my hands flapping, fingers tangled in rubber bands. The nipple is an autistic object, she writes. Five years earlier, Bruno Bettelheim analyzed drawings from his autistic child patients, in search of nipples. Nipples he found. Nipples, and breasts, black breasts and white breasts, racialized interpretations of autistic drawings (the white breasts are the "good" ones), nipples, finger paintings plentiful in nipples, oh, the rhetoricity of the nipple.[2]

I am stimming as I read these things, clinicians and their autistic objects. Tustin suggests that stimming, that autistic gesture writ large, is a kind of psychogenic nipple play: autistics are always searching for breasts, for that which they supposedly lost. Breasts are to autistics as car keys are to neurotypicals. I imagine Tustin rummaging through a pocketful of breasts, a fruitless search. I look at the dust jacket on my book, where a reviewer in 1995 notes that Tustin's work is still relevant "today." How long must we dwell in today?

**Reading three.** Nineteen sixty-seven. Bertram Ruttenberg and Enid Wolf declare that echolalia—the repetition of words—is a kind of autistic autoeroticism (or, is *autistic autoeroticism* redundant?).[3] "Nipple," I mutter to myself. "Nipple, nipple, nipple." I think about arousal and the so-called prison that is autism, a prison so-called by breast-obsessed shrinks and the protégés of B. F. Skinner. I think about rhetorical arousal, erotic rhetorics, autistic eros. I wonder about the nipple as an autistic placeholder: the meaning in movement, the queering of pinwheels in a field, where autistic objects of all sorts commune.

Pinwheels, like many a shiny object, catch my gaze. In some ways, I would offer the pinwheel as a prototypical autistic object, much like shrinks of days past would claim the nipple as a prototypical autistic object. Pinwheels can resemble breasts, albeit hypnotic breasts: the pushpin or metallic brad sits centrally, areolar in its duty, clasping together a series of fanning paper blades. These breasts—or, rather, pinwheels—span the field, fading toward an invisible infinity against the horizon. "Spin, pinwheel," I breathily murmur, placing a solitary finger against a looming petal. "Be the maternal object of my bisexual desire."

I am not sure if I follow pinwheels, or if they follow me.

While at the airport some months back, en route home from a conference, I caught the glance of a stationary pinwheel perched in a newsstand. The conference, Conversations on Autism and Sign Language (CASL), was brain defying, in a good way. At the time of CASL, I was imagining this book more tripartitely, as an engagement of the autistic, queer, and deaf. The autistic culture movement models itself after numerous countercultural movements, and queer and Deaf cultures have tended to dominate such comparatives.[4] Some of this modeling has to do with awes over what have come to be viewed as successes in areas such as civil rights, community participation, and identity formation. Some of this modeling is also analogical and strategic: autistics talk of cultural eradication much in the ways that Deaf people do with regard to cochlear implants, oralism, and/or prenatal screening. As well, autistics tend to replace the word *autism* with items such as LGBT or *queerness* in clinical texts as a means of highlighting ableism, and, anecdotally speaking, a not-insignificant number of us identify ourselves along intersections of autism and queerness.

But, more than issues of pride or culture, or argument by analogy, autistics hold interlocking, at times convergent, histories with deaf people and those who identify as queer. Autistics are often clinically conceived as queer, both in the identitarian sense and in the "this is abnormal and defies all logic and theory" sense. Likewise, autism has also been clinically conceived as a sensory and processing disability, wherein autistics experience interventions and training similar to those of deaf and hard-of-hearing people. Helen Keller and Annie Sullivan are the icons of behaviorism, as is Jean-Marc Gaspard Itard (trainer, erm I mean teacher, of Victor of Aveyron, and chief physician at the National Institute for Deaf-Mutes in Paris). Autistics, queers, and the deaf have been frequently subject to behavioral methodologies with similar or shared geneses, ranging from those of B. F. Skinner to Ole Ivar Lovaas to George Rekers and Robert Stoller. Applied behavior analysis, auditory-verbal therapy, and reparative therapies often share as their goal the performance of normalcy by means of behavioral overwriting. These therapies have less to do with undoing autism, deafness, or queerness than they do with training subjects to behave as though they were neurotypical, hearing, cisgender, or straight. Because of these interweaving histories, autistic culture has come to figure itself as a kind of child of the deaf-queer—while at the same time using the moments in which autism diverges as entry points for retheorization of language, presence, and community.

And so, there I was at the CASL conference, an airport pinwheel transporting me through time. Among the conference's aims was for autism researchers to consider lessons from Deaf culture, deaf studies, and sign languages, and what those communities and bodies of scholarship might teach us about autism and communication. Autistic, embodied language is scarcely recognized as language, and autistic people often look to sign languages and iconic communicative forms as instructive for their own self-definition. And while Deaf culture has now (at least for linguists) gained a distinction as actually being a culture because it has a language(s), autistic culture faces battles with regard to its legitimacy.[5] Autistic anthropologist Dawn Prince-Hughes famously described autism as a "culture of one."[6] What autistic language lacks, according to many researchers, is a sociality: for every autistic person there is an entirely different, and sometimes mutually unintelligible, autistic language. "Autistic language users," Kristina Chew suggests, "think metonymically, connecting and ordering concepts according to seemingly chance and arbitrary occurrences in an 'autistic idiolect.'"[7] Rooting out the system behind an autistic person's idiolect is among the primary challenges that parents identify, a challenge compounded by research agendas that all too quickly behold these autistic rhetorics as pathological non-rhetorics.

As I have noted throughout this book, and probably to the point of redundancy, autism has been bound to non-rhetoricity, or demi-rhetoricity, in myriad ways. We lack a theory of mind. We lack symbolic capacity and empathy. We lack tact and we lack a concept of gender, and with it a concept of self. I could keep going on all things lack because our lackluster lack list grows daily. One of our trademark lacks, a lack that supposedly evinces and touches upon many an autistic symptom, involves our idiosyncratic usage of pronouns. Since Kanner's seminal autism publication in 1943, autistics have been known for our pronoun weirdness. Among other examples, autistics have tendencies toward pronominal reversal, wherein we might reference another person as "me" and ourselves as "you." As well, research has suggested that autistic people display greater preferences for proper nouns over pronouns, often self-referencing in the third-person. (So, for instance, I might refer to myself as Melanie rather than "me" or "I"—for example, "Melanie is arguing that autistic people are rhetorically crafty and cunning. Also, Melanie loves the Electric Light Orchestra.")

Unsurprisingly, clinicians generally equate autistic pronoun (mis)use to theory of mind deficits, or profound egocentrism. Peter Hobson, for instance, suggests that autistic pronoun use indicates a profound lack of identification with others.[8] In calling upon identification, Hobson describes an interlocking set of phenomena that sound remarkably Burkean and thereby remarkably rhetorical: identification, per Hobson, "seems to characterize a process that is both critical for self-other connectedness and differentiation" and likewise demands "self-reflective awareness but also symbolic thinking."[9] Like Kenneth Burke, Hobson characterizes identification as inseparable from division, or what Burke termed consubstantiality. As Burke relates: "If men were not apart from one another, there would be no need for the rhetorician to proclaim their unity. If men were wholly and truly of one substance, absolute communication would be of man's very essence. It would not be an ideal, as it now is, partly embodied in material conditions and partly frustrated by these same conditions."[10] Hobson invokes identification to suggest that pronouns serve as exemplars of autistic people's lack of theory of mind—a lack that prevents autistics from accessing others, but also from accessing our own selves. What is there to claim of an autistic culture when an autistic-authored *you* typifies our existence as nonexistence, as arhetorical isolationism?

I find failure in Burke, much like I find failure in pinwheels. In claiming failure, I am not claiming wrongness or errancy, but rather possibilities and potentialities. An asymmetrical patterning of blade colors transforms the sensory-scape of the pin-spin: a longer wash of bright purple, a subtler hint of neon orange, a radically altered pinwheel experiential. What Burke suggests is that identification, and rhetoric, can only exist because of failure. A world without failure is a world without rhetoric.

The gaze, the psychoanalytic gaze: autistics are insects, and we will break their appendages one by one.

The gaze suggests many things. I find it telling that shrinks and scholars concern themselves so frequently with autistics and eye contact, and yet they refuse to consider the violences of their own (sometimes metaphorical, sometimes literal) gazes. As Stephen Kuusisto relates, eyes have long been metaphorized, fetishized as placeholders for wisdom, or insight, or pithy quips about souls and windows and maybe also love or affect.[11]

In avoiding the eyes of others, I am indeed missing out on things. In this regard, researchers are right: there is much that I do not learn or experience when I avert my eyes. And yet—there is much that I do learn, do experience, do feel and intimate and express and attract and repel. I might not know or recognize your face, but I know your scent, what you wore last Thursday, the exact date on which we first met, the rhythm of your pace, the resting cut of your hair against your shoulder, the pulsing force field of the space between our bodies. There are intimacies and knowledges that exceed the eye-to-eye, that exceed the I-to-I. We might call this the ga(y)ze, the queering of field, reference, and looking.

Sometimes I wonder if Tustin and Bettelheim were substituting breasts for eyes. There is something queerly ocular in the nipple, the cripple, the crip-nipple. *Spin, pinwheel, spin.*

Of course, I'm more interested in queering autistic pronouns than I am in thinking about how pronouns supposedly surface our collective inhumanity. In thinking about what it means to be pronominally queer, I am beholden to Ibby Grace, Noah Britton, and Aaron Shield, all of whom, at the CASL conference and beyond, have suggested that autistic pronouns call upon desires for precision. In self-referencing as *Melanie* rather than *I*, Melanie more thoroughly pinpoints, identifies, and consubstantiates hir Melanie-ness. It is not that *Melanie*, in and of itself, is necessarily more concrete than first-person pronouns. Rather, *Melanie*-as-pronoun-substitute reveals queer particularities about Melanie: In what ways does *Melanie* bend gender? In what ways does *Melanie* fuck up rhetorical exchange? In what ways does *Melanie* summon curious eyes, uncomfortable eyes, WTF eyes, eyes that blink with "did she really just third-personify herself?"

Autly substitutions and reversals are not always borne of the purposiveness that we so often (and wrongly) attribute to other queer pronouns. Self-referencing as *Melanie* or *you* (as opposed to *I/me*) is more of a reflex, an involuntary tic, an embodied grammar. I cannot stop Melanie-ing in the same way that I cannot stop breathing.

Do you want to look at me while I do this?

*Come, spin the pinwheel.*

The gaze, the psychoanalytic gaze.

It is here I close, sitting in a field. The field was literal, but it has grown symbolic. I gesture symbolically in part out of concern for readers who need symbolism in order to understand meaninglessness.

When we think about orders of discourse, we tend to think of anything but someone walking up to a fast-food counter and asking for a milk shake with a side order of discourse. Of course, when I say *we*, I really mean *you*—the neurotypical among you, the *you* that isn't among a neurodivergent *we*.

What is neuroqueer referentiality? If we disregard spectra and poles, how else might we index and disorient our relations? How to queer *us* and *them*?

Pronouns are tricky, much like rhetoric is tricky. But I close here because pronouns are indexical. In calling pronouns indexical, I am in some ways calling upon studies in linguistics and rhetoric. But more plainly, I mean to say that pronouns are relational, are indexes that configure how we interact with and come to know one another. They are an expanse that washes over, dripping with connectivity and queer intimacies. Pronouns, as Margaret Price maintains, enable gazing publics to consider the ways in which neuroqueer subjects reclaim "symptoms" by means of counter-diagnosis: "Pronouns operate as a rich feature . . . in disability discourses: that is, they offer a significant window onto the ways that power dynamics of disability are maintained. The 'us-them' binary, often invoked in DS [disability studies] literature, is a ready example."[12] Following Price's lead, were I to invoke the previous two chapters, I might suggest autistethnography as one means of neuroqueer indexing, of disorientation. Autistic rhetorics may be idiosyncratic, but they are also intertextual in their idiosyncracies. The overshare—the autistethnographic impulse—functions as one means through which autists ground themselves and inter/relate with others, human and non. These narratives, whether recorded or fleetingly embodied, can provide entry points into thinking more capaciously (and precisely) about cultural and institutional memory. For (pro)nouns are mnemonic: how I reference myself (much like how I reference others) relates how I relate. It calls into being all of the my-ness of my bodymind. It indicates an epistemic, a kind of knowing.

I would suggest that pro(nouns) indicate standpoints, but the autistic are in continuous motion. As such, there is no place to stand. Pro(nouns) might be better thought as stimpoints—unlocalizable, kakokairotic, multiple, and self-soothing. Or, put another way, autistic pronouns might be read as a kind of stim, a deeply embodied placeholder that can signify multiple meanings and relationships.

In the field, the sky grows dark. The wind tussles pinwheel edges, and a faux-luminum chorus of blades purrs across the grass. *Who are we*, I wonder. *What is autistic community, autistic rhetoric?*

Somewhere, another solitary *you* sifts through a collection of cereal box tops, rhetoricizing into the night.

INTRODUCTION

1   John Duffy and Rebecca Dorner, "The Pathos of 'Mindblindness': Autism, Science, and Sadness in 'Theory of Mind' Narratives," *Journal of Literary and Cultural Disability Studies* 5, no. 2 (2011): 201.

2   Margaret Price, *Mad at School: Rhetorics of Mental Disability and Academic Life* (Ann Arbor: University of Michigan Press, 2010), 240.

3   Kassiane Sibley, "The Helper Personality Scares Me," *Radical Neurodivergence Speaking* (blog), July 16, 2013, http://timetolisten.blogspot.com/2013/07/the-helper -personality-scares-me.html. Presumably nonautistic, helper personalities are those whose raison d'être is to help disabled people and yet, in the harshest of ironies, instead actively harm disabled people, often refusing to listen to the very people they claim to help. As Sibley notes, "Some people who are helpers? Their chosen method of helping actively hurts people. And they cannot process this— they are Good People and Help Others, they can't possibly be doing damage."

4   Duffy and Dorner, "The Pathos of 'Mindblindness,'" 202.

5   Sam Goldstein and Sally Ozonoff, "Historical Perspective and Overview," in *Assessment of Autism Spectrum Disorders*, ed. Sam Goldstein, Jack A. Naglieri, and Sally Ozonoff (New York: Guilford, 2009), 5.

6   Chloe Silverman, *Understanding Autism: Parents, Doctors, and the History of a Disorder* (Princeton, NJ: Princeton University Press, 2012), 373.

7   On scatolia, see, for example, Jessica Case and Mary Konstantareas, "Brief Report: Interventions for Inappropriate Handling of Feces in Adults with Autism Spectrum Disorders," *Journal on Developmental Disabilities* 17, no. 2 (2011): 73–78; Autism Speaks, "Challenging Behaviors Tool Kit," 2012, https://www.autismspeaks .org/family-services/tool-kits/challenging-behaviors-tool-kit.

8   A potent example of this hails from Alabama's Department of Mental Health and Mental Retardation. In a handout authored by Richard E. Powers, fecal smearing is represented as "manipulative behavior, attention-seeking behavior or delirium" (p. 1). Powers returns to the first item—manipulation—multiple times

in the three-page document, maintaining variously that "fecal 'flinging' by mildly retarded persons suggests manipulative behavior" and "fecal smearing in a borderline IQ or mildly retarded in [*sic*] strongly suggestive of manipulative behavior." Richard E. Powers, "Medical and Psychiatric Management of Fecal Smearing in Adult Persons with Mental Retardation and Developmental Disabilities (MR/DD)," Alabama Department of Mental Health and Mental Retardation, 2005, 2–3, http://www.ddmed.org/pdfs/26.pdf.

9   Joelle Smith, "Smearing of Feces: How Common Is It?," *Evil Autie: Musings from an Autistic Who Refuses to Be "Good"* (blog), April 6, 2014, http://evilautie.org/2014/04/06/smearing-of-feces-how-common-is-it/.

10  Smith, "Smearing of Feces."

11  The IACC, or the Interagency Autism Coordinating Committee, is a federally appointed body of researchers, parents, and autistic people that advises the U.S. government on issues relating to legislation and policy concerns specific to autism research and family support.

12  This, of course, doesn't stop people from denying it. See, for example, Autism Speaks's blog, especially the "In Their Words" column.

13  Elizabeth Grace, "Autistethnography," in *Both Sides of the Table: Autoethnographies of Educators Learning and Teaching with/in [Dis]ability*, ed. Phil Smith (New York: Peter Lang, 2013), 89–102.

14  Indeed, a number of rhetoric scholars have bemoaned this fact—that rhetoric remains pointedly human focused, despite bodies of work that argue otherwise. For critiques of rhetoric's nonhuman elisions, see Casey Boyle and Nathaniel A. Rivers, "A Version of Access," *Technical Communication Quarterly* 25, no. 1 (January 2, 2016): 29–47; Debra Hawhee, *Bodily Arts: Rhetoric and Athletics in Ancient Greece* (Austin: University of Texas Press, 2005); Byron Hawk, *A Counter-history of Composition: Toward Methodologies of Complexity* (Pittsburgh: University of Pittsburgh Press, 2007); Thomas Rickert, *Ambient Rhetoric: The Attunements of Rhetorical Being* (Pittsburgh: University of Pittsburgh Press, 2013).

15  Craig R. Smith, *Rhetoric and Human Consciousness: A History*, 4th ed. (Long Grove, IL: Waveland, 2013), 5.

16  Paul Heilker and Melanie Yergeau, "Autism and Rhetoric," *College English* 73, no. 5 (2011): 485–97.

17  Heather M. Brown and Perry D. Klein, "Writing, Asperger Syndrome and Theory of Mind," *Journal of Autism and Developmental Disorders* 41 (2011): 1464–74; Benjamin T. Brown et al., "Brief Report: Making Experience Personal: Internal States Language in the Memory Narratives of Children with and without Asperger's Disorder," *Journal of Autism and Developmental Disorders* 42 (2012): 441–46; Sylvie Goldman, "Brief Report: Narratives of Personal Events in Children with Autism and Developmental Language Disorders," *Journal of Autism and Developmental Disorders* 38 (2008): 1982–88; Molly Losh and Peter C. Gordon, "Quantifying Narrative Ability in Autism Spectrum Disorder: A Computational Linguistic Analysis of Narrative Coherence," *Journal of Autism and Developmental Disorders* 44, no. 12 (2014): 2016–3025.

18   A. Schuler, "Beyond Echoplaylia: Promoting Language in Children with Autism," *Autism* 7, no. 4 (2003): 456; Ann Jurecic, "Neurodiversity," *College English* 69, no. 5 (2007): 432; David Newnham, "News from Nowhere?," *Guardian Weekend Supplement*, March 25, 1995, http://www.mugsy.org/nowhere.htm.

19   Autism Speaks, "The Launch of a New Public Service Ad Campaign and a Series of Special Events Highlight Autism Speaks' Efforts during Autism Awareness Month," March 20, 2006, https://www.autismspeaks.org/about-us/press-releases/launch-new-public-service-ad-campaign-and-series-special-events-highlight-au; Ad Council, "Autism—Print—Hypothermia," Autism Speaks, 2007, https://www.autismspeaks.org/docs/d_200704_Autism_Print_Hypothermia.pdf; Ad Council, "Autism Awareness," 2006, https://web.Archive.org/web/20080705025112/http://www.adcouncil.org/default.aspx?id=333; Ad Council and Autism Speaks, *Autism Speaks—Lightning*, YouTube video, January 11, 2013, https://www.youtube.com/watch?v=HZ1yiw1LEkY; Autism Speaks Walk, "Autism Speaks Walk Participant Guide," 2016, 5, http://autismspeakswalk.org.

20   Deborah R. Barnbaum, *The Ethics of Autism: Among Them, but Not of Them* (Bloomington: University of Indiana Press, 2008).

21   Barnbaum, *The Ethics of Autism*, 154.

22   Barnbaum, *The Ethics of Autism*, 174.

23   This is likewise a loaded question, dependent in part on how one conceives the terms *choice* or *neurology*. As Davi Johnson Thornton, *Brain Culture: Neuroscience and Popular Media* (New Brunswick, NJ: Rutgers University Press, 2011) and Victoria Pitts-Taylor, "The Plastic Brain: Neoliberalism and the Neuronal Self," *Health* 14, no. 6 (2010): 635–52, have compellingly argued, we are currently living in a culture of the brain, a sociopolitical moment in which humans are reduced to "cerebral subjects" (Francisco Ortega, "The Cerebral Subject and the Challenge of Neurodiversity," *BioSocieties* 4 [2009]: 425–45). In chapter 2, I consider the ways in which this cerebral subjectivity is implicated in neuroscientific rhetoric on brain plasticity, especially in the context of behavioral interventions. With the rhetoric of the plastic brain comes the idea that our brains are forever trainable, malleable, changeable. As Christine Skolnik ("Rhetoric and the Plastic Brain," unpublished manuscript, 2012) notes, our every action impels change in our neurostructures. Whether we take medication, engage in cognitive-behavioral therapy, read self-help books, or even open a window and smell a neighbor's pie, we are arguably changing our brains. Does this mean, then, that one can choose one's neurology? While plastic rhetorics suggest this might be true, it also signals a perverse opposition: Cerebral subjectivity compels us to remediate our presumed pathologies, creating a rhetorical involuntarity of compulsory rehabilitation and coerced treatment. What choice is choice when there is no choice?

24   In this chapter, I use *mental disability* and *neurodivergence* somewhat interchangeably. In disability studies scholarship, *mental disability* has become the primary term of work to signify enminded, enbrained difference. Conversely, *neurodivergence*, coined by Kassiane Sibley, circulates primarily in activist spaces and is my

preferred mode of reference. While neurodivergence is often associated with the formerly autism-specific leanings of the neurodiversity movement, Sibley and others invoke it to incorporate anyone who identifies against neuronormativity. I follow Sibley's lead in my use of the term.

25  Tim Luckett, Anita Bundy, and Jacqueline Roberts, "Do Behavioural Approaches Teach Children with Autism to Play or Are They Pretending?," *Autism* 11, no. 4 (2007): 374.

26  Jenell Johnson, "The Skeleton on the Couch: The Eagleton Affair, Rhetorical Disability, and the Stigma of Mental Illness," *Rhetoric Society Quarterly* 40, no. 5 (2010): 459–78; Catherine Prendergast, "On the Rhetorics of Mental Disability," in *Embodied Rhetorics: Disability in Language and Culture*, ed. James C. Wilson and Cynthia Lewiecki-Wilson (Carbondale: Southern Illinois University Press, 2001), 45–60; Katie Rose Guest Pryal, "The Genre of the Mood Memoir and the Ethos of Psychiatric Disability," *Rhetoric Society Quarterly* 40, no. 5 (2010): 479–501.

27  Todd V. Oakley, "The Human Rhetorical Potential," *Written Communication* 16, no. 1 (1999): 102.

28  George A. Kennedy, "A Hoot in the Dark: The Evolution of General Rhetoric," *Philosophy and Rhetoric* 25, no. 1 (1992): 1–21; Alex Reid, "Composing Objects: Prospects for a Digital Rhetoric," *Enculturation* 14 (2012), http://enculturation.net/composing-objects.

29  Jill Boucher, "Putting Theory of Mind in Its Place: Psychological Explanations of the Socio-Emotional-Communicative Impairments in Autistic Spectrum Disorder," *Autism* 16, no. 3 (2012): 229.

30  Peter Carruthers, "Autism as Mind-Blindness: An Elaboration and Partial Defence," in *Theories of Theories of Mind*, ed. Peter Carruthers and Peter K. Smith (Cambridge: Cambridge University Press, 1996), 257–73; Victoria McGeer, "Autistic Self-Awareness," *Philosophy, Psychiatry, and Psychology* 11, no. 3 (2004): 235–51; Charlotte Montgomery et al., "Do Adults with High Functioning Autism or Asperger Syndrome Differ in Empathy and Emotion Recognition?," *Journal of Autism and Developmental Disorders* 46, no. 6 (2016): 1931–40.

31  R. Peter Hobson, "Explaining Autism: Ten Reasons to Focus on the Developing Self," *Autism* 14, no. 5 (2010): 398.

32  Kenneth Burke, *A Grammar of Motives* (Berkeley: University of California Press, 1969), 105.

33  Victor Vitanza, "Writing the Tic," *Kairos* 12, no. 3 (2008), http://kairos.technorhetoric.net/12.3/topoi/gallery/index.html.

34  James Berlin, *Rhetoric and Reality: Writing Instruction in American Colleges, 1900–1985* (Carbondale: Southern Illinois University Press, 1987), 16–17.

35  Bruno Bettelheim, *The Empty Fortress: Infantile Autism and the Birth of the Self* (New York: Free Press, 1967), 7–8, 66–78, 90.

36  For a more extended account of this phenomenon, see chapter 3.

37  Kenneth Burke, "(Nonsymbolic) Motion / (Symbolic) Action," *Critical Inquiry* 4, no. 4 (1978): 809–38.

38  Marc J. Lanovaz and Ingrid E. Sladeczek, "Vocal Stereotypy in Individuals with Autism Spectrum Disorders: A Review of Behavioral Interventions," *Behavior Modification* 36, no. 2 (2012): 146–64; Schuler, "Beyond Echoplaylia."

39  Francesca Happé, "Understanding Minds and Metaphors: Insights from the Study of Figurative Language in Autism," *Metaphor and Symbolic Activity* 10, no. 4 (1995): 282.

40  Michelle Garcia Winner, "What Is Social Thinking?," video presentation, *Social Thinking*, 2016, https://www.socialthinking.com/LandingPages/Mission; Carol A. Gray and Joy D. Garand, "Social Stories: Improving Responses of Students with Autism with Accurate Social Information," *Focus on Autism and Other Developmental Disabilities* 8, no. 1 (1993): 1–10; Carol Gray, *The New Social Story Book* (Arlington, TX: Future Horizons, 2015).

41  *Allism* is a community term often preferred to *nonautistic* or *neurotypical*. As I discuss in chapter 4, *allism* arose out of a desire to mark the nonautistic and to theorize able-bodied defaults more robustly than the mere absence of autism. As well, while *neurotypical* originally did the work of connoting nonautism, it has grown more capacious and less autism specific as a term: One can be neurodivergent and be allistic, for example. But so too does *allism* grow out of community consciousness of the nonspecificity of able-centric terms. Indeed, as Robert McRuer notes, "if it's hard to deny that something called normalcy exists, it's even harder to pinpoint what that something is." Robert McRuer, *Crip Theory: Cultural Signs of Queerness and Disability* (New York: New York University Press, 2006), 7. That is to say: While *allism* as a term might seem to cement the stereotype that autistic people are self-centered and nonautistic people are not, its usage by autistics tends to be a wry commentary on the absurdity of this very binary.

42  O. Ivar Lovaas, *Teaching Developmentally Disabled Children: The ME Book* (Baltimore, MD: University Park Press, 1981).

43  Wendy [Wenn] Lawson, *Autism: Taking Over* (Saarbrucken, Germany: Lambert Academic Publishing, 2011).

44  Dawn Prince-Hughes, *Songs of the Gorilla Nation: My Journey through Autism* (New York: Harmony, 2005), 4–5.

45  Erin Manning and Brian Massumi, *Thought in the Act: Passages in the Ecology of Experience* (Minneapolis: University of Minnesota Press, 2014), 4.

46  Hawhee, *Bodily Arts*; Bruno Latour, *Reassembling the Social: An Introduction to Actor-Network-Theory* (Oxford: Oxford University Press, 2005); Rickert, *Ambient Rhetoric*; Malea Powell, "Stories Take Place: A Performance in One Act (2012 CCCC Chair's Address)," *College Composition and Communication* 64, no. 2 (2012): 383–406; Lois Agnew et al., "Octalog III: The Politics of Historiography in 2010," *Rhetoric Review* 30, no. 2 (2011): 109–34.

47  José Esteban Muñoz, *Cruising Utopia: The Then and There of Queer Futurity* (New York: New York University Press, 2009), 1.

48  Muñoz, *Cruising Utopia*, 11.

49  Jonathan Alexander, "Queer Composition Redux: Impossibility toward Futurity," *Writing Instructor*, March 2015, http://parlormultimedia.com/twitest/alexander-2015-03.

50  See also McRuer, *Crip Theory.*

51  Alexander, "Queer Composition Redux."

52  Jay T. Dolmage, *Disability Rhetoric* (Syracuse, NY: Syracuse University Press, 2014).

53  Alison Kafer, *Feminist, Queer, Crip* (Bloomington: Indiana University Press, 2013), 2.

54  Autism does, however, have a long history of being represented mechanically
    and mechanistically. We can trace these histories back to Bruno Bettelheim's
    March 1959 *Scientific American* article, "Joey: A 'Mechanical' Boy," much like
    we can observe computeristic metaphors in the structuring logics of texts such
    as Grandin's *Thinking in Pictures* or characters like Abed Nadir in the TV show
    *Community.*

55  Dan Zahavi and Josef Parnas, "Conceptual Problems in Infantile Autism Research:
    Why Cognitive Science Needs Phenomenology," *Journal of Consciousness Studies* 10,
    nos. 9–10 (2003): 53–71.

56  Rickert, *Ambient Rhetoric,* 159.

57  Phil Bratta and Malea Powell, "Introduction to the Special Issue: Entering the
    Cultural Rhetorics Conversations," *Enculturation* 21 (2016), http://enculturation
    .net/entering-the-cultural-rhetorics-conversations.

58  S. Baron-Cohen, A. M. Leslie, and U. Frith, "Does the Autistic Child Have a
    Theory of Mind?," *Cognition* 21 (1985): 37–46. Prior to Baron-Cohen et al.'s article,
    ToM had been theorized in relation to nonhuman primates. See, for example,
    David Premack and Guy Woodruff, "Does the Chimpanzee Have a Theory of
    Mind?," *Behavioral and Brain Sciences* 1, no. 4 (1978): 515–26.

59  Anne McGuire, *The War on Autism* (Ann Arbor: University of Michigan Press,
    2016), 26.

60  Bernard Rimland, "Editorial: Recovery Is Possible," *Autism Research Review Inter-
    national* 8, no. 2 (1994): 3.

61  Francesca Happé, "The Autobiographical Writings of Three Asperger Syndrome
    Adults: Problems of Interpretation and Implications for Theory," in *Autism and
    Asperger Syndrome,* ed. Uta Frith (Cambridge: Cambridge University Press, 1991), 207.

62  Happé, "The Autobiographical Writings of Three Asperger Syndrome Adults," 212.

63  Christina Kauschke, Bettina van der Beek, and Inge Kamp-Becker, "Narratives of
    Girls and Boys with Autism Spectrum Disorders: Gender Differences in Narrative
    Competence and Internal State Language," *Journal of Autism and Developmental
    Disorders* 46, no. 3 (2016): 840–52.

64  Janet Bang, Jesse Burns, and Aparna Nadig, "Brief Report: Conveying Subjec-
    tive Experience in Conversation: Production of Mental State Terms and Personal
    Narratives in Individuals with High Functioning Autism," *Journal of Autism and
    Developmental Disorders* 43, no. 7 (2013): 1732–40, doi:10.1007/s10803-012-1716-4.

65  Rosa M. Garcia-Perez, R. Peter Hobson, and Anthony Lee, "Narrative Role-Taking
    in Autism," *Journal of Autism and Developmental Disorders* 38 (2008): 163.

66  Helen Tager-Flusberg, "Language and Understanding Minds: Connections in
    Autism," in *Understanding Other Minds: Perspectives from Developmental Cognitive
    Neuroscience,* 2nd ed., ed. Simon Baron-Cohen, Helen Tager-Flusberg, and Donald J.
    Cohen (Oxford: Oxford University Press, 2000), 125.

67  I will let readers decide if I am here being sarcastic. There are many diagnostic tools on narrative competence that might assist you in this matter. For instance, if I am being sarcastic, is my sarcasm effective? Am I accurately predicting, inferring, or mentalizing your potential reactions to this statement? If I were to hand you a Likert Scale, how and where would you rate my (non)sarcasm?

68  Irene Rose, "Autistic Autobiography or Autistic Life Narrative?," *Journal of Literary Disability* 2, no. 1 (2008): 46.

69  Rose, "Autistic Autobiography or Autistic Life Narrative?," 47.

70  Grace, "Autistethnography."

71  Grace, "Autistethnography," 89.

72  Grace, "Autistethnography," 89, 100.

73  Prince-Hughes, *Songs of the Gorilla Nation*, 7.

74  Tobin Siebers, *Disability Theory* (Ann Arbor: University of Michigan Press, 2008).

75  George A. Rekers and O. Ivar Lovaas, "Behavioral Treatment of Deviant Sex-Role Behaviors in a Male Child," *Journal of Applied Behavior Analysis* 7, no. 2 (1974): 173–74; Alyric, "Indistinguishable from Their Peers," *A Touch of Alyricism* (blog), June 23, 2008, http://alyric.blogspot.com/2008/06/indistinguishable-from-their -peers.html.

76  Simon Baron-Cohen, "Theories of the Autistic Mind," *Psychologist* 21, no. 2 (2008): 112–16.

77  Most autism orgs (read: nonautistic autism orgs) recommend twenty to sixty hours of EIBI per week.

78  On being actively antisocial, see Fiona Kumari Campbell, "Re-cognising Disability: Cross-Examining Social Inclusion through the Prism of Queer Anti-sociality," *Jindal Global Law Review* 4, no. 2 (2013): 209–38; Rachel Groner, "Sex as 'Spock': Autism, Sexuality, and Autobiographical Narrative," in *Sex and Disability*, ed. Robert McRuer and Anna Mollow (Durham, NC: Duke University Press, 2012), 263–81; Lee Edelman, *No Future: Queer Theory and the Death Drive* (Durham, NC: Duke University Press, 2004).

79  Micki McGee, "Cruel Optimism for the Neurologically Queer," *Social Text: Periscope*, January 13, 2013, http://socialtextjournal.org/periscope_article/cruel -optimism-for-the-neurologically-queer/.

80  Nick Walker, "Neuroqueer: An Introduction," *Neurocosmopolitanism* (blog), May 2, 2014, http://neurocosmopolitanism.com/neuroqueer-an-introduction/.

81  Dolmage, *Disability Rhetoric*, 114.

82  Dolmage, *Disability Rhetoric*, 114–15.

83  Julia Miele Rodas, " 'On the Spectrum': Rereading Contact and Affect in Jane Eyre," *Nineteenth-Century Gender Studies* 4, no. 2 (2008): par. 20, http://www .ncgsjournal.com/issue42/rodas.htm.

84  Jay Dolmage, "Framing Disability, Developing Race: Photography as Eugenic Technology," *Enculturation* 17 (2014), http://enculturation.net/framingdisability.

85  John Harvey Kellogg, *Proceedings of the Race Betterment Conference* (Battle Creek, MI, 1928); Jonathan G. Silin, *Sex, Death, and the Education of Children: Our Passion for Ignorance in the Age of AIDS* (New York: Teachers College Press, 1995); Gary

Woodill, "Controlling the Sexuality of Developmentally Disabled Persons: Historical Perspectives," *Journal on Developmental Disabilities* 1, no. 1 (1992): 1–14.

86 S. G. Howe, *Report Made to the Legislature of Massachusetts, upon Idiocy* (Boston: Coolidge and Wiley, 1848), http://mirlyn.lib.umich.edu/Record/001133226; John Harvey Kellogg, *Plain Facts for Old and Young* (Burlington, IA: Segner and Condit, 1881), http://catalog.hathitrust.org/Record/010600804; Eric Rofes, *A Radical Rethinking of Sexuality and Schooling: Status Quo or Status Queer?* (Lanham, MD: Rowman and Littlefield, 2005), 60; Woodill, "Controlling the Sexuality of Developmentally Disabled Persons."

87 In a display of profound violence, Lovaas, Rekers, and colleagues routinely misgendered their child subjects. The mere title Feminine Boy Project, after all, adopts a changeling premise not unlike autism's stories, wherein a child's presumed core self is "cis boy" and transness and gender nonconformity somehow cover—obscure, threaten, imprison—the child's inner and real boyness.

88 Rekers and Lovaas, "Behavioral Treatment of Deviant Sex-Role Behaviors in a Male Child," 174.

89 Rekers and Lovaas, "Behavioral Treatment of Deviant Sex-Role Behaviors in a Male Child," 173; Richard Green, *The Sissy Boy Syndrome: The Development of Homosexuality* (New Haven, CT: Yale University Press, 1987).

90 Phyllis Burke, *Gender Shock: Exploding the Myths of Male and Female* (New York: Anchor, 1996), 47.

91 Giorgio Albertini et al., "Compulsive Masturbation in Infantile Autism Treated by Mirtazapine," *Pediatric Neurology* 34, no. 5 (2006): 417–18; Murat Coskun and Nahit Motavalli Mukaddes, "Mirtazapine Treatment in a Subject with Autistic Disorder and Fetishism," *Journal of Child and Adolescent Psychopharmacology* 18, no. 2 (April 1, 2008): 206–9, doi:10.1089/cap.2007.0014; Murat Coskun et al., "Effectiveness of Mirtazapine in the Treatment of Inappropriate Sexual Behaviors in Individuals with Autistic Disorder," *Journal of Child and Adolescent Psychopharmacology* 19, no. 2 (April 1, 2009): 203–6, doi:10.1089/cap.2008.020; Mathew Nguyen and Tanya Murphy, "Mirtazapine for Excessive Masturbation in an Adolescent with Autism" [letter to the editor], *Journal of the American Academy of Child and Adolescent Psychiatry* 40, no. 8 (2001): 868–69, doi:10.1097/00004583-200108000-00004; David J. Posey et al., "A Naturalistic Open-Label Study of Mirtazapine in Autistic and Other Pervasive Developmental Disorders," *Journal of Child and Adolescent Psychopharmacology* 11, no. 3 (September 1, 2001): 267–77, doi:10.1089/10445460152595586.

92 Deborah L. Shelton, "Autism Doctor Loses License in Illinois, Missouri," *Chicago Tribune*, November 5, 2012, http://articles.chicagotribune.com/2012-11-05/news/ct -met-autism-doctor-20121106_1_autism-doctor-david-geier-mark-geier.

93 Gary C. Woodward, *The Perfect Response: Studies of the Rhetorical Personality* (Lanham, MD: Lexington, 2010), 91.

94 Barnbaum, *The Ethics of Autism*, 154.

95 Uta Frith and Francesca Happé, "Theory of Mind and Self-Consciousness: What Is It Like to Be Autistic?," *Mind and Language* 14, no. 1 (1999): 18.

96   Andrea Greenbaum, "Nurturing Difference: The Autistic Student in Professional Writing Programs," *Journal of the Assembly for Advanced Perspectives on Learning* 16 (2011): 46.

97   Newnham, "News from Nowhere?"

98   Francesca Happé, *Autism: An Introduction to Psychological Theory* (New York: Psychology Press, 1994), 68.

99   Craig Snyder and Peter Bell, "To Petition the Government for a Redress of Grievances," in *Autism Spectrum Disorders*, ed. David Amaral, Daniel Geschwind, and Geraldine Dawson (Oxford: Oxford University Press, 2011), 1369–76; Lea Winerman, "Autism Diagnoses Bring Slew of Costs for Families," *PBS News Hour*, April 13, 2011, http://www.pbs.org/newshour/updates/health-jan-june11 -autismcosts_04-13/.

100  Judy Endow, *Learning the Hidden Curriculum: The Odyssey of One Autistic Adult* (Shawnee Mission, KS: Autism Asperger, 2012); Brenda Smith Myles and Richard L. Simpson, "Understanding the Hidden Curriculum: An Essential Social Skill for Children and Youth with Asperger Syndrome," *Intervention in School and Clinic* 36, no. 5 (2001).

ONE. INTENTION

1   In using the term *psychodynamic*, I am here referring to the idea that autism is understood, theoretically, as an internal state or psychological force. Psychodynamic approaches to autism include but are not limited to psychoanalysis. Although psychodynamism is still alive and well in the realm of autism treatment and research, such methodologies have largely been displaced by behavioral approaches to autism, as I discuss in chapter 2.

2   Slavoj Žižek, *The Sublime Object of Ideology* (London: Verso, 1989), 75.

3   Quoted in Kate Barrows, *Autism in Childhood and Autistic Features in Adults: A Psychoanalytic Perspective* (London: Karnac, 2008), 33.

4   Frances Tustin, *Autistic Barriers in Neurotic Patients* (London: Karnac, 1986), 305.

5   Judy Holiday, "In[ter]vention: Locating Rhetoric's Ethos," *Rhetoric Review* 28, no. 4 (2009): 390.

6   Holiday, "In[ter]vention."

7   Bruno Bara et al., "Intentional Minds: A Philosophical Analysis of Intention Tested through fMRI Experiments Involving People with Schizophrenia, People with Autism, and Healthy Individuals," *Frontiers in Human Neuroscience* 5 (2011): 7, doi:10.3389/fnhum.2011.00007.

8   Bara et al., "Intentional Minds," 2.

9   Mikhail Kissine, *From Utterances to Speech Acts* (Cambridge: Cambridge University Press, 2013), 143.

10  José Esteban Muñoz, *Cruising Utopia: The Then and There of Queer Futurity* (New York: New York University Press, 2009), 65.

11  Lydia Brown, "The Politics of Coming Out," *Autistic Hoya* (blog), October 11, 2012, http://www.autistichoya.com/2012/10/the-politics-of-coming-out.html.

12 Here, for example, I am invoking the nonautistic public's reception of memoirs by more famous individuals, such as Temple Grandin, John Elder Robison, or Donna Williams. My intent isn't to suggest that such works aren't important to autistic history, identity, or culture. Rather, these texts have taken on such status in the public imagination that they obscure the ongoingness of autistic being. G. Thomas Couser, for instance, has described these trends as rhetorics of overcoming, wherein a disability narrative is only seen as complete if its disabled subject somehow rises above disability, or accomplishes mundane tasks that then become heroic tasks due to disability's presence. Of course, autistic beings and doings do not end at the memoir; autism exceeds the bounds of paperbacks.

13 Denying the trustworthiness of autistic narrative is unfortunately common. In the foreword to Temple Grandin's *Emergence*, for instance, Bernard Rimland described Grandin as a "recovered (or recovering) autistic" who he at first believed could not possibly be autistic because she had gone to college and could use the telephone. Bernard Rimland, foreword to *Emergence: Labelled Autistic*, by Temple Grandin and Margaret Scariano (New York: Warner, 1986), 1.

14 Autism trade presses include Jessica Kingsley, Autism/Asperger Publishing Company, and New Horizons.

15 Brown, "The Politics of Coming Out."

16 Byron Hawk, *A Counter-history of Composition: Toward Methodologies of Complexity* (Pittsburgh: University of Pittsburgh Press, 2007), 164.

17 Lennard Davis, *Bending over Backwards: Disability, Dismodernism, and Other Difficult Positions* (New York: New York University Press, 2002), 13.

18 Holiday, "In[ter]vention," 389.

19 Jay T. Dolmage, *Disability Rhetoric* (Syracuse, NY: Syracuse University Press, 2014); Shannon Walters, "Animal Athena: The Interspecies Mētis of Women Writers with Autism," *JAC* 30, nos. 3–4 (2010): 683–711.

20 Dolmage, *Disability Rhetoric*, 219.

21 Gloria Anzaldúa, *Borderlands/La Frontera: The New Mestiza*, 3rd ed. (San Francisco: Aunt Lute, 2007).

22 Anzaldúa, *Borderlands/La Frontera*, 104–5.

23 Anzaldúa, *Borderlands/La Frontera*, 104.

24 An outgrowth of Lorna Wing's seminal work, autism is frequently construed as a triad of impairments, including impaired social interaction, impaired communication, and repetitive and restrictive behaviors and interests (often known as RRBI). The last item—RRBI—is often framed behaviorally and/or motorically, as these are the motions that are most typically read or made legible on the autistic body. Thus RRBI encompass the obsessional, the sensorial, the ticced or self-stimulational, as well as the ways in which autistic bodies mill and dwell in the world. Importantly, the DSM-5 has worked to collapse the triad into more of a dyad, combining the social and communicative domains into/as one singular impairment (or, put alternatively, as a series of impairments whose boundaries are tenuous at best). Lorna Wing, "Asperger's Syndrome: A Clinical Account," *Psychological Medicine* 11 (1981): 115–29.

25  Lorna Wing, Judith Gould, and Christopher Gillberg, "Autism Spectrum Disorders in the DSM-V: Better or Worse than the DSM-IV?," *Research in Developmental Disabilities* 32, no. 2 (2011): 769.

26  The ICD, or the International Statistical Classification of Diseases and Related Health Problems, codes various health classifications and is organized by the World Health Organization. The ICD-10, in particular, is the U.S. variant of the document and is used in insurance and billing, epidemiological tracking, and diagnostic classification.

27  See, for example, Deborah Fein et al., "Optimal Outcome in Individuals with a History of Autism," *Journal of Child Psychology and Psychiatry* 54, no. 2 (2013): 195–205; Elizabeth Kelley et al., "Residual Language Deficits in Optimal Outcome Children with a History of Autism," *Journal of Autism and Developmental Disorders* 36, no. 6 (2006): 807–28.

28  Obscure movie references might be another symptom of my autism, man (see *The Big Lebowski*).

29  Plato, *Parmenides*, trans. Benjamin Jowett (Project Gutenberg, 2013), 107.

30  Plato, *Parmenides*, 109.

31  Aristotle, *Physics*, trans. R. P. Hardie and R. K. Gaye (University of Adelaide, eBooks @ Adelaide, 2015), 251–52, https://ebooks.adelaide.edu.au/a/aristotle /physics/index.html.

32  Aristotle, *Physics*, 251.

33  Malea Powell et al., "Our Story Begins Here: Constellating Cultural Rhetorics," *Enculturation* 18 (2014), http://enculturation.net/our-story-begins-here.

34  Jeanne Fahnestock, *Rhetorical Figures in Science* (Oxford: Oxford University Press, 1999), 88; Jordynn Jack, "'The Extreme Male Brain?' Incrementum and the Rhetorical Gendering of Autism," *Disability Studies Quarterly* 31, no. 3 (2011).

35  Fahnestock, *Rhetorical Figures in Science*, 101.

36  Angela Ciaramidaro et al., "Schizophrenia and Autism as Contrasting Minds: Neural Evidence for the Hypo-Hyper-Intentionality Hypothesis," *Schizophrenia Bulletin* 41, no. 1 (2015): 171–79.

37  See also Bernard Rimland, *Infantile Autism: The Syndrome and Its Implications for a Neural Theory of Behavior* (New York: Appleton-Century-Crofts, 1964); or Mark Brosnan et al., "Can an 'Extreme Female Brain' Be Characterised in Terms of Psychosis?," *Personality and Individual Differences* 49, no. 7 (2010): 738–42, all of whom likewise suggest that autism and psychosis reside at opposing ends of neural continua. According to Rimland, autism represents unorientation and schizophrenia represents disorientation (167). Normalcy, as it were, is simply orientation.

38  Karen Zelan, *Between Their World and Ours: Breakthroughs with Autistic Children* (New York: St. Martin's, 2003), 10.

39  For an example of this argument, see Deborah Barnbaum, *The Ethics of Autism: Among Them, but Not of Them* (Bloomington: University of Indiana Press, 2008). In it, Barnbaum contends that because autistics lack a fully developed ToM (and thereby a theory that other humans exist), there can never be an autistic community: to claim an autistic community would be oxymoronic.

40  Simon Baron-Cohen, *Mindblindness: An Essay on Autism and Theory of Mind* (Boston: MIT Press, 1997).

41  Uta Frith and Francesca Happé, "Theory of Mind and Self-Consciousness: What Is It Like to Be Autistic?," *Mind and Language* 14, no. 1 (1999): 6, 2.

42  David Williams, "Theory of Own Mind in Autism: Evidence of a Specific Deficit in Self-Awareness?," *Autism* 14, no. 5 (2010): 481.

43  Victoria E. A. Brunsdon and Francesca Happé, "Exploring the 'Fractionation' of Autism at the Cognitive Level," *Autism* 18, no. 1 (2014): 17–30.

44  Brunsdon and Happé, "Exploring the 'Fractionation' of Autism at the Cognitive Level," 17.

45  See also Elise B. Robinson et al., "A Multivariate Twin Study of Autistic Traits in 12-Year-Olds: Testing the Fractionable Autism Triad Hypothesis," *Behavior Genetics* 42, no. 2 (2012): 245–55; and David M. Williams and Dermot M. Bowler, "Autism Spectrum Disorder: Fractionable or Coherent?," *Autism* 18, no. 1 (2014): 2–5.

46  Richard M. Weaver, *The Ethics of Rhetoric* (Chicago: Henry Regnery, 1953), 212.

47  Jasbir K. Puar, "Prognosis Time: Towards a Geopolitics of Affect, Debility and Capacity," *Women and Performance: A Journal of Feminist Theory* 19, no. 2 (2009): 161–72.

48  Puar, "Prognosis Time," 167.

49  Jasbir K. Puar, *Terrorist Assemblages: Homonationalism in Queer Times* (Durham, NC: Duke University Press, 2007).

50  Puar, *Terrorist Assemblages*, 213.

51  Kelly Fritsch, "Gradations of Debility and Capacity: Biocapitalism and the Neo-liberalization of Disability Relations," *Canadian Journal of Disability Studies* 4, no. 2 (2015): 28.

52  Rebecca Mallett and Katherine Runswick-Cole, "Commodifying Autism: The Cultural Contexts of 'Disability' in the Academy," in *Disability and Social Theory: New Developments and Directions*, ed. Dan Goodley, Bill Hughes, and Lennard Davis (New York: Palgrave Macmillan, 2012), 33–51.

53  Chapter 2, on applied behavior analysis, is one such example of interventionism.

54  Stuart Murray, "Autism Functions / The Function of Autism," *Disability Studies Quarterly* 31, no. 1 (2010), http://dsq-sds.org/article/view/1048/1229.

55  Catherine Prendergast, "On the Rhetorics of Mental Disability," in *Embodied Rhetorics: Disability in Language and Culture*, ed. James C. Wilson and Cynthia Lewiecki-Wilson (Carbondale: Southern Illinois University Press, 2001), 45–60; Margaret Price, *Mad at School: Rhetorics of Mental Disability and Academic Life* (Ann Arbor: University of Michigan Press, 2011).

56  Helen Tager-Flusberg, "Language and Understanding Minds: Connections in Autism," in *Understanding Other Minds: Perspectives from Developmental Cognitive Neuroscience*, 2nd ed., ed. Simon Baron-Cohen, Helen Tager-Flusberg, and Donald J. Cohen (Oxford: Oxford University Press, 2000), 124.

57  Muñoz, *Cruising Utopia*, 81.

58  Muñoz, *Cruising Utopia*, 65.

59 Ami Klin et al., "The Enactive Mind, or from Actions to Cognition: Lessons from Autism," *Philosophical Transactions of the Royal Society B: Biological Sciences* 358, no. 1430 (2003): 357.

60 Susan Dodd, *Understanding Autism* (Marrickville, NSW: Elsevier Australia, 2005), 58.

61 Lucille Hess, "I Would Like to Play but I Don't Know How: A Case Study of Pretend Play in Autism," *Child Language Teaching and Therapy* 22, no. 1 (2006): 98.

62 Dolmage, *Disability Rhetoric*, 2.

63 James E. Kinneavy, "The Basic Aims of Discourse," *College Composition and Communication* 20, no. 5 (1969): 297–304.

64 Jacqueline Jones Royster and Gesa E. Kirsch, *Feminist Rhetorical Practices: New Horizons for Rhetoric, Composition, and Literacy Studies* (Carbondale: Southern Illinois University Press, 2012).

65 James Berlin, *Rhetoric and Reality: Writing Instruction in American Colleges, 1900–1985* (Carbondale: Southern Illinois University Press, 1987), 3.

66 Bruno Bettelheim, *The Empty Fortress: Infantile Autism and the Birth of the Self* (New York: Free Press, 1967).

67 Suzanne Wright, "Autism Speaks to Washington—a Call for Action," Autism Speaks, November 11, 2013, https://www.autismspeaks.org/news/news-item/autism-speaks-washington-call-action.

68 Baron-Cohen, *Mindblindness*.

69 MSSNG, "Autism Speaks Launches MSSNG: Groundbreaking Genome-Sequencing Program," 2014, https://www.autismspeaks.org/science/science-news/autism-speaks-launches-mssng-groundbreaking-genome-sequencing-program. On their project page for MSSNG, Autism Speaks writes, "Pronounced 'missing,' the name has vowels deliberately omitted to represent the missing pieces of the autism puzzle. It is symbolic of the missing information about autism that the project is designed to find."

70 Wayne C. Booth, *The Rhetoric of Rhetoric: The Quest for Effective Communication* (Malden, MA: Blackwell, 2004).

71 Wing, "Asperger's Syndrome."

72 Dilip Parameshwar Gaonkar, "Rhetoric and Its Double: Reflections on the Rhetorical Turn in the Human Sciences," in *The Rhetorical Turn: Invention and Persuasion in the Conduct of Inquiry*, ed. Herbert W. Simons (Chicago: University of Chicago Press, 1990), 341–66; Carolyn R. Miller, "Should We Name the Tools? Concealing and Revealing the Art of Rhetoric," in *The Public Work of Rhetoric: Citizen-Scholars and Civic Engagement*, ed. John M. Ackerman and David J. Coogan (Columbia: University of South Carolina Press, 2010), 19–38.

73 Olga Bogdashina, *Sensory Perceptual Issues in Autism: Different Sensory Experiences, Different Perceptual Worlds* (London: Jessica Kingsley, 2003).

74 Donna Williams, *Autism and Sensing: The Unlost Instinct* (London: Jessica Kingsley, 1998).

75 Muñoz, *Cruising Utopia*, 66.

76 Erin Manning, *The Minor Gesture* (Durham, NC: Duke University Press, 2016), 20–21.

77   Manning, *The Minor Gesture*, 41.

78   Manning, *The Minor Gesture*, 137.

79   Phil Schwarz, "Building Alliances: Community Identity and the Role of Allies in Autistic Self-Advocacy," in *Ask and Tell: Self-Advocacy and Disclosure for People on the Autism Spectrum*, ed. Stephen M. Shore (Shawnee Mission, KS: Autism Asperger, 2004), 147.

80   Ian [Star] Ford, *A Field Guide to Earthlings: An Autistic/Asperger View of Neurotypical Behavior* (Albuquerque, NM: Ian Ford Software, 2010).

81   Ford, *A Field Guide to Earthlings*, 21.

82   Kenneth Burke, *Dramatism and Development* (Barre, MA: Clark University Press, 1972), 21.

83   Suzanne Wright, "Transcript—Suzanne Wright Speaks at the Vatican," *Unstrange Mind* (blog), 2014, https://unstrangemind.wordpress.com/transcripts/transcript-suzanne-wright-speaks-at-the-vatican/.

84   Joshua St. Pierre, "Distending Straight-Masculine Time: A Phenomenology of the Disabled Speaking Body," *Hypatia* 30, no. 1 (2015): 49–65.

85   Gayle Salamon, *Assuming a Body: Transgender and Rhetorics of Materiality* (New York: Columbia University Press, 2010), 49–50.

86   Salamon, *Assuming a Body*, 51.

87   Bara et al., "Intentional Minds"; Tim Crane, "The Mental States of Persons and Their Brains," *Royal Institute of Philosophy Supplement* 76 (2015): 253–70.

88   Brian D. Mills et al., "White Matter Microstructure Correlates of Narrative Production in Typically Developing Children and Children with High Functioning Autism," *Neuropsychologia* 51 (2013): 1933.

89   Joana Bisol Balardin et al., "Relationship between Surface-Based Brain Morphometric Measures and Intelligence in Autism Spectrum Disorders," *Autism Research* 8, no. 5 (October 1, 2015): 556, doi:10.1002/aur.1470.

90   R. J. Holt et al., "'Reading the Mind in the Eyes': An fMRI Study of Adolescents with Autism and Their Siblings," *Psychological Medicine* 44, no. 15 (2015): 3223.

91   Caspar J. Goch et al., "Quantification of Changes in Language-Related Brain Areas in Autism Spectrum Disorders Using Large-Scale Network Analysis," *International Journal of Computer Assisted Radiology and Surgery* 9, no. 3 (2014): 357–65.

92   Todd V. Oakley, "The Human Rhetorical Potential," *Written Communication* 16, no. 1 (1999): 102; Andrea Greenbaum, "Nurturing Difference: The Autistic Student in Professional Writing Programs," *Journal of the Assembly for Advanced Perspectives on Learning* 16 (2011): 40–47; Ann Jurecic, "Neurodiversity," *College English* 69, no. 5 (2007): 421–42.

93   Isabelle Dussauge and Anelis Kaiser, "Re-queering the Brain," in *Neurofeminism: Issues at the Intersection of Feminist Theory and Cognitive Science*, ed. Robyn Bluhm, Anne Jaap Jacobson, and Heidi Lene Maibom (London: Palgrave Macmillan, 2012), 121–44.

94   Dussauge and Kaiser, "Re-queering the Brain," 137.

95   Dussauge and Kaiser, "Re-queering the Brain," 124.

96   Francesca Happé, "The Autobiographical Writings of Three Asperger Syndrome Adults: Problems of Interpretation and Implications for Theory," in *Autism and Asperger Syndrome*, ed. Uta Frith (Cambridge: Cambridge University Press, 1991), 217.

97   See, for example, Julia Miele Rodas, *Autistic Disturbances: Theorizing Autism Poetics from the* DSM *to Robinson Crusoe* (Ann Arbor: University of Michigan Press, forthcoming); Erin Manning, *Always More Than One: Individuation's Dance* (Durham, NC: Duke University Press, 2013); Jason Nolan and Melanie McBride, "Embodied Semiosis: Autistic 'Stimming' as Sensory Praxis," in *International Handbook of Semiotics*, ed. Peter P. Trifonas (New York: Springer, 2015), 1069–78; Michael Monje, "Why #Fiction? (#Autism #Book Club Questions)," *Shaping Clay*, April 3, 2015, http://www.mmonjejr.com/2015/04/why-fiction-autism-book-club -questions.html.

98   Jordynn Jack, *Autism and Gender: From Refrigerator Mothers to Computer Geeks* (Champaign: University of Illinois Press, 2014), 2.

99   Chaim Perelman and C. Olbrechts-Tyteca, *The New Rhetoric: A Treatise on Argumentation* (South Bend, IN: University of Notre Dame Press, 1991); Lisa Ede and Andrea Lunsford, "Audience Addressed / Audience Invoked: The Role of Audience in Composition Theory and Pedagogy," *College Composition and Communication* 35, no. 2 (1984): 155–71.

100  Elizabeth O'Nions et al., "Examining the Genetic and Environmental Associations between Autistic Social and Communication Deficits and Psychopathic Callous-Unemotional Traits," PLOS ONE 10, no. 9 (2015): 2.

101  Jenell Johnson, "The Skeleton on the Couch: The Eagleton Affair, Rhetorical Disability, and the Stigma of Mental Illness," *Rhetoric Society Quarterly* 40, no. 5 (2010): 462.

102  Johnson, "The Skeleton on the Couch," 463.

103  Galen, *Method of Medicine*, books 1–4, ed. and trans. Ian Johnston and G. H. R. Horsley (Cambridge, MA: Harvard University Press, 2011), 419.

104  Galen, *Method of Medicine*, 397.

105  Dolmage, *Disability Rhetoric*.

106  Amy Sequenzia, "On Not Being 'Pretty,'" *Ollibean* (blog), August 5, 2015, http:// ollibean.com/on-not-being-pretty/.

107  John Horgan, *The Undiscovered Mind: How the Human Brain Defies Replication, Medication, and Explanation* (New York: Touchstone, 1999), 228.

108  Kenneth Burke, *On Symbols and Society* (Chicago: University of Chicago Press, 1989), 120.

109  Kenneth Burke, "(Nonsymbolic) Motion / (Symbolic) Action," *Critical Inquiry* 4, no. 4 (1978): 836.

110  Brian Massumi, *Parables for the Virtual: Movement, Affect, Sensation* (Durham, NC: Duke University Press, 2002), 3.

111  Anne M. Donnellan, "Invented Knowledge and Autism: Highlighting Our Strengths and Expanding the Conversation," *Journal of the Association for Persons with Severe Handicaps* 24, no. 3 (1999): 232.

112  Margaret Price, "The Politics of the Portal," in *Cripping the Computer: A Critical Moment in Composition Studies*, ed. Elizabeth Brewer and Melanie Yergeau (unpublished manuscript, 2017).

113  Alison Kafer, *Feminist, Queer, Crip* (Bloomington: Indiana University Press, 2013), 34.

114  Ariane Zurcher and Emma Zurcher-Long, "Intention," *Emma's Hope Book* (blog), September 9, 2014, http://emmashopebook.com/2014/09/09/intention/.

115  Zurcher and Zurcher-Long, "Intention."

116  Emma Zurcher-Long, "The Fan Stays Off," *Emma's Hope Book* (blog), April 9, 2015, http://emmashopebook.com/2015/04/09/the-fan-stays-off/.

117  Melanie Yergeau et al., "Multimodality in Motion: Disability and Kairotic Spaces," *Kairos: A Journal of Rhetoric, Technology, and Pedagogy* 18, no. 1 (2013), http://kairos .technorhetoric.net/18.1/coverweb/yergeau-et-al/index.html.

118  Massumi, *Parables for the Virtual*.

119  Burke, *On Symbols and Society*, 79.

120  Burke, *On Symbols and Society*, 84; Ian Hacking, "How We Have Been Learning to Talk about Autism: A Role for Stories," in *Cognitive Disability and Its Challenge to Moral Philosophy*, ed. Eva F. Kittay and Licia Carlson (Malden, MA: Wiley-Blackwell, 2010), 261–78.

121  Diane Davis, "Creaturely Rhetorics," *Philosophy and Rhetoric* 44, no. 1 (2011): 88.

122  Fiona Kumari Campbell, "Re-cognising Disability: Cross-Examining Social Inclusion through the Prism of Queer Anti-sociality," *Jindal Global Law Review* 4, no. 2 (2013): 209–38.

123  Kafer, *Feminist, Queer, Crip*, 17.

124  E. L. McCallum and Mikko Tuhkanen, "Introduction: Becoming Unbecoming: Untimely Meditations," in *Queer Times, Queer Becomings* (Albany: State University of New York Press, 2011), 6.

125  Zach Richter, *Awkward Gestures* (blog), 2015, http://zachrichter.weebly.com /awkward-gestures-blog; Kafer, *Feminist, Queer, Crip*; Craig Meyer, "Infusing Dysfluency into Rhetoric and Composition: Overcoming the Stutter" (PhD diss., Ohio University, 2013).

126  St. Pierre, "Distending Straight-Masculine Time," 49.

127  St. Pierre, "Distending Straight-Masculine Time," 52.

128  Simon Baron-Cohen, *Essential Difference: Male and Female Brains and the Truth about Autism* (New York: Basic Books, 2003), 8.

129  Baron-Cohen, *Essential Difference*, 100.

130  Baron-Cohen, *Essential Difference*, 109.

131  Mark Brosnan, Rajiv Daggar, and John Collomosse, "The Relationship between Systemising and Mental Rotation and the Implications for the Extreme Male Brain Theory of Autism," *Journal of Autism and Developmental Disorders* 40 (2010): 739.

132  Brosnan, Daggar, and Collomosse, "The Relationship between Systemising and Mental Rotation," 741.

133  Jack, *Autism and Gender*; Jack, "'The Extreme Male Brain?'"

134  Cordelia Fine, *Delusions of Gender: How Our Minds, Society, and Neurosexism Create Difference* (New York: Norton, 2010), 174.

135 Simon Baron-Cohen, *The Science of Evil: On Empathy and the Origins of Cruelty* (New York: Basic Books, 2011).

136 Nick Walker, "Throw Away the Master's Tools: Liberating Ourselves from the Pathology Paradigm," *Neurocosmopolitanism* (blog), August 16, 2013, http:// neurocosmopolitanism.com/throw-away-the-masters-tools-liberating-ourselves -from-the-pathology-paradigm/.

137 Rolf J. F. Ypma et al., "Default Mode Hypoconnectivity Underlies a Sex-Related Autism Spectrum," *Biological Psychiatry: Cognitive Neuroscience and Neuroimaging* 1, no. 4 (2016): 364.

138 Ypma et al., "Default Mode Hypoconnectivity," 368.

139 Simon Baron-Cohen et al., "Attenuation of Typical Sex Differences in 800 Adults with Autism vs. 3,900 Controls," PLOS ONE 9, no. 7 (July 16, 2014): e102251, doi:10.1371/journal.pone.0102251.

140 Baron-Cohen et al., "Attenuation of Typical Sex Differences," 7.

141 On transactional relationship, Laura A. Jacobs et al., "Gender Dysphoria and Co-occurring Autism Spectrum Disorders: Review, Case Examples, and Treatment Considerations," LGBT Health 1, no. 4 (2014): 278.

142 Davis, "Creaturely Rhetorics," 89.

143 Massumi, *Parables for the Virtual*, 6.

144 Written and self-published by Michael Alan, *I Wish My Kids Had Cancer* chronicles Alan's experiences with fathering two autistic children, whose disabilities, as the title suggests, Alan believes are worse than potentially fatal conditions. Michael Alan, *I Wish My Kids Had Cancer: A Family Surviving the Autism Epidemic* (Baltimore, MD: PublishAmerica, 2008). Zombie walks are becoming increasingly common, with such events having transpired in U.S. locales ranging from Michigan to South Carolina. Participants are typically encouraged to dress like the undead and parade around a town or local thoroughfare in order to raise funds for autism research. A Sault Ste. Marie walk, for example, boasts that walkers will "creep for autism" in order to "help raise awareness." Corner Pieces, "Zombie Walk for Autism," 2013, http://www.eventbrite.com/e/zombie-walk-for-autism-tickets -8623281467.

145 Wright, "Autism Speaks to Washington."

146 Sarah Kurchak, "I'm Autistic, and Believe Me, It's a Lot Better than Measles," *Medium*, February 6, 2015, https://medium.com/the-archipelago/im-autistic-and -believe-me-its-a-lot-better-than-measles-78cb039f4bea.

147 Kurchak, "I'm Autistic."

148 Leo Kanner, "Austistic Disturbances of Affective Contact," *Nervous Child* 2, no. 3 (1943): 217–50.

149 Hans Asperger, " 'Autistic Psychopathy' in Childhood," in *Autism and Asperger Syndrome*, ed. Uta Frith (Cambridge: Cambridge University Press, 1991), 39.

150 Sigmund Freud, *Beyond the Pleasure Principle*, trans. C. J. M. Hubback (London: International Psycho-Analytical Press, 1922); Denys Ribas, "Autism as the Defusion of Drives," *International Journal of Psychoanalysis* 79 (1998): 529–38; Hyman Spotnitz, *Psychotherapy of Preoedipal Conditions: Schizophrenia and Severe Character*

Disorders (Lanham, MD: Jason Aronson, 1976); Frances Tustin, *Autism and Childhood Psychosis* (London: Karnac, 1995).

151  Eileen E. Brennan, "Encountering Autism: Learning to Listen to the Fear," in *The Use of Psychoanalysis in Working with Children's Emotional Lives*, ed. Michael O'Laughlin (Lanham, MD: Jason Aronson, 2013), 310.

152  Laurence Barrer and Guy Gimenez, "First Time Description of Dismantling Phenomenon," *Frontiers in Psychology* 6, no. 510 (2015): 3.

153  Ian Hacking, "Humans, Aliens, and Autism," *Daedalus* 138, no. 3 (2009): 44; Uta Frith, *Autism: Explaining the Enigma*, 2nd ed. (Malden, MA: Blackwell, 2003), 1; Maureen Aarons and Tessa Gittens, *The Handbook of Autism: A Guide for Parents and Professionals* (New York: Routledge, 2002), 33.

154  Aristotle, *Physics*.

155  In this, I am indebted to Cynthia Lewiecki-Wilson's suggestion that autistic movements are not intentions but rather their own drives, which are queerly and partially rhetorical. In this way, the autistic exceeds the intentional, representing rhetorical practices that are more capacious in form and effect.

156  As quoted in Stan A. Lindsay, *Implicit Rhetoric: Kenneth Burke's Extension of Aristotle's Concept of Entelechy* (Lanham, MD: University Press of America, 1998), 18.

157  Kenneth Burke, *A Rhetoric of Motives* (New York, NY: Prentice-Hall, 1955), 14.

158  Burke, *A Rhetoric of Motives*, 17.

159  Hawk, *A Counter-history of Composition*, 164.

160  Dolmage, *Disability Rhetoric*, 157.

161  Anzaldúa, *Borderlands / La Frontera*, 64.

162  Debra Hawhee, *Bodily Arts: Rhetoric and Athletics in Ancient Greece* (Austin: University of Texas Press, 2005), 50.

163  Stan A. Lindsay, *Psychotic Entelechy: The Dangers of Spiritual Gifts Theology* (Lanham, MD: University Press of America, 2006).

164  Lindsay, *Psychotic Entelechy*, 9.

165  Lindsay, *Psychotic Entelechy*, 13.

166  Bryan Hubbard, "Reassessing Truman, the Bomb, and Revisionism: The Burlesque Frame and Entelechy in the Decision to Use Atomic Weapons against Japan," *Western Journal of Communication* 62, no. 3 (1998): 328–85; Michael J. Steudeman, "Entelechy and Irony in Political Time: The Preemptive Rhetoric of Nixon and Obama," *Rhetoric and Public Affairs* 16, no. 1 (2013): 59–96.

167  Lindsay, *Psychotic Entelechy*, 14.

168  David Morris, *The Sense of Space* (Albany: State University of New York Press, 2004).

169  Qwo-Li Driskill, "Double-Weaving Two-Spirit Critiques: Building Alliances between Native and Queer Studies," *GLQ: A Journal of Lesbian and Gay Studies* 16, nos. 1–2 (2010): 69–92; Andrea Riley-Mukavetz, "On Working from or with Anger: Or How I Learned to Listen to My Relatives and Practice All Our Relations," *Enculturation* 21 (2016), http://enculturation.net/on-working-from-or-with-anger.

170  Kenneth Burke, *Counter-statement* (Los Angeles: University of California Press, 1968), 180.

171  Rimland, *Infantile Autism*.

172  Rimland, *Infantile Autism*, 206–7.

173  Simon Baron-Cohen, "The Biology of the Imagination," *Enetelechy: Mind and Culture* 9 (2007), http://www.entelechyjournal.com/simonbaroncohen.htm.

174  Lee Edelman, *No Future: Queer Theory and the Death Drive* (Durham, NC: Duke University Press, 2004).

175  Muñoz, *Cruising Utopia*, 28.

176  Hawk, *A Counter-history of Composition*, 255.

177  Zoe Gross, "Killing Words," ASAN, April 10, 2012, http://autisticadvocacy.org/2012/04/killing-words/.

178  Burke, *Counter-statement*, 180.

179  Bruno Latour, *The Pasteurization of France*, trans. Alan Sheridan and John Law (Cambridge, MA: Harvard University Press, 1993).

180  Bettelheim, *The Empty Fortress*, 90.

181  Burke, *A Rhetoric of Motives*, 20.

182  Hawk, *A Counter-history of Composition*, 126.

183  Booth, *The Rhetoric of Rhetoric*.

184  Booth, *The Rhetoric of Rhetoric*, 4.

185  Miller, "Should We Name the Tools?"

186  Price, *Mad at School*, 142.

187  Sparrow R. Jones, *The ABCs of Autism Acceptance* (Fort Worth, TX: Autonomous Press, 2016).

188  N. I. Nicholson, "Racial Profiling and the Black Autistic: The Case of Neli Latson," *The Digital Hyperlexic* (blog), December 11, 2014, https://thedigitalhyperlexic.wordpress.com/2014/12/11/racial-profiling-and-the-black-autistic-the-case-of-neli-latson/.

189  Jonathan Alexander and Jacqueline Rhodes, "Queer Rhetoric and the Pleasures of the Archive," *Enculturation* 13 (2012), http://www.enculturation.net/queer-rhetoric-and-the-pleasures-of-the-archive.

190  Dolmage, *Disability Rhetoric*, 2–4.

191  Alexander and Rhodes, "Queer Rhetoric and the Pleasures of the Archive."

192  Kafer, *Feminist, Queer, Crip*, 13.

193  Robert McRuer, *Crip Theory: Cultural Signs of Queerness and Disability* (New York: New York University Press, 2006).

194  Sami Schalk, "Coming to Claim Crip: Disidentification with/in Disability Studies," *Disability Studies Quarterly* 33, no. 2 (2013), http://dsq-sds.org/article/view/3705/3240; McRuer, *Crip Theory*.

195  Schalk, "Coming to Claim Crip."

196  As quoted in Norma Carr-Ruffino, *Diversity Success Strategies* (New York: Routledge, 2009), 250.

197  Kassiane Sibley, "Feminist Wire, You May Not Colonize My Community," *Radical Neurodivergence Speaking* (blog), August 29, 2013, http://timetolisten.blogspot.com/2013/08/feminist-wire-you-may-not-colonize-my.html.

198  Nick Walker, "Neuroqueer: An Introduction," *Neurocosmopolitanism* (blog), May 2, 2014, http://neurocosmopolitanism.com/neuroqueer-an-introduction/.

199   Thomas Rickert, *Ambient Rhetoric: The Attunements of Rhetorical Being* (Pittsburgh: University of Pittsburgh Press, 2013), 160.

200   George A. Kennedy, "A Hoot in the Dark: The Evolution of General Rhetoric," *Philosophy and Rhetoric* 25, no. 1 (1992): 1–21; Rickert, *Ambient Rhetoric*; Sara Ahmed, "Happy Objects," in *The Affect Theory Reader*, ed. Melissa Gregg and Gregory J. Seigworth (Durham, NC: Duke University Press, 2010), 29–51.

201   Ford, *A Field Guide to Earthlings*, 202.

202   Ford, *A Field Guide to Earthlings*, 201.

203   Ford, *A Field Guide to Earthlings*, 202.

204   Audre Lorde, *Sister Outsider: Essays and Speeches* (Berkeley, CA: Crossing Press, 2007); Nick Walker, "Throw Away the Master's Tools: Liberating Ourselves from the Pathology Paradigm," *Neurocosmopolitanism* (blog), August 16, 2013, http://neurocosmopolitanism.com/throw-away-the-masters-tools-liberating-ourselves-from-the-pathology-paradigm/; Sara Ahmed, *Living a Feminist Life* (Durham, NC: Duke University Press, 2017).

205   In relaying this example, I do not mean to invoke Sarah Palin's death panels, or similar hyperbole around health care and supposed death. I do, however, mean to summon issues such as caregiver murder, restraint deaths, death by cop, euthanasia, institutionalization and incarceration, segregated schooling, sheltered workshops, forced medical treatment, surgical experimentation, ugly laws, and so on.

206   Malea Powell, "Stories Take Place: A Performance in One Act (2012 CCCC Chair's Address)," *College Composition and Communication* 64, no. 2 (2012): 383–406.

TWO. INTERVENTION

1   Amit Pinchevski, "Displacing Incommunicability: Autism as an Epistemological Boundary," *Communication and Critical/Cultural Studies* 2, no. 2 (2005): 163–84.

2   George Kennedy, *Comparative Rhetoric: An Historical and Cross-Cultural Introduction* (Oxford: Oxford University Press, 1998).

3   Rachel Groner, "Sex as 'Spock': Autism, Sexuality, and Autobiographical Narrative," in *Sex and Disability*, ed. Robert McRuer and Anna Mollow (Durham, NC: Duke University Press, 2012), 65.

4   Karen A. Foss, "Harvey Milk and the Queer Rhetorical Situation: A Rhetoric of Contradiction," in *Queering Public Address: Sexualities in American Historical Discourse* (Columbia: University of South Carolina Press, 2007), 86.

5   Byron Hawk, *A Counter-history of Composition: Toward Methodologies of Complexity* (Pittsburgh: University of Pittsburgh Press, 2007), 282.

6   See BACB, "About Behavior Analysis," Behavior Analyst Certification Board, n.d., http://bacb.com/about-behavior-analysis/; Albert J. Kearney, *Understanding Applied Behavior Analysis: An Introduction to ABA for Parents, Teachers, and Other Professionals* (London: Jessica Kingsley, 2007); Travis Thompson, "Autism and Behavior Analysis: History and Current Status," in *The Wiley Blackwell Handbook of Operant and Classical Conditioning*, ed. Frances K. McSweeney and Eric S. Murphy (Malden, MA: Wiley-Blackwell, 2014), 483–508; Steph, "Why I Left ABA," *Socially*

*Anxious Advocate* (blog), May 22, 2015, https://sociallyanxiousadvocate.wordpress
.com/2015/05/22/why-i-left-aba/.

7   Alicia Broderick, "Autism as Rhetoric: Exploring Watershed Rhetorical Moments
    in Applied Behavior Analysis Discourse," *Disability Studies Quarterly* 31, no. 3
    (2011), http://dsq-sds.org/article/view/1674/1597.

8   Broderick, "Autism as Rhetoric."

9   Barry M. Prizant, "Straight Talk about Autism: Treatment Options and Parent
    Choice: Is ABA the Only Way?," *Autism Spectrum Quarterly*, spring 2009.

10  The recommendations include, but are not limited to, the surgeon general, the Na-
    tional Institutes of Mental Health, and the American Academy of Pediatrics (Au-
    tism Speaks, "Self-Funded Employer Tool Kit," 2012, https://www.autismspeaks
    .org/sites/default/files/docs/gr/erisa_tool_kit_9.12_0.pdf).

11  O. Ivar Lovaas, "The Development of a Treatment-Research Project for Develop-
    mentally Disabled and Autistic Children," *Journal of Applied Behavior Analysis* 26,
    no. 4 (1993): 627; Mary, "Testimonial: 'Best Decision I Ever Made for My Son,'"
    ABI: Applied Behavioral Interventions, 2015, http://abiautism.com/about-abi
    /testimonial-best-decision-i-ever-made-for-my-son/; Gil Eyal et al., *The Autism
    Matrix* (Cambridge: Polity, 2010), 201.

12  Sparrow R. Jones, "ABA," in *The Real Experts: Readings for Parents of Autistic
    Children,* ed. Michelle Sutton (Fort Worth, TX: Autonomous Press, 2015), loc.
    745.

13  Christina Adams, *A Real Boy: A True Story of Autism, Early Intervention, and Recovery*
    (New York: Berkley, 2005).

14  Beth Ryan, "Touch Nose. Gummi Bear: ABA in Our Family," *Love Explosions* (blog),
    September 13, 2013, http://loveexplosions.net/2013/09/13/touch-nose-gummi-bear
    -aba-in-our-family/.

15  George A. Rekers et al., "Child Gender Disturbances: A Clinical Rationale for
    Intervention," *Psychotherapy: Theory, Research, and Practice* 14, no. 1 (1977): 5.

16  Martijn Dekker, "On Our Own Terms: Emerging Autistic Culture," Autscape, 1999,
    http://www.autscape.org/2015/programme/handouts/Autistic-Culture-07-Oct-1999
    .pdf; Erin Human, "Autistic Culture: A Primer," *E Is for Erin* (blog), January 14,
    2016, https://eisforerin.com/2016/01/14/autistic-primer/.

17  Wendy [Wenn] Lawson, *Concepts of Normality: The Autistic and Typical Spectrum*
    (London: Jessica Kingsley, 2008), 84.

18  On therapies for same-sex attraction, see, for instance, Travis Webster, "Pray the
    Gay Away: Rhetorical Dilemmas of the American Ex-Gay Movement" (PhD diss.,
    Michigan State University, 2012).

19  Autism Speaks, "Autism Prevalence on the Rise," *Autism Speaks* (blog), Octo-
    ber 2010, https://autismspeaksblog.files.wordpress.com/2010/10/prevalence
    -graph1.jpg. Conversely, reparative therapy has been blacklisted and banned by the
    American Psychological Association. It would be easy to make the claim that it is a
    matter of subjectivity—that is, ABA is bad for queers but good for autistics, because
    their disabilities require any and all intensity of intervention and normalization.
    Consider, however, the queerness of disability, as well as the comorbidities that

often attend queerness. Therapeutic modalities, much like diagnostic constructions themselves, have always found ways to backdoor and pathologize the queer.

20  Alison Kafer, *Feminist, Queer, Crip* (Bloomington: Indiana University Press, 2013), 16.

21  Jay T. Dolmage, *Disability Rhetoric* (Syracuse: Syracuse University Press, 2014), 16.

22  Tim Luckett, Anita Bundy, and Jacqueline Roberts, "Do Behavioural Approaches Teach Children with Autism to Play or Are They Pretending?," *Autism* 11, no. 4 (2007): 365–88.

23  Luckett, Bundy, and Roberts, "Do Behavioural Approaches Teach Children with Autism to Play," 374.

24  Lovaas, "The Development of a Treatment-Research Project."

25  Lovaas, "The Development of a Treatment-Research Project," 618.

26  Lovaas, "The Development of a Treatment-Research Project," 620.

27  D. Moser and A. Grant, "Screams, Slaps, and Love: A Surprising, Shocking Treatment Helps Far-Gone Mental Cripples," *Life*, May 7, 1965.

28  Moser and Grant, "Screams, Slaps, and Love," 93.

29  Adam Feinstein, *A History of Autism: Conversations with the Pioneers* (Malden, MA: Wiley-Blackwell, 2010), 132.

30  Chloe Silverman, *Understanding Autism: Parents, Doctors, and the History of a Disorder* (Princeton, NJ: Princeton University Press, 2012), 111.

31  Kenneth Burke, *Language as Symbolic Action: Essays of Life, Literature, and Method* (Los Angeles: University of California Press, 1966), 428.

32  Paul Chance, "'After You Hit a Child, You Can't Just Get Up and Leave Him; You Are Hooked to That Kid': A Conversation with Ivar Lovaas about Self-Mutilating Children and How Their Parents Make It Worse," *Psychology Today*, January 1974, 76; O. Ivar Lovaas, *The Autistic Child: Language Development through Behavior Modification* (New York: Irvington, 1977), 13.

33  David Michael Rorvik, "The Gender Enforcers: Seeing to It the Boys Will Be Boys," *Rolling Stone*, October 9, 1975.

34  George A. Rekers and O. Ivar Lovaas, "Behavioral Treatment of Deviant Sex-Role Behaviors in a Male Child," *Journal of Applied Behavior Analysis* 7, no. 2 (1974): 174. As I noted in chapter 1, one hallmark of Rekers and Lovaas's work is their insistence on calling their child subjects "feminine boys," what is surely a misgendering of the children who were in their care. We do not, however, know fully who these children were, nor do we know their gender identities. For these reasons, I refer to Rekers and Lovaas's child subjects as gender-variant and gender-nonconforming children. All references to cisgender or effeminate boys represent the language of Lovaas and his colleagues, not my own.

35  See Richard Green, *The "Sissy Boy Syndrome": The Development of Homosexuality* (New Haven, CT: Yale University Press, 1987).

36  Rekers and Lovaas, "Behavioral Treatment of Deviant Sex-Role Behaviors," 38.

37  George A. Rekers, *Growing Up Straight: What Every Family Should Know about Homosexuality* (Chicago: Moody, 1982); George A. Rekers, *Shaping Your Child's Sexual Identity* (Grand Rapids, MI: Baker, 1982).

38   George A. Rekers, "Review of Research on Homosexual Parenting, Adoption, and Foster Parenting," NARTH, 2004, 2, https://web.archive.org/web/20080228024533 /http://www.narth.com/docs/RationaleBasisFinal0405.pdf; George A. Rekers et al., "Childhood Gender Identity Change: Operant Control over Sex-Typed Play and Mannerisms," *Journal of Behavioral Therapy and Experimental Psychiatry* 7 (1976): 51; Rekers, *Growing Up Straight*, 14.

39   Judith Butler, *Undoing Gender* (New York: Routledge, 2004), 89; George A. Rekers, Professor George.com, Archive.org, 2011, https://web.archive.org/web /20110208224932/http://www.professorgeorge.com/ProfessorGeorge.com /Welcome_to_ProfessorGeorge.com.html.

40   Jim Burroway, "What Are Little Boys Made Of? An Original BTB Investigation," *Box Turtle Bulletin* (blog), June 7, 2011, http://www.boxturtlebulletin.com/what-are -little-boys-made-of-main; Scott Bronstein and Jessi Joseph, "Therapy to Change 'Feminine' Boy Created a Troubled Man, Family Says," CNN, June 10, 2011, http:// www.cnn.com/2011/US/06/07/sissy.boy.experiment/. For an extended example of Rekers's empirical assessment of the horrors of homosexually behaving parents and family members, see his 2004 NARTH report, "Review of Research on Homo- sexual Parenting, Adoption, and Foster Parenting."

41   Rekers, "Professor George.com."

42   Research in ABA has been conducted on other disabled communities, beyond that of autistic people. As well, many behavior analysts will make the argument that ABA is merely the applied science of learning principles—that ABA is part of the natural order, and everyday life is merely an invisible exercise of operant principles. I tackle this particular viewpoint later in this chapter under my discussion of environmental- ism. But, suffice to say, I submit that any argument regarding ABA's naturalness and everydayness doesn't hold its own muster. There is a radical difference between a parent who places her allistic daughter in time-out for drawing on the walls and a behavior analyst who binds an autistic child's hands in sticky tape for joyfully flapping her fingers. (For an autistic account of this example—holding down children's arms to prevent stimming—see Julia Bascom, "Quiet Hands," *Just Stimming* (blog), October 5, 2011, https://juststimming.wordpress.com/2011/10/05/quiet-hands/, which is arguably anti-ABA canon in autistic activism circles.) As well, I am wary of any claim or claim- ant that declares something to be of a natural order. That way lies eugenics.

43   Broderick, "Autism as Rhetoric."

44   UPIAS and the Disability Alliance, "Fundamental Principles of Disability," ed. Mark Priestley, Vic Finkelstein, and Ken Davis (Centre for Disability Studies, University of Leeds, 1975), http://disability-studies.leeds.ac.uk/files/library/UPIAS -fundamental-principles.pdf.

45   Simi Linton, *Claiming Disability: Knowledge and Identity* (New York: New York University Press, 1998); Tom Shakespeare, *Disability Rights and Wrongs* (New York: Routledge, 2006).

46   Shakespeare, *Disability Rights and Wrongs*, 15.

47   James C. Wilson and Cynthia Lewiecki-Wilson, *Embodied Rhetorics: Disability in Language and Culture* (Carbondale: Southern Illinois University Press, 2001), 9.

48 Tom Shakespeare and Nicole Watson, "The Social Model of Disability: An Outdated Ideology?," in *Research in Social Science and Disability: Exploring Theories and Expanding Methodologies: Where We Are and Where We Need to Go*, vol. 2, ed. Sharon N. Barnartt and Barbara M. Altman (Bingley, U.K.: Emerald, 2001), 11.

49 Dolmage, *Disability Rhetoric*; Nirmala Erevelles, "Thinking with Disability Studies," *Disability Studies Quarterly* 34, no. 2 (2014), http://dsq-sds.org/article/view/4248 /3587; Robert McRuer, *Crip Theory: Cultural Signs of Queerness and Disability* (New York: New York University Press, 2006); Margaret Price, "The Bodymind Problem and the Possibilities of Pain," *Hypatia* 30, no. 1 (2015): 268–84; Tobin Siebers, *Disability Theory* (Ann Arbor: University of Michigan Press, 2008); Wilson and Lewiecki-Wilson, *Embodied Rhetorics*.

50 As a disclaimer: in addition to being an academic, I am an autistic activist. At various junctures, I have served on either committees or the boards of each of these organizations.

51 See, for example, Amy Sequenzia, "My Uncooperative Body," *Autism Women's Network* (blog), October 28, 2013, http://autismwomensnetwork.org/my -uncooperative-body/; Emma Zurcher-Long, "The Fan Stays Off," *Emma's Hope Book* (blog), April 9, 2015, http://emmashopebook.com/2015/04/09/the-fan-stays -off/; Barb R. Rentenbach and Lois A. Prislovsky, *I Might Be You: An Exploration of Autism and Connection* (author, 2012); Tito Rajarshi Mukhopadhyay, *Plankton Dreams: What I Learned in Special Ed* (London: Open Humanities Press, 2015).

52 One such important engagement is the dual special issues on cripistemologies coedited by Merri Lisa Johnson and Robert McRuer in the *Journal of Literary and Cultural Disability Studies* 8, nos. 2–3.

53 Fiona Kumari Campbell, "Re-cognising Disability: Cross-Examining Social Inclusion through the Prism of Queer Anti-sociality," *Jindal Global Law Review* 4, no. 2 (2013): 209–38.

54 Campbell, "Re-cognising Disability," 215.

55 Cynthia Kim, "Acceptance as a Well Being Practice," *Musings of an Aspie* (blog), January 14, 2015, http://musingsofanaspie.com/2015/01/14/acceptance-as-a-well -being-practice/.

56 Campbell, "Re-cognising Disability," 215.

57 Campbell, "Re-cognising Disability," 238.

58 UPIAS and the Disability Alliance, "Fundamental Principles of Disability," 3.

59 Ole Ivar Lovaas, *Teaching Developmentally Disabled Children: The ME Book* (Baltimore, MD: University Park Press, 1981), 2.

60 Campbell, "Re-cognising Disability," 223.

61 Lovaas, *Teaching Developmentally Disabled Children*.

62 Lovaas, *Teaching Developmentally Disabled Children*, x.

63 Lovaas, *Teaching Developmentally Disabled Children*, 5.

64 Eyal et al., *The Autism Matrix*, 147.

65 Lovaas, "The Development of a Treatment-Research Project," 623.

66 Lovaas, "The Development of a Treatment-Research Project," 622.

67 Lovaas, "The Development of a Treatment-Research Project," 623.

68  Bernard Rimland, "A Risk/Benefit Perspective on the Use of Aversives," *Journal of Autism and Childhood Schizophrenia* 8, no. 1 (1978): 101.

69  O. Ivar Lovaas et al., "Some Generalization and Follow-Up Measures on Autistic Children in Behavior Therapy," *Journal of Applied Behavior Analysis* 6, no. 1 (1973): 163.

70  Roger Shattuck, *The Forbidden Experiment: The Story of the Wild Boy of Aveyron* (New York: Farrar, Straus and Giroux, 1980), 104.

71  With these examples I am also reminded of a Mickee Faust video titled *Annie Dearest* (Tallahassee, FL: Diane Wilkins Productions, 2002), https://www.youtube.com/watch?v=MXNUN5OCZdY, an ironic crip parody of the infamous water pump scene from *The Miracle Worker*. *Annie Dearest* serves as an anachronistic mashup of Annie Sullivan's iconic role as Teacher and Joan Crawford's representation as abusive mother in the film *Mommie Dearest*. At the end of the video, as Helen finally learns to say "WA-TER" (after having been drenched at the water pump, swirled in the toilet bowl, and bent over backward by a high-pressure fire hose), Teacher appears with a hanger and, in a nod to Crawford, incites Helen to say "wire hanger." The credits of the film close with the adage, "The Only Way They Learn."

72  Lovaas, *Teaching Developmentally Disabled Children*, 4.

73  Silverman, *Understanding Autism*.

74  Eyal et al., *The Autism Matrix*, 155.

75  Sally J. Rogers and Geraldine Dawson, *Early Start Denver Model for Young Children with Autism: Promoting Language, Learning, and Engagement* (New York: Guilford, 2010).

76  Rogers and Dawson, *Early Start Denver Model*, xi.

77  Jennifer Germon, *Gender: A Genealogy of an Idea* (London: Palgrave Macmillan, 2009), 65; Burroway, "What Are Little Boys Made Of?"; Green, *The "Sissy Boy" Syndrome*.

78  Green, *The "Sissy Boy" Syndrome*, 295.

79  Green, *The "Sissy Boy" Syndrome*.

80  Green, *The "Sissy Boy" Syndrome*, 297.

81  Rekers and Lovaas, "Behavioral Treatment of Deviant Sex-Role Behaviors," 178.

82  Rekers and Lovaas, "Behavioral Treatment of Deviant Sex-Role Behaviors," 179.

83  Rekers and Lovaas, "Behavioral Treatment of Deviant Sex-Role Behaviors."

84  George A. Rekers et al., "Sex-Role Stereotypy and Professional Intervention for Childhood Gender Disturbance," *Professional Psychology* 9, no. 1 (1978): 127–36.

85  Rekers et al., "Sex-Role Stereotypy and Professional Intervention," 127.

86  Rekers et al., "Sex-Role Stereotypy and Professional Intervention," 127, 134; George A. Rekers, Judith A. Sanders, and Cyd C. Strauss, "Developmental Differentiation of Adolescent Body Gestures," *Journal of Genetic Psychology* 138 (1981): 124.

87  Lovaas, *The Autistic Child*.

88  Lovaas, *The Autistic Child*, 125.

89  Lovaas, *The Autistic Child*, 125–26.

90  Michelle Dawson, "The Misbehaviour of Behaviourists," No Autistics Allowed, January 29, 2004, http://www.sentex.net/~nexus23/naa_aba.html.

91  Chance, "'After You Hit a Child,'" 76.

92  Jeannie Davide-Rivera, *Twirling Naked in the Streets and No One Noticed: Growing Up with Undiagnosed Autism* (David and Goliath, 2013), 62.

93  Cheryl Glenn, *Rhetoric Retold: Regendering the Tradition from Antiquity through the Renaissance* (Carbondale: Southern Illinois University Press, 1997), 10; Jacqueline Jones Royster and Gesa E. Kirsch, *Feminist Rhetorical Practices: New Horizons for Rhetoric, Composition, and Literacy Studies* (Carbondale: Southern Illinois University Press, 2012), 15–16; Andrea A. Lunsford, "On Reclaiming Rhetorica," in *Reclaiming Rhetorica: Women in the Rhetorical Tradition*, ed. Andrea A. Lunsford (Pittsburgh: University of Pittsburgh Press, 1995), 7.

94  Angela Haas, "Race, Rhetoric, and Technology: A Case Study of Decolonial Technical Communication Theory, Methodology, and Pedagogy," *Journal of Business and Technical Communication* 26, no. 3 (2012): 277–310; Malea Powell, "Stories Take Place: A Performance in One Act (2012 CCCC Chair's Address)," *College Composition and Communication* 64, no. 2 (2012): 383–406.

95  Broderick, "Autism as Rhetoric."

96  O. Ivar Lovaas, "Behavioral Treatment and Normal Education and Intellectual Functioning in Young Autistic Children," *Journal of Consulting and Clinical Psychology* 55, no. 1 (1987): 3–9.

97  Lovaas, "Behavioral Treatment and Normal Education," 3.

98  Lovaas's findings were and continue to be hotly debated. To date, his findings have yet to be replicated. As well, numerous scholars, both then and now, have commented on flaws in the study design, the lack of participant controls, and the stacking of clients who were so-called high-functioning autistics (Feinstein, *A History of Autism*).

99  Broderick, "Autism as Rhetoric"; Feinstein, *A History of Autism*.

100  Catherine Maurice, *Let Me Hear Your Voice: A Family's Triumph over Autism* (New York: Alfred A. Knopf, 1993), 44, 306.

101  Dawson, "The Misbehaviour of Behaviourists."

102  In the United States, Autism Speaks routinely makes similar moves around comparisons between autism and cancer. In their "Self-Funded Employer Tool Kit" (2012, https://www.autismspeaks.org/sites/default/files/docs/gr/erisa_tool_kit_9 .12_0.pdf), for example, Autism Speaks offers several letter templates that parents can modify and mail to their insurance companies in order to persuade them to cover ABA. One such letter bears the following passage: "For employees whose children are affected by autism, the proposed policy, which includes speech, occupational, and physical therapy, but excludes ABA, is like having coverage for treatment of cancer that excludes chemotherapy" (p. 55).

103  Ariane Zurcher, "Tackling That Troublesome Issue of ABA and Ethics," *Emma's Hope Book* (blog), October 10, 2012, http://emmashopebook.com/2012/10/10 /tackling-that-troublesome-issue-of-aba-and-ethics/.

104  Zurcher, "Tackling That Troublesome Issue of ABA and Ethics."

105  Zurcher, "Tackling That Troublesome Issue of ABA and Ethics."

106  Zurcher, "Tackling That Troublesome Issue of ABA and Ethics."

107  Lovaas, "The Development of a Treatment-Research Project."

108  Lovaas, "The Development of a Treatment-Research Project," 621.

109  Rimland, "A Risk/Benefit Perspective on the Use of Aversives," 101.

110  Ruth Christ Sullivan, "Risks and Benefits in the Treatment of Autistic Children: Introduction," *Journal of Autism and Childhood Schizophrenia* 8, no. 1 (1978): 99.

111  Francine M. Bernstein, "Thirty-Three: Francine M. Bernstein," in *Families of Adults with Autism: Stories and Advice for the Next Generation*, ed. Jane Johnson, Stephen M. Edelson, and Anne Van Rensselaer (London: Jessica Kingsley, 2008), 166–72; Rosalind C. Oppenheim, *Effective Teaching Methods for Autistic Children* (Springfield, IL: Charles C. Thomas, 1974).

112  Bernstein, "Thirty-Three," 168; Michael Higgins, "Shock Therapy Called Cruel: Kin Disagree," *Chicago Tribune*, March 8, 2007, http://articles.chicagotribune.com /2007-03-08/news/0703080165_1_electric-shock-robert-bernstein-group-home; Lindsey Tanner, "Shock Treatment Sought for Autistic Man," *Washington Post*, March 14, 2007, http://www.washingtonpost.com/wp-dyn/content/article/2007/03 /14/AR2007031401732_pf.html.

113  G. Martin and J. Pear, *Behavior Modification: What It Is and How to Do It* (Englewood Cliffs, NJ: Prentice-Hall, 1978).

114  Meredith K Ultra, "I'm Sorry, but That's Not Earning Your Token," *Ink and Daggers* (blog), February 25, 2015, http://ink-and-daggers.tumblr.com/post/112076858794 /im-sorry-but-thats-not-earning-your-token.

115  Meredith K Ultra, "Untitled," *Ink and Daggers* (blog), February 25, 2015, http://ink -and-daggers.tumblr.com/post/127321531039.

116  Liane H. Willey, *Pretending to Be Normal: Living with Asperger's Syndrome* (London: Jessica Kingsley, 1999).

117  Willey, *Pretending to Be Normal.*

118  Rekers et al., "Child Gender Disturbances," 8.

119  Rekers et al., "Child Gender Disturbances," 9.

120  Kit Mead, "Missing What You Never Had: Autistic and Queer," in *QDA: A Queer Disability Anthology*, ed. Raymond Luczak (Minneapolis: Squares and Rebels, 2015).

121  Elaine M. Day, *Aspies Alone Together: My Story and a Survival Guide for Women Living with Asperger Syndrome* (CreateSpace, 2014), 10–11.

122  Deborah Fein et al., "Optimal Outcome in Individuals with a History of Autism," *Journal of Child Psychology and Psychiatry* 54, no. 2 (2013): 199.

123  Fein et al., "Optimal Outcome in Individuals with a History of Autism," 202.

124  Jones, "ABA"; see also Siebers, *Disability Theory.*

125  Jones, "ABA."

126  Lovaas, *The Autistic Child,* 12.

127  Teodoro Ayllon and Nathan Azrin, *The Token Economy: A Motivational System for Therapy and Rehabilitation* (New York: Appleton-Century-Crofts, 1968).

128  Ayllon and Azrin, *The Token Economy,* 4.

129  Ayllon and Azrin, *The Token Economy*, 194, 26.

130  Jake Pyne, "The Governance of Gender Non-conforming Children: A Dangerous Enclosure," *Annual Review of Critical Psychology* 11 (2014): 79–96.

131  Pyne, "The Governance of Gender Non-conforming Children," 85–86.

132  Robert LaRue, "Functional Analysis," Association for Science in Autism Treatment, http://www.asatonline.org/research-treatment/clinical-corner/functional-analysis/.

133  Nicole M. Rodriguez et al., "Functional Analysis and Treatment of Arranging and Ordering by Individuals with an Autism Spectrum Disorder," *Journal of Applied Behavior Analysis* 45, no. 1 (2012): 5.

134  George A. Rekers, O. Ivar Lovaas, and Benson Low, "The Behavioral Treatment of a 'Transsexual' Preadolescent Boy," *Journal of Abnormal Child Psychology* 2, no. 2 (1974): 106.

135  Rekers, Lovaas, and Low, "The Behavioral Treatment of a 'Transsexual' Preadolescent Boy," 101–2.

136  See Sara Ahmed, *Willful Subjects* (Durham, NC: Duke University Press, 2014).

137  Kassiane Sibley, "Indistinguishable from Peers—an Introduction," *Radical Neurodivergence Speaking* (blog), September 13, 2013, http://timetolisten.blogspot.com/2013/09/indistinguishable-from-peers.html.

138  Jocelyn J. LeBlanc and Michela Fagiolini, "Autism: A 'Critical Period' Disorder?," *Neural Plasticity*, 2011, 1, doi:10.1155/2011/921680.

139  Kafer, *Feminist, Queer, Crip*.

140  Catherine Malabou, *What Should We Do with Our Brain?* (New York: Fordham University Press, 2008).

141  As quoted in Gail B. Peterson, "A Day of Great Illumination: B.F. Skinner's Discovery of Shaping," *Journal of the Experimental Analysis of Behavior* 82, no. 3 (2004): 318.

142  Peterson, "A Day of Great Illumination," 319.

143  Incidentally, Skinner found such success with his pigeons that he was funded by the U.S. National Research Defense Committee to work on a (now declassified) World War II–era program, called Project Pigeon, in which pigeons were to be trained to guide missiles. The program never was put into use, of course, because of its impracticality. See B. F. Skinner, "Pigeons in a Pelican," *American Psychologist* 15, no. 1 (1960): 28–37.

144  Davi Johnson Thornton, *Brain Culture: Neuroscience and Popular Media* (New Brunswick, NJ: Rutgers University Press, 2011); Christine Skolnik, "Rhetoric and the Plastic Brain" (unpublished manuscript, 2012).

145  Jordynn Jack and L. Gregory Appelbaum, "'This Is Your Brain on Rhetoric': Research Directions for Neurorhetorics," *Rhetoric Society Quarterly* 40, no. 5 (2010): 411–37.

146  Thornton, *Brain Culture*.

147  Thornton, *Brain Culture*, 84.

148  Kafer, *Feminist, Queer, Crip*, 79.

149  Skolnik, *Rhetoric and the Plastic Brain*.

150 Anne McGuire, *The War on Autism* (Ann Arbor: University of Michigan Press, 2016), 80.

151 LeBlanc and Fagiolini, "Autism," 1.

152 Thornton, *Brain Culture*, 62.

153 As Catherine Malabou notes, "plasticity directly contradicts rigidity. It is its exact antonym" (*What Should We Do with Our Brain?*, 5).

154 In June 2015, the U.S. Government Accountability Office released a report on federal autism funding allocations and fluctuations between 2008 and 2012. Most striking were the meager funds dedicated to life span issues, which accounted for only 1.5 percent of the total budget (ASAN, "ASAN Statement on GAO Report of Autism Research Funding," Autistic Self Advocacy Network, August 14, 2015, http://autisticadvocacy.org/2015/08/asan-statement-on-gao-report-on-autism -research-funding/) and which, when adjusted for inflation, saw a decline of 15 percent between the years 2008 and 2012 (U.S. Government Accountability Office, "Federal Autism Research: Updated Information on Funding from Fiscal Years 2008 through 2012," report [Washington, DC: U.S. Government Accountability Office, June 30, 2015], http://www.gao.gov/products/GAO-15-583R, 17). Given the inflated rhetoric surrounding autism prevalence, the decrease in adult-oriented re-search is particularly shocking; after all, autistic children grow into autistic adults. Numerous autism organizations have invoked the metaphor of the tsunami to describe the problem that autistic adults pose for service provision infrastructures, yet the same organizations continue to operate with the figure of the child as their raison d'être. If nothing else signals the extent to which autism discourse is alarm-ingly preventionist in orientation, surely money and budget priorities must.

155 Peter F. Gerhardt, "The Promise of ABA: Creating Meaningful Lives throughout Adolescence and Adulthood," *Autism Advocate*, 2008, 24.

156 Victoria Pitts-Taylor, "The Plastic Brain: Neoliberalism and the Neuronal Self," *Health* 14, no. 6 (2010): 648.

157 Malabou, *What Should We Do with Our Brain?*, 5.

158 James C. Wilson, *Weather Reports from the Autism Front: A Father's Memoir of His Autistic Son* (Jefferson, NC: McFarland, 2008), 75.

159 Erin Manning, *Relationscapes: Movement, Art, Philosophy* (Cambridge, MA: MIT Press, 2012), 16, 6.

160 Dawn Prince-Hughes, *Circus of Souls: How I Discovered That We Are All Freaks Pass-ing as Normal* (CreateSpace, 2013), 19.

THREE. INVITATION

1 Peter Vermeulen, "Context Blindness in Autism Spectrum Disorder: Not Using the Forest to See the Trees as Trees," *Focus on Autism and Other Developmental Dis-abilities* 30, no. 3 (2015): 25.

2 Edward Schiappa, "Second Thoughts on the Critiques of Big Rhetoric," *Philosophy and Rhetoric* 34, no. 3 (2001): 260–75.

3 Schiappa, "Second Thoughts on the Critiques of Big Rhetoric," 272.

4   William Keith et al., "Taking Up the Challenge: A Response to Simons," *Quarterly Journal of Speech* 85 (1999): 331.

5   Lloyd F. Bitzer, "The Rhetorical Situation," *Philosophy and Rhetoric* 1 (1968): 5.

6   We might, of course, say something similar about any kind of disclosure, or even any kind of attire. If I wear an Ohio State football shirt while in rival city Ann Arbor, for example, I might receive any number of comments, both hostile and affirmative. My wearing of an OSU shirt is invitational in that it signifies a shared set of discourses—or presumed discourse community/s—to any number of people (in much the same way my button might inspire antipathy or ambivalence in others). However, to be clear, I do believe something different is at work when disability or marginality enters the disclosure fold, as I explain in the pages that follow. When marginal identity comes into play, profound questions around ethos, rhetoricity, humanity, and institutional power arise. One cannot disclose a disabled body without risking some hefty rhetorical and historical baggage.

7   Jenell Johnson, "The Skeleton on the Couch: The Eagleton Affair, Rhetorical Disability, and the Stigma of Mental Illness," *Rhetoric Society Quarterly* 40, no. 5 (2010): 459–78.

8   Dinah Murray, "Introduction," in *Coming Out Asperger: Diagnosis, Disclosure, and Self-Confidence*, ed. Dinah Murray (London: Jessica Kingsley, 2006), 13.

9   Judy Endow, *Learning the Hidden Curriculum: The Odyssey of One Autistic Adult* (Shawnee Mission, KS: Autism Asperger, 2012).

10  Margaret Price, "'Her Pronouns Wax and Wane': Psychosocial Disability, Autobiography, and Counter-diagnosis," *Journal of Literary and Cultural Disability Studies* 3, no. 1 (2009): 11–33.

11  Edward P. J. Corbett, "The Rhetoric of the Open Hand and the Rhetoric of the Closed Fist," *College Composition and Communication* 20, no. 5 (1969): 295.

12  Judi Randi, Tina Newman, and Elena L. Grigorenko, "Teaching Children with Autism to Read for Meaning: Challenges and Possibilities," *Journal of Autism and Developmental Disorders* 40, no. 7 (2010): 890–902.

13  While I think that this statement would surprise folks who do pharmacological research into autism, my assumption is that my ex-therapist didn't mean this uber-literally. That is, there is no specific pill that's being overtly marketed as a treatment for queer autism. Then again, Risperdal works on/for anything, and it also comes with the added bonus of extra breasts (why stop at two?) and seizures.

14  Lisa Zunshine, "Theory of Mind and Fictions of Embodied Transparency," *Narrative* 16, no. 1 (2008): 66–92. In her earlier work on fiction and theory of mind, Zunshine at times employed autistic people as a theoretical foil, as an example of people lacking in ToM. Importantly, in a coauthored piece with Ralph Savarese in 2014, Zunshine bravely retracted her past statements about autism, writing, "We cannot simply rely on mainstream scientific discourse and echo its impersonal 'outside-in' view." Ralph J. Savarese and Lisa Zunshine, "The Critic as Neurocosmopolite; Or, What Cognitive Approaches to Literature Can Learn from Disability Studies," *Narrative* 22, no. 1 (2014): 34.

15  Judith [Jack] Halberstam, *The Queer Art of Failure* (Durham, NC: Duke University Press, 2011), 3.

16  Halberstam, *The Queer Art of Failure*, 12.

17  Erin Manning, *Always More than One: Individuation's Dance* (Durham, NC: Duke University Press, 2013), 151–52.

18  See also Julia Miele Rodas, *Autistic Disturbances: Theorizing Autism Poetics from the DSM to Robinson Crusoe* (Ann Arbor: University of Michigan Press, forthcoming).

19  Sally Miller Gearhart, "The Womanization of Rhetoric," *Women's Studies International Quarterly* 2 (1979): 195–201; Sonja K. Foss and Cindy L. Griffin, "Beyond Persuasion: A Proposal for an Invitational Rhetoric," *Communication Monographs* 62 (1995): 2–18.

20  Sonja K. Foss and Cindy L. Griffin, "A Feminist Perspective on Rhetorical Theory: Toward a Clarification of Boundaries," *Western Journal of Communication* 56, no. 4 (1992): 331.

21  Kenneth Burke, *A Rhetoric of Motives* (New York: Prentice-Hall, 1955), 20.

22  Foss and Griffin, "Beyond Persuasion," 3.

23  In making this statement, I wish to separate the rhetorical actions of pharmaceutical companies from neurodivergent people's agentive use of medication. My stance on psychiatric medication is this: what matters most is neurodivergent people having active control of and participation in their medical care and decisions. Many neurodivergent people claim positive experiences with medication, and many fervently argue that medication sustains them, provides more optimal quality of life, and/or quite literally keeps them alive. These are not minuscule feelings and require others' deepest respect if neurodivergent people are to be recognized as having capacity to make personal choices regarding their most intimate needs, indeed, as having capacity even to self-assess their own identity and experiences of/with neurodivergent life. Unfortunately, however, many neurodivergent people relate stories of coercion and abuse in contexts of medicine and care. The medical-industrial complex plays a large role in the forcible medicalization of mental illness and neurodivergent people. The very idea that neurodivergence is a pathology in need of eradication drives medical markets unto themselves.

24  Foss and Griffin, "Beyond Persuasion," 11.

25  Foss and Griffin, "Beyond Persuasion," 10.

26  Jeffrey W. Murray, "The Face in Dialogue, Part II: Invitational Rhetoric, Direct Moral Suasion, and the Asymmetry of Dialogue," *Southern Communication Journal* 69, no. 4 (2004): 333–47.

27  Murray, "The Face in Dialogue," 335.

28  Nina M. Lozano-Reich and Dana L. Cloud, "The Uncivil Tongue: Invitational Rhetoric and the Problem of Inequality," *Western Journal of Communication* 73, no. 2 (2009): 221.

29  Lozano-Reich and Cloud, "The Uncivil Tongue," 222.

30  Some poignant examples of trolling behavior on the part of pro-ABA practitioners include the comment streams on Meredith K Ultra's *Ink and Daggers* blog or autistic activist Lydia Brown's behaviorism-related posts at *Autistic Hoya*.

31 Deborah Fein et al., "Optimal Outcome in Individuals with a History of Autism," *Journal of Child Psychology and Psychiatry* 54, no. 2 (2013): 195–205; O. Ivar Lovaas, "Behavioral Treatment and Normal Education and Intellectual Functioning in Young Autistic Children," *Journal of Consulting and Clinical Psychology* 55, no. 1 (1987): 3–9.

32 Suzanne Wright, "Autism Changes Everything," *Parade*, January 27, 2008, https://web.archive.org/web/20081202080054/http://www.parade.com/articles/editions/2008/edition_01-27-2008/Autism_Changes_Everything.

33 Autism Votes, "State Initiatives," 2008, https://web.archive.org/web/20080607043126/http://www.autismvotes.org/site/c.frKNI3PCImE/b.3909861/k.B9DF/State_Initiatives.htm. The Autism Votes campaign, an initiative of Autism Speaks, was eventually subsumed under the organization's more generalized advocacy branch. In 2008, Autism Votes implored site visitors to take action in their home states and provided an interactive U.S. map that ranked state coverage of ABA in color codes ranging from green to yellow to red. On the state of ABA insurance reimbursement, Autism Votes remarked, "The insurance legislation supported by Autism Speaks specifically targets coverage of Applied Behavior Analysis (ABA) and other structured behavioral therapies, which are the most effective forms of treatment and have the best outcomes, both in human costs and in long-term economic benefits. Nationwide, few private insurance companies or other employee benefit plans cover Applied Behavior Analysis and other behavioral therapies."

34 Phyllis Burke, *Gender Shock: Exploding the Myths of Male and Female* (New York: Anchor, 1996).

35 Richard Green, *The "Sissy Boy Syndrome": The Development of Homosexuality* (New Haven, CT: Yale University Press, 1987), ix–x.

36 Maureen A. Mathison, "Complicity as Epistemology: Reinscribing the Historical Categories of 'Woman' through Standpoint Feminism," *Communication Theory* 7, no. 2 (1997): 156.

37 Elizabeth (Ibby) Grace, "Behaviorism Everywhere," *NeuroQueer* (blog), April 15, 2014, http://neuroqueer.blogspot.com/2014/04/behaviorism-everywhere-by-ib-grace.html.

38 K. J. Rawson, "Queering Feminist Rhetorical Canonization," in *Rhetorica in Motion: Feminist Rhetorical Methods and Methodologies*, ed. Eileen E. Schell and K. J. Rawson (Pittsburgh: University of Pittsburgh Press, 2010), 39–52.

39 Have you encountered the good news that is ELO's "Mr. Blue Sky"? If not, please close this book and direct your web browser to YouTube. You're welcome.

40 Steve Silberman, "The Geek Syndrome," *Wired*, December 1, 2001, https://www.wired.com/2001/12/aspergers/.

41 Inquiring minds wish to know: the romantic, fruit, or calendar kind of dates?

42 Claire Hughes, Rosie Ensor, and Alex Marks, "Individual Differences in False Belief Understanding Are Stable from 3 to 6 Years of Age and Predict Children's Mental State Talk with School Friends," *Journal of Experimental Child Psychology* 108, no. 1 (2011): 97.

43  Rachel Cohen-Rottenberg, "Disorder in Society, Disorder in Self," *Shift: Journal of Alternatives*, May 27, 2011, http://www.shiftjournal.com/2011/05/27/disorder-in -society-disorder-in-self/.

44  Cohen-Rottenberg, "Disorder in Society, Disorder in Self."

45  George A. Kennedy, *Classical Rhetoric and Its Christian and Secular Tradition from Ancient to Modern Times*, 2nd ed. (Chapel Hill: University of North Carolina Press, 1999), 81.

46  M. Ariel Cascio, "Rigid Therapies, Rigid Minds: Italian Professionals' Perspectives on Autism Interventions," *Culture, Medicine, and Psychiatry* 39, no. 2 (2015): 235.

47  K. I. Al-Ghani, *Learning about Friendship: Stories to Support Social Skills Training in Children with Asperger Syndrome and High Functioning Autism* (London: Jessica Kingsley, 2010), 95.

48  Corbett, "The Rhetoric of the Open Hand."

49  Corbett, "The Rhetoric of the Open Hand," 288.

50  Corbett, "The Rhetoric of the Open Hand," 293.

51  Brenda Jo Brueggemann, *Deaf Subjects: Between Identities and Places* (New York: New York University Press, 2009); Shannon Walters, *Rhetorical Touch: Disability, Identification, Haptics* (Columbia: University of South Carolina Press, 2014).

52  Walters, *Rhetorical Touch*, 199.

53  Walters, *Rhetorical Touch*, 198.

54  Brueggemann, *Deaf Subjects*, 41.

55  Brueggemann, *Deaf Subjects*, 44.

56  Cynthia Kim, "The Myth of Passing," *Musings of an Aspie* (blog), October 24, 2013, http://musingsofanaspie.com/2013/10/24/the-myth-of-passing/.

57  N. I. Nicholson, "Nothing about Us without ALL of Us: That Means Autistics of Colour, Too," *The Digital Hyperlexic* (blog), January 24, 2016, https:// thedigitalhyperlexic.wordpress.com/2016/01/24/nothing-about-us-without-all-of -us-that-means-autistics-of-colour-too/.

58  Cheryl Marie Wade, "I Am Not One of The," in *The Disability Studies Reader*, 4th ed., ed. Lennard J. Davis (New York: Routledge, 2013), 526.

59  Petra Kuppers, "Deconstructing Images: Performing Disability," *Contemporary Theatre Review* 11, no. 3–4 (2001): 39.

60  For a fuller discussion of the violences of developmentalism, see Anne McGuire, *The War on Autism* (Ann Arbor: University of Michigan Press, 2016).

61  Eustacia Cutler, "Autism and Child Pornography: A Toxic Combination," *Daily Beast*, August 5, 2013, http://www.thedailybeast.com/articles/2013/08/05/autism -and-child-pornography-a-toxic-combination.html.

62  Tony Attwood, Isabelle Henault, and Nick Dubin, *The Autism Spectrum, Sexuality and the Law: What Every Parent and Professional Needs to Know* (London: Jessica Kingsley, 2014); Malcolm Gladwell, "Thresholds of Violence: How School Shootings Catch On," *New Yorker*, October 19, 2015, http://www.newyorker.com /magazine/2015/10/19/thresholds-of-violence.

63  Laura Hershey, "From Poster Child to Protester," Independent Living Institute, 1993, http://www.independentliving.org/docs4/hershey93.html.

64  Autism Speaks, "About Autism: What You Need to Know," 2013, 2.

65  An Archive.org search of Autism Speaks's websites and documents from 2005 to the present day reveals changes in the way the organization has compared autism to other disabilities and illnesses. Importantly, in 2005, the comparative was "autism" against "Down Syndrome, childhood diabetes, and childhood cancer combined." In this comparison, there is a distinctive emphasis on the latter two as childhood conditions. Yet by 2007, Autism Speaks shifted comparative tactics, replacing Down syndrome with AIDS. By 2011, many of the childhood modifiers for cancer, AIDS, and diabetes, such as *pediatric* or *juvenile*, had been dropped altogether in their promotional materials. One possible reason for the shift may have been autism's changing prevalence, which in 2005 hovered around 1 in 150 and by 2015 had risen to 1 in 68. Autism Speaks, "Autism Prevalence on the Rise," *Autism Speaks* (blog), October 2010, https://autismspeaksblog.files.wordpress.com /2010/10/prevalence-graph1.jpg; CDC, "Data & Statistics," Centers for Disease Control and Prevention, August 12, 2015, http://www.cdc.gov/ncbddd/autism/data .html. However, the removal of childhood modifiers has a particularly deleterious rhetorical effect: it implies, quite falsely and problematically, that more money goes to adults, who are agentive and have opportunity to make personal choices that impact their health, and that these adult conditions are far less prevalent than autism, the supposed stealer of children's souls.

66  Autism Speaks, "Sponsorship Packet—5th Annual Milwaukee Walk Now for Autism Speaks," 2013, http://www.kintera.org/atf/cf/%7BBEBB52F7-5AE4-49F7 -A192-BF4B7DD999C6%7D/2013%20WALK%20NOW%20FOR%20AUTISM%20 SPEAKS%20MILWAUKEE%20SPONSORSHIP%20PACKAGES.PDF.

67  Gil Eyal et al., *The Autism Matrix* (Cambridge: Polity, 2010).

68  Tracy A. Becerra et al., "Autism Spectrum Disorders and Race, Ethnicity, and Nativity: A Population-Based Study," *Pediatrics* 134, no. 1 (2014): e63–e71; David S. Mandell et al., "Racial/Ethnic Disparities in the Identification of Children with Autism Spectrum Disorder," *American Journal of Public Health* 99, no. 3 (2009): 493–98; Katherine E. Zuckerman et al., "Pediatrician Identification of Latino Children at Risk for Autism Spectrum Disorder," *Pediatrics* 132, no. 3 (2013): 445–53.

69  Paul Heilker, "Autism, Rhetoric, and Whiteness," *Disability Studies Quarterly* 32, no. 4 (2012), http://dsq-sds.org/article/view/1756/3181.

70  It is with great trepidation that I use the term *misdiagnosis*. As Eli Clare ("Yearn-ing for Carrie Buck," keynote presentation at Queer Practices, Places, and Lives II, Ohio State University, 2014) relates, there is no such thing as misdiagnosis because misdiagnosis assumes there is a right diagnosis. That is, all diagnoses are the product of pathology and oppression. Nonetheless, I use *misdiagnosis* here, in part, to signify those diagnostic constructs that are too often stratified along racial lines, rendering autistics of color as multiply and willfully deviant. As well, autistic individuals, especially autistics who identify among multiple axes of marginal identity, have long narrated the frustration of being slapped with diagnoses that did not fit them, often expressing profound relief upon learning they are autistic.

71  Nirmala Erevelles, "Crippin' Jim Crow: Disability Dis-location and the School to Prison Pipeline," in *Disability Incarcerated: Imprisonment and Disability in the United States and Canada*, ed. Liat Ben-Moshe, Chris Chapman, and Allison C. Carey (New York: Palgrave Macmillan, 2014), 92.

72  Erevelles, "Crippin' Jim Crow," 95.

73  ASAN, "ASAN Statement on #JusticeForKayleb," Autistic Self Advocacy Network, April 14, 2015, http://autisticadvocacy.org/2015/04/asan-statement-on -justiceforkayleb/; Morénike Giwa Onaiwu, "#JusticeForKayleb NOW," *Just Being Me . . . Who Needs "Normalcy" Anyway?* (blog), April 15, 2015, http:// whoneedsnormalcy.blogspot.com/2015/04/justiceforkayleb-now.html.

74  Kerima Çevik, "Justice for Kayleb Moon Robinson #AliveWhileBlack and Autistic," *InterSected* (blog), April 14, 2015, http://intersecteddisability.blogspot.com/2015 /04/justice-for-kayleb-moon-robinson.html.

75  Onaiwu, "#JusticeForKayleb NOW."

76  N. I. Nicholson, "The Souls of Black Autistic Folk, Part III: Difference and the Question of Visibility," *Woman with Asperger's* (blog), April 30, 2013, https:// womanwithaspergers.wordpress.com/2013/04/30/the-souls-of-black-autistic-folk -part-iii-difference-and-the-question-of-visibility/.

77  Kerima Çevik, "Autism Speaks: Speaking for Typical White Males," Infogr.am, 2013, https://infogr.am/autism-speaks-diversity-in-representation.

78  Autism Speaks has long refused to appoint autistic people to meaningful leadership positions within its organization. It wasn't until December 2015 that Autism Speaks appointed its first autistic board members, Stephen Shore and Valerie Paradiz, a move that many in the autistic community have interpreted as a tokenistic gesture rather than real change. Theirs is a dance we have seen before. In 2010, best-selling autistic author John Elder Robison was appointed to Autism Speaks's Scientific Advisory and Scientific Treatment boards. Contrary to popular belief, Robison was never appointed to the board of directors; rather, his appointment was a dual committee appointment, and he served as the lone autistic appointee on committees that included about twenty to thirty people each. In 2013, when Autism Speaks released its controversial "A Call for Action," Robison swiftly resigned his posts, claiming that despite all of his efforts, the organization refused to listen to him or take him seriously.

79  Simon Baron-Cohen, *Essential Difference: Male and Female Brains and the Truth about Autism* (New York: Basic Books, 2003).

80  This testing instrument was designed at the Cambridge University Autism Research Centre (ARC). Notably, the Autism Spectrum Quotient (known as the AQ) was not designed for diagnostic testing. In the words of the ARC, its initial purpose was to "test if adults with high-functioning autism or Asperger Syndrome are just an extreme on a dimension of autistic traits that runs right through the general population" ("Autism Spectrum Quotient," 2017, https://www .autismresearchcentre.com/project_7_asquotient/). However, many clinicians use the AQ as part of their diagnostic testing repertoire, especially when working with teens and adults.

81 Jean Kearns Miller, "Foreword," in *Women from Another Planet? Our Lives in the Universe of Autism*, ed. Jean Kearns Miller (Bloomington, IN: AuthorHouse, 2003), xxi.

82 Jane Meyerding, "Growing Up Genderless," in *Women from Another Planet? Our Lives in the Universe of Autism*, ed. Jean Kearns Miller (Bloomington, IN: AuthorHouse, 2003), 157.

83 Meyerding, "Growing Up Genderless," 169.

84 Daina Krumins, "Coming Alive in a World of Texture," in *Women from Another Planet? Our Lives in the Universe of Autism*, ed. Jean Kearns Miller (Bloomington, IN: AuthorHouse, 2003), 87.

85 Krumins, "Coming Alive in a World of Texture," 89.

86 Kenneth Burke, *Language as Symbolic Action: Essays of Life, Literature, and Method* (Los Angeles: University of California Press, 1966), 17–18.

87 Byron Hawk, *A Counter-history of Composition: Toward Methodologies of Complexity* (Pittsburgh: University of Pittsburgh Press, 2007).

88 Stephanie Kerschbaum, *Toward a New Rhetoric of Difference* (Urbana, IL: NCTE, 2014).

89 Price, "'Her Pronouns Wax and Wane.'"

90 Price, "'Her Pronouns Wax and Wane,'" 17.

91 Price, "'Her Pronouns Wax and Wane.'"

92 Phil Schwarz, "Building Alliances: Community Identity and the Role of Allies in Autistic Self-Advocacy," in *Ask and Tell: Self-Advocacy and Disclosure for People on the Autism Spectrum*, ed. Stephen M. Shore (Shawnee Mission, KS: Autism Asperger, 2004), 143–76. For those unfamiliar with the term, *unconventional diaspora* is often used in disability circles to signify that disability cultures are generally not cultures based in one's biological family. While some disabilities (including autism) can be hereditary, it is often the case that disabled children might be the only disabled person in their families, or even in their classes or cohorts at school. The same, of course, could be said of many other cultural formations, including and especially queer cultures or transracial adoptees. These cultures, then, are transmitted and shaped largely outside familial bounds, creating queer/er kinds of kinship, intimacies, rhetorics, and practices.

93 Murray, "Introduction," 9.

94 Murray, "Introduction," 10.

95 Hawk, *A Counter-history of Composition*, 219.

96 Stephen Shore, *Beyond the Wall: Personal Experiences with Autism and Asperger Syndrome*, 2nd ed. (Shawnee Mission, KS: Autism Asperger, 2003), 137.

97 Morénike Giwa Onaiwu, "Why I Decided to 'Come Out' of the Autism Closet," *Just Being Me . . . Who Needs "Normalcy" Anyway?* (blog), October 1, 2015, http://whoneedsnormalcy.blogspot.com/2015/10/why-i-decided-to-come-out-of-autism.html.

98 Corbin Kramer, *Autism in Fiction and Everything in Between* (video), Digital Archive of Literacy Narratives, 2010, http://daln.osu.edu/handle/2374.DALN/1132.

99 Johnson, "The Skeleton on the Couch."

100 Johnson, "The Skeleton on the Couch," 465.

101 Jon Baio and CDC, "Prevalence of Autism Spectrum Disorder among Children Aged 8 Years—Autism and Developmental Disabilities Monitoring Network, 11 Sites, United States, 2010," *Morbidity and Mortality Weekly Report*, March 28, 2014. In the CDC's case, their sample is restricted to eight-year-old children.

102 NHS Information Centre et al., "Estimating the Prevalence of Autism Spectrum Conditions in Adults: Extending the 2007 Adult Psychiatric Morbidity Survey" (NHS / Health and Social Care Information Centre, 2012); T. Brugha et al., "Epidemiology of Autism Spectrum Disorders in Adults in the Community in England," *Archives of General Psychiatry* 68, no. 5 (2011): 459–65.

103 The CDC's most recent autism prevalence study, for instance, took shape as a phone survey among parents of eight-year-old children. As in any study, samples bear profound limitations for the conclusions we might draw. And yet, the "1 in 68" number from the CDC has taken on profound argumentative power in autism advocacy. (Autism Speaks's newest slogan, for instance, is "1 in 68 can't wait." While the object of the words *can't wait* is unclear, it's highly unlikely that they mean *can't wait for the Electric Light Orchestra to reunite and tour*.)

104 Cynthia Kim, "Acceptance as a Well Being Practice," *Musings of an Aspie* (blog), January 14, 2015, http://musingsofanaspie.com/2015/01/14/acceptance-as-a-well -being-practice/.

105 Kim, "Acceptance as a Well Being Practice."

106 Kim, "Acceptance as a Well Being Practice."

107 Julia Rodas, "Diagnosable: Mothering at the Threshold of Disability," in *Disability and Mothering: Liminal Spaces of Embodied Knowledge*, ed. Cynthia Lewiecki-Wilson and Jen Cellio (Syracuse, NY: Syracuse University Press, 2011), 113–26.

108 A number of countries impose quotas and/or restrictions on receiving immigrants with disabilities, including autism, because of disability's supposed drain on social assistance, health care, and other governmental safety nets. Australia has frequently made headlines for a number of high-profile cases in which families faced deportation because of an autistic child or family member. See, for instance, Julie Hare, "Autistic Boy's Family Appeals to Scott Morrison," *The Australian*, December 11, 2013, http://www.theaustralian.com.au/higher-education/autistic-boys -family-appeals-to-scott-morrison/story-e6frgcjx-1226780128297013.

109 Nick Walker, "Throw Away the Master's Tools: Liberating Ourselves from the Pathology Paradigm," *Neurocosmopolitanism* (blog), August 16, 2013, http:// neurocosmopolitanism.com/throw-away-the-masters-tools-liberating-ourselves -from-the-pathology-paradigm/.

110 Rodas, "Diagnosable," 119.

111 M. Kelter, "The Myth of 'Official': Autism and Self-Diagnosis Skeptics," *Invisible Strings* (blog), July 20, 2015, http://theinvisiblestrings.com/the-myth-of-official -autism-and-self-diagnosis-skeptics/.

112 Andrew (Zefram) Main, "Allism: An Introduction to a Little-Known Condition," Zefram, January 30, 2003, http://www.fysh.org/~zefram/allism/allism_intro.txt.

113 Savannah Logsdon-Breakstone, "Autistic, Allistic, Neurodiverse, and Neurotypical: Say What?," *Cracked Mirror in Shalott* (blog), April 12, 2013,

http://crackedmirrorinshalott.wordpress.com/2013/04/12/autistic-allistic
-neurodiverse-and-neurotypical-say-what/; Main, "Allism."

114  Dani Ryskamp, *Field Notes on Allistics* (blog), 2017, http://fieldnotesonallistics
.tumblr.com/.

115  Ryskamp, *Field Notes on Allistics.*

116  Muskie, Institute for the Study of the Neurologically Typical, 2002, https://web
-beta.archive.org/web/20160304042053/http://isnt.autistics.org.

117  The ISNT website imagines a world in which the DSM is instead named the DSN—
*The Diagnostic and Statistical Manual of "Normal" Disorders* (wherein the word
*medical* is substituted with *normal*).

118  Muskie, Institute for the Study of the Neurologically Typical.

119  Roy Grinker, *Unstrange Minds: Remapping the World of Autism* (New York: Basic
Books, 2007), 178.

120  Endow, *Learning the Hidden Curriculum.*

121  Endow, *Learning the Hidden Curriculum,* 73.

122  Walker, "Throw Away the Master's Tools."

FOUR. INVENTION

1  Horrifically, all of these items are contemporarily being proffered by various
organizations and professionals as autism cures.

2  Nick Walker, "Aikido, Somatics, and Liberation of the Autistic Self," in *Scholars
with Autism Achieving Dreams,* ed. Lars Perner (Sedona, AZ: Auricle, 2012), 101.

3  Brenda Brueggemann and Julia Voss, "Articulating Betweenity: Literacy, Language,
Identity, and Technology in the Deaf/Hard-of-Hearing Collection," in *Stories That
Speak to Us: Exhibits from the Digital Archive of Literacy Narratives,* ed. H. Lewis
Ulman, Scott Lloyd DeWitt, and Cynthia L. Selfe (Logan, UT: Computers and Com-
position Digital Press, 2013), http://ccdigitalpress.org/stories/brueggemann.html.

4  Brueggemann and Voss, "Articulating Betweenity."

5  Gloria Anzaldúa, *Borderlands/La Frontera: The New Mestiza,* 3rd ed. (San Francisco:
Aunt Lute, 2007).

6  Anzaldúa, *Borderlands/La Frontera,* 101.

7  Anzaldúa, *Borderlands/La Frontera.*

8  José Esteban Muñoz, *Cruising Utopia: The Then and There of Queer Futurity* (New
York: New York University Press, 2009).

9  Muñoz, *Cruising Utopia,* 2.

10  Karen A. Foss, "Harvey Milk and the Queer Rhetorical Situation: A Rhetoric of
Contradiction," in *Queering Public Address: Sexualities in American Historical Discourse* (Columbia: University of South Carolina Press, 2007).

11  Casey O'Callaghan, "Sounds and Events," in *Sounds and Perception: New Philosophical Essays,* ed. Matthew Nudds and Casey O'Callaghan (Oxford: Oxford University
Press, 2009), 1–22.

12  Lydia Brown, "Autistic Empowerment: The Civil Rights Model," *Autistic
Hoya* (blog), March 27, 2012, http://www.autistichoya.com/2012/03/autistic

-empowerment-civil-rights-model.html; Kerima Çevik, "Understanding the Disability Rights Movement: On the Washington Post's Neurodiversity Article," *The Autism Wars* (blog), July 21, 2015, http://theautismwars.blogspot.com/2015/07 /understanding-of-disability-rights.html.

13  Kerima Çevik, "Surviving Inclusion: At the Intersection of Minority, Disability and Resegregation," *Ollibean* (blog), June 24, 2015, http://ollibean.com/surviving -inclusion-at-the-intersection-of-minority-disability-and-resegregation/; Nirmala Erevelles, "Crippin' Jim Crow: Disability Dis-location and the School to Prison Pipeline," in *Disability Incarcerated: Imprisonment and Disability in the United States and Canada*, ed. Liat Ben-Moshe, Chris Chapman, and Allison C. Carey (New York: Palgrave Macmillan, 2014), 82–99.

14  H-Dirksen L. Bauman and Joseph J. Murray, "Deaf Gain: An Introduction," in *Deaf Gain: Raising the Stakes for Human Diversity*, ed. H-Dirksen L. Bauman and Joseph J. Murray (Minneapolis: University of Minnesota Press, 2014), xv–xlii.

15  See also Cindee Calton, "What We Learned from Sign Languages When We Stopped Having to Defend Them," in *Deaf Gain: Raising the Stakes for Human Diversity*, ed. H-Dirksen L. Bauman and Joseph J. Murray, 112–29 (Washington, DC: Gallaudet University Press, 2014); Kristen Harmon, "Addressing Deafness: From Hearing Loss to Deaf Gain," *Profession*, 2010, 124–30; Alison Kafer, *Feminist, Queer, Crip* (Bloomington: Indiana University Press), 2013.

16  Harmon, "Addressing Deafness."

17  For ease of reference, I offer two primary critiques. The first is Bauman and Murray's reliance on evolutionary psychology in praise of deafness. In particular, the authors use ableist logics (in particular, that of mental fitness and visual acuity) in order to deflate ableist logics. Ableism cannot cancel out ableism. The second involves their decidedly neoliberal approach: the authors develop a defense of deafness predicated on deaf people's employability and competitiveness in the marketplace. A neoliberal approach will always exclude and oppress bodies/minds who do not produce—and premising a disabled person's worth on their labor runs serious risk.

18  See Gideon O. Burton, "Canons of Rhetoric: Invention," in Silva Rhetoricae, 2016, http://rhetoric.byu.edu.

19  Bre Garrett, Denise Landrum-Geyer, and Jason Palmeri, "Re-inventing Invention: A Performance in Three Acts," in *The New Work of Composing*, ed. Debra Journet, Cheryl Ball, and Ryan Trauman (Logan, UT: Computers and Composition Digital Press, 2012).

20  Debra Hawhee, "Kairotic Encounters," in *Perspectives on Rhetorical Invention*, ed. Janet M. Atwill and Janice M. Lauer (Knoxville: University of Tennessee Press, 2002), 24.

21  Anzaldúa, *Borderlands / La Frontera*, 100–103.

22  The centrality of sign language to Deaf culture, I might add, has long been debated within deaf studies and deaf communities, in large part because it represents a site of exclusion: for example, asking, "Are you d/Deaf enough?" See Brenda Jo Brueggemann, *Deaf Subjects: Between Identities and Places* (New York: New York University Press, 2009).

23  Lisa Zunshine, *Strange Concepts and the Stories They Make Possible: Cognition, Culture, Narrative* (Baltimore, MD: Johns Hopkins University Press, 2011).

24  Judy Holiday, "In[ter]vention: Locating Rhetoric's Ethos," *Rhetoric Review* 28, no. 4 (2009): 388.

25  Judith [Jack] Halberstam, *The Queer Art of Failure* (Durham, NC: Duke University Press, 2011).

26  Sara Ahmed, *Queer Phenomenology: Orientations, Objects, Others* (Durham, NC: Duke University Press, 2006), 170.

27  Brueggemann, *Deaf Subjects*; Shannon Walters, *Rhetorical Touch: Disability, Identification, Haptics* (Columbia: University of South Carolina Press, 2014).

28  Ahmed, *Queer Phenomenology*, 170.

29  Ahmed, *Queer Phenomenology*, 161.

30  Leo Kanner, "Austistic Disturbances of Affective Contact," *Nervous Child* 2, no. 3 (1943): 217.

31  Bernard Rimland, *Infantile Autism: The Syndrome and Its Implications for a Neural Theory of Behavior* (New York: Appleton-Century-Crofts, 1964).

32  Didier Houzel, "The Psychoanalysis of Infantile Autism," *Journal of Child Psychotherapy* 30 (2004): 225–37; Lesley Maroni, "Say Hello to the Scream Extractor: Working with an Autistic Child with Psychotic Mechanisms," *Journal of Child Psychotherapy* 34 (2008): 222–39.

33  Frances Tustin, *Autism and Childhood Psychosis* (London: Karnac, 1995); Frances Tustin, *Autistic Barriers in Neurotic Patients* (London: Karnac, 1986); Bruno Bettelheim, *The Empty Fortress: Infantile Autism and the Birth of the Self* (New York: Free Press, 1967).

34  Bertram A. Ruttenberg and Enid G. Wolf, "Evaluating the Communication of the Autistic Child," *Journal of Speech and Hearing Disorders* 32, no. 4 (1967): 314–24.

35  Kanner, "Austistic Disturbances of Affective Contact," 246.

36  Vickie Pasterski, Liam Gilligan, and Richard Curtis, "Traits of Autism Spectrum Disorders in Adults with Gender Dysphoria," *Archives of Sexual Behavior* 43, no. 2 (2013): 387–93; Rebecca M. Jones et al., "Brief Report: Female-to-Male Transsexual People and Autistic Traits," *Journal of Autism and Developmental Disorders* 42 (2012): 301–6.

37  Edgardo Menvielle, "A Comprehensive Program for Children with Gender Variant Behaviors and Gender Identity Disorders," *Journal of Homosexuality* 59, no. 3 (2012): 363.

38  N. M. Mukaddes, "Gender Identity Problems in Autistic Children," *Child: Care, Health and Development* 28, no. 6 (2002): 529.

39  Laura A. Jacobs et al., "Gender Dysphoria and Co-occurring Autism Spectrum Disorders: Review, Case Examples, and Treatment Considerations," *LGBT Health* 1, no. 4 (2014): 277–82.

40  Jacobs et al., "Gender Dysphoria and Co-occurring Autism Spectrum Disorders," 278.

41  Nonbinary.org runs a wiki dedicated to demigenders, which it defines as "partial connection" to gender/s that do not rely on "percentage" or halving. Nonbinary

.org, "Demigender," Nonbinary.org Wiki, August 2015, https://web-beta.archive
.org/web/20170113162325/http://nonbinary.org/wiki/Demigender.

42  AVENwiki, "Demisexual," 2014, http://www.asexuality.org/wiki/index.php?title
=Demisexual.

43  See, for instance, Julie Sondra Decker, *The Invisible Orientation: An Introduction
to Asexuality* (New York: Skyhorse, 2014). At many junctures, Decker illustrates
asexuality via the figure of the incrementum, where asexuality and sexuality occupy opposite poles and graysexuality resides in the expansive middle. It is important to note, however, that Decker's scalar representations of a sexuality-asexuality
continuum are but one kind of representation within her book. That is, Decker
takes great care to elaborate the potentially infinite nuances—and manners of
positioning or describing—asexuality within asexual (or ace) communities.

44  Much like autistics have created terminology to designate those lacking in autism
(allism), asexual people have made similar moves in naming those who are not
asexual. *Allosexual*, like allism, borrows the Greek *allos* (other) as a way of signifying sexual orientations that are other-directed. Moreover, using *allosexual* rather
than *sexual* works to expand notions of asexuality beyond that of absence or what's
missing, which the *a-* prefix often suggests. Allosexuality, then, enables constructs of asexuality that do not have to rely on antithetical poles of substance and
absence, but rather describe varying configurations of inter/relation, attraction,
and arousal. There is presently heated debate in asexual communities around the
term *allosexual*, due to its usage and origins within sexology research and thus its
connections to norms and violences. In response, activists have offered *zedsexual*
as a corresponding term. I here use allosexual, however, as one means of pointing
out both absurdities and violences in clinical frameworks: Toward whom do we
turn, and toward whom are we coerced to turn? When is turning toward the other
(allos) presumed more moral than turning toward the self (autos)?

45  Catherine Malabou, *What Should We Do with Our Brain?* (New York: Fordham
University Press, 2008).

46  Queerplatonic and *wtfromantic* signal shifting, uncertain, and contingent relations
to notions of romance and intimacy. *Wtfromantic*, for example, is an identity that
at once harnesses the queer and the disabled: *wtfromantics* may narrate an inability to understand the concept of romance unto itself, or they may narrate an inability to understand whether they have ever experienced romantic attraction.

47  Stephanie Kerschbaum, *Toward a New Rhetoric of Difference* (Urbana, IL: NCTE,
2014), 69.

48  Kafer, *Feminist, Queer, Crip*, 34.

49  E., "On (A)sexuality," *The Third Glance* (blog), January 3, 2012, http://
thethirdglance.wordpress.com/2012/01/03/on-asexuality/.

50  See, for example, Anthony F. Bogaert, *Understanding Asexuality* (Lanham,
MD: Rowman and Littlefield, 2012); Karli J. Cerankowski and Megan Milks,
"Introduction: Why Asexuality? Why Now?," in *Asexualities: Feminist and
Queer Perspectives*, ed. Karli J. Cerankowski and Megan Milks, 1–14 (New York:
Routledge, 2014); Decker, *The Invisible Orientation*.

51   *Ace* is slang for asexual. See also *asexy*.

52   Stephanie L. Kerschbaum, "Avoiding the Difference Fixation: Identity Categories, Markers of Difference, and the Teaching of Writing," *College Composition and Communication* 63, no. 4 (2012): 626.

53   Eunjung Kim, "Asexualities and Disabilities in Constructing Normalcy," in *Asexualities: Feminist and Queer Perspectives*, ed. Karli J. Cerankowski and Megan Milks (New York: Routledge, 2014), 266.

54   E., "On (A)sexuality"; Alyssa Hillary, "The Erasure of Queer Autistic People," in *Criptiques*, ed. Caitlin Wood (Lexington, KY: May Day, 2014), 121–46.

55   Dereka Rushbrook, "Cities, Queer Space, and the Cosmopolitan Tourist," GLQ: A *Journal of Lesbian and Gay Studies* 8, nos. 1–2 (2002): 203.

56   Rushbrook, "Cities, Queer Space, and the Cosmopolitan Tourist," 200.

57   Erica Chu, "Radical Identity Politics: Asexuality and Contemporary Articulations of Identity," in *Asexualities: Feminist and Queer Perspectives* (New York: Routledge, 2014), 90.

58   Chu, "Radical Identity Politics, 83.

59   Importantly, asexuality is not synonymous with celibacy. Celibacy is an action or an expression rather than an orientation or identity. Much like an allosexual person may abstain from sexual activity, an asexual person may engage in sexual activity.

60   Chavisory, "Hermocrates: Because Everyone Feels This Strong Urge to Label Every Tiny Variant in Sexuality," Tumblr, *Chavisory's Post-It Notes*, August 19, 2012, http://chavisory.tumblr.com/post/29762771583/hermocrates-because-everyone-feels-this-strong.

61   Sarah E. S. Sinwell, "Aliens and Asexuality: Media Representation, Queerness, and Asexual Visibility," in *Asexualities: Feminist and Queer Perspectives*, ed. Karli J. Cerankowski and Megan Milks (New York: Routledge, 2014), 166; David Jay, "Desexualization v. Asexuality" (forum post), AVEN: Asexual Visibility and Education Network, April 6, 2003, http://www.asexuality.org/en/topic/499-desexualization-v-asexuality/.

62   Erving Goffman, *Stigma: Notes on the Management of Spoiled Identity* (New York: Simon and Schuster, 1963).

63   Alyssa Hillary, "Home," Alyssa Hillary, 2015, https://alyssahillary.wordpress.com/.

64   Edward Schiappa, "Second Thoughts on the Critiques of Big Rhetoric," *Philosophy and Rhetoric* 34, no. 3 (2001): 260–75.

65   Jim Sinclair, "Don't Mourn for Us," Autism Network International, 1993, http://www.autreat.com/dont_mourn.html.

66   Kafer, *Feminist, Queer, Crip*, 45.

67   Mel Baggs, *In My Language* (video), YouTube, January 14, 2007, https://www.youtube.com/watch?v=JnylM1hI2jc.

68   Baggs, *In My Language*.

69   O'Callaghan, "Sounds and Events," 22.

70   O'Callaghan, "Sounds and Events," 1.

71   W. Kawohl and K. Podoll, "Contour Copying or Echoplasia—a New Echo Phenomenon in a Person with Gilles de La Tourette Syndrome," *Psychopathology* 41 (2008): 201.

72   Kawohl and Podoll, "Contour Copying or Echoplasia."

73   See, for example, Temple Grandin and Sean Barron, *The Unwritten Rules of Social Relationships: Decoding Social Mysteries through the Unique Perspectives of Autism* (Arlington, TX: Future Horizons, 2005), or Liane H. Willey, *Safety Skills for Asperger Women: Saving a Perfectly Good Female Life* (Philadelphia: Jessica Kingsley, 2011).

74   Judy Endow, *Learning the Hidden Curriculum: The Odyssey of One Autistic Adult* (Shawnee Mission, KS: Autism Asperger, 2012).

75   Rachel Cohen-Rottenberg, *Blazing My Trail: Living and Thriving with Autism* (Brattleboro, VT: Rachel B. Cohen-Rottenberg, 2011), 9.

76   Ido Kedar, "Theories That Bind Us," *Ido in Autismland* (blog), July 15, 2015, http://idoinautismland.com/?p=353.

77   Ralph J. Savarese, "Moving the Field: The Sensorimotor Perspective on Autism (Commentary on 'Rethinking Autism: Implications of Sensory and Motor Differences,' an Article by Anne Donnellan, David Hill, and Martha Leary)," *Frontiers in Integrative Neuroscience* 7 (2013), http://journal.frontiersin.org/article/10.3389/fnint.2013.00006/full.

78   Ariane Zurcher, "Scripts—a Communication Bridge," *Emma's Hope Book* (blog), October 9, 2014, http://emmashopebook.com/2014/10/09/scripts-a-communication-bridge/.

79   Zurcher, "Scripts."

80   Jennifer L. Cook and Geoffrey Bird, "Atypical Social Modulation of Imitation in Autism Spectrum Conditions," *Journal of Autism and Developmental Disorders* 42, no. 6 (2012): 1050.

81   Cynthia Kim, "Echolalia and Scripting: Straddling the Border of Functional Language," *Musings of an Aspie* (blog), October 9, 2014, http://musingsofanaspie.com/2014/10/09/echolalia-and-scripting-straddling-the-border-of-functional-language/.

82   Kim, "Echolalia and Scripting.

83   D. Grossi et al., "On the Differential Nature of Induced and Incidental Echolalia in Autism," *Journal of Intellectual Disability Research* 57, no. 10 (2013): 903.

84   Grossi et al., "On the Differential Nature of Induced and Incidental Echolalia," 904.

85   Bettelheim, *The Empty Fortress.*

86   Julia Bascom, "The Obsessive Joy of Autism," *Just Stimming* (blog), April 5, 2011, https://juststimming.wordpress.com/2011/04/05/the-obsessive-joy-of-autism/.

87   Phil Schwarz, "Building Alliances: Community Identity and the Role of Allies in Autistic Self-Advocacy," in *Ask and Tell: Self-Advocacy and Disclosure for People on the Autism Spectrum,* ed. Stephen M. Shore (Shawnee Mission, KS: Autism Asperger, 2004), 147.

88   Savarese, "Moving the Field."

89   Savarese, "Moving the Field."

90   Jason Nolan and Melanie McBride, "Embodied Semiosis: Autistic 'Stimming' as Sensory Praxis," in *International Handbook of Semiotics,* ed. Peter P. Trifonas (New York: Springer, 2015), 1069–78.

91 Nolan and McBride, "Embodied Semiosis," 1070.

92 Nolan and McBride, "Embodied Semiosis," 1075.

93 Kirsten Lindsmith, "Stimming 101, or: How I Learned to Stop Worrying and Love the Stim," *The Artism Spectrum* (blog), May 16, 2014, https://kirstenlindsmith .wordpress.com/2014/05/16/stimming-101-or-how-i-learned-to-stop-worrying-and -love-the-stim/.

94 Michel Foucault, *The History of Sexuality*, vol. 1, trans. Robert Hurley (New York: Pantheon, 1978).

95 Nolan and McBride, "Embodied Semiosis," 1075.

96 Laura N. Rice and Robert Elliott, *Facilitating Emotional Change: The Moment-by-Moment Process* (New York: Guilford, 1993), 65.

97 J. P. Byrnes, "Piaget's Cognitive Developmental Theory," in *Language, Memory, and Cognition in Infancy and Early Childhood*, ed. Janette B. Benson and Marshall M. Haith (Oxford: Academic Press, 2010), 384.

98 David Morris, *The Sense of Space* (Albany: State University of New York Press, 2004), 66.

99 Amy Sequenzia, "My Uncooperative Body," *Autism Women's Network* (blog), October 28, 2013, http://autismwomensnetwork.org/my-uncooperative-body/.

100 Sequenzia, "My Uncooperative Body."

101 Debra Hawhee, *Bodily Arts: Rhetoric and Athletics in Ancient Greece* (Austin: University of Texas Press, 2005).

102 Hawhee, *Bodily Arts*, 147.

103 Hawhee, *Bodily Arts*.

104 Rachel Cohen-Rottenberg, *The Uncharted Path: My Journey with Late-Diagnosed Autism* (Brattleboro, VT: Rachel B. Cohen-Rottenberg, 2010), 120.

105 Jay T. Dolmage, *Disability Rhetoric* (Syracuse, NY: Syracuse University Press, 2014).

106 Paul Heilker and Melanie Yergeau, "Autism and Rhetoric," *College English* 73, no. 5 (2011): 485–97.

107 It is in these regards that I hold distinct privilege. I am white; I sometimes have access to reliable speech, even if that access isn't frequent or long-term; I also have a doctorate, and my experiences with forced hospitalization have been short-term rather than permanent residential placements. As well, perhaps the biggest shortcoming of this book is that it's written for an academic audience—necessary in some ways, but quite exclusionary in most ways.

EPILOGUE

1 Frances Tustin, *Autism and Childhood Psychosis* (London: Karnac, 1995).

2 Bruno Bettelheim, *The Empty Fortress: Infantile Autism and the Birth of the Self* (New York: Free Press, 1967), 146–51.

3 Bertram A. Ruttenberg and Enid G. Wolf, "Evaluating the Communication of the Autistic Child," *Journal of Speech and Hearing Disorders* 32, no. 4 (1967): 314–24.

4 Phil Schwarz, "Building Alliances: Community Identity and the Role of Allies in Autistic Self-Advocacy," in *Ask and Tell: Self-Advocacy and Disclosure for People*

on the *Autism Spectrum*, ed. Stephen M. Shore (Shawnee Mission, KS: Autism Asperger, 2004), 143–76.

5   I'm footnoting the statement that Deaf culture has a language because it's not completely true. Deaf culture is often represented as being a culture (or cultures) because of sign languages, but deaf studies and disability studies scholars, not to mention activists and nonacademics, have long argued that sign languages are not, in toto, Deaf culture. To conflate signing with Deaf culture would be to deny the inclusion of innumerable deaf and hard-of-hearing people and rhetorical practices. See Brenda Jo Brueggemann, *Deaf Subjects: Between Identities and Places* (New York: New York University Press, 2009); Joseph M. Valente, Benjamin Bahan, and H-Dirksen L. Bauman, "Sensory Politics and the Cochlear Implant Debates," in *Cochlear Implants: Evolving Perspectives*, ed. Raylene Paludneviciene and Irene W. Leigh (Washington, DC: Gallaudet University Press, 2011), 245–58.

6   Dawn Prince-Hughes, *Songs of the Gorilla Nation: My Journey through Autism* (New York: Harmony, 2005), 7.

7   Kristina Chew, "Fractioned Idiom: Metonymy and the Language of Autism," in *Autism and Representation* (New York: Routledge, 2007), 133.

8   R. Peter Hobson, "Autism and the Philosophy of Mind," in *The Oxford Handbook of Philosophy and Psychiatry*, ed. K. W. M. Fulford et al. (Oxford: Oxford University Press, 2013), 826–27.

9   Hobson, "Autism and the Philosophy of Mind," 827.

10  Kenneth Burke, *A Rhetoric of Motives* (New York: Prentice-Hall, 1955), 22.

11  Stephen Kuusisto, *Planet of the Blind* (New York: Delta, 1998).

12  Margaret Price, "'Her Pronouns Wax and Wane': Psychosocial Disability, Autobiography, and Counter-diagnosis," *Journal of Literary and Cultural Disability Studies* 3, no. 1 (2009): 15.

Aarons, Maureen, and Tessa Gittens. *The Handbook of Autism: A Guide for Parents and Professionals*. New York: Routledge, 2002.

Adams, Christina. *A Real Boy: A True Story of Autism, Early Intervention, and Recovery*. New York: Berkley, 2005.

Ad Council and Autism Speaks. *Autism Speaks—Lightning*. YouTube video, January 11, 2013. https://www.youtube.com/watch?v=HZ1yiw1LEkY.

Agnew, Lois, Laurie Gries, Zosha Stuckey, Tolar Burton Vicki, Jay Dolmage, Jessica Enoch, Ronald L. Jackson, et al. "Octalog III: The Politics of Historiography in 2010." *Rhetoric Review* 30, no. 2 (2011): 109–34.

Ahmed, Sara. "Happy Objects." In *The Affect Theory Reader*, edited by Melissa Gregg and Gregory J. Seigworth, 29–51. Durham, NC: Duke University Press, 2010.

———. *Living a Feminist Life*. Durham, NC: Duke University Press, 2017.

———. *Queer Phenomenology: Orientations, Objects, Others*. Durham, NC: Duke University Press, 2006.

———. *Willful Subjects*. Durham, NC: Duke University Press, 2014.

Alan, Michael. *I Wish My Kids Had Cancer: A Family Surviving the Autism Epidemic*. Baltimore, MD: PublishAmerica, 2008.

Albertini, Giorgio, Emilena Polito, Marco Sarà, and Paolo Onorati. "Compulsive Masturbation in Infantile Autism Treated by Mirtazapine." *Pediatric Neurology* 34, no. 5 (2006): 417–18.

Alexander, Jonathan. "Queer Composition Redux: Impossibility toward Futurity." *Writing Instructor*, March 2015. http://parlormultimedia.com/twitest/alexander-2015-03.

Alexander, Jonathan, and Jacqueline Rhodes. "Queer Rhetoric and the Pleasures of the Archive." *Enculturation* 13 (2012). http://www.enculturation.net/queer-rhetoric-and-the-pleasures-of-the-archive.

Al-Ghani, K. I. *Learning about Friendship: Stories to Support Social Skills Training in Children with Asperger Syndrome and High Functioning Autism*. London: Jessica Kingsley, 2010.

Alyric. "Indistinguishable from Their Peers." *A Touch of Alyricism* (blog), June 23, 2008. http://alyric.blogspot.com/2008/06/indistinguishable-from-their-peers.html.

Amen, Daniel G. *Making a Good Brain Great: The Amen Clinic Program for Achieving and Sustaining Optimal Mental Performance*. New York: Three Rivers, 2005.

Anzaldúa, Gloria. *Borderlands / La Frontera: The New Mestiza*. 3rd ed. San Francisco: Aunt Lute, 2007.

Aristotle. *Physics*. Translated by R. P. Hardie and R. K. Gaye. University of Adelaide, eBooks @ Adelaide, 2015. https://ebooks.adelaide.edu.au/a/aristotle/physics/index.html.

ASAN. "ASAN Statement on GAO Report of Autism Research Funding." Autistic Self Advocacy Network, August 14, 2015. http://autisticadvocacy.org/2015/08/asan-statement-on-gao-report-on-autism-research-funding/.

———. "ASAN Statement on #JusticeForKayleb." Autistic Self Advocacy Network, April 14, 2015. http://autisticadvocacy.org/2015/04/asan-statement-on-justice forkayleb/.

Asperger, Hans. "'Autistic Psychopathy' in Childhood." In *Autism and Asperger Syndrome*, edited by Uta Frith, 37–92. Cambridge: Cambridge University Press, 1991.

Attwood, Tony, Isabelle Henault, and Nick Dubin. *The Autism Spectrum, Sexuality and the Law: What Every Parent and Professional Needs to Know*. London: Jessica Kingsley, 2014.

Autism Research Centre, University of Cambridge. "Autism Spectrum Quotient." 2017. https://www.autismresearchcentre.com/project_7_asquotient.

Autism Speaks. "About Autism: What You Need to Know." 2013. https://www.autismspeaks.org/sites/default/files/afyo_about_autism.pdf.

———. "Autism Prevalence on the Rise." *Autism Speaks* (blog), October 2010. https://autismspeaksblog.files.wordpress.com/2010/10/prevalence-graph1.jpg.

———. "Challenging Behaviors Tool Kit." 2012. https://www.autismspeaks.org/family-services/tool-kits/challenging-behaviors-tool-kit.

———. "The Launch of a New Public Service Ad Campaign and a Series of Special Events Highlight Autism Speaks' Efforts during Autism Awareness Month." March 20, 2006. https://www.autismspeaks.org/about-us/press-releases/launch-new-public-service-ad-campaign-and-series-special-events-highlight-au.

———. "Self-Funded Employer Tool Kit." 2012. https://www.autismspeaks.org/sites/default/files/docs/gr/erisa_tool_kit_9.12_0.pdf.

———. "Sponsorship Packet—5th Annual Milwaukee Walk Now for Autism Speaks." 2013. http://www.kintera.org/atf/cf/%7BBEBB52F7-5AE4-49F7-A192-BF4B7DD999C6%7D/2013%20WALK%20NOW%20FOR%20AUTISM%20SPEAKS%20MILWAUKEE%20SPONSORSHIP%20PACKAGES.PDF.

Autism Speaks Walk. Walk Participant Guide. 2016. http://autismspeakswalk.org.

Autism Votes. "State Initiatives." 2008. https://web.archive.org/web/20080607043126/http://www.autismvotes.org/site/c.frKNI3PCImE/b.3909861/k.B9DF/State_Initiatives.htm.

AVENwiki. "Demisexual." 2014. http://www.asexuality.org/wiki/index.php?title=Demisexual.

Ayllon, Teodoro, and Nathan Azrin. *The Token Economy: A Motivational System for Therapy and Rehabilitation*. New York: Appleton-Century-Crofts, 1968.

BACB. "About Behavior Analysis." Behavior Analyst Certification Board, August 29, 2015. http://bacb.com/about-behavior-analysis/.

Baggs, Mel. *In My Language*. Video. YouTube, January 14, 2007. https://www.youtube
.com/watch?v=JnylM1hI2jc.

Baglieri, Susan, and Arthur Shapiro. *Disability Studies and the Inclusive Classroom: Critical
Practices for Creating Least Restrictive Attitudes*. New York: Routledge, 2012.

Baio, Jon, and CDC. "Prevalence of Autism Spectrum Disorder among Children Aged
8 Years—Autism and Developmental Disabilities Monitoring Network, 11 Sites,
United States, 2010." *Morbidity and Mortality Weekly Report*, March 28, 2014.

Balardin, Joana Bisol, João Ricardo Sato, Gilson Vieira, Yeu Feng, Eileen Daly, Clodagh
Murphy, Anthony J. Bailey, et al. "Relationship between Surface-Based Brain Morphometric Measures and Intelligence in Autism Spectrum Disorders." *Autism Research* 8,
no. 5 (October 1, 2015): 556–66. doi:10.1002/aur.1470.

Bang, Janet, Jesse Burns, and Aparna Nadig. "Brief Report: Conveying Subjective Experience in Conversation: Production of Mental State Terms and Personal Narratives
in Individuals with High Functioning Autism." *Journal of Autism and Developmental
Disorders* 43, no. 7 (2013): 1732–40. doi:10.1007/s10803-012-1716-4.

Bara, Bruno, Angela Ciaramidaro, Henrik Walter, and Mauro Adenzato. "Intentional
Minds: A Philosophical Analysis of Intention Tested through fMRI Experiments
Involving People with Schizophrenia, People with Autism, and Healthy Individuals."
*Frontiers in Human Neuroscience* 5 (2011): 7. doi:10.3389/fnhum.2011.00007.

Bard. "VLog: Problem with Goldilocks Rhetoric." *Prism*Song* (vlog), August 8, 2011.
http://prismsong.blogspot.com/2011/08/vlog-problem-with-goldilocks-rhetoric
.html.

Barnbaum, Deborah R. *The Ethics of Autism: Among Them, but Not of Them*. Bloomington:
University of Indiana Press, 2008.

Baron-Cohen, Simon. "The Biology of the Imagination." *Enetelechy: Mind and Culture* 9
(2007). http://www.entelechyjournal.com/simonbaroncohen.htm.

——. *Essential Difference: Male and Female Brains and the Truth about Autism*. New York:
Basic Books, 2003.

——. *Mindblindness: An Essay on Autism and Theory of Mind*. Boston: MIT Press, 1997.

——. *The Science of Evil: On Empathy and the Origins of Cruelty*. New York: Basic Books,
2011.

——. "Theories of the Autistic Mind." *Psychologist* 21, no. 2 (2008): 112–16.

Baron-Cohen, S., A. M. Leslie, and U. Frith. "Does the Autistic Child Have a Theory of
Mind?" *Cognition* 21 (1985): 37–46.

Baron-Cohen, Simon, Sarah Cassidy, Bonnie Auyeung, Carrie Allison, Maryam
Achoukhi, Sarah Robertson, Alexa Pohl, and Meng-Chuan Lai. "Attenuation of Typi-
cal Sex Differences in 800 Adults with Autism vs. 3,900 Controls." *PLOS ONE* 9, no. 7
(July 16, 2014): e102251. doi:10.1371/journal.pone.0102251.

Barrer, Laurence, and Guy Gimenez. "First Time Description of Dismantling Phenomenon." *Frontiers in Psychology* 6, no. 510 (2015): 1–5.

Barrows, Kate. *Autism in Childhood and Autistic Features in Adults: A Psychoanalytic Perspective*. London: Karnac, 2008.

Bascom, Julia. "The Obsessive Joy of Autism." *Just Stimming* (blog), April 5, 2011. https://
juststimming.wordpress.com/2011/04/05/the-obsessive-joy-of-autism/.

———. "Quiet Hands." *Just Stimming* (blog), October 5, 2011. https://juststimming
.wordpress.com/2011/10/05/quiet-hands/.

Bauman, H-Dirksen L., and Joseph J. Murray. "Deaf Gain: An Introduction." In
*Deaf Gain: Raising the Stakes for Human Diversity*, edited by H-Dirksen L. Bauman and Joseph J. Murray, xv–xlii. Minneapolis: University of Minnesota Press,
2014.

Becerra, Tracy A., Ondine S. von Ehrenstein, Julia E. Heck, Jorn Olsen, Onyebuchi A.
Arah, Shafali S. Jeste, Michael Rodriguez, and Beate Ritz. "Autism Spectrum Disorders
and Race, Ethnicity, and Nativity: A Population-Based Study." *Pediatrics* 134, no. 1
(2014): e63–e71.

Berlin, James. *Rhetoric and Reality: Writing Instruction in American Colleges, 1900–1985.*
Carbondale: Southern Illinois University Press, 1987.

Bernstein, Francine M. "Thirty-Three: Francine M. Bernstein." In *Families of Adults with
Autism: Stories and Advice for the Next Generation*, edited by Jane Johnson, Stephen
M. Edelson, and Anne Van Rensselaer, 166–72. London: Jessica Kingsley, 2008.

Bettelheim, Bruno. *The Empty Fortress: Infantile Autism and the Birth of the Self.* New York:
Free Press, 1967.

———. "Joey: A 'Mechanical Boy.'" *Scientific American*, March 1959.

Bitzer, Lloyd F. "The Rhetorical Situation." *Philosophy and Rhetoric* 1 (1968): 1–14.

Bogaert, Anthony F. *Understanding Asexuality.* Lanham, MD: Rowman and Littlefield,
2012.

Bogdashina, Olga. *Communication Issues in Autism and Asperger Syndrome: Do We Speak
the Same Language?* London: Jessica Kingsley, 2005.

———. *Sensory Perceptual Issues in Autism: Different Sensory Experiences, Different Perceptual Worlds.* London: Jessica Kingsley, 2003.

Booth, Wayne C. *The Rhetoric of Rhetoric: The Quest for Effective Communication.* Malden,
MA: Blackwell, 2004.

Boucher, Jill. "Putting Theory of Mind in Its Place: Psychological Explanations of the
Socio-Emotional-Communicative Impairments in Autistic Spectrum Disorder." *Autism*
16, no. 3 (2012): 226–46.

Boyle, Casey, and Nathaniel A. Rivers. "A Version of Access." *Technical Communication
Quarterly* 25, no. 1 (January 2, 2016): 29–47. doi:10.1080/10572252.2016.1113702.

Bratta, Phil, and Malea Powell. "Introduction to the Special Issue: Entering the Cultural
Rhetorics Conversations." *Enculturation* 21 (2016). http://enculturation.net/entering
-the-cultural-rhetorics-conversations.

Brennan, Eileen E. "Encountering Autism: Learning to Listen to the Fear." In *The
Use of Psychoanalysis in Working with Children's Emotional Lives*, edited by Michael
O'Laughlin, 305–22. Lanham, MD: Jason Aronson, 2013.

Broderick, Alicia. "Autism as Rhetoric: Exploring Watershed Rhetorical Moments in
Applied Behavior Analysis Discourse." *Disability Studies Quarterly* 31, no. 3 (2011).
http://dsq-sds.org/article/view/1674/1597.

Bronstein, Scott, and Jessi Joseph. "Therapy to Change 'Feminine' Boy Created a
Troubled Man, Family Says." CNN, June 10, 2011. http://www.cnn.com/2011/US/06/07
/sissy.boy.experiment/.

Brosnan, Mark, Chris Ashwin, Ian Walker, and Joseph Donaghue. "Can an 'Extreme Female Brain' Be Characterised in Terms of Psychosis?" *Personality and Individual Differences* 49, no. 7 (2010): 738–42.

Brosnan, Mark, Rajiv Daggar, and John Collomosse. "The Relationship between Systemising and Mental Rotation and the Implications for the Extreme Male Brain Theory of Autism." *Journal of Autism and Developmental Disorders* 40 (2010): 739–41.

Brown, Benjamin T., Gwynn Morris, Robert E. Nida, and Lynne Baker-Ward. "Brief Report: Making Experience Personal: Internal States Language in the Memory Narratives of Children with and without Asperger's Disorder." *Journal of Autism and Developmental Disorders* 42 (2012): 441–46.

Brown, Heather M., and Perry D. Klein. "Writing, Asperger Syndrome and Theory of Mind." *Journal of Autism and Developmental Disorders* 41 (2011): 1464–74.

Brown, Lydia. "Autistic Empowerment: The Civil Rights Model." *Autistic Hoya* (blog), March 27, 2012. http://www.autistichoya.com/2012/03/autistic-empowerment-civil -rights-model.html.

———. "The Politics of Coming Out." *Autistic Hoya* (blog), October 11, 2012. http://www .autistichoya.com/2012/10/the-politics-of-coming-out.html.

Brueggemann, Brenda Jo. *Deaf Subjects: Between Identities and Places.* New York: New York University Press, 2009.

Brueggemann, Brenda Jo, and Julia Voss. "Articulating Betweenity: Literacy, Language, Identity, and Technology in the Deaf/Hard-of-Hearing Collection." In *Stories That Speak to Us: Exhibits from the Digital Archive of Literacy Narratives,* edited by H. Lewis Ulman, Scott Lloyd DeWitt, and Cynthia L. Selfe. Logan, UT: Computers and Composition Digital Press, 2013. http://ccdigitalpress.org/stories/brueggemann.html.

Brugha, T., S. McManus, J. Bankart, F. Scott, S. Purdon, J. Smith, P. Bebbington, R. Jenkins, and H. Meltzer. "Epidemiology of Autism Spectrum Disorders in Adults in the Community in England." *Archives of General Psychiatry* 68, no. 5 (2011): 459–65.

Brunsdon, Victoria E. A., and Francesca Happé. "Exploring the 'Fractionation' of Autism at the Cognitive Level." *Autism* 18, no. 1 (January 1, 2014): 17–30. doi:10.1177/1362361313499456.

Burke, Kenneth. *Counter-statement.* Los Angeles: University of California Press, 1968.

———. *Dramatism and Development.* Barre, MA: Clark University Press, 1972.

———. *A Grammar of Motives.* Berkeley: University of California Press, 1969.

———. *Language as Symbolic Action: Essays of Life, Literature, and Method.* Los Angeles: University of California Press, 1966.

———. "(Nonsymbolic) Motion / (Symbolic) Action." *Critical Inquiry* 4, no. 4 (1978): 809–38.

———. *On Symbols and Society.* Chicago: University of Chicago Press, 1989.

———. *A Rhetoric of Motives.* New York: Prentice-Hall, 1955.

Burke, Phyllis. *Gender Shock: Exploding the Myths of Male and Female.* New York: Anchor, 1996.

Burroway, Jim. "What Are Little Boys Made Of? An Original BTB Investigation." *Box Turtle Bulletin* (blog), June 7, 2011. http://www.boxturtlebulletin.com/what-are-little -boys-made-of-main.

Butler, Judith. *Undoing Gender*. New York: Routledge, 2004.

Byrnes, J. P. "Piaget's Cognitive Developmental Theory." In *Language, Memory, and Cognition in Infancy and Early Childhood*, edited by Janette B. Benson and Marshall M. Haith, 381–89. Oxford: Academic Press, 2010.

Calton, Cindee. "What We Learned from Sign Languages When We Stopped Having to Defend Them." In *Deaf Gain: Raising the Stakes for Human Diversity*, edited by H-Dirksen L. Bauman and Joseph J. Murray, 112–29. Washington, DC: Gallaudet University Press, 2014.

Campbell, Fiona Kumari. "Re-cognising Disability: Cross-Examining Social Inclusion through the Prism of Queer Anti-sociality." *Jindal Global Law Review* 4, no. 2 (2013): 209–38.

Carr-Ruffino, Norma. *Diversity Success Strategies*. New York: Routledge, 2009.

Carruthers, Peter. "Autism as Mind-Blindness: An Elaboration and Partial Defence." In *Theories of Theories of Mind*, edited by Peter Carruthers and Peter K. Smith, 257–73. Cambridge: Cambridge University Press, 1996.

Cascio, M. Ariel. "Rigid Therapies, Rigid Minds: Italian Professionals' Perspectives on Autism Interventions." *Culture, Medicine, and Psychiatry* 39, no. 2 (2015): 235–53.

Case, Jessica, and Mary Konstantareas. "Brief Report: Interventions for Inappropriate Handling of Feces in Adults with Autism Spectrum Disorders." *Journal on Developmental Disabilities* 17, no. 2 (2011): 73–78.

CDC. "Data & Statistics." Centers for Disease Control and Prevention, August 12, 2015. http://www.cdc.gov/ncbddd/autism/data.html.

Cerankowski, Karli J., and Megan Milks. "Introduction: Why Asexuality? Why Now?" In *Asexualities: Feminist and Queer Perspectives*, edited by Karli J. Cerankowski and Megan Milks, 1–14. New York: Routledge, 2014.

Çevik, Kerima. "Autism Speaks: Speaking for Typical White Males." Infogr.am, 2013. https://infogr.am/autism-speaks-diversity-in-representation.

———. "Justice for Kayleb Moon Robinson #AliveWhileBlack and Autistic." *InterSected* (blog), April 14, 2015. http://intersecteddisability.blogspot.com/2015/04/justice-for-kayleb-moon-robinson.html.

———. "Surviving Inclusion: At the Intersection of Minority, Disability and Resegregation." *Ollibean* (blog), June 24, 2015. http://ollibean.com/surviving-inclusion-at-the-intersection-of-minority-disability-and-resegregation/.

———. "Understanding the Disability Rights Movement: On the Washington Post's Neurodiversity Article." *The Autism Wars* (blog), July 21, 2015. http://theautismwars.blogspot.com/2015/07/understanding-of-disability-rights.html.

Chance, Paul. "'After You Hit a Child, You Can't Just Get Up and Leave Him; You Are Hooked to That Kid': A Conversation with Ivar Lovaas about Self-Mutilating Children and How Their Parents Make It Worse." *Psychology Today*, January 1974.

Chavisory. "Hermocrates: Because Everyone Feels This Strong Urge to Label Every Tiny Variant in Sexuality." *Chavisory's Post-It Notes*, August 19, 2012. http://chavisory.tumblr.com/post/29762771583/hermocrates-because-everyone-feels-this-strong.

Chew, Kristina. "Fractioned Idiom: Metonymy and the Language of Autism." In *Autism and Representation*, 133–44. New York: Routledge, 2007.

Chu, Erica. "Radical Identity Politics: Asexuality and Contemporary Articulations of Identity." In *Asexualities: Feminist and Queer Perspectives*, 79–99. New York: Routledge, 2014.

Ciaramidaro, Angela, Sven Bölte, Sabine Schlitt, Daniela Hainz, Fritz Poutska, Barnhard Weber, Bruno G. Bara, Christine Frietag, and Henrik Walter. "Schizophrenia and Autism as Contrasting Minds: Neural Evidence for the Hypo-Hyper-Intentionality Hypothesis." *Schizophrenia Bulletin* 41, no. 1 (2015): 171–79.

Clare, Eli. "Yearning for Carrie Buck." Keynote presentation at Queer Practices, Places, and Lives II, Ohio State University, 2014.

Cohen-Rottenberg, Rachel. *Blazing My Trail: Living and Thriving with Autism*. Brattleboro, VT: Rachel B. Cohen-Rottenberg, 2011.

———. "Disorder in Society, Disorder in Self." *Shift: Journal of Alternatives*, May 27, 2011. http://www.shiftjournal.com/2011/05/27/disorder-in-society-disorder-in-self/.

———. *The Uncharted Path: My Journey with Late-Diagnosed Autism*. Brattleboro, VT: Rachel B. Cohen-Rottenberg, 2010.

Cook, Jennifer L., and Geoffrey Bird. "Atypical Social Modulation of Imitation in Autism Spectrum Conditions." *Journal of Autism and Developmental Disorders* 42, no. 6 (2012): 1045–51.

Corbett, Edward P. J. "The Rhetoric of the Open Hand and the Rhetoric of the Closed Fist." *College Composition and Communication* 20, no. 5 (1969): 288–96.

Coskun, Murat, Sevcan Karakoc, Fuat Kircelli, and Nahit Motavalli Mukaddes. "Effectiveness of Mirtazapine in the Treatment of Inappropriate Sexual Behaviors in Individuals with Autistic Disorder." *Journal of Child and Adolescent Psychopharmacology* 19, no. 2 (April 1, 2009): 203–6. doi:10.1089/cap.2008.020.

Coskun, Murat, and Nahit Motavalli Mukaddes. "Mirtazapine Treatment in a Subject with Autistic Disorder and Fetishism." *Journal of Child and Adolescent Psychopharmacology* 18, no. 2 (April 1, 2008): 206–9. doi:10.1089/cap.2007.0014.

Crane, Tim. "The Mental States of Persons and Their Brains." *Royal Institute of Philosophy Supplement* 76 (2015): 253–70.

Cutler, Eustacia. "Autism and Child Pornography: A Toxic Combination." *Daily Beast*, August 5, 2013. http://www.thedailybeast.com/articles/2013/08/05/autism-and-child -pornography-a-toxic-combination.html.

Davide-Rivera, Jeannie. *Twirling Naked in the Streets and No One Noticed: Growing Up with Undiagnosed Autism*. David and Goliath, 2013.

Davis, Diane. "Creaturely Rhetorics." *Philosophy and Rhetoric* 44, no. 1 (2011): 88–94.

Davis, Lennard. *Bending over Backwards: Disability, Dismodernism, and Other Difficult Positions*. New York: New York University Press, 2002.

Dawson, Michelle. "The Misbehaviour of Behaviourists." No Autistics Allowed, January 29, 2004. http://www.sentex.net/~nexus23/naa_aba.html.

Day, Elaine M. *Aspies Alone Together: My Story and a Survival Guide for Women Living with Asperger Syndrome*. CreateSpace, 2014.

Decker, Julie S. *The Invisible Orientation: An Introduction to Asexuality*. New York: Skyhorse, 2014.

Dekker, Martijn. "On Our Own Terms: Emerging Autistic Culture." Autscape, 1999. http://www.autscape.org/2015/programme/handouts/Autistic-Culture-07-Oct-1999 .pdf.

Dodd, Susan. *Understanding Autism*. Marrickville, NSW: Elsevier Australia, 2005.

Dolmage, Jay T. *Disability Rhetoric*. Syracuse, NY: Syracuse University Press, 2014.

———. "Framing Disability, Developing Race: Photography as Eugenic Technology." *Enculturation* 17 (2014). http://enculturation.net/framingdisability.

Donnellan, Anne M. "Invented Knowledge and Autism: Highlighting Our Strengths and Expanding the Conversation." *Journal of the Association for Persons with Severe Handicaps* 24, no. 3 (1999): 230–36.

Driskill, Qwo-Li. "Double-Weaving Two-Spirit Critiques: Building Alliances between Native and Queer Studies." *GLQ: A Journal of Lesbian and Gay Studies* 16, nos. 1–2 (2010): 69–92.

Duffy, John, and Rebecca Dorner. "The Pathos of 'Mindblindness': Autism, Science, and Sadness in 'Theory of Mind' Narratives." *Journal of Literary and Cultural Disability Studies* 5, no. 2 (2011): 201–16.

Dussauge, Isabelle, and Anelis Kaiser. "Re-queering the Brain." In *Neurofeminism: Issues at the Intersection of Feminist Theory and Cognitive Science*, edited by Robyn Bluhm, Anne Jaap Jacobson, and Heidi Lene Maibom, 121–44. London: Palgrave Macmillan, 2012.

E. "On (A)sexuality." *The Third Glance* (blog), January 3, 2012. http://thethirdglance .wordpress.com/2012/01/03/on-asexuality/.

Eastham, David. *Understand: Fifty Memowriter Poems*. Ottawa: Oliver Pate, 1985.

Ede, Lisa, and Andrea Lunsford. "Audience Addressed / Audience Invoked: The Role of Audience in Composition Theory and Pedagogy." *College Composition and Communication* 35, no. 2 (1984): 155–71.

Edelman, Lee. *No Future: Queer Theory and the Death Drive*. Durham, NC: Duke University Press, 2004.

Endow, Judy. *Learning the Hidden Curriculum: The Odyssey of One Autistic Adult*. Shawnee Mission, KS: Autism Asperger, 2012.

Erevelles, Nirmala. "Crippin' Jim Crow: Disability Dis-location and the School to Prison Pipeline." In *Disability Incarcerated: Imprisonment and Disability in the United States and Canada*, edited by Liat Ben-Moshe, Chris Chapman, and Allison C. Carey, 82–99. New York: Palgrave Macmillan, 2014.

———. "Thinking with Disability Studies." *Disability Studies Quarterly* 34, no. 2 (2014), http://dsq-sds.org/article/view/4248/3587.

Eyal, Gil, Brendan Hart, Emine Onculer, Neta Oren, and Natasha Rossi. *The Autism Matrix*. Cambridge: Polity, 2010.

Fahnestock, Jeanne. *Rhetorical Figures in Science*. Oxford: Oxford University Press, 1999.

Faust, Mickee. *Annie Dearest*. Video. Faust Films. Tallahassee, FL: Diane Wilkins Productions, 2002. https://www.youtube.com/watch?v=MXNUN5OCZdY.

Fein, Deborah, Marianne Barton, Inge-Marie Eigsti, Elizabeth Kelley, Letitia Naigles, Robert T. Schultz, Michael Stevens, et al. "Optimal Outcome in Individuals with a History of Autism." *Journal of Child Psychology and Psychiatry* 54, no. 2 (2013): 195–205.

Feinstein, Adam. *A History of Autism: Conversations with the Pioneers.* Malden, MA: Wiley-Blackwell, 2010.

Fine, Cordelia. *Delusions of Gender: How Our Minds, Society, and Neurosexism Create Difference.* New York: Norton, 2010.

Ford, Ian [Star]. *A Field Guide to Earthlings: An Autistic/Asperger View of Neurotypical Behavior.* Albuquerque, NM: Ian Ford Software, 2010.

Foss, Karen A. "Harvey Milk and the Queer Rhetorical Situation: A Rhetoric of Contradiction." In *Queering Public Address: Sexualities in American Historical Discourse.* Columbia: University of South Carolina Press, 2007.

Foss, Sonja K., and Cindy L. Griffin. "Beyond Persuasion: A Proposal for an Invitational Rhetoric." *Communication Monographs* 62 (1995): 2–18.

———. "A Feminist Perspective on Rhetorical Theory: Toward a Clarification of Boundaries." *Western Journal of Communication* 56, no. 4 (1992): 330–49.

Foucault, Michel. *The History of Sexuality*, vol. 1. Translated by Robert Hurley. New York: Pantheon, 1978.

Freud, Sigmund. *Beyond the Pleasure Principle.* Translated by C. J. M. Hubback. London: International Psycho-Analytical Press, 1922.

Frith, Uta. "Autism—Are We Any Closer to Explaining the Enigma?" *The Psychologist* 27, no. 10 (October 2014): 744–45.

———. *Autism: Explaining the Enigma.* 2nd ed. Malden, MA: Blackwell, 2003.

Frith, Uta, and Francesca Happé. "Theory of Mind and Self-Consciousness: What Is It Like to Be Autistic?" *Mind and Language* 14, no. 1 (1999): 1–22.

Galen. *Method of Medicine*, books 1–4. Edited and translated by Ian Johnston and G. H. R. Horsley. Cambridge, MA: Harvard University Press, 2011.

Gaonkar, Dilip Parameshwar. "Rhetoric and Its Double: Reflections on the Rhetorical Turn in the Human Sciences." In *The Rhetorical Turn: Invention and Persuasion in the Conduct of Inquiry*, edited by Herbert W. Simons, 341–66. Chicago: University of Chicago Press, 1990.

Garcia-Perez, Rosa M., R. Peter Hobson, and Anthony Lee. "Narrative Role-Taking in Autism." *Journal of Autism and Developmental Disorders* 38 (2008): 156–68.

Garcia Winner, Michelle. "What Is Social Thinking?" Video presentation. *Social Thinking*, 2016. https://www.socialthinking.com/LandingPages/Mission.

Garrett, Bre, Denise Landrum-Geyer, and Jason Palmeri. "Re-inventing Invention: A Performance in Three Acts." In *The New Work of Composing*, edited by Debra Journet, Cheryl Ball, and Ryan Trauman. Logan, UT: Computers and Composition Digital Press / Utah State University Press, 2012.

Gearhart, Sally Miller. "The Womanization of Rhetoric." *Women's Studies International Quarterly* 2 (1979): 195–201.

Gerhardt, Peter F. "The Promise of ABA: Creating Meaningful Lives throughout Adolescence and Adulthood." *Autism Advocate* 53, no. 4 (2008).

Germon, Jennifer. *Gender: A Genealogy of an Idea.* London: Palgrave Macmillan, 2009.

Gladwell, Malcolm. "Thresholds of Violence: How School Shootings Catch on." *New Yorker*, October 19, 2015. http://www.newyorker.com/magazine/2015/10/19/thresholds-of-violence.

Glenn, Cheryl. *Rhetoric Retold: Regendering the Tradition from Antiquity through the Renaissance.* Carbondale: Southern Illinois University Press, 1997.

Goch, Caspar J., Bram Stieltjes, Romy Henze, Jan Hering, Luise Poustka, Hans-Peter Meinzer, and Klaus H. Maier-Hein. "Quantification of Changes in Language-Related Brain Areas in Autism Spectrum Disorders Using Large-Scale Network Analysis." *International Journal of Computer Assisted Radiology and Surgery* 9, no. 3 (2014): 357–65.

Goffman, Erving. *Stigma: Notes on the Management of Spoiled Identity.* New York: Simon and Schuster, 1963.

Goldman, Sylvie. "Brief Report: Narratives of Personal Events in Children with Autism and Developmental Language Disorders." *Journal of Autism and Developmental Disorders* 38 (2008): 1982–88.

Goldstein, Sam, and Sally Ozonoff. "Historical Perspective and Overview." In *Assessment of Autism Spectrum Disorders*, edited by Sam Goldstein, Jack A. Naglieri, and Sally Ozonoff, 1–17. New York: Guilford, 2009.

Grace, Elizabeth (Ibby). "Autistethnography." In *Both Sides of the Table: Autoethnographies of Educators Learning and Teaching with/in [Dis]ability*, edited by Phil Smith, 89–102. New York: Peter Lang, 2013.

———. "Behaviorism Everywhere." *NeuroQueer* (blog), April 15, 2014. http://neuroqueer .blogspot.com/2014/04/behaviorism-everywhere-by-ib-grace.html.

Grandin, Temple, and Sean Barron. *The Unwritten Rules of Social Relationships: Decoding Social Mysteries through the Unique Perspectives of Autism.* Arlington, TX: Future Horizons, 2005.

Gray, Carol. *The New Social Story Book.* Arlington, TX: Future Horizons, 2015.

Gray, Carol A., and Joy D. Garand. "Social Stories: Improving Responses of Students with Autism with Accurate Social Information." *Focus on Autism and Other Developmental Disabilities* 8, no. 1 (1993): 1–10.

Green, Richard. *The "Sissy Boy Syndrome": The Development of Homosexuality.* New Haven, CT: Yale University Press, 1987.

Greenbaum, Andrea. "Nurturing Difference: The Autistic Student in Professional Writing Programs." *Journal of the Assembly for Advanced Perspectives on Learning* 16 (2011): 40–47.

Grinker, Roy. *Unstrange Minds: Remapping the World of Autism.* New York: Basic Books, 2007.

Groner, Rachel. "Sex as 'Spock': Autism, Sexuality, and Autobiographical Narrative." In *Sex and Disability*, edited by Robert McRuer and Anna Mollow, 263–81. Durham, NC: Duke University Press, 2012.

Gross, Zoe. "Killing Words." ASAN, April 10, 2012. http://autisticadvocacy.org/2012/04 /killing-words/.

Grossi, D., R. Marcone, T. Cinquegrana, and M. Gallucci. "On the Differential Nature of Induced and Incidental Echolalia in Autism." *Journal of Intellectual Disability Research* 57, no. 10 (2013): 903–12.

Gunning, Tom. "Animation and Alienation: Bergson's Critique of the Cinématographe and the Paradox of Mechanical Motion." *Moving Image* 14, no. 1 (2014): 1–9.

Haas, Angela. "Race, Rhetoric, and Technology: A Case Study of Decolonial Technical Communication Theory, Methodology, and Pedagogy." *Journal of Business and Technical Communication* 26, no. 3 (2012): 277–310.

Hacking, Ian. "How We Have Been Learning to Talk about Autism: A Role for Stories." In *Cognitive Disability and Its Challenge to Moral Philosophy*, edited by Eva F. Kittay and Licia Carlson, 261–78. Malden, MA: Wiley-Blackwell, 2010.

——. "Humans, Aliens, and Autism." *Daedalus* 138, no. 3 (2009): 44–59.

Halberstam, Judith [Jack]. *The Queer Art of Failure*. Durham, NC: Duke University Press, 2011.

Happé, Francesca. *Autism and Theory of Mind in Everyday Life*. New York: Psychology Press, 1994.

——. "The Autobiographical Writings of Three Asperger Syndrome Adults: Problems of Interpretation and Implications for Theory." In *Autism and Asperger Syndrome*, edited by Uta Frith, 207–42. Cambridge: Cambridge University Press, 1991.

——. "Understanding Minds and Metaphors: Insights from the Study of Figurative Language in Autism." *Metaphor and Symbolic Activity* 10, no. 4 (1995): 275–95.

Hare, Julie. "Autistic Boy's Family Appeals to Scott Morrison." *The Australian*, December 11, 2013. http://www.theaustralian.com.au/higher-education/autistic-boys-family-appeals-to-scott-morrison/story-e6frgcjx-1226780128297.

Harmon, Kristen. "Addressing Deafness: From Hearing Loss to Deaf Gain." *Profession* (2010): 124–30.

Hawhee, Debra. *Bodily Arts: Rhetoric and Athletics in Ancient Greece*. Austin: University of Texas Press, 2005.

——. "Kairotic Encounters." In *Perspectives on Rhetorical Invention*, edited by Janet M. Atwill and Janice M. Lauer, 16–35. Knoxville: University of Tennessee Press, 2002.

Hawk, Byron. *A Counter-history of Composition: Toward Methodologies of Complexity*. Pittsburgh: University of Pittsburgh Press, 2007.

Heilker, Paul. "Autism, Rhetoric, and Whiteness." *Disability Studies Quarterly* 32, no. 4 (2012). http://dsq-sds.org/article/view/1756/3181.

Heilker, Paul, and Melanie Yergeau. "Autism and Rhetoric." *College English* 73, no. 5 (2011): 485–97.

Hershey, Laura. "From Poster Child to Protester." Independent Living Institute, 1993. http://www.independentliving.org/docs4/hershey93.html.

Hess, Lucille. "I Would Like to Play but I Don't Know How: A Case Study of Pretend Play in Autism." *Child Language Teaching and Therapy* 22, no. 1 (2006): 97–116.

Higgins, Michael. "Shock Therapy Called Cruel: Kin Disagree." *Chicago Tribune*, March 8, 2007. http://articles.chicagotribune.com/2007-03-08/news/0703080165_1_electric-shock-robert-bernstein-group-home.

Hillary, Alyssa. "The Erasure of Queer Autistic People." In *Criptiques*, edited by Caitlin Wood, 121–46. Lexington, KY: May Day, 2014.

——. "Home." Alyssa Hillary, 2015. https://alyssahillary.wordpress.com/.

Hobson, R. Peter. "Autism and the Philosophy of Mind." In *The Oxford Handbook of Philosophy and Psychiatry*, edited by K. W. M. Fulford, Martin Davies, Richard G. T. Gipps,

George Graham, John Z. Sadler, Giovanni Stanghellini, and Tim Thornton, 820–34. Oxford: Oxford University Press, 2013.

———. "Explaining Autism: Ten Reasons to Focus on the Developing Self." *Autism* 14, no. 5 (2010): 391–407.

Holiday, Judy. "In[ter]vention: Locating Rhetoric's Ethos." *Rhetoric Review* 28, no. 4 (2009): 390.

Holt, R. J., L. R. Chura, J. Suckling, E. vom dem Hagen, A. J. Calder, E. T. Bullmore, S. Baron-Cohen, and M. D. Spencer. "'Reading the Mind in the Eyes': An fMRI Study of Adolescents with Autism and Their Siblings." *Psychological Medicine* 44, no. 15 (2015): 3215–27.

Horgan, John. *The Undiscovered Mind: How the Human Brain Defies Replication, Medication, and Explanation.* New York: Touchstone, 1999.

Houzel, Didier. "The Psychoanalysis of Infantile Autism." *Journal of Child Psychotherapy* 30 (2004): 225–37.

Howe, S. G. *Report Made to the Legislature of Massachusetts, upon Idiocy.* Boston: Coolidge and Wiley, 1848. http://mirlyn.lib.umich.edu/Record/001133226.

Hubbard, Bryan. "Reassessing Truman, the Bomb, and Revisionism: The Burlesque Frame and Entelechy in the Decision to Use Atomic Weapons against Japan." *Western Journal of Communication* 62, no. 3 (1998): 328–85.

Hughes, Claire, Rosie Ensor, and Alex Marks. "Individual Differences in False Belief Understanding Are Stable from 3 to 6 Years of Age and Predict Children's Mental State Talk with School Friends." *Journal of Experimental Child Psychology* 108, no. 1 (2011): 96–112.

Human, Erin. "Autistic Culture: A Primer." *E Is for Erin* (blog), January 14, 2016. http://eisforerin.com/2016/01/14/autistic-primer/.

Jack, Jordynn. *Autism and Gender: From Refrigerator Mothers to Computer Geeks.* Champaign: University of Illinois Press, 2014.

———. "'The Extreme Male Brain?' Incrementum and the Rhetorical Gendering of Autism." *Disability Studies Quarterly* 31, no. 3 (2011).

Jack, Jordynn, and L. Gregory Appelbaum. "'This Is Your Brain on Rhetoric': Research Directions for Neurorhetorics." *Rhetoric Society Quarterly* 40, no. 5 (2010): 411–37.

Jacobs, Laura A., Katherine Rachlin, Laura Erickson-Schroth, and Aron Janssen. "Gender Dysphoria and Co-occurring Autism Spectrum Disorders: Review, Case Examples, and Treatment Considerations." *LGBT Health* 1, no. 4 (2014): 277–82.

Jay, David. "Desexualization v. Asexuality." Forum post. AVEN: Asexual Visibility and Education Network, April 6, 2003. http://www.asexuality.org/en/topic/499-desexualization-v-asexuality/.

Johnson, Jenell. "The Skeleton on the Couch: The Eagleton Affair, Rhetorical Disability, and the Stigma of Mental Illness." *Rhetoric Society Quarterly* 40, no. 5 (2010): 459–78.

Jones, Rebecca M., Sally Wheelwright, Krista Farrell, Emma Martin, Richard Green, Domenico Di Ceglie, and Simon Baron-Cohen. "Brief Report: Female-to-Male Transsexual People and Autistic Traits." *Journal of Autism and Developmental Disorders* 42 (2012): 301–6.

Jones, Sparrow R. "ABA." In *The Real Experts: Readings for Parents of Autistic Children*, edited by Michelle Sutton. Fort Worth, TX: Autonomous Press, 2015.

———. *The ABCs of Autism Acceptance*. Fort Worth, TX: Autonomous Press, 2016.

Jurecic, Ann. "Neurodiversity." *College English* 69, no. 5 (2007): 421–42.

Kafer, Alison. "Compulsory Bodies: Reflections on Heterosexuality and Able-Bodiedness." *Journal of Women's History* 15, no. 3 (2003): 77–89.

———. *Feminist, Queer, Crip*. Bloomington: Indiana University Press, 2013.

Kanner, Leo. "Austistic Disturbances of Affective Contact." *Nervous Child* 2, no. 3 (1943): 217–50.

Katherine. "Language, Thought, Feminism, Autism, Wildness." *Katherine Lives in the Real World* (blog), February 1, 2015. https://web-beta.archive.org/web/20160622105143/https://katherinelivesintherealworld.wordpress.com/2015/02/01/language-thought -feminism-autism-wildness-part1/.

Kauschke, Christina, Bettina van der Beek, and Inge Kamp-Becker. "Narratives of Girls and Boys with Autism Spectrum Disorders: Gender Differences in Narrative Competence and Internal State Language." *Journal of Autism and Developmental Disorders* 46, no. 3 (2016): 840–52.

Kawohl, W., and K. Podoll. "Contour Copying or Echoplasia—a New Echo Phenomenon in a Person with Gilles de La Tourette Syndrome." *Psychopathology* 41 (2008): 201–2.

Kearney, Albert J. *Understanding Applied Behavior Analysis: An Introduction to ABA for Parents, Teachers, and Other Professionals*. London: Jessica Kingsley, 2007.

Kedar, Ido. "Theories That Bind Us." *Ido in Autismland* (blog), July 15, 2015. http://idoinautismland.com/?p=353.

Keith, William, Steve Fuller, Alan Gross, and Michael Leff. "Taking Up the Challenge: A Response to Simons." *Quarterly Journal of Speech* 85 (1999): 330–38.

Kelley, Elizabeth, Jennifer J. Paul, Deborah Fein, and Letitia R. Naigles. "Residual Language Deficits in Optimal Outcome Children with a History of Autism." *Journal of Autism and Developmental Disorders* 36, no. 6 (2006): 807–28.

Kellogg, John Harvey. *Plain Facts for Old and Young*. Burlington, IA: Segner and Condit, 1881. http://catalog.hathitrust.org/Record/010600804.

———. *Proceedings of the Race Betterment Conference*. Battle Creek, MI: The Race Betterment Foundation, 1928.

Kelter, M. "The Myth of 'Official': Autism and Self-Diagnosis Skeptics." *Invisible Strings* (blog), July 20, 2015. http://theinvisiblestrings.com/the-myth-of-official-autism-and -self-diagnosis-skeptics/.

Kennedy, George A. *Classical Rhetoric and Its Christian and Secular Tradition from Ancient to Modern Times*. 2nd ed. Chapel Hill: University of North Carolina Press, 1999.

———. *Comparative Rhetoric: An Historical and Cross-Cultural Introduction*. Oxford: Oxford University Press, 1998.

———. "A Hoot in the Dark: The Evolution of General Rhetoric." *Philosophy and Rhetoric* 25, no. 1 (1992): 1–21.

Kerschbaum, Stephanie L. "Avoiding the Difference Fixation: Identity Categories, Markers of Difference, and the Teaching of Writing." *College Composition and Communication* 63, no. 4 (2012): 616–44.

———. *Toward a New Rhetoric of Difference*. Urbana, IL: NCTE, 2014.

Kim, Cynthia. "Acceptance as a Well Being Practice." *Musings of an Aspie* (blog), January 14, 2015. http://musingsofanaspie.com/2015/01/14/acceptance-as-a-well-being -practice/.

———. "Echolalia and Scripting: Straddling the Border of Functional Language." *Musings of an Aspie* (blog), October 9, 2014. http://musingsofanaspie.com/2014/10/09/echolalia -and-scripting-straddling-the-border-of-functional-language/.

———. "The Myth of Passing." *Musings of an Aspie* (blog), October 24, 2013. http:// musingsofanaspie.com/2013/10/24/the-myth-of-passing/.

Kim, Eunjung. "Asexualities and Disabilities in Constructing Normalcy." In *Asexualities: Feminist and Queer Perspectives*, edited by Karli J. Cerankowski and Megan Milks, 249–82. New York: Routledge, 2014.

Kinneavy, James E. "The Basic Aims of Discourse." *College Composition and Communication* 20, no. 5 (1969): 297–304.

Kissine, Mikhail. *From Utterances to Speech Acts*. Cambridge: Cambridge University Press, 2013.

Klin, Ami, Warren Jones, Robert Schultz, and Fred Volkmar. "The Enactive Mind, or from Actions to Cognition: Lessons from Autism." *Philosophical Transactions of the Royal Society B: Biological Sciences* 358, no. 1430 (2003): 345–60.

Kramer, Corbin. *Autism in Fiction and Everything in Between*. Video. Digital Archive of Literacy Narratives, 2010. http://daln.osu.edu/handle/2374.DALN/1132.

Krumins, Daina. "Coming Alive in a World of Texture." In *Women from Another Planet? Our Lives in the Universe of Autism*, edited by Jean Kearns Miller, 85–91. Bloomington, IN: AuthorHouse, 2003.

Kuppers, Petra. "Deconstructing Images: Performing Disability." *Contemporary Theatre Review* 11, nos. 3–4 (2001): 25–40.

Kurchak, Sarah. "I'm Autistic, and Believe Me, It's a Lot Better than Measles." *Medium*, February 6, 2015. https://medium.com/the-archipelago/im-autistic-and-believe-me-its -a-lot-better-than-measles-78cb039f4bea.

Kuusisto, Stephen. *Planet of the Blind*. New York: Delta, 1998.

Lanovaz, Marc J., and Ingrid E. Sladeczek. "Vocal Stereotypy in Individuals with Autism Spectrum Disorders: A Review of Behavioral Interventions." *Behavior Modification* 36, no. 2 (2012): 146–64.

LaRue, Robert. "Functional Analysis." Association for Science in Autism Treatment. Accessed February 7, 2015. http://www.asatonline.org/research-treatment/clinical-corner /functional-analysis/.

Latour, Bruno. *The Pasteurization of France*. Translated by Alan Sheridan and John Law. Cambridge, MA: Harvard University Press, 1993.

———. *Reassembling the Social: An Introduction to Actor-Network-Theory*. Oxford: Oxford University Press, 2005.

Lawson, Wendy [Wenn]. *Autism: Taking Over*. Saarbrucken, Germany: Lambert Academic Publishing, 2011.

———. *Concepts of Normality: The Autistic and Typical Spectrum*. London: Jessica Kingsley, 2008.

LeBlanc, Jocelyn J., and Michela Fagiolini. "Autism: A 'Critical Period' Disorder?" *Neural Plasticity*, 2011, 1–17. doi:10.1155/2011/921680.

Lewiecki-Wilson, Cynthia, and Jen Cellio. "Diagnosable: Mothering at the Threshold of Disability." In *Introduction: On Liminality and Cultural Embodiment*, edited by Cynthia Lewiecki-Wilson and Jen Cellio, 1–15. Syracuse, NY: Syracuse University Press, 2011.

Lindsay, Stan A. *Implicit Rhetoric: Kenneth Burke's Extension of Aristotle's Concept of Entelechy*. Lanham, MD: University Press of America, 1998.

———. *Psychotic Entelechy: The Dangers of Spiritual Gifts Theology*. Lanham, MD: University Press of America, 2006.

Lindsmith, Kirsten. "Stimming 101, or: How I Learned to Stop Worrying and Love the Stim." *The Artism Spectrum* (blog), May 16, 2014. https://kirstenlindsmith.wordpress.com/2014/05/16/stimming-101-or-how-i-learned-to-stop-worrying-and-love-the-stim/.

Linton, Simi. *Claiming Disability: Knowledge and Identity*. New York: New York University Press, 1998.

Logsdon-Breakstone, Savannah. "Autistic, Allistic, Neurodiverse, and Neurotypical: Say What?" *Cracked Mirror in Shalott* (blog), April 12, 2013. http://crackedmirrorinshalott.wordpress.com/2013/04/12/autistic-allistic-neurodiverse-and-neurotypical-say-what/.

Lorde, Audre. *Sister Outsider: Essays and Speeches*. Berkeley, CA: Crossing Press, 2007.

Losh, Molly, and Peter C. Gordon. "Quantifying Narrative Ability in Autism Spectrum Disorder: A Computational Linguistic Analysis of Narrative Coherence." *Journal of Autism and Developmental Disorders* 44, no. 12 (2014): 2016–3025.

Lovaas, O. Ivar. *The Autistic Child: Language Development through Behavior Modification*. New York: Irvington, 1977.

———. "Behavioral Treatment and Normal Education and Intellectual Functioning in Young Autistic Children." *Journal of Consulting and Clinical Psychology* 55, no. 1 (1987): 3–9.

———. "The Development of a Treatment-Research Project for Developmentally Disabled and Autistic Children." *Journal of Applied Behavior Analysis* 26, no. 4 (1993): 617–30.

———. *Teaching Developmentally Disabled Children: The ME Book*. Baltimore: University Park Press, 1981.

Lovaas, O. Ivar, Robert Koegel, James Q. Simmons, and Judith Stevens Long. "Some Generalization and Follow-Up Measures on Autistic Children in Behavior Therapy." *Journal of Applied Behavior Analysis* 6, no. 1 (1973): 131–66.

Lozano-Reich, Nina M., and Dana L. Cloud. "The Uncivil Tongue: Invitational Rhetoric and the Problem of Inequality." *Western Journal of Communication* 73, no. 2 (2009): 220–26.

Luckett, Tim, Anita Bundy, and Jacqueline Roberts. "Do Behavioural Approaches Teach Children with Autism to Play or Are They Pretending?" *Autism* 11, no. 4 (2007): 365–88.

Lunsford, Andrea A. "On Reclaiming Rhetorica." In *Reclaiming Rhetorica: Women in the Rhetorical Tradition*, edited by Andrea A. Lunsford, 3–8. Pittsburgh: University of Pittsburgh Press, 1995.

Main, Andrew (Zefram). "Allism: An Introduction to a Little-Known Condition." Zefram, January 30, 2003. http://www.fysh.org/~zefram/allism/allism_intro.txt.

Malabou, Catherine. *What Should We Do with Our Brain?* New York: Fordham University Press, 2008.

Mallett, Rebecca, and Katherine Runswick-Cole. "Commodifying Autism: The Cultural Contexts of 'Disability' in the Academy." In *Disability and Social Theory: New Developments and Directions*, edited by Dan Goodley, Bill Hughes, and Lennard Davis, 33–51. New York: Palgrave Macmillan, 2012.

Mandell, David S., Lisa D. Wiggins, Laura A. Carpenter, Julie Daniels, Carolyn DiGuiseppi, Maureen S. Durkin, Ellen Giarelli, et al. "Racial/Ethnic Disparities in the Identification of Children with Autism Spectrum Disorder." *American Journal of Public Health* 99, no. 3 (2009): 493–98.

Manning, Erin. *Always More than One: Individuation's Dance.* Durham, NC: Duke University Press, 2013.

———. *The Minor Gesture.* Durham, NC: Duke University Press, 2016.

———. *Relationscapes: Movement, Art, Philosophy.* Cambridge, MA: MIT Press, 2012.

Manning, Erin, and Brian Massumi. *Thought in the Act: Passages in the Ecology of Experience.* Minneapolis: University of Minnesota Press, 2014.

Maroni, Lesley. "Say Hello to the Scream Extractor: Working with an Autistic Child with Psychotic Mechanisms." *Journal of Child Psychotherapy* 34 (2008): 222–39.

Martin, G., and J. Pear. *Behavior Modification: What It Is and How to Do It.* Englewood Cliffs, NJ: Prentice-Hall, 1978.

Mary. "Testimonial: 'Best Decision I Ever Made for My Son.'" ABI: Applied Behavioral Interventions, 2015. https://web.archive.org/web/20150203110803/http://abiautism.com/about-abi/testimonials/.

Massumi, Brian. *Parables for the Virtual: Movement, Affect, Sensation.* Durham, NC: Duke University Press, 2002.

Mathison, Maureen A. "Complicity as Epistemology: Reinscribing the Historical Categories of 'Woman' through Standpoint Feminism." *Communication Theory* 7, no. 2 (1997): 149–61.

Maurice, Catherine. *Let Me Hear Your Voice: A Family's Triumph over Autism.* New York: Alfred A. Knopf, 1993.

McCallum, E. L., and Mikko Tuhkanen. "Introduction: Becoming Unbecoming: Untimely Meditations." In *Queer Times, Queer Becomings*, 1–21. Albany: State University of New York Press, 2011.

McGee, Micki. "Cruel Optimism for the Neurologically Queer." *Social Text: Periscope*, January 13, 2013. http://socialtextjournal.org/periscope_article/cruel-optimism-for-the-neurologically-queer/.

McGeer, Victoria. "Autistic Self-Awareness." *Philosophy, Psychiatry, and Psychology* 11, no. 3 (2004): 235–51.

McGuire, Anne. *The War on Autism.* Ann Arbor: University of Michigan Press, 2016.

McRuer, Robert. *Crip Theory: Cultural Signs of Queerness and Disability.* New York: New York University Press, 2006.

Mead, Kit. "Missing What You Never Had: Autistic and Queer." In *QDA: A Queer Disability Anthology*, edited by Raymond Luczak. Minneapolis: Squares and Rebels, 2015.

Menvielle, Edgardo. "A Comprehensive Program for Children with Gender Variant Behaviors and Gender Identity Disorders." *Journal of Homosexuality* 59, no. 3 (2012): 357–68.

Merleau-Ponty, Maurice. *Phenomenology of Perception*. Translated by Donald A. Landes. New York: Routledge, 2014.

Meyer, Craig. "Infusing Dysfluency into Rhetoric and Composition: Overcoming the Stutter." PhD diss., Ohio University, 2013.

Meyerding, Jane. "Growing Up Genderless." In *Women from Another Planet? Our Lives in the Universe of Autism*, edited by Jean Kearns Miller, 157–70. Bloomington, IN: AuthorHouse, 2003.

Miller, Carolyn R. "Should We Name the Tools? Concealing and Revealing the Art of Rhetoric." In *The Public Work of Rhetoric: Citizen-Scholars and Civic Engagement*, edited by John M. Ackerman and David J. Coogan, 19–38. Columbia: University of South Carolina Press, 2010.

Miller, Jean Kearns. "Foreword." In *Women from Another Planet? Our Lives in the Universe of Autism*, edited by Jean Kearns Miller, xvii–xxiv. Bloomington, IN: AuthorHouse, 2003.

Mills, Brian D., Janie Lai, Timothy T. Brown, Matthew Erhart, Eric Halgren, Judy Reilly, Anders Dale, Mark Appelbaum, and Pamela Moses. "White Matter Microstructure Correlates of Narrative Production in Typically Developing Children and Children with High Functioning Autism." *Neuropsychologia* 51 (2013): 1933–41.

Monje, Michael. "Why #Fiction? (#Autism #Book Club Questions)." *Shaping Clay*, April 3, 2015. http://www.mmonjejr.com/2015/04/why-fiction-autism-book-club-questions.html.

Montgomery, Charlotte, Carrie Allison, Meng-Chuan Lai, Sarah Cassidy, Peter E. Langdon, and Simon Baron-Cohen. "Do Adults with High Functioning Autism or Asperger Syndrome Differ in Empathy and Emotion Recognition?" *Journal of Autism and Developmental Disorders* 46, no. 6 (2016): 1931–40.

Morris, David. *The Sense of Space*. Albany: State University of New York Press, 2004.

Moser, D., and A. Grant. "Screams, Slaps, and Love: A Surprising, Shocking Treatment Helps Far-Gone Mental Cripples." *Life*, May 7, 1965.

MSSNG. "Autism Speaks Launches MSSNG: Groundbreaking Genome-Sequencing Program." 2014. https://www.autismspeaks.org/science/science-news/autism-speaks-launches-mssng-groundbreaking-genome-sequencing-program.

Mukaddes, N. M. "Gender Identity Problems in Autistic Children." *Child: Care, Health and Development* 28, no. 6 (2002): 529–32.

Mukhopadhyay, Tito Rajarshi. *Plankton Dreams: What I Learned in Special Ed*. London: Open Humanities Press, 2015.

Muñoz, José Esteban. *Cruising Utopia: The Then and There of Queer Futurity*. New York: New York University Press, 2009.

Murray, Dinah. "Introduction." In *Coming Out Asperger: Diagnosis, Disclosure, and Self-Confidence*, edited by Dinah Murray, 9–18. London: Jessica Kingsley, 2006.

Murray, Jeffrey W. "The Face in Dialogue, Part II: Invitational Rhetoric, Direct Moral Suasion, and the Asymmetry of Dialogue." *Southern Communication Journal* 69, no. 4 (2004): 333–47.

Murray, Stuart. "Autism Functions / The Function of Autism," *Disability Studies Quarterly* 31, no. 1 (2010), http://dsq-sds.org/article/view/1048/1229.

Newnham, David. "News from Nowhere?" *Guardian Weekend Supplement*, March 25, 1995. http://www.mugsy.org/nowhere.htm.

Nguyen, Mathew, and Tanya Murphy. "Mirtazapine for Excessive Masturbation in an Adolescent with Autism" [letter to the editor]. *Journal of the American Academy of Child and Adolescent Psychiatry* 40, no. 8 (2001): 868–69. doi:10.1097/00004583-200108000-00004.

NHS Information Centre, Community and Mental Health Team, T. Brugha, S. A. Cooper, S. McManus, S. Purdon, J. Sh, F. J. Scott, N. Spiers, and F. Tyrer. "Estimating the Prevalence of Autism Spectrum Conditions in Adults: Extending the 2007 Adult Psychiatric Morbidity Survey." NHS / Health and Social Care Information Centre, 2012.

Nicholson, N. I. "Nothing about Us without ALL of Us: That Means Autistics of Colour, Too." *The Digital Hyperlexic* (blog), January 24, 2016. https://thedigitalhyperlexic .wordpress.com/2016/01/24/nothing-about-us-without-all-of-us-that-means-autistics -of-colour-too/.

———. "Racial Profiling and the Black Autistic: The Case of Neli Latson." *The Digital Hyperlexic* (blog), December 11, 2014. https://thedigitalhyperlexic.wordpress.com/2014 /12/11/racial-profiling-and-the-black-autistic-the-case-of-neli-latson/.

———. "The Souls of Black Autistic Folk, Part III: Difference and the Question of Visibility." *Woman with Asperger's* (blog), April 30, 2013. https://womanwithaspergers.wordpress .com/2013/04/30/the-souls-of-black-autistic-folk-part-iii-difference-and-the-question -of-visibility/.

Nolan, Jason, and Melanie McBride. "Embodied Semiosis: Autistic 'Stimming' as Sensory Praxis." In *International Handbook of Semiotics*, edited by Peter P. Trifonas, 1069–78. New York: Springer, 2015.

Nonbinary.org. "Demigender." Nonbinary.org Wiki, August 2015. https://web-beta .archive.org/web/20170113162325/http://nonbinary.org/wiki/Demigender.

Oakley, Todd V. "The Human Rhetorical Potential." *Written Communication* 16, no. 1 (1999): 93–128.

O'Callaghan, Casey. "Sounds and Events." In *Sounds and Perception: New Philosophical Essays*, edited by Matthew Nudds and Casey O'Callaghan, 1–22. Oxford: Oxford University Press, 2009.

Onaiwu, Morénike Giwa. "#JusticeForKayleb NOW." *Just Being Me . . . Who Needs "Normalcy" Anyway?* (blog), April 15, 2015. http://whoneedsnormalcy.blogspot.com/2015 /04/justiceforkayleb-now.html.

———. "Why I Decided to 'Come Out' of the Autism Closet." *Just Being Me . . . Who Needs "Normalcy" Anyway?* (blog), October 1, 2015. http://whoneedsnormalcy.blogspot.com /2015/10/why-i-decided-to-come-out-of-autism.html.

O'Nions, Elizabeth, Beata Tick, Fruhling Rijsdijk, Francesca Happé, Robert Plomin, Angelica Ronald, and Essi Viding. "Examining the Genetic and Environmental Associations between Autistic Social and Communication Deficits and Psychopathic Callous-Unemotional Traits." *PLOS ONE* 10, no. 9 (2015): e0134331, 1–12.

Oppenheim, Rosalind C. *Effective Teaching Methods for Autistic Children*. Springfield, IL: Charles C. Thomas, 1974.

———. "They Said Our Child Was Hopeless." *Saturday Evening Post*, June 17, 1961.

Ortega, Francisco. "The Cerebral Subject and the Challenge of Neurodiversity." *BioSocieties* 4 (2009): 425–45.

Pasterski, Vickie, Liam Gilligan, and Richard Curtis. "Traits of Autism Spectrum Disorders in Adults with Gender Dysphoria." *Archives of Sexual Behavior* 43, no. 2 (2013): 387–93.

Perelman, Chaim, and C. Olbrechts-Tyteca. *The New Rhetoric: A Treatise on Argumentation*. South Bend, IN: University of Notre Dame Press, 1991.

Peterson, Gail B. "A Day of Great Illumination: B.F. Skinner's Discovery of Shaping." *Journal of the Experimental Analysis of Behavior* 82, no. 3 (2004): 317–28.

Pinchevski, Amit. "Displacing Incommunicability: Autism as an Epistemological Boundary." *Communication and Critical/Cultural Studies* 2, no. 2 (2005): 163–84.

Pitts-Taylor, Victoria. "The Plastic Brain: Neoliberalism and the Neuronal Self." *Health* 14, no. 6 (2010): 635–52.

Plato. *Parmenides*. Translated by Benjamin Jowett. Project Gutenberg, 2013. https://www.gutenberg.org/ebooks/1687.

Posey, David J., Krista D. Guenin, Arlene E. Kohn, Naomi B. Swiezy, and Christopher J. McDougle. "A Naturalistic Open-Label Study of Mirtazapine in Autistic and Other Pervasive Developmental Disorders." *Journal of Child and Adolescent Psychopharmacology* 11, no. 3 (September 1, 2001): 267–77. doi:10.1089/10445460152595586.

Powell, Malea. "Stories Take Place: A Performance in One Act (2012 CCCC Chair's Address)." *College Composition and Communication* 64, no. 2 (2012): 383–406.

Powell, Malea, Daisy Levy, Andrea Riley-Mukavetz, Marilee Brooks-Gillies, Maria Novotny, Jennifer Fisch-Ferguson, and Cultural Rhetorics Theory Lab. "Our Story Begins Here: Constellating Cultural Rhetorics." *Enculturation* 18 (2014). http://enculturation.net/our-story-begins-here.

Powers, Richard E. "Medical and Psychiatric Management of Fecal Smearing in Adult Persons with Mental Retardation and Developmental Disabilities (MR/DD)." Alabama Department of Mental Health and Mental Retardation, 2005. http://www.ddmed.org/pdfs/26.pdf.

Premack, David, and Guy Woodruff. "Does the Chimpanzee Have a Theory of Mind?" *Behavioral and Brain Sciences* 1, no. 4 (1978): 515–26.

Prendergast, Catherine. "On the Rhetorics of Mental Disability." In *Embodied Rhetorics: Disability in Language and Culture*, edited by James C. Wilson and Cynthia Lewiecki-Wilson, 45–60. Carbondale: Southern Illinois University Press, 2001.

Price, Margaret. "The Bodymind Problem and the Possibilities of Pain." *Hypatia* 30, no. 1 (2015): 268–84.

———. "'Her Pronouns Wax and Wane': Psychosocial Disability, Autobiography, and Counter-diagnosis." *Journal of Literary and Cultural Disability Studies* 3, no. 1 (2009): 11–33.

———. *Mad at School: Rhetorics of Mental Disability and Academic Life*. Ann Arbor: University of Michigan Press, 2010.

———. "The Politics of the Portal." In *Cripping the Computer: A Critical Moment in Composition Studies*, edited by Elizabeth Brewer and Melanie Yergeau. Unpublished manuscript, 2017.

Prince-Hughes, Dawn. *Circus of Souls: How I Discovered That We Are All Freaks Passing as Normal.* CreateSpace, 2013.

———. *Songs of the Gorilla Nation: My Journey through Autism.* New York: Harmony, 2005.

Prizant, Barry M. "Straight Talk about Autism: Treatment Options and Parent Choice: Is ABA the Only Way?" *Autism Spectrum Quarterly*, spring 2009.

Pryal, Katie Rose Guest. "The Genre of the Mood Memoir and the Ethos of Psychiatric Disability." *Rhetoric Society Quarterly* 40, no. 5 (2010): 479–501.

Puar, Jasbir K. "Prognosis Time: Towards a Geopolitics of Affect, Debility and Capacity." *Women and Performance: A Journal of Feminist Theory* 19, no. 2 (2009): 161–72.

———. *Terrorist Assemblages: Homonationalism in Queer Times.* Durham, NC: Duke University Press, 2007.

Pyne, Jake. "The Governance of Gender Non-conforming Children: A Dangerous Enclosure." *Annual Review of Critical Psychology* 11 (2014): 79–96.

Randi, Judi, Tina Newman, and Elena L. Grigorenko. "Teaching Children with Autism to Read for Meaning: Challenges and Possibilities." *Journal of Autism and Developmental Disorders* 40, no. 7 (2010): 890–902.

Rawson, K. J. "Queering Feminist Rhetorical Canonization." In *Rhetorica in Motion: Feminist Rhetorical Methods and Methodologies*, edited by Eileen E. Schell and K. J. Rawson, 39–52. Pittsburgh: University of Pittsburgh Press, 2010.

Reid, Alex. "Composing Objects: Prospects for a Digital Rhetoric." *Enculturation* 14 (2012). http://enculturation.net/composing-objects.

Rekers, George A. *Growing Up Straight: What Every Family Should Know about Homosexuality.* Chicago: Moody, 1982.

———. Professor George.com. Archive.org, 2011. https://web.archive.org/web/2011 0208224932/http://www.professorgeorge.com/ProfessorGeorge.com/Welcome_to_ ProfessorGeorge.com.html.

———. "Review of Research on Homosexual Parenting, Adoption, and Foster Parenting." NARTH, 2004. https://web.archive.org/web/20080228024533/http://www.narth.com /docs/RationaleBasisFinal0405.pdf.

———. *Shaping Your Child's Sexual Identity.* Grand Rapids, MI: Baker, 1982.

Rekers, George A., Peter M. Bentler, Alexander C. Rosen, and O. Ivar Lovaas. "Child Gender Disturbances: A Clinical Rationale for Intervention." *Psychotherapy: Theory, Research, and Practice* 14, no. 1 (1977): 2–11.

Rekers, George A., and O. Ivar Lovaas. "Behavioral Treatment of Deviant Sex-Role Behaviors in a Male Child." *Journal of Applied Behavior Analysis* 7, no. 2 (1974): 173–90.

Rekers, George A., Alexander C. Rosen, O. Ivar Lovaas, and Peter M. Bentler. "Sex-Role Stereotypy and Professional Intervention for Childhood Gender Disturbance." *Professional Psychology* 9, no. 1 (1978): 127–36.

Rekers, George A., Judith A. Sanders, and Cyd C. Strauss. "Developmental Differentiation of Adolescent Body Gestures." *Journal of Genetic Psychology* 138 (1981): 123–31.

Rekers, George A., Cindy E. Yates, Thomas J. Willis, Alexander C. Rosen, and Mitchell Taubman. "Childhood Gender Identity Change: Operant Control over Sex-Typed Play and Mannerisms." *Journal of Behavioral Therapy and Experimental Psychiatry* 7 (1976): 51–57.

Rentenbach, Barb R., and Lois A. Prislovsky. *I Might Be You: An Exploration of Autism and Connection.* Author, 2012.

Ribas, Denys. "Autism as the Defusion of Drives." *International Journal of Psychoanalysis* 79 (1998): 529–38.

Rice, Laura N., and Robert Elliott. *Facilitating Emotional Change: The Moment-by-Moment Process.* New York: Guilford, 1993.

Richter, Zach. *Awkward Gestures* (blog), 2015. http://zachrichter.weebly.com/awkward -gestures-blog.

Rickert, Thomas. *Ambient Rhetoric: The Attunements of Rhetorical Being.* Pittsburgh: University of Pittsburgh Press, 2013.

Riley-Mukavetz, Andrea. "On Working from or with Anger: Or How I Learned to Listen to My Relatives and Practice All Our Relations." *Enculturation* 21 (2016). http:// enculturation.net/on-working-from-or-with-anger.

Rimland, Bernard. "Editorial: Recovery Is Possible." *Autism Research Review International* 8, no. 2 (1994): 3.

———. "Foreword." In *Emergence: Labelled Autistic*, by Temple Grandin and Margaret Scariano, 1–4. New York: Warner, 1986.

———. *Infantile Autism: The Syndrome and Its Implications for a Neural Theory of Behavior.* New York: Appleton-Century-Crofts, 1964.

———. "A Risk/Benefit Perspective on the Use of Aversives." *Journal of Autism and Childhood Schizophrenia* 8, no. 1 (1978): 100–104.

Robinson, Elise B., Karestan C. Koenen, Marie C. McCormick, Kerim Munir, Victoria Hallett, Francesca Happé, Robert Plomin, and Angelica Ronald. "A Multivariate Twin Study of Autistic Traits in 12-Year-Olds: Testing the Fractionable Autism Triad Hypothesis." *Behavior Genetics* 42, no. 2 (2012): 245–55.

Rodas, Julia Miele. *Autistic Disturbances: Theorizing Autism Poetics from the DSM to Robinson Crusoe.* Ann Arbor: University of Michigan Press, forthcoming.

———. "Diagnosable: Mothering at the Threshold of Disability." In *Disability and Mothering: Liminal Spaces of Embodied Knowledge*, edited by Cynthia Lewiecki-Wilson and Jen Cellio, 113–26. Syracuse, NY: Syracuse University Press, 2011.

———. "'On the Spectrum': Rereading Contact and Affect in Jane Eyre." *Nineteenth-Century Gender Studies* 4, no. 2 (2008). http://www.ncgsjournal.com/issue42/rodas.htm.

Rodriguez, Nicole M., Rachel H. Thompson, Kevin Schlichenmeyer, and Corey S. Stocco. "Functional Analysis and Treatment of Arranging and Ordering by Individuals with an Autism Spectrum Disorder." *Journal of Applied Behavior Analysis* 45, no. 1 (2012): 1–22.

Rofes, Eric. *A Radical Rethinking of Sexuality and Schooling: Status Quo or Status Queer?* Lanham, MD: Rowman and Littlefield, 2005.

Rogers, Sally J., and Geraldine Dawson. *Early Start Denver Model for Young Children with Autism: Promoting Language, Learning, and Engagement.* New York: Guilford, 2010.

Rorvik, David Michael. "The Gender Enforcers: Seeing to It the Boys Will Be Boys." *Rolling Stone*, October 9, 1975.

Rose, Irene. "Autistic Autobiography or Autistic Life Narrative?" *Journal of Literary Disability* 2, no. 1 (2008): 44–54.

Royster, Jacqueline Jones, and Gesa E. Kirsch. *Feminist Rhetorical Practices: New Horizons for Rhetoric, Composition, and Literacy Studies.* Carbondale: Southern Illinois University Press, 2012.

Rushbrook, Dereka. "Cities, Queer Space, and the Cosmopolitan Tourist." GLQ: *A Journal of Lesbian and Gay Studies* 8, nos. 1–2 (2002): 183–206.

Ruttenberg, Bertram A., and Enid G. Wolf. "Evaluating the Communication of the Autistic Child." *Journal of Speech and Hearing Disorders* 32, no. 4 (1967): 314–24.

Ryan, Beth. "Touch Nose. Gummi Bear: ABA in Our Family." *Love Explosions* (blog), September 13, 2013. http://loveexplosions.net/2013/09/13/touch-nose-gummi-bear-aba-in-our-family/.

Ryan, Marie-Laure. "Narratology and Cognitive Science: A Problematic Relation." *Style* 44, no. 4 (2010): 469–95.

Ryskamp, Dani. *Field Notes on Allistics* (blog), 2015. http://fieldnotesonallistics.tumblr.com/.

Salamon, Gayle. *Assuming a Body: Transgender and Rhetorics of Materiality.* New York: Columbia University Press, 2010.

Savarese, Ralph J. "Moving the Field: The Sensorimotor Perspective on Autism (Commentary on 'Rethinking Autism: Implications of Sensory and Motor Differences,' an Article by Anne Donnellan, David Hill, and Martha Leary)." *Frontiers in Integrative Neuroscience* 7 (2013). http://journal.frontiersin.org/article/10.3389/fnint.2013.00006/full.

Savarese, Ralph J., and Lisa Zunshine. "The Critic as Neurocosmopolite; Or, What Cognitive Approaches to Literature Can Learn from Disability Studies." *Narrative* 22, no. 1 (2014): 17–44.

Schaffner, Kenneth F. "Reduction and Reductionism in Psychiatry." In *The Oxford Handbook of Philosophy and Psychiatry*, edited by K. W. M. Fulford, Martin Davies, Richard G. T. Gipps, George Graham, John Z. Sadler, Giovanni Stanghellini, and Tim Thornton, 1004–22. Oxford: Oxford University Press, 2013.

Schalk, Sami. "Coming to Claim Crip: Disidentification with/in Disability Studies." *Disability Studies Quarterly* 33, no. 2 (2013). http://dsq-sds.org/article/view/3705/3240.

Schiappa, Edward. "Second Thoughts on the Critiques of Big Rhetoric." *Philosophy and Rhetoric* 34, no. 3 (2001): 260–75.

Schuler, A. "Beyond Echoplaylia: Promoting Language in Children with Autism." *Autism* 7, no. 4 (2003): 455–69.

Schwarz, Phil. "Building Alliances: Community Identity and the Role of Allies in Autistic Self-Advocacy." In *Ask and Tell: Self-Advocacy and Disclosure for People on the Autism Spectrum*, edited by Stephen M. Shore, 143–76. Shawnee Mission, KS: Autism Asperger, 2004.

Sequenzia, Amy. "Attitudes—Communication." *Ollibean* (blog), September 2, 2014. http://ollibean.com/2014/09/02/attitudes-communication/.

———. "My Uncooperative Body." *Autism Women's Network* (blog), October 28, 2013. http://autismwomensnetwork.org/my-uncooperative-body/.

———. "On Not Being 'Pretty.'" *Ollibean* (blog), August 5, 2015. http://ollibean.com/on-not-being-pretty/.

Shakespeare, Tom. *Disability Rights and Wrongs.* New York: Routledge, 2006.

Shakespeare, Tom, and Nicole Watson. "The Social Model of Disability: An Outdated Ideology?" In *Research in Social Science and Disability: Exploring Theories and Expanding Methodologies: Where We Are and Where We Need to Go,* edited by Sharon N. Barnartt and Barbara M. Altman, 2:9–28. Bingley, U.K.: Emerald Group, 2001.

Shanker, Stuart, and Stanley Greenspan. *The First Idea: How Symbols, Language, and Intelligence Evolved from Our Primate Ancestors to Modern Humans.* Cambridge, MA: Da Capo, 2004.

Shattuck, Roger. *The Forbidden Experiment: The Story of the Wild Boy of Aveyron.* New York: Farrar, Straus and Giroux, 1980.

Shelton, Deborah L. "Autism Doctor Loses License in Illinois, Missouri." *Chicago Tribune,* November 5, 2012. http://articles.chicagotribune.com/2012-11-05/news/ct-met-autism-doctor-20121106_1_autism-doctor-david-geier-mark-geier.

Shore, Stephen. *Beyond the Wall: Personal Experiences with Autism and Asperger Syndrome.* 2nd ed. Shawnee Mission, KS: Autism Asperger, 2003.

Sibley, Kassiane. "Feminist Wire, You May Not Colonize My Community." *Radical Neurodivergence Speaking* (blog), August 29, 2013. http://timetolisten.blogspot.com/2013/08/feminist-wire-you-may-not-colonize-my.html.

———. "The Helper Personality Scares Me." *Radical Neurodivergence Speaking* (blog), July 16, 2013. http://timetolisten.blogspot.com/2013/07/the-helper-personality-scares-me.html.

———. "Indistinguishable from Peers—an Introduction." *Radical Neurodivergence Speaking* (blog), September 13, 2013. http://timetolisten.blogspot.com/2013/09/indistinguishable-from-peers.html.

Siebers, Tobin. *Disability Theory.* Ann Arbor: University of Michigan Press, 2008.

Silberman, Steve. "The Geek Syndrome." *Wired,* December 1, 2001. https://www.wired.com/2001/12/aspergers/.

———. *Neurotribes: The Legacy of Autism and the Future of Neurodiversity.* New York: Avery, 2015.

Silin, Jonathan G. *Sex, Death, and the Education of Children: Our Passion for Ignorance in the Age of AIDS.* New York: Teachers College Press, 1995.

Silverman, Chloe. *Understanding Autism: Parents, Doctors, and the History of a Disorder.* Princeton, NJ: Princeton University Press, 2012.

Sinclair, Jim. "Don't Mourn for Us." Autism Network International, 1993. http://www.autreat.com/dont_mourn.html.

Sinwell, Sarah E. S. "Aliens and Asexuality: Media Representation, Queerness, and Asexual Visibility." In *Asexualities: Feminist and Queer Perspectives,* edited by Karli J. Cerankowski and Megan Milks, 162–73. New York: Routledge, 2014.

Skinner, B. F. "Pigeons in a Pelican." *American Psychologist* 15, no. 1 (1960): 28–37.

Skolnik, Christine. "Rhetoric and the Plastic Brain." Unpublished manuscript, 2012.

Smith, Craig R. *Rhetoric and Human Consciousness: A History*. 4th ed. Long Grove, IL: Waveland, 2013.

Smith, Joel. "Smearing of Feces: How Common Is It?" *Evil Autie: Musings from an Autistic Who Refuses to Be "Good"* (blog), April 6, 2014. http://evilautie.org/2014/04/06 /smearing-of-feces-how-common-is-it/.

Smith Myles, Brenda, and Richard L. Simpson. "Understanding the Hidden Curriculum: An Essential Social Skill for Children and Youth with Asperger Syndrome." *Intervention in School and Clinic* 36, no. 5 (2001).

Smukler, David. "Unauthorized Minds: How 'Theory of Mind' Theory Misrepresents Autism." *Mental Retardation* 43, no. 1 (2005): 11–24.

Snyder, Craig, and Peter Bell. "To Petition the Government for a Redress of Grievances." In *Autism Spectrum Disorders*, edited by David Amaral, Daniel Geschwind, and Geraldine Dawson, 1369–76. Oxford: Oxford University Press, 2011.

Spotnitz, Hyman. *Psychotherapy of Preoedipal Conditions: Schizophrenia and Severe Character Disorders*. Lanham, MD: Jason Aronson, 1976.

Steph. "Why I Left ABA." *Socially Anxious Advocate* (blog), May 22, 2015. https:// sociallyanxiousadvocate.wordpress.com/2015/05/22/why-i-left-aba/.

Steudeman, Michael J. "Entelechy and Irony in Political Time: The Preemptive Rhetoric of Nixon and Obama." *Rhetoric and Public Affairs* 16, no. 1 (2013): 59–96.

St. Pierre, Joshua. "Distending Straight-Masculine Time: A Phenomenology of the Disabled Speaking Body." *Hypatia* 30, no. 1 (2015): 49–65.

Sullivan, Ruth Christ. "Risks and Benefits in the Treatment of Autistic Children: Introduction." *Journal of Autism and Childhood Schizophrenia* 8, no. 1 (1978): 99–100.

Tager-Flusberg, Helen. "Autistic Children's Talk about Psychological States: Deficits in the Early Acquisition of a Theory of Mind." *Child Development* 63, no. 1 (1992): 161–72.

———. "Language and Understanding Minds: Connections in Autism." In *Understanding Other Minds: Perspectives from Developmental Cognitive Neuroscience*, 2nd ed., edited by Simon Baron-Cohen, Helen Tager-Flusberg, and Donald J. Cohen, 124–49. Oxford: Oxford University Press, 2000.

Tanner, Lindsey. "Shock Treatment Sought for Autistic Man." *Washington Post*, March 14, 2007. http://www.washingtonpost.com/wp-dyn/content/article/2007/03/14 /AR2007031401732_pf.html.

Thompson, Travis. "Autism and Behavior Analysis: History and Current Status." In *The Wiley Blackwell Handbook of Operant and Classical Conditioning*, edited by Frances K. McSweeney and Eric S. Murphy, 483–508. Malden, MA: Wiley-Blackwell, 2014.

Thornton, Davi Johnson. *Brain Culture: Neuroscience and Popular Media*. New Brunswick, NJ: Rutgers University Press, 2011.

Tustin, Frances. *Autism and Childhood Psychosis*. London: Karnac, 1995.

———. *Autistic Barriers in Neurotic Patients*. London: Karnac, 1986.

Ultra, Meredith K. "I'm Sorry, but That's Not Earning Your Token." *Ink and Daggers* (blog), February 25, 2015. http://ink-and-daggers.tumblr.com/post/112076858794/im -sorry-but-thats-not-earning-your-token.

———. "Untitled." *Ink and Daggers* (blog), February 25, 2015. http://ink-and-daggers .tumblr.com/post/127321531039.

UPIAS, and the Disability Alliance. "Fundamental Principles of Disability." Edited by Mark Priestley, Vic Finkelstein, and Ken Davis. Centre for Disability Studies, University of Leeds, 1975. http://disability-studies.leeds.ac.uk/files/library/UPIAS -fundamental-principles.pdf.

U.S. Government Accountability Office. "Federal Autism Research: Updated Information on Funding from Fiscal Years 2008 through 2012." Report. Washington, DC: U.S. Government Accountability Office, June 30, 2015. http://www.gao.gov/products/GAO -15-583R.

Valente, Joseph M., Benjamin Bahan, and H-Dirksen L. Bauman. "Sensory Politics and the Cochlear Implant Debates." In *Cochlear Implants: Evolving Perspectives*, edited by Raylene Paludneviciene and Irene W. Leigh, 245–58. Washington, DC: Gallaudet University Press, 2011.

Vermeulen, Peter. *Autism as Context Blindness*. Shawnee Mission, KS: Autism Asperger, 2012.

———. "Context Blindness in Autism Spectrum Disorder: Not Using the Forest to See the Trees as Trees." *Focus on Autism and Other Developmental Disabilities* 30, no. 3 (2015): 25.

Vitanza, Victor. "Writing the Tic." *Kairos* 12, no. 3 (2008). http://kairos.technorhetoric .net/12.3/topoi/gallery/index.html.

Wade, Cheryl Marie. "I Am Not One of The." In *The Disability Studies Reader*, 4th ed., edited by Lennard J. Davis, 526. New York: Routledge, 2013.

Walker, Nick. "Aikido, Somatics, and Liberation of the Autistic Self." In *Scholars with Autism Achieving Dreams*, edited by Lars Perner, 93–112. Sedona, AZ: Auricle, 2012.

———. "Neuroqueer: An Introduction." *Neurocosmopolitanism* (blog), May 2, 2014. http:// neurocosmopolitanism.com/neuroqueer-an-introduction/.

———. "Throw Away the Master's Tools: Liberating Ourselves from the Pathology Paradigm." *Neurocosmopolitanism* (blog), August 16, 2013. http://neurocosmopolitanism .com/throw-away-the-masters-tools-liberating-ourselves-from-the-pathology -paradigm/.

Walters, Shannon. "Animal Athena: The Interspecies Mētis of Women Writers with Autism." *JAC* 30, nos. 3–4 (2010): 683–711.

———. *Rhetorical Touch: Disability, Identification, Haptics*. Columbia: University of South Carolina Press, 2014.

Weaver, Richard M. *The Ethics of Rhetoric*. Chicago: Henry Regnery, 1953.

Webster, Travis. "Pray the Gay Away: Rhetorical Dilemmas of the American Ex-Gay Movement." PhD diss., Michigan State University, 2012.

Willey, Liane H. *Pretending to Be Normal: Living with Asperger's Syndrome*. London: Jessica Kingsley, 1999.

———. *Safety Skills for Asperger Women: How to Save a Perfectly Good Female Life*. Philadelphia: Jessica Kingsley, 2012.

Williams, David. "Theory of *Own* Mind in Autism: Evidence of a Specific Deficit in Self-Awareness?" *Autism* 14, no. 5 (2010): 474–94.

Williams, David M., and Dermot M. Bowler. "Autism Spectrum Disorder: Fractionable or Coherent?" *Autism* 18, no. 1 (2014): 2–5.

Williams, Donna. *Autism and Sensing: The Unlost Instinct*. London: Jessica Kingsley, 1998.

Wilson, James C. *Weather Reports from the Autism Front: A Father's Memoir of His Autistic Son*. Jefferson, NC: McFarland, 2008.

Wilson, James C., and Cynthia Lewiecki-Wilson. *Embodied Rhetorics: Disability in Language and Culture*. Carbondale: Southern Illinois University Press, 2001.

Winerman, Lea. "Autism Diagnoses Bring Slew of Costs for Families." PBS *News Hour*, April 13, 2011, http://www.pbs.org/newshour/updates/health-jan-june11-autismcosts_04-13/.

Wing, Lorna. "Asperger's Syndrome: A Clinical Account." *Psychological Medicine* 11 (1981): 115–29.

Wing, Lorna, Judith Gould, and Christopher Gillberg. "Autism Spectrum Disorders in the DSM-V: Better or Worse than the DSM-IV?" *Research in Developmental Disabilities* 32, no. 2 (2011): 768–73.

Wired Staff. "Take the AQ Test." *Wired*, December 2001. https://www.wired.com/2001/12/aqtest/.

Woodill, Gary. "Controlling the Sexuality of Developmentally Disabled Persons: Historical Perspectives." *Journal on Developmental Disabilities* 1, no. 1 (1992): 1–14.

Woodward, Gary C. *The Perfect Response: Studies of the Rhetorical Personality*. Lanham, MD: Lexington, 2010.

Wright, Suzanne. "Autism Changes Everything." *Parade*, January 27, 2008. https://web.archive.org/web/20081202080054/http://www.parade.com/articles/editions/2008/edition_01-27-2008/Autism_Changes_Everything.

———. "Autism Speaks to Washington—a Call for Action." Autism Speaks, November 11, 2013. https://www.autismspeaks.org/news/news-item/autism-speaks-washington-call-action.

———. "Transcript—Suzanne Wright Speaks at the Vatican." *Unstrange Mind* (blog), 2014. https://unstrangemind.wordpress.com/transcripts/transcript-suzanne-wright-speaks-at-the-vatican/.

Yergeau, Melanie, Elizabeth Brewer, Stephanie Kerschbaum, Sushil Oswal, Margaret Price, Michael Salvo, Cynthia L. Selfe, and Franny Howes. "Multimodality in Motion: Disability and Kairotic Spaces." *Kairos: A Journal of Rhetoric, Technology, and Pedagogy* 18, no. 1 (2013). http://kairos.technorhetoric.net/18.1/coverweb/yergeau-et-al/index.html.

Ypma, Rolf J. F., Rachel L. Moseley, Rosemary J. Holt, Naresh Rughooputh, Dorothea L. Floris, Lindsay R. Chura, Michael D. Spencer, et al. "Default Mode Hypoconnectivity Underlies a Sex-Related Autism Spectrum." *Biological Psychiatry: Cognitive Neuroscience and Neuroimaging* 1, no. 4 (2016): 364–71.

Zahavi, Dan, and Josef Parnas. "Conceptual Problems in Infantile Autism Research: Why Cognitive Science Needs Phenomenology." *Journal of Consciousness Studies* 10, nos. 9–10 (2003): 53–71.

Zelan, Karen. *Between Their World and Ours: Breakthroughs with Autistic Children*. New York: St. Martin's, 2003.

Žižek, Slavoj. *The Sublime Object of Ideology*. London: Verso, 1989.

Zuckerman, Katherine E., Kimber Mattox, Karen Donelan, Oyundari Batbayar, Anita Baghaee, and Christina Bethell. "Pediatrician Identification of Latino Children at Risk for Autism Spectrum Disorder." *Pediatrics* 132, no. 3 (2013): 445–53.

Zunshine, Lisa. *Strange Concepts and the Stories They Make Possible: Cognition, Culture, Narrative.* Baltimore, MD: Johns Hopkins University Press, 2011.

———. "Theory of Mind and Fictions of Embodied Transparency." *Narrative* 16, no. 1 (2008): 66–92.

Zurcher, Ariane. "Scripts—a Communication Bridge." *Emma's Hope Book* (blog), October 9, 2014. http://emmashopebook.com/2014/10/09/scripts-a-communication-bridge/.

———. "Tackling That Troublesome Issue of ABA and Ethics." *Emma's Hope Book* (blog), October 10, 2012. http://emmashopebook.com/2012/10/10/tackling-that-troublesome-issue-of-aba-and-ethics/.

Zurcher, Ariane, and Emma Zurcher-Long. "Intention." *Emma's Hope Book* (blog), September 9, 2014. http://emmashopebook.com/2014/09/09/intention/.

Zurcher-Long, Emma. "The Fan Stays off." *Emma's Hope Book* (blog), April 9, 2015. http://emmashopebook.com/2015/04/09/the-fan-stays-off/.

Ciaramidaro, Angela, 46
circuitous logic, 11, 19, 36, 173
cisnormativity, 159–60, 185
civil rights rhetoric, 108, 152, 179–80
Clare, Eli, 248n70
clinical logics, 2–3, 6, 14, 32; best of both
    worlds, too high- or low-functioning, 32,
    50–51; as echolalic, 197; reductionist moves,
    51–52
closed-fist metaphor, 152–53, 171
Cloud, Dana L., 146–47
coalitional histories, 179–80, 208–9
cognitive modules, 4, 19–20, 58
cognitive studies, 7, 22, 26, 91–92, 212
Cohen-Rottenberg, Rachel, 151, 194, 204
Collomosse, John, 69, 225n37
colonial rhetoric, 117
"coming aut," 160–68
Coming Out Asperger (Murray), 162
compliance and coercion, domain of, 10, 18,
    106, 124–25, 195. See also applied behavior
    analysis (ABA)
concentration camp analogy, 14
consumer/survivor/ex-patient (c/s/x) move-
    ment, 115–16, 145
contamination, racist and transmisogynist, 18
context, 137–39
continua, 225n37; autism-allism (or self-other)
    continuum, 45, 51; freeze-framed points, 45,
    45, 52–53, 63–64, 151, 167, 182; of impair-
    ment, 45, 47, 51; social brain continuum, 69.
    See also spectra
Conversations on Autism and Sign Language
    (CASL), 208, 209
Cook, Jennifer, 196–97
Corbett, Edward, 142, 152–53, 171
corporal punishment, 97, 103, 120–21, 125
counter-diagnosis, 140, 161, 165, 169, 212
counter-rhetoric, 25, 149
countersocial rhetorics, 67–73, 69, 71
Couser, G. Thomas, 224n12
crip culture, 67, 109–10, 188
cripple, as term, 85
crip-queer rhetorics, 27, 84–85, 129, 173, 192
crip theory, 41, 67, 85
crip time, 188
crisis, rhetorics of, 10–11
"critical period disorder," 132
critical race theory, 109
Cruising Utopia (Muñoz), 18
cult leaders, 77
Cultural Rhetorics Theory Lab, 45

culture, 161
curb cuts, 107, 109
Curious Incident of the Dog in the Night-Time, The
    (Haddon), 89–90, 116
Curious Incident of the Vote at the Book Club, 89
Cutler, Eustacia, 155

Daggar, Rajiv, 69, 225n37
data-driven interventions, 95, 96, 101, 105–6
Davide-Rivera, Jeannie, 117
Davis, Diane, 67, 71
Davis, Lennard, 40, 86
Dawson, Michelle, 116, 119
Day, Elaine, 124
deadening, 56, 110, 129
Deaf culture, 179, 180, 208, 209, 253n17,
    253n22, 259n5
Deaf Gain, 180
Deaf Gain (Bauman and Murray), 180
Deaf Subjects: Between Identities and Places
    (Brueggemann), 153
death, 79–80, 97, 234n205
death, trope of, 14, 73, 78; narrative entelechy,
    75–76; worse-than-death, 73, 79–80, 119
death drive, 74, 76, 78
debility and capacity, 48–49
Decker, Julie Sondra, 255n43
dehumanization, 9–10, 34, 38–39, 77
Deleuze, Gilles, 13, 52
demi figure, 178
demigenders, 33, 178, 186, 254–55n41
demi-rhetoricity, 32, 33, 58, 178; autistic fuck
    yous, 91–92; continuum of impairment, 45,
    47, 51; Deaf Gain, 180; duration and, 187–88;
    fractionable autism theories, 47–48, 64; leg-
    ible through bodily behavior, 63; neoliberal
    ideologies and, 48–50; as non-rhetoricity, 46;
    paradoxes of motion and, 43–52; queering,
    178, 182–84; re/claiming, 182–92; self-
    surveillance and, 128; social models used
    to support, 105
demisexualities, 33, 178, 189, 190–91
demi-symbolicity, 56
desexualization, 30, 190, 191–92
destruction, as autistic method, 78–79
developmental disability, autism as, 42
developmentalism, 131–32, 155, 202
diagnosis: in adulthood, 156, 163–65; cisnor-
    mativity of, 159–60; counter-diagnosis, 140,
    161, 165, 169, 212; DSM criteria, 20; girls,
    women, and nonbinary-identifying individu-
    als, 123; losing, 124; modern, development

of, 42, 73–74; neuroqueer culture created from, 67; neuroqueering, 168–72; as process, 160, 162, 168; race issues, 156–57; refusal of, 165–66; self-diagnosis, 163, 166–67; as storytelling, 1–2

*Diagnostic and Statistical Manual of Mental Disorders (DSM)*, 20

diagnostic looping, 66

dialectic, 151, 152

dichotomies, 84, 85

difference, 160

diplomatic rhetoric, 149–54

disability: impairment, distinctions between, 107; as rhetorical condition, 66, 90–91; rhetorics (inter)dependent on, 87

disability culture, 21, 40, 109

disability rhetorics, 19, 41, 84

disability rights activism, 85, 108, 179–80

disability rights rhetoric: Lovaas's use of, 95, 111–12; social model of disability, 106–7

disability studies: as narrativistic field, 26; paradoxes engaged by, 48–49; social model of disability, 107–9

disabled subject, 9

disbelief, 25

disclosure, 33, 137–38, 206, 244n6; diplomacy and, 151–53; embodied effects, 140–41; inferences, 141–42; as metonym for diagnostic assessment, 138, 139, 142, 147–48, 172; performative understanding of, 183; residual effects, 20; rhetorically charged, 140–41; violence done by, 146, 153, 158, 180, 191–92

discrete trials, 96–97, 113, 121

disease comparisons, 7–8, 73, 119–20, 155–56, 231n144, 240n102, 248n65

disidentification, 85

disorientation, 27, 93, 182, 183, 188, 212, 225n37

dis-rhetoricity, 19

Dodd, Susan, 52

"Does the Autistic Child Have a Theory of Mind?" (Baron-Cohen, Leslie, and Frith), 21

Dolmage, Jay, 19, 27–28, 54, 62, 84, 99, 108; mētis, 41, 76

Donnellan, Anne, 65

Don't Ask, Don't Tell policy (U.S. military), 161

Dorner, Rebecca, 1–2, 3, 6

drag, ABA as inversion of, 123

Driskill, Qwo-Li, 77

DSM-5, 161, 224n24

Duffy, John, 1–2, 3, 6

duration, 65–66, 90, 110, 187–88, 198

Dussauge, Isabelle, 58–59

E (autistic blogger), 189–90

early intensive behavioral intervention (EIBI), 26

early intervention discourse, 131–32

Eastham, David, 21

echoing, 55

echolalia, 34, 62, 74, 98, 178, 184, 193, 208; affect and, 195–96. *See also* language, autistic

echophenomena, 178–79, 182, 193–94; echographia, 194; echomimia, 193, 197; echoplasia, 194; echopraxia, 178, 193; as mediated disruption, 197; as reverbing, 199

echophenomenology, 193–99

Ede, Lisa, 60

Edelman, Lee, 78

Ed Wiley Lending Library, 39

Electric Light Orchestra, 22, 98, 246n39, 251n103

electric shock, 97, 112, 120, 149

elliptic rhetoric, 33, 139, 140–44, 149, 155, 172–73

embodied communication, 181, 195–96

emergence, 20

*Emergence: Labelled Autistic* (Grandin), 21, 224n13

empathy: autistic, 117; sex-typed brain theories, 68–71, 69

*Empty Fortress, The* (Bettelheim), 79–80

Endow, Judy, 33, 140, 172–73, 194

England, autism prevalence, 163–64

entelechies, 38, 39–40, 65, 71, 133; autistic, 75; filamentlike, 79; finishedness, 75–77; identity, 160–61; meltdowns as, 176; narrative, 75–76; neural, 75, 78; normative, 75–78, 160; psychotic, 76–78; queer, 78–79, 93; of symbolic action, 75–77

environmentalism, 103–6, 115; immersion approach, 111–13, 125–26; practicing, 106–15; prosthetic environment, 103, 110, 112, 117, 125; rhetorics of, 120–21; total environment, 110, 115

ephemeral rhetoricity, 38, 39, 51, 178

epidemic, logics of, 27

epistemology, 54

Erevelles, Nirmala, 157, 179

essentialization, 2, 61, 68

*Ethics of Autism, The* (Barnbaum), 8

ethos, 42, 60–61, 139

eugenicist narratives, 28, 82, 141, 194

*Evil Autie* (Smith), 4

evolutionary psychology, 253n17

ex-ABA movement, 29, 115–16, 245n30

exceptionality, 21

involuntarity, 7–8; apraxia, 55; assumptions about willingness to share, 62; demi-rhetoricity and, 48; domains of, 7; entelechial understanding of, 71; god theories, 11–12; logics of, 9–10; as project of dehumanization, 10; violence wrought by, 9–10. *See also* theory of mind (ToM)

involution, 13, 20, 40, 179

irreducible relationality, 71–72

Itard, Jean-Marc Gaspard, 112, 209

*I Wish My Kids Had Cancer* (Alan), 73, 231n144

Jack, Jordynn, 4, 45, 69

Jacobs, Laura A., 185

Johnson, Jenell, 60, 139, 163

Jones, Sparrow R., 97, 124

*Journal of Applied Behavior Analysis*, 101

*Journal of Autism and Developmental Disorders*, 7

Judge Rotenberg Educational Center, 97, 121

Jurecic, Ann, 58

*Just Stimming* (Bascom), 34

Kafer, Alison, 19, 65, 85, 99, 129, 133, 188; on crip-queer kinship, 192

kairos, 62, 65–66, 138

kakoethos, 60–64, 65, 79, 139; counter-diagnosis, 163, 166–67, 172

kakokairos, 62, 79

Kanner, Leo, 28, 73, 74, 101, 210

Kawohl, W., 193

Kedar, Ido, 34, 55, 194

Keith, William, 137

Keller, Helen, 112, 209, 239n71

Kellogg, John Harvey, 28, 184

Kelter, M., 166–67

Kennedy, George A., 87, 91, 151

Kerschbaum, Stephanie, 160–61, 189

Kim, Cynthia, 34, 109, 154, 164–65, 197

Kim, Eunjung, 189

Kinneavy, James E., 54

Kinsey's continuum, 189

Kirsch, Gesa E., 54, 84

Kissine, Mikhail, 37

knowledge structures, 54, 202

"Kraig"/"Kyle" (Kirk Murphy), 29, 113–15, 125, 126, 127

Kramer, Corbin, 163

Krumins, Daina, 159

Kuppers, Petra, 154

Kurchak, Sarah, 73

Kuusisto, Stephen, 211

lack, autism represents, 7, 14, 50–51, 51, 59, 69, 133, 210. *See also* failure

Landrum-Geyer, Denise, 181

language, autistic, 7, 181, 193; access barriers, 83–84; brain studies, 58; idiolect, 209–10; mapping of brain, 57–58. *See also* echolalia; nonspeaking/nonwriting autistics

LaRue, Robert, 127

Latour, Bruno, 79

Latson, Reginald "Neli," 82–83

Lawson, Wenn, 17

Learn the Signs campaign (Autism Speaks), 7–8

LeBlanc, Jocelyn, 128–29, 132

Leslie, Alan, 21

*Let Me Hear Your Voice* (Maurice), 119

Lewiecki-Wilson, Cynthia, 107, 108, 232n155

*Life*, 102, 120

Lindsay (*Autist's Corner*), 23

Lindsay, Stan, 76–77

Lindsmith, Kirsten, 201

linear/developmental trajectories, 42, 45, 177; autism-allism (or self-other) continuum, 45, 51; queering of, 181, 182, 183, 188–89

literality, 22, 41, 52, 55–56, 59, 171

Lorde, Audre, 88

*Loud Hands: Autistics, Speaking*, 23

Loud Hands Project, 39

Lovaas, Ole Ivar, 16, 29, 32, 35, 95, 97, 109, 126, 207, 209, 240n98; *The Autistic Child*, 125; "Behavioral Treatment" retrospective, 118–19; devaluing of, 148–49; gender interventions, 98, 236n34; *Life* article, 102; rhetorical capacities as focus, 101–2; in *Rolling Stone*, 103; stereotypy, view of, 114–15; *Teaching Developmentally Disabled Children*, 110, 128

Lozano-Reich, Nina M., 146–47

Luckett, Tim, 10, 100

Lunsford, Andrea, 60

Lupron, 29

lusting, rhetorical, 192, 204

lying, rhetorical, 42, 43, 55, 62, 84, 86; attributed to neuronal motion, 58

mad pride, 115

*Making a Good Brain Great* (Amen), 130

Malabou, Catherine, 129, 133, 151, 188, 243n153

malignancy, 60

Manning, Erin, 17, 55, 134, 144

marginalized people, 29–30, 49, 85–86, 117–18, 244n6

Maroni, Lesley, 184

masking, 123

Massumi, Brian, 17, 52, 64, 66, 72

masturbation, 28, 184, 201–2

materiality, 56, 107–8

Mathison, Maureen, 148

Maurice, Catherine, 119

McAuliffe, Terry, 82

McBride, Melanie, 200–201, 202

McCabe, London, 80

McCallum, E. L., 67

McCarthy, Jenny, 16–17, 87, 163

McGee, Micki, 26

McGuire, Anne, 131–32

McKean, Thomas, 21

McRuer, Robert, 27, 85, 108, 219n41

Mead, Kit, 123

meaning, 13, 57, 205–6; ABA not concerned with, 128; embodied intentionality, 65; madness and, 78, 79; neuroqueer lives lack, 133; primacy of, 83–88; privileging of, 13, 83, 86; queer rhetoric and, 84; in rhetorical studies, 180–81; three levels, 87

mechanism, attributed to autism, 14, 16, 17, 19, 58, 220n54

media accounts, 2–3

medicalized storying, 7, 9

medical model of disability, 67, 107, 109

meltdowns, 55, 89, 175–77, 204

mental age, 155

mental disability, 10, 217–18n24; violence attributed to, 81

mental illness, 10, 29, 77

Menvielle, Edgardo, 185

mereness, 56

Merleau-Ponty, Maurice, 52, 57, 202

mestiza, 41, 177

metaphor, 54–55, 75

meta-stories, 9

mētis, 41, 76

Meyerding, Jane, 159

Michaels-Dillon, Athena Lynn, 27

Miedzianik, David, 21

Miller, Carolyn, 81

Miller, Jean Kearns, 159

mindblindness, 12, 15, 16, 18–19, 27, 54, 143

mind-body disconnection, 195

"Misbehaviour of Behaviourists, The" (Dawson), 116

misdiagnosis, 156–57, 248n70

Modified Checklist for Autism in Toddlers, 158

modularity, 19–20, 47, 58, 125

Moon-Robinson, Kayleb, 157–58

morality: in ABA, 104, 128, 146–47; allistic as superior, 143; autism as moral failing, 39, 182; eradicating autism as moral good, 99

Morris, David, 77, 202, 203

motion, autistic, 1, 8, 13, 31; continuity of, 72–73; as drive, 37–38, 232n155; duration and disconnection, 65–66; languaging/apraxia, 55; motion/action dichotomy, 56, 63–66; as neuronal, 4, 15, 59; as nonsymbolic, 15, 17; paradoxes of, 43–52; perception and, 55–56; rocking, 56; sidling, rhetorical, 18, 19, 41, 76, 92; striving, 75–77; Zeno's paradoxes, 43–47, 44, 45. See also bodies/bodymind; sensorimotor schemas

motion/action dichotomy, 56, 63–66

motor planning, 195

motor schemas, 179, 182

MSSNG, 54, 227n69

Mukaddes, N. M., 185

Mukhopadhyay, Tito, 55

Muñoz, José Esteban, 18, 38, 51–52, 78, 177, 178, 182; queerness as not-yet-here, 39, 85, 182

murders of autistic people, 79–80, 82, 234n205

Murphy, Kaytee, 113–15

Murphy, Kirk ("Kraig"/"Kyle"), 29, 113–15, 125, 126, 127

Murray, Dinah, 139, 162, 165

Murray, Jeffrey, 146

Murray, Joseph, 180

*Musings of an Aspie* (Kim), 34

*My Autobiography* (Miedzianik), 21

Myles, Brenda Smith, 33, 140, 172

narrative methodologies, 26

National Association for Research and Therapy of Homosexuality (NARTH), 104

National Society for Autistic Children, 112

negativistic terminology, 4

neoliberalism, 48–50, 130, 253n17

neurodivergence, 7, 10, 19, 169, 217–18n24

*neurodiversity*, 4

neuro-hegemonies, 88

neurons, entelechial, 78

neuroplastic logics, 130–31

*NeuroQueer* blog, 23, 148

neuroqueerness: abject potentiality of, 7, 18, 41–42; as contested site, 26–27; diagnosis and, 67, 168–72; interrelation of disability and queerness, 99–100; inventing, 176–82; overwriting of, 33, 100, 128, 208; practicing, 116–17, 144; resistance to definition, 27;

rhetoric: as art of persuasion, 13, 14, 54;
   autistics occluded from, 5–6, 10, 12, 20, 43,
   36; braining, rejection of, 88; as circulation of power through discourse, 62, 205;
   constructs, 14; diplomatic, 149–54; as
   distribution, 18; domains of, 3, 6, 10, 13,
   18, 54; emergent capacity, 20; everythingness and everywhereness, 137, 192; failure
   and disability paired, 143–44; human-
   centeredness, 11, 13; invitational, 144–49;
   as meaningless, 87; neuroplastic logics,
   130–31; as obligation, 71; as precondition
   for humanness, 6, 11, 86; project of, 35, 38;
   resides/lies/lives, 35, 43, 92; thereness of,
   40–43
rhetorical action, 35, 71, 245n23; autistic motion
   and, 20, 64, 66, 102, 179; denied to autistics,
   10, 12, 20, 43
"rhetorical brain," 130
rhetorical degradation, 36, 38
rhetorical effects, 61, 86, 173, 248n65
rhetorical potentials of autism, 7, 18, 41–42
rhetorical practice, 90
Rhetorical Touch (Walters), 153
Rhetoric of Motives, A (Burke), 75
rhetoric of plasticity, 130–32
Rhetoric of Rhetoric, The (Booth), 81
rhetorics, voluntary, 6–13
rhetrickery, 54, 81
Rhodes, Jacqueline, 84
Rich, Adrienne, 131
Rickert, Thomas, 20, 86, 87
rigidity, attributed to autistics, 151–52
Riley-Mukavetz, Andrea, 77
Rimland, Bernard, 21, 78, 112, 121, 224n13,
   225n37
Risperdal, 244n13
Roberts, Ed, 85
Roberts, Jacqueline, 10, 100
Robison, John Elder, 249n78
rocking, 8, 56, 114, 176, 181, 197, 201
Rodas, Julia Miele, 28, 165–66
Rodriguez, Nicole M., 127
Rolling Stone, 103
Rose, Irene, 24
Rosen, Alexander C., 98
Royster, Jacqueline Jones, 54, 84
Rubin, Sue, 34, 205
Rushbrook, Dereka, 190
Ruttenberg, Bertram, 208
Ryan, Beth, 98
Ryskamp, Dani, 170–71

safe spaces, 146–49
Salamon, Gayle, 56–57
Sanchez, Raul, 88
saturation, 104, 110
savant-beings, 2–3
Savarese, D. J., 55
Savarese, Ralph, 195, 200, 244n14
Schalk, Sami, 85
schemas, 202
schēmata, 203–4
Schiappa, Edward, 137, 192
schizophrenia, 73, 168, 225n37
school-to-prison pipeline, 157
Schwarz, Phil, 199
Science of Evil, The (Baron-Cohen), 68, 69
"scientific sadness," 6
scientism, 58, 68
"Screams, Slaps, and Love: A Surprising,
   Shocking Treatment Helps Far-Gone Mental
   Cripples" (Life), 102
scripting, 53–54, 59, 197–98; nonfunctional
   scripts, 197
self-advocacy, 166–67
self-diagnosis, 163, 166–68
self-help manuals, 194
self-injurious behavior, 134, 144, 204–5; corporal punishment for, 120–21
self-narrating zoo exhibit, 173
sensorimotor schemas, 195, 200–205; self-
   injury, 204–5
Sequenzia, Amy, 34, 63, 203
severe/mild binaries, 25, 32, 51, 139
sex-role deviance, 123
"sex-role stereotypy," 114
sexuality, 178; as defiant, 56–57; moralistic
   approach to, 28
Shakespeare, Tom, 107–8
shaping, 96–97, 102, 125
Shaping Your Child's Sexual Identity (Rekers), 104
Shields, Aaron, 211
shit smearing, 3–4, 6–7, 14–15, 31, 62, 91,
   215–16n8; as communication, 17
shitty narratives, 3–4; "shock and outdo" approach, 4
Shore, Stephen, 161, 162, 249n78
Sibley, Kassiane, 2, 85, 128, 217n24
Siebers, Tobin, 108
signification, perceptual and symbolic, 54–55
sign languages, 259n5
Silberman, Steve, 150
Silverman, Chloe, 3, 102, 112
Simon, Herbert, 137

Sinclair, Jim, 169, 173, 192
Singer, Judy, 169
Sinwell, Sarah, 191
"Sissy Boy Syndrome," The (Green), 113, 115, 148
Skinner, B. F., 64, 129–30, 208, 209, 242n143
Skolnik, Christine, 130, 131–32, 217n23
slavery metaphor, 198–99
smiling example, 125
Smith, Craig, 6
Smith, Joel, 4
social bodies, 60
social brain continuum, 69
sociality, 6; compulsory, 27–28, 60; intentionality and, 36–38; lack of, 69
socially appropriate norms, 104
social model of disability, 67; disabled viewpoints, 106–17; used to discredit neuroqueer rhetorics, 104–5
social significance, 114–15
social skills curricula, 15
Social Stories, 15
social symbolic, 42
Social Thinking, 15
Songs of the Gorilla Nation (Prince), 17
Soon Will Come the Light (McKean), 21
spatiality, 41, 66, 139, 177
special education, as resegregation, 179
spectra, 40, 51; degree of rhetoricity, 91; as master trope for disability, 33, 50, 139; sexual, 189. See also continua
spray bottles of vinegar, 97, 122
squishes, 187–88
Stapleton, Kelli, 80
stereotypy, 13, 98, 201; gender variance as, 114–15; masking, 123. See also stimming (self-stimulation)
sterilization, 29
stimming (self-stimulation), 1, 34, 98, 144, 201–3. See also stereotypy
stimpoints, 178, 182
Stoddard, Melissa, 80
Stoller, Robert, 113, 209
storying, 1–2, 20–21, 24; narrating neuroqueer histories, 28–31
St. Pierre, Joshua, 68
straight time, 188
street cred, 167
striving, 75–77, 84
suicide, 29; autism worse than, 80–81; queer, 80, 95, 121
Sullivan, Annie, 112, 209, 239n71
Sullivan, Ruth, 121

surveillance, 94, 96, 100, 105–6; gender-checking self-governance, 123–24, 128; of gender-variant children, 125–28; practicing, 124–28; token economies, 125–26
survival, autistic, 28
symbolic actions, 51–60; ABA reduction of, 125; entelechies of, 75–77; reduced to nonsymbolic motion, 15, 17
symbolic filtering, 56, 62
symbolicity: in allistic narratives, 58, 87; as deadening, 56
symbolism, 35–36, 40; as brain damage in autistics, 58; as mere brain module, 57
symptoms, 2, 28, 90–92; autistic practices as, 90; god theories and, 11
syndrome, 48

Tager-Flusberg, Helen, 22
Teaching Developmentally Disabled Children: The ME Book (Lovaas), 110, 128
TeenSexToday.com, 104
terministic screens, 64, 77, 160
terms of work, 19, 24, 64, 68; crip, 85; invitation and persuasion, 145
Terrorist Assemblages (Puar), 49
testimonio, 24
testosterone theories, 68, 71
theory of mind (ToM), 11, 15, 21, 42, 105, 210, 225n39; antifuturistic logic, 19; applied to autistic writing, 22, 30, 47; applied to transgender autistic people, 71; assumptions about autistic perception, 63; demi-rhetoricity and, 47–48; domains of, 19–20; fractionable autism theories and, 48, 64; intentionality and, 37; modules, 19–20, 58; as "perfect phrase," 29; ToM studies, 19
thereness, 40–41, 43
There's a Boy in Here (Barron and Barron), 21
thingness, 56, 74, 84
Third Glance, The, blog, 189–90
Thornton, Davi Johnson, 130–32
tics, 201
timeliness, 65–66
toe walking, 168
toilet training, 6–7
token economies, 125–26
Token Economy, The (Ayllon and Azrin), 126
torture, 97
totality, 110, 115
touch, 153
transpeople, 70–71, 185. See also gender-variant children